D.H. Lawrence and Germany

The Politics of Influence

COSTERUS NEW SERIES 164

Series Editors:
C.C. Barfoot, Theo D'haen
and Erik Kooper

D.H. Lawrence and Germany

The Politics of Influence

Carl Krockel

Rodopi Amsterdam-New York, NY 2007

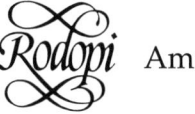

Cover illustration: Franz Marc, *Turm der blauen Pferde / Tower of the blue horses* (1913), Oil on canvas, 200 x 130 cm, destroyed in the war. Unfortunately we were unable to contact the owners of the copyrights, despite consequent efforts to do so. If anyone feels their rights have been offended in any way, please do not hesitate to contact the publisher or the author.

Cover design: Aart Jan Bergshoeff

The paper on which this book is printed meets the requirements of "ISO 9706:1994, Information and documentation - Paper for documents - Requirements for permanence".

ISBN-13: 978-90-420-2126-6
©Editions Rodopi B.V., Amsterdam - New York, NY 2007
Printed in the Netherlands

For my mother and father

Contents

List of Illustrations ... ix

Introduction ... 1

I   Towards a Modernist Tragedy:
The White Peacock ... 19

II   Between Wagner and Nietzsche:
The Trespasser ... 51

III   Versions of Modernist Realism:
Sons and Lovers and *Buddenbrooks* ... 73

IV   Unity and Fragmentation in
The Rainbow ... 107

V   Myth and History in
Women in Love ... 159

VI   Rewriting *Wilhelm Meisters Lehrjahre* in
The Lost Girl ... 197

VII   A Reflection on Past Influences:
Mr Noon ... 219

VIII   Leadership and the "Dead Ideal":
Aaron's Rod and *Kangaroo* ... 241

IX   The Völkisch Ideologies in
The Plumed Serpent ... 269

Conclusion: *The Lady Chatterley Novels* ... 301

Select Bibliography ... 309

Index ... 323

List of Illustrations

Figure 1: Franz Marc, Die großen blauen Pferde (1911).   155

Figure 2: Franz Marc, Turm der blauen Pferde (1911).   156

Figure 3: Wassily Kandinsky, Komposition IV (1911).   157

Figure 4: Wassily Kandinsky, Bild mit schwarzen Bogen (1912).   158

INTRODUCTION

In *D. H. Lawrence: Novelist*, a foundation stone of Lawrence criticism, F. R. Leavis chose as one of his epigraphs a quotation from Lawrence: "And I am English, and my Englishness is my very vision."[1] If I were to choose an epigraph for this book, it would be: "But I belong to Europe. Though not to England" (Letters, IV, 362).

There is a pertinent relationship between these quotations, despite their being written respectively in 1915 and 1922. The first comes from a letter written to Lady Cynthia Asquith, consoling her over the death of her brother in the war; Lawrence is so disgusted by the war that he feels he must leave England for America. The second quotation is from a letter to Catherine Carswell, in which he complains about America, and says that he wants to return to Europe. Lawrence only identifies with England or the European mainland either because he is about to leave them or because he wishes to return: his declarations of allegiance spring from a frustrated yearning, from a feeling of not belonging to any homeland. A question these two contradictory statements raise is not whether Lawrence belongs to English or European culture – after all, the two are not mutually exclusive. Instead, we might ask how both of them can be true, and what issues are involved in locating Lawrence's cultural heritage.

It is difficult to argue persuasively that Lawrence should be examined exclusively in a British or German context, especially when one of his ambitions was to write a novel in each of the six continents. His understanding of the German language was always awkward; he never mastered its grammar in his letters to his German relatives. He would call it "beastly" and "alien to my psychology and my very tissue". However, Ford Madox Ford asked him for reviews of German literature because of his knowledge of German philosophy,[2] and Lawrence would often compromise with translations into English if his linguistic skills were inadequate.[3] His early years were spent in England, yet English culture had strong connections to Germany before the First World War, and many German ideas contributed to his development both directly and indirectly. He married a German woman, Frieda Weekley (*née* von Richthofen), and

---

[1] F. R. Leavis, *D. H. Lawrence: Novelist* (London: Penguin, 1955), 6.
[2] See Jennifer Michaels-Tonks, *D. H. Lawrence: The Polarity of North and South, Germany and Italy in His Prose Works* (Bonn: Bouvier, 1976), 38.
[3] *The Letters of D. H. Lawrence*, I, 554, 545.

his personal and artistic maturity coincided with their arrival in Bavaria. In terms of Lawrence's notion of marriage, his relationship with Frieda at times made him merge with her German identity, and at other times oppose himself to it. During the First World War he considered his passionate battles with her as their own war, and yet both of them were harassed by the English authorities, and sang German folk songs during the Armistice. Germany had provided him with a means of escape from England, yet in turn he wandered to Italy, then Ceylon, Australia, America, and finally back to Europe again.

Since Lawrence's cultural identity is so diverse, its definition by critics has mainly been a product of their own perspectives, in particular their ideological motives. I consider myself as no exception to this. Leavis identified Lawrence with England in an attempt to stem the tide of controversy against the author. When Leavis asked in his monograph of 1955: "What, above all, is Lawrence?", his immediate answer was that "Lawrence is a great artist, a creative writer". At the same time he recognized that Lawrence's "greatness" does not provide an ideological defence against, for instance, V. S. Pritchett's diagnosis that "Lawrence represented the last phase of the Romantic Movement: random, irresponsible egotism, power for power's sake, the blood cult of Rosenberg".[4] As a dominant cultural force in England, the Romantic movement had been displaced by a Victorian emphasis on Realism, which Leavis regarded as part of the "Great Tradition". But in Germany Romanticism remained powerful well into the twentieth century, especially through its idealist philosophy and musical tradition. It inspired the Expressionist movement, but was also perceived as a contributory element in fascism. English writers regarded it as the cultural source of German militarism in the First World War, and this impression persisted into the Second World War. When Leavis emphasizes Lawrence's "Englishness", then, he is trying to dissociate the author from the German Romantic tradition.

The controversy over Lawrence's cultural identity was fuelled by Bertrand Russell in 1953, when he characterized the author as a proto-German fascist. Russell recalled his relationship with Lawrence during the First World War: "I was a firm believer in democracy, whereas he had developed the whole philosophy of Fascism before the politicians had thought of it." Russell focused on Lawrence's "mystical philosophy of

---

[4] Leavis, *D. H. Lawrence: Novelist*, 17, 21.

'blood'": "This seemed to me frankly rubbish, and I rejected it vehemently, though I did not then know that it led straight to Auschwitz." Russell was not content to see his parallel between Lawrence and Nazism as coincidental, but posited that Lawrence's thought was exclusively German in origin, because he was only the mouthpiece of his German wife: "He had the eloquence, but she had the ideas."[5] The link is particularly weak, since at worst Russell could only accuse Frieda of being interested in Freudianism.

Despite Leavis' intervention, in 1970 Kate Millett filled the gap in Russell's argument by grouping Freud with fascism into what she called the "Counterrevolution" between 1930 and 1960 against female liberation. Hitler's assertion that man reasons while woman feels was linked to Freud's definition of the female personality as passive, masochistic and narcissistic. Millett then conflated Freudianism and fascism in her analysis of Lawrence. She asserted that the sexual passivity of Connie in *Lady Chatterley's Lover* follows from Freud's prescription of female passivity. Millett also linked Lilly and Aaron's relationship in *Aaron's Rod* to the Nazis as "a combination of political fascism and male supremacy".[6]

We can see two extreme readings of Lawrence at work here: Leavis argues that he belongs to the "Great Tradition" that is founded on Enlightenment values; Russell and Millett accuse him of rejecting the Enlightenment for an authoritarian politics of the "blood" and male supremacy. The argument revolves around Lawrence's relationship to German culture, particularly to fascism, and its supposed debts to Freudianism and Romanticism. When Leavis returned Lawrence to English culture, he was ingeniously avoiding these ideological issues. Actually, Leavis shares Russell's philosophical stance, but reverses his argument: instead of attacking Lawrence from a Realist, or logical positivist viewpoint, he defends Lawrence from it.

These philosophical assumptions have also been prominent in German historiography, especially in the context of the origins of German fascism. Certain German historians have interpreted fascism as a reaction against liberal, Enlightenment culture. For instance, George L. Mosse's influential study *The Crisis of German Ideology* (1964) argues that fascist

---

[5] Bertrand Russell, *The Autobiography of Bertrand Russell* (London: George Allen and Unwin, 1968), II, 21-23.
[6] Kate Millett, *Sexual Politics* (London: Virago Press, 1977), 167, 178, 277.

trends emerged in protest against the economic, social and cultural upheaval of industrialism.[7] This argument bears similarities to Georg Lukács' premise, for instance in *Goethe and His Age* (1968) that fascism originated in "the simple truth that Germany's cultural evolution was the result of a struggle between progress and reaction". Lukács argues that Germany's protracted semi-feudalism left the bourgeois intelligentsia servile to "Junker" ideology, unlike the intelligentsias in Britain and France which mastered the aristocracy in their revolutions of 1688 and 1789 respectively. Instead of taking political power the German bourgeoisie depended on the authoritarian Junkers for order, leaving itself in the subservient position; it lacked any civic courage or the ability to make responsible independent decisions, and was only able to replicate its superiors' "ruthless inhuman brutality towards inferiors".[8] The subservient relationship between bourgeois and Junker classes provided the foundation for the reactionary national unification of 1870, the starting point of modern German history, and later for the totalitarian Third Reich in 1933.

Mosse and Lukács consider progress and regression as having independent origins, not as being implicated in one another. Lukács assumes that the progress of a benign liberalism dominated over regressive tendencies in Britain and France, without having any oppressive elements inherent in it. Mosse's argument begins to falter when he arrives at the focus of his study, National Socialism; for instance he is unable to explain Houston Stewart Chamberlain's ideology in which technological progress could strengthen the power of the *Volk*.[9] Leavis, Russell and Millett all share Mosse and Lukács' historical assumptions, which have persisted into contemporary criticism of Lawrence. Even in the recently published third volume of the Cambridge biography of Lawrence, David Ellis compares Mosse's definition of *völkisch* myth to the mythology of *The Plumed Serpent*. Crucially, though, Ellis leaves open the question of whether *völkisch* necessarily corresponds to "fascist".[10]

---

[7] See George L. Mosse, *The Crisis of German Ideology* (New York: Grosset and Dunlop, 1964).
[8] See Georg Lukács, *Goethe and His Age* (London: Merlin Press, 1968), 10, 9.
[9] See Mosse, *The Crisis of German Ideology*, 132.
[10] See David Ellis, *D. H. Lawrence: Dying Game* (Cambridge: Cambridge University Press, 1998), 218, 656.

We can see an alternative reading of German Fascism, and Western history, in Theodor Adorno and Max Horkheimer's *Dialectic of Enlightenment* (1972). This work has been crucial in my characterization of Lawrence's relationship with Germany. Adorno and Horkheimer analyse fascism as a dialectical consequence of rational and technological progress since the Enlightenment, not as a rejection of it:

> The fallen nature of modern man cannot be separated from social progress. On the one hand the growth of economic productivity furnishes the conditions for a world of greater justice; on the other hand it allows the technical apparatus and the social groups which administer it a disproportionate superiority to the rest of the population. The individual is wholly devalued in relation to the economic powers, which at the same time press the control of society over nature to hitherto unsuspected heights. Even though the individual disappears before the apparatus which he serves, that apparatus provides for him as never before. In an unjust state of life, the impotence and pliability of the masses grow with the quantitative increase in commodities allowed them.

While we gain control over nature through technology, we become increasingly alienated from nature, and as individuals more helpless before it. Adorno and Horkheimer insist that social freedom is inseparable from enlightened thought. Yet reason loses its relation to truth when "what men want to learn from nature is how to use it in order to wholly dominate it and other men" in the economic "progress" of industrialization.[11] Through the alienation of labour the worker no longer identifies himself with the product of his labour, as a craftsman does. He becomes one of the unskilled masses, subject to economic and political manipulation. Fascist rationalization exercised an unbridled exploitation of individuals in the machines of war, and the factory-like efficiency of concentration camps.

Anne Fernihough recognizes the parallel between Lawrence and Adorno's thought, and ascribes it to their shared involvement in the ideas of "romantic anti-capitalism and anti-technology"[12] prevalent in German cultural circles before and after the First World War. In particular, she is

---

[11] Theodor Adorno and Max Horkheimer, *Dialectic of Enlightenment* (New York: Herder and Herder, 1972), 4.

[12] Anne Fernihough, *D. H. Lawrence: Aesthetics and Ideology* (Oxford: Clarendon Press, 1993), 40.

alluding to Frieda's lover, the Freudian Otto Gross. His profound influence on Lawrence discredits Millett and Russell's conflation of Freud and Nazism in their views of Lawrence. Gross' philosophy of eroticism was opposed to Prussian patriarchy which had encouraged the abrupt rise of industrialization in Germany after unification. Indeed, Millett's characterization of Nazism is itself indebted to Wilhelm Reich, whose synthesis of Freudianism and sociology is descended, if indirectly, from Gross himself,[13] and directly from Adorno and Horkheimer. In effect, one could argue that Lawrence and Millett's thought belongs to a shared philosophical tradition, despite their being apparent antipodes. Appreciating this irony, later feminists such as Carol Dix and Sheila Macleod have emulated aspects of Millett's approach in their celebration of Lawrence's work.[14] Lawrence's greatest novels emulate Gross' affirmation of desire against the rationalization of modern society, and Adorno is part of this tradition in Germany.

According to Adorno and Horkheimer, nature in human subjectivity and the environment is expressed through myth which resists rational, scientific analysis. Myth is articulated in a self-repeating, eternal symbolism which defies Enlightenment progress and objectivity. Fascism occurs when rationalism monopolizes the language of myth, and mythologizes its own ideological foundations, to authorize itself tautologically over nature.[15]

In their extreme forms Romantic art claims to overcome man's alienation from nature in its symbolic, cyclical expressiveness, while Realist art objectifies nature in time and space. In both cases, nature and reason struggle to dominate each other with potentially dangerous results. Adorno and Horkheimer comment that "myth has always been obscure and enlightening at the same time".[16] The crucial issue is the relation between nature and reason, of maintaining a dialogue between them, not a dialectic which synthesizes them with each other. Art has the power to maintain this dialogue.

In his studies on German music Adorno attempted to answer how art could maintain the balance between reason and nature, and we can apply

---

[13] See Martin Green, *The von Richthofen Sisters: The Triumphant and Tragic Modes of Love* (New York: Basic Books, 1974), 282-83.
[14] See Carol Dix, *D. H. Lawrence and Women* (London: Macmillan, 1980); Sheila MacLeod, *Lawrence's Men and Women* (London: Heinemann, 1985).
[15] See Adorno, Horkheimer, *Dialectic of Enlightenment*, 11, 17.
[16] *Ibid.*, xiv.

some of his conclusions to Lawrence. To begin with, Beethoven's music enacts the dialectic of the Realist novel and Hegelian philosophy, between the individual melody and the musical whole, like the protagonist and society, the individual and the *Geist* of history. The melody develops through its variations within the framework of tonal harmony, to constitute the form of the sonata.[17] Beethoven belongs to the early period of capitalism in which the individual had freedom within the framework of customs to change his society.[18] Yet Beethoven's sonata form often threatens to smother the individuality of the melodies that comprise it. His music is comparable to the nineteenth-century Realist novel where the structural whole restricts the freedom of characters; it also shares the tyranny of reason over individuals that is central to capitalist society.[19] Adorno compares Beethoven's style to that of Goethe's novels, where individuals such as Ottilie in *Die Wahlverwandtschaften* and Wilhelm Meister renounce their desires for the sake of the social whole. I will concentrate on Lawrence's relation to Goethe in terms of this issue. In his novels Lawrence registers the limits of the Realist form in modern culture. In the openings of *The White Peacock* and *Sons and Lovers* he attempts to give his characters a dynamic relation with society, as in the Realist tradition, but they are soon paralysed within this scheme. In *The Lost Girl* he plays with the Realist genre, breaking its conventions to set his heroine's physical impulses free of social convention.

According to Adorno, Wagner responds both positively and negatively to this dialectic of the Enlightenment in Beethoven's music. His Romantic music claims to speak the language of nature. Melodies are organized as *Leitmotive*, which are akin to myth in their repetition, unlike Beethoven's developing variations. Through sonority Wagner transgresses the tonal system of harmony (a product of the Enlightenment) into the dissonance of longing, overwhelming rationality with feeling. Throughout this book I use the term *Motiv* to signify Lawrence's emulation of Wagner's Romantic style in his repetitive, symbolic language. Lawrence repeats words till they accumulate an expression of the characters' emotions and desires, especially during their erotic encounters. Through this musical language Lawrence is attempting

---

[17] See Theodor Adorno, *Beethoven: The Philosophy of History* (Cambridge: Polity Press, 1998), 10, 13-14.
[18] See Theodor Adorno, *In Search of Wagner* (London: NLB, 1981), 44.
[19] See Adorno, *Beethoven: The Philosophy of History*, 17-18, 119-20.

to give voice to his characters' subjectivity within the blank sameness of a rationalized, industrial society.

Like Leavis and Russell, Adorno is also sceptical about German Romanticism. He is alert to the risk of Wagner's music reifying feelings, instead of articulating our individual nature in feelings: the spectators at Bayreuth give up their individual volition to lose themselves in the music's overwhelming repetition, like a crowd before a speech by Hitler. The lack of dynamism of the *Motiv* within the musical structure reflects the individual's powerlessness within society: "Impotent by repeating itself, music abandons the struggle within the temporal framework it mastered in the symphony."[20] The seductive ambiguities within Wagner's art reflect the dangers, and richness of German Romanticism. These dangers are fundamental to the structural use of the *Motiv* in Lawrence's novels from *The White Peacock* onwards. He turns to a Wagnerian reality of erotic love that transcends an alienating social reality, but often it proves to be an alternative of reified feelings only. His characters become irretrievably caught in a structure of *Leitmotive* as repeated events and actions. In reaction to this problem, though, Lawrence struggles to transform society through his characters' desires, not merely to escape from it.

For Adorno, Schoenberg's music offers a solution to the inertia within Wagner's music, and to the dialectic of Enlightenment within modern society. Schoenberg's musical phrases break from tonality to express unconscious emotions directly, unlike Wagner's "feeling" that cannot be rationalized within the structure of the work: "The seismographic registration of traumatic shock becomes, at the same time, the technical structural law of music."[21] The individual's nature is asserted through these shocks and traumas that resist reification. As we shall see, Lawrence achieves the literary equivalent of this effect in "The Prussian Officer", and to a certain extent in *The Rainbow*, *Women in Love* and *Aaron's Rod*.

Schoenberg, however, was unable to sustain an artistic principle which denies order. He established an alternative order to tonality in serialism, which still foregrounds the significance of individual forms. Lawrence achieved a comparable solution by juxtaposing Romantic and

---

[20] Adorno, *In Search of Wagner*, 37.
[21] Theodor Adorno, *The Philosophy of Modern Music* (New York: Seabury Press, 1973), 39, 42.

Realist forms of order. His most consistent achievement is to mediate between these styles, to dramatize the tension between the individual and the social whole in different ways and with various outcomes. In *Sons and Lovers* he transforms the Romanticism of his characters' subjective desires into a Realism of their physical, erotic relationships with each other. In turn, this Modernist form of Realism has the potentiality to transform the social reality that the characters inhabit. However, the problem of eroticism as a mere Romantic escapism from society remains in his later fiction. Lawrence's career forms an ongoing struggle to envisage a way of asserting the individuality of his characters without reducing them to an exclusive literary style.

To conclude this opening theoretical discussion, I wish to modify the debate between Leavis, Russell and Millett about Lawrence's Realism. Leavis was sensitive to the diverse qualities of Lawrence's art, despite being unable to reconcile them with his ideological stance towards Lawrence. In 1930 he had characterized *Women in Love* as "a parallel to the turgid, cyclonic disasters of Blake's prophetic books",[22] but in his 1955 monograph he chooses *Women in Love* as Lawrence's greatest work, and defends him against any charge of Romanticism. Leavis declares that "Lawrence belongs to the same ethical and religious tradition as George Eliot"; then he acknowledges "a great difference" between Eliot's tendency to the ethical and Lawrence's to the religious. "Religious" here can be traced back to the Romantic. In his appraisal of *Women in Love*, Leavis implicitly retains his earlier impression of its Blakean elements: "how different *The Rainbow* is from *Women in Love* we may fairly convey by observing that there is much about *The Rainbow* that makes us see it as being, clearly and substantially, in a line from George Eliot." In other words, for Leavis *Women in Love* is Lawrence's greatest novel, yet it does not follow from the tradition of Eliot's Realism but from the Romantic tradition.[23]

Anne Fernihough appreciates Lawrence's contradictory postures, commenting that "it would be extremely difficult to 'place' a writer like Lawrence, whose tendency was to take up and drop certain positions as it suited his rhetorical purposes".[24] Part of Fernihough's argument focuses on the question of "organicism", and its idealist implications. She shows

---

[22] F. R. Leavis, *D. H. Lawrence*, reprinted in *For Continuity* (Cambridge: Minority Press, 1933), 123.
[23] Leavis, *D. H. Lawrence: Novelist*, 123, 132, 116, 207.
[24] Fernihough, *Aesthetics and Ideology*, 3.

how Lawrence interacts his idealist tendencies with material experiences, to introduce contradictions into his work, "fracturing" its organicism. Nevertheless, without exploring the countertendencies within *The Plumed Serpent*, she resorts to criticizing the novel for its reification of material experience.

Where my approach differs from Fernihough's is in its concentration on the historical and personal processes that take place in Lawrence's struggle between different literary discourses. Lawrence takes up contradictory positions in his novels as a deliberate strategy to achieve a dynamic expression of reality. In her reading of Lawrence, Fernihough does not draw attention to how his ideas develop over the course of his career; she places quotations which may have been separated from each other by many years into the same arguments. She tends to dismiss his apparently reactionary postures and credit him his radical insights, as if they were independent of each other. Instead this book shows how Lawrence works through various positions in tandem with his personal and historical circumstances: Lawrence's failures are integral to his achievements.

The self-contradictory nature of Lawrence's art, then, is its saving grace. This book incorporates the ideas of his most hostile opponents with those of his most ardent defenders, to form a complex and dynamic interpretation of him. Instead of avoiding the arguments about Lawrence's relation to Germany as Leavis did, I shall play them against interpretations of German history, to evaluate Lawrence in a more concrete, historical way.

My vision of Lawrence is a response to the criticism of the most significant Lawrencean scholars of the last twenty years, including Michael Black, John Worthen, Mark Kinkead-Weekes, George Hyde, Michael Bell and David Ellis, all of whom I refer to throughout this book. In their work they search beyond the issues set out by Leavis, Russell and Millett, exploring the multifaceted achievement of Lawrence's fiction. Other studies on my field of research, such as those by Jennifer Michaels-Tonks, Mitzi M. Brunsdale, Billy James Pace, Eleanor Hewson Green and Colin Milton,[25] have tended to concentrate on outlining references in

---

[25] See Michaels-Tonks, *D. H. Lawrence: The Polarity of North and South, Germany and Italy in His Prose Works*; Mitzi M. Brunsdale, *The German Effect on D. H. Lawrence and His Works 1885-1912* (Berne: Peter Lang, 1978); Billy James Pace, *D. H. Lawrence's Use in His Novels of Germanic and Celtic Myth from the Music Dramas of Richard Wagner* (Arkansas: University of Arkansas, 1973); Eleanor Hewson Green, *The*

Lawrence's work to Germany without focusing on the historical, cultural and ideological issues at stake. I have made these issues the subject of this book.

The single most important development in D. H. Lawrence studies in recent years has been the Cambridge edition of his works and letters. This enterprise, which includes eight volumes of his correspondence, offers the researcher an enormous amount of information about Lawrence, which has fed into my reading of his texts. The Cambridge edition has enabled me to discover complex developments in Lawrence's life and thought, especially in terms of his contacts with Germany, that were unavailable to previous researchers in this field. To convey these developments, this book is structured chronologically, and it incorporates biographical facts only where they are pertinent to its critical arguments. I have limited my study to the novels, which embody Lawrence's main developments as a writer, and I refer to other works, including poetry, drama and non-fiction where they substantiate my readings.

The first chapter on *The White Peacock* begins with Lawrence's initial attempt to emulate George Eliot's structure of two pairs of lovers in *Middlemarch*. Eliot based the structure of her novel on Goethe's *Die Wahlverwandtschaften*, in which two pairs of lovers are motivated by their "elective affinities" with each other. This chemical theory, which Lawrence was directly aware of, contributed to the empirical and objective style of the nineteenth-century Realist novel. Yet Goethe, and Eliot in *The Mill on the Floss*, abandoned "affinities" when its sexual element threatened their ethical values. They revert to tragedy in which their characters renounce their "affinities" with each other. While composing *The White Peacock* Lawrence was deeply impressed by Schopenhauer's "Metaphysics of Love" which foregrounded sexual opposition over personal affinity. In Lettie Beardsall and George Saxton, Lawrence reveals the individual's split between the body's desires for otherness and the personal need for affinity. As a Schopenhauerian tragedy of this split, Lawrence's novel is structured around repeated, frustrating encounters between the characters is based on repetition, without the development of Goethe and Eliot's novels. The structural

---

Works of D. H. Lawrence with Relation to Schopenhauer and Nietzsche (Nottingham: University of Nottingham, 1973); Colin Milton, *Lawrence and Nietzsche: A Study in Influence* (Aberdeen: Aberdeen University Press, 1987).

repetition of *The White Peacock* aligns it with the operas of Wagner, which are based on the repetition of "Leitmotive" to express a Schopenhauerian pessimism. Lawrence, then, has discovered the revolutionary potential of his characters' physical desires, but is unable to affirm them.

In *The Trespasser* Lawrence further develops his use of Wagner, not only in the *Leitmotiv* principle, but also by emulating the musical quality of Wagner's *Tonsprache* in his librettos. Through this poetic style based on assonance and alliteration, Lawrence's prose transcends an objectified reality of the Realist novel into a world of Helena and Siegmund's inner feelings. Yet this style leaves his characters weak as individuals on their return to society. In the struggle to envisage an alternative to this Romantic transcendence, Lawrence is indebted to the philosophy of Nietzsche. He attempts to express the Dionysian energies of his characters instead of their transcendence of reality. He envisages for them Zarathustra's affirmative *grosser Mittag* ("great noon") instead of Wagner's *Nacht* ("night") of *Tristan und Isolde*; he grants them the possibility of grasping each moment in its *ewige Wiederkehr* ("eternal recurrence") instead of renouncing it as a futile repetition of the Schopenhauerian *Wille*. Yet tragically Helena and Siegmund still turn from life, to resignation.

In the third chapter I compare *Sons and Lovers* with Thomas Mann's *Buddenbrooks*. Both are the focus of debates on the Realist genre in modern literature, yet they follow the anti-Realist traditions of Schopenhauerian philosophy and Wagnerian opera. Lawrence, however, also breaks from this tradition through the revolution in his life and art effected by his future wife Frieda Weekley. Through her, he begins to conceive tragedy as a celebration of the protagonist's heroic struggle against death, not as a parable preaching resignation. Particularly important is the influence of Frieda's former lover, Otto Gross, and his Freudian and Nietzschean ideas. Lawrence adopts Freud's developmental theory to portray Paul Morel as a victim of his Oedipal relationship with his parents, and of their Schopenhauerian conflict of wills. Through Freud, Lawrence returns to a realistic analysis of Paul in terms of his relationship with other characters. Lawrence also relates Freud's notion of the libido to Nietzsche's Dionysian vitality, and attempts to affirm them in Paul's relationship with Clara Baxter. Instead of a Romantic transcendence of their material lives, Lawrence envisages their sexual encounters as a transformation of them. Yet in this new perspective he struggles with Gross' idealism of the erotic, and acknowledges its limitations as a force with which to change society. At the end of the novel Paul lapses into a Wagnerian "nothingness" before the will of the universe, but begins to recoup himself in the knowledge of his individual desires.

Lawrence, then, has developed from his initial rejection of the Realist genre and adherence to Romanticism, towards establishing his mature style. *The Rainbow*, as his most rich and complex novel in its relation to German culture, continues this development. It shares with the art of the Blaue Reiter group the dualistic expression of characters' individual desires, and tendency to unify them into a religious vision. The novel is organized around contending value systems. In his "Study of Thomas Hardy" Lawrence revealed his debt to both Schopenhauer's theory of the *Wille* as the dark source of living forms, and Goethe's *Morphologie* in which life continuously divides itself into forms of greater consciousness and light. In the first generation, Tom Brangwen and Lydia Lensky, Lawrence counters his imagery of Wagnerian darkness with Goethe's imagery of light from *Faust*, to express the characters' flux between the primal will and their consciousness of the outside world. In the next generation Lawrence introduces Novalis' imagery from *Hymnen an die Nacht* to reinforce his Wagnerian Romanticism in Will Brangwen. Anna opposes Will by affirming the darkness and light within herself. In giving birth to Ursula she enacts Lawrence's Nietzschean ideas against Romanticism: she embodies Gross' *Umwertung aller Werte* through motherhood, and participates in Nietzsche's *ewige Wiederkehr* as the eternal recurrence of the Brangwen generations. In Ursula Lawrence further develops his contending German themes. Her lover Skrebensky embodies the liberal imperialist ideas of Max Weber, who affirms the Nietzschean *Wille zur Macht* of the nation. She opposes him with Lawrence's erotic reading of Nietzsche, attacking him through her aggressive sexuality. Then Lawrence sets Ursula against the ideas of Thomas Mann. In her lesbian relationship with Winifred Inger and his description of the younger Tom Brangwen's mines he parodies the imagery of Mann's *Der Tod in Venedig*. Again Lawrence is creating a Nietzschean dialogue between Mann's affirmation of the individual's conscious *Wille zur Macht* over the corruption of society and his bodily impulses, and Gross' affirmation of the body against mental and social corruption. Yet Lawrence accords with both Weber and Mann, not with Gross' erotic utopianism, in Ursula's struggle to enforce her will upon her pupils at school. Again, he is critical of Gross' ideas, despite their primary importance to him. Towards the end of the novel in Ursula's encounters with Skrebensky, Lawrence's dialectic between darkness and light, the primal will and consciousness, disintegrates as he affirms the will to the exclusion of consciousness. This problem bears upon his treatment of Ursula's encounters with the horses, then the rainbow, which is compared to similar subject-matter in the paintings of Marc and Kandinsky. Lawrence's position straddles Marc's idealistic vision of unity, and Kandinsky's vision of unity in diversity.

Women in Love departs from *The Rainbow* in terms of Lawrence's needs for a religious sense of unity and for the particularity of his characters' experiences. Lawrence continues his cultural oppositions from *The Rainbow*, with Gerald Crich's management of his mines symbolizing the German nation in its history of Unification, the rule of Bismarck and its class divisions which led to the First World War. Gerald's philosophy resembles the Protestant ethic that Max Weber had analysed in capitalist culture. Through analysing Gerald's character in terms of repression and obsessional neurosis, Lawrence is able to show the psychological conditions of capitalism, and of modern Germany's history. Gerald's relationship with Gudrun reveals how these conditions erupt into war. On the other side, Ursula and Birkin attempt to overcome the extremes of idealism and Wagnerian Romanticism in their relationship together. Lawrence attempts to convey the consummation of their relationship as a triumph over the conditions symbolized between Gerald and Gudrun, but as in the closing sections of *The Rainbow*, his alternative to the problems of contemporary history is more of an escape than an answer to them. The achievement of *Women in Love*, though, lies in its acknowledgement of these failings.

After the war Lawrence directly approached the problem of idealism in contemporary history. In *The Lost Girl* he attempted to answer the idealism of liberal German culture, especially of Weber, by parodying Goethe's *Wilhelm Meisters Lehrjahre* and the Realist genre. Where Wilhelm joins an acting troupe, then rejects it for his duties to society by eventually specializing in the medical profession, Alvina joins the Natcha-kee-Tawaras, abandoning her career as a nurse. Lawrence's style approaches that of Novalis' *Heinrich von Ofterdingen*, his Romantic riposte to *Wilhelm Meister*. Lawrence and Novalis foreground their characters' subjectivity, in comparison to Goethe's omniscient and objective style. In *Wilhelm Meister* Goethe personified the Romantic longing to escape from middle-class society in the mysterious figure of Mignon, who longs to return to Italy; in *The Lost Girl* Alvina's Italian lover Ciccio plays the role of Mignon, and instead of wasting away like her, he manages to persuade Alvina to return with him to Italy. In their relationship Lawrence employs ideas from *Psychoanalysis and the Unconscious* about the need to overcome the idealism of the mind with the impulses of the body. Ciccio liberates Alvina through her body, but dispossesses her of a conscious free will. The novel ends on the uncertainty of having substituted the idealism of consciousness with an idealism of the body. Again, Lawrence has encountered the dangers of his Romantic inheritance.

During this period Lawrence also wrote *Mr Noon*, the second half of which is set in Germany, enabling him to review the country's influence on him since meeting Frieda. Lawrence parodies Goethe's *Faust*, to continue his dialogue with German liberal culture, both in Gilbert Noon's exploitation of women and in the bourgeois idealism of his German acquaintances. In Gilbert's relationship with Johanna, Lawrence uncovers a link between Frieda and Gross' eroticism and Wagnerian Romanticism, then he correlates their idealism with that of war. Here Lawrence is revising the idealism that has entered his novels since the impact of Gross in *Sons and Lovers*. The novel ends unfinished in a crisis of ideas, as Gilbert Noon turns from his marriage towards the passing regiments of German soldiers, glimpsing at an alternative through them.

In *Aaron's Rod* and *Kangaroo* Lawrence struggles with this crisis in his ideas, turning from eroticism to male independence, then attempting to formulate a political vision from this. *Aaron's Rod* bears many similarities with a contemporary novel by Hesse, *Demian*, which attempts to envisage a way forward from the idealism of the war. Hesse's novel lapses back into an idealism of Goethe and Marc to justify the war; meanwhile, *Aaron's Rod* resists any single solutions to the crises in post-war Europe, instead merely insisting on the individual attitudes of its characters. The crisis in the novel is summed up by Lilly Rawdon's concluding affirmation of individuality and slavery, which Lawrence pursues in *Kangaroo*. The political positions of these novels are speculative answers to the failure of liberalism and socialism in post-war Germany. I explore the various possible interpretations of Kangaroo's Diggers' movement in terms of fascism in the violent authoritarianism of members such as Jack Callcott, socialism like Edgar Jaffe's Independent Socialists in the failed Bavarian Revolution, and Zionism in the Jewish identity and *völkisch* quality of some of Kangaroo's ideas. Richard Lovatt Somers rejects these movements as symbolized by Kangaroo in their shared ideal of social unity. He returns to the original premise of *Aaron's Rod*, of his freedom as an individual.

Finally, in *The Plumed Serpent* Lawrence pursues the *völkisch* ideas implicit in *Kangaroo* through his vision of the revived Aztec religion in Mexico. I attempt to answer whether these ideas correspond to fascism, or to an alternative *völkisch* movement in Germany, Zionism. The novel's relationship to Germany can be traced back to Lawrence's ambivalent attitude to the rise of right-wing politics there in early 1924, after the economic crisis and Munich Putsch. I compare *The Plumed Serpent* to its earlier version *Quetzalcoatl*, written before Lawrence's stay in Germany, to assess its impact on the final version. Although *Quetzalcoatl* appears less authoritarian than *The Plumed Serpent* in that the heroine Kate rejects Ramón's cult, *The Plumed Serpent* is more liberal in its flexible treatment of "blood" and race, compared to the Fascist definition of these terms. However, *The Plumed Serpent* still has authoritarian tendencies in the way its Romantic mythology overwhelms the individuality of its characters.

This book, then, analyses Lawrence's relationship to Germany in terms of the "dialectic of Enlightenment". Lawrence opposes both industrial civilization and the Realist novel as means of suppressing the freedom of individuals. Via George Eliot, Goethe provides him with the German model of Realism in *Die Wahlverwandtschaften* and *Wilhelm Meisters Lehrjahre*. Lawrence's German acquaintances, Edgar Jaffe and Alfred Weber, along with Max Weber, also celebrate Goethe as the voice of liberal Germany, and of the individual's obligation to his social duties, as in the Protestant ethic. Lawrence opposes Goethe with Schopenhauer and Wagner who concentrate on the primal *Wille* of individuals, but fail to affirm the individual in his relation to society. Nietzsche in turn provides the antidote to their "Romantic pessimism" in his affirmation of the individual's Dionysian *Wille zur Macht*. Lawrence reformulates this as the libidinal impulse through the example of Otto Gross' combination of Nietzsche and Freud. Unlike his Romantic predecessors, though, Lawrence manages to hold objective reality in dialogue with the characters' Romantic impulses, but there is the danger of Romanticism dominating and constituting Lawrence's own idealism, which becomes a politically contentious issue in his later novels. His novels as a whole dramatize the irresolvable conflict between these positions, and their respective sources in German culture.

I
TOWARDS A MODERNIST TRAGEDY:
THE WHITE PEACOCK

In "A Modern Lover", dated January 1910, Lawrence's fictionalized persona Cyril Mersham "traced the graph" of his early ideas from Charlotte Brontë and George Eliot outwards to Russian and French literature, and to the German writings of Schopenhauer and Nietzsche (*LAH*, 33). Lawrence's first novel, *The White Peacock* (1912), emerges from the tradition of the Victorian novel, in particular George Eliot and Thomas Hardy. Like Lawrence's broad range of interests, Victorian culture was a product of international elements. Through figures such as Samuel Taylor Coleridge, Thomas Carlyle and George Henry Lewes, Britain enjoyed a close cultural relationship with Germany; later, during the First World War, the two countries would become long-term enemies, violently severing their cultural ties. In this opening chapter I shall reveal the direct and indirect presence of German culture in *The White Peacock*. In order to survey the wide panorama of relationships in Lawrence's complex and hesitant early development, I shall also refer to earlier drafts of the novel and secondary sources.

During the composition of the novel, from its first version as "Laetitia" at Easter 1906 to the final correcting of proofs in autumn 1910, Lawrence traversed almost a century of German thought from Goethe through Schopenhauer to Wagner. He attempted to emulate the structure of George Eliot's *Middlemarch* (1871-72), which in turn was borrowed from Goethe's *Die Wahlverwandtschaften* (1809). Both George Eliot and Goethe used a framework of two pairs of lovers to compare the chemical affinities among them, and to analyse relationships in an objective, scientific way. Sexual affinity threatens the social conventions underlying these novels, and is thus sacrificed by Goethe, and by George Eliot in *The Mill on the Floss*, by their reversion to tragedy in which characters renounce their affinities, and their lives. In an attempt to avoid this tragic conclusion, Lawrence emulated Schopenhauer's "Metaphysics of Love" ("Metaphysik der Geschlechtsliebe") in *Parerga und Paralipomena* (1851), to stress sexual opposition rather than personal affinity between his characters.

However, in its conflict with social relations, sexuality still only yields a tragedy of pessimism in *The White Peacock*, which Lawrence learned from two other adherents of Schopenhauer's philosophy, Thomas Hardy and Richard Wagner. Towards the end of the novel, where he emulates Wagner's musical effects in terms of the *Leitmotiv*, Lawrence strains unsuccessfully against Schopenhauer's philosophy while glimpsing at a form of tragedy which can affirm his characters' vitality.

Lawrence's problem in *The White Peacock* is also that of the Edwardian period in which he writes: his dependence on the cultural innovations of the previous century, and his consequent entrapment in its social conventions. In what follows I shall explore how he is subject to this problem and how he attempts to break from it, towards the tragedies of his later novels.

George Eliot and Goethe's "affinities"
Lawrence began *The White Peacock* by trying to emulate George Eliot's style, yet without much conviction. Jessie Chambers recalls how he first proposed writing the novel in the spring of 1906:

> "The usual plan is to take two couples and develop their relationships," he said. "Most of George Eliot's are on that plan. Anyhow, I don't want a plot, I should be bored with it. I shall try two couples for a start."[1]

It is difficult to argue that "most" of George Eliot's novels are founded on the structure of two couples. A notable exception, however, is *Middlemarch* whose second half focuses respectively on the relationships of Dorothea Casaubon with Will Ladislaw, and of Rosamond Vincy with Tertius Lydgate.[2]

A possible source of George Eliot's "plan" for *Middlemarch* is Goethe's *Die Wahlverwandtschaften* whose plot revolves around the respective relationships between Eduard and Ottilie, and between the Hauptmann and Charlotte. The English translation of Goethe's title, *Elective Affinities*, is closer to the title of the Swedish chemist Tobern Olof Bergmann's book, *De attractionibus electivis,* which Goethe

---

[1] E.T. [Jessie Chambers], *D. H. Lawrence: A Personal Record* (London: Frank Cass, 1965), 103.
[2] See Michael Black, "A Bit of Both: George Eliot and D. H. Lawrence", *Critical Review*, XXIX (1989), 89-109.

borrowed. The basic principle involved is the attraction between chemicals through their common properties, as Eduard elaborates:

> "Consider water, or oil, or quicksilver, and you will find a unity and coherence of their parts. They will not relinquish this unified state except through the action or force of some other agent. If this is removed, they will immediately come together again."[3]

"Es fehlt nicht viel" ("it doesn't require much"), according to Charlotte, to apply this theory of chemical relationships to social relationships: "But most similar of all to these inanimate things are the masses which stand against one another in the world: the classes, the professions, the nobility and the third estate, the soldier and the civilian."[4]

As Erich Heller comments, Goethe's scientific research was partly a strategy to restore the balance of power between analytical reason and the creative imagination.[5] Scientific theory yields an objective portrayal of human relationships in *Die Wahlverwandtschaften*; it authorizes the plausibility of these relationships, regardless of whether they transgress social convention. Through science, Goethe liberates his art from received morality.

German culture played a dominant role in George Eliot's life, beginning with her shift from Evangelicism to free-thought when she studied German historical criticism of the Bible in the 1840s.[6] Her lover George Lewes acknowledged her contribution to his analysis of *Die Wahlverwandtschaften* in his pioneering biography of Goethe[7] and, as we shall see later, *The Mill on the Floss* shares similar scenes to

---

[3] Johann Wolfgang Goethe, *Gedenkausgabe der Werke, Briefe und Gespräche*, twenty-six vols (Zurich: Artemis, 1949-64), IX, 40: "Stelle dir nur das Wasser, das Öl, das Quecksilber vor, so wirst du eine Einigkeit, einen Zusammenhang ihrer Teile finden. Diese Einung verlassen sie nicht, außer durch Gewalt oder sonstige Bestimmung. Ist diese beseitigt, so treten sie gleich wieder zusammen."
[4] Goethe, *Gedenkausgabe*, IX, 41. "Die meiste Ähnlichkeit jedoch mit diesen seelenlosen Wesen haben die Massen, die in der Welt sich einander gegenüber stellen, die Stände, die Berufsbestimmungen, der Adel und der dritte Stand, der Soldat und der Zivilist."
[5] See Erich Heller, *The Disinherited Mind* (London: Bowes and Bowes, 1975), 20.
[6] Rosemary Ashton, *The German Idea* (Cambridge: Cambridge University Press, 1980), 147-48.
[7] See George Henry Lewes, *The Life of Goethe* (London: J. M. Dent, 1908), 525.

those in Goethe's novel. George Eliot may be thinking about *Die Wahlverwandtschaften* in parts of her 1855 article, "The Morality of Wilhelm Meister", where she describes how Goethe "quietly follows the stream of fact and of life; and waits patiently for the moral processes of nature as we all do for her material processes".[8] George Eliot's appraisal of Goethe as "the man who helps us to rise to a lofty point of observation, so that we may see things in their relative proportions", is comparable to Georg Lukács' characterization of Goethe's "consistently thought-out systemization of these relationships, contrasts and nuances, and his ability to transform all these features into a vivid plot which can characterize them".[9] For Lukács, in the plot of *Die Wahlverwandtschaften* Goethe comes closest to the designs of the nineteenth-century Realist novel, of which *Middlemarch* is a supreme example.

The chemical theory is the structural backbone of Goethe and George Eliot's Realism. Chemicals are only electively affined when their attraction excludes other chemicals. In his narrative Goethe uses the framework of two pairs of lovers, whose attraction to different aspects of each other reveals their psychological "properties". Eduard and Charlotte are married, having known each other since childhood; the Hauptmann arrives, and links up with Eduard in their horticultural plans while excluding Charlotte for being too fanciful. Charlotte is satisfied by the arrival of the childlike Ottilie, and is also finding her own measured nature in affinity with the Hauptmann's. Meanwhile, Ottilie appeals to Eduard's childlike side, but the Hauptmann finds her ideas disturbing. And so the narrative continues.

In *Middlemarch* George Eliot systematically elaborates on what Goethe only suggests in *Die Wahlverwandtschaften*, since each of her four characters is also bound to wider social relationships through affinity. In the two couples she explores her moral vision of a liberal utopia based on sympathy: each individual is in a process of becoming, relating to others in order to realize his or her self, while helping them to do the same. In the final Book of the novel this scheme is most perfectly expressed, and is reminiscent of Goethe's own narrative mode. Dorothea and Lydgate's shared desire for social reform links

---

[8] George Eliot, *Selected Critical Writings* (Oxford: Oxford University Press, 1992), 131.
[9] Lukács, *Goethe and His Age*, 67.

them together, her wealth providing a hospital to enable him to make the most of his medical abilities; fascinated by her beauty, Ladislaw comforts Lydgate's neglected wife Rosamond. Ladislaw then renounces Rosamond for Dorothea, since her belief in his abilities is necessary for him to achieve anything; likewise, she needs his sympathy as support for her aspirations. Lydgate and Ladislaw discuss their frustration and loneliness, and comfort each other, while Rosamond is comforted by the compassion of Dorothea, who understands her feeling of alienation from the man she loves. Rosamond and Lydgate are reconciled, because he now has the means to support her (through Dorothea), and Ladislaw and Dorothea unite (with Rosamond's help). This complex network of relationships between individuals is George Eliot's alternative to traditional duty, as represented in the oppressive relationship between Tom and Maggie in *The Mill on the Floss*. Affinities provide a rational principle by which to organize an enlightened society.

Lawrence was certainly aware of Goethe's theory of affinities, if only through reading Ernst Haeckel's account of it in *The Riddle of the Universe*:[10]

> Goethe, in his classical romance, *Affinities*, compared the relations of pairs of lovers with the phenomenon of the same name in the formation of chemical combinations. The irresistible passion that draws Eduard to the sympathetic Ottilia, or Paris to Helen, and leaps over all bounds of reason and morality, is the same powerful "unconscious" attractive force which impels the living spermatozoon of the egg of the animal or plant – the same impetuous movement which unites two atoms of hydrogen to one atom of oxygen for the formation of the molecule of water.[11]

Haeckel's pantheism helped Lawrence to break from his Christian upbringing, for a monism based on the material universe.[12]

The White Peacock begins with the two male characters, George Saxton and Cyril Beardsall; George is in love with Cyril's sister, Lettie, and Cyril is in love with George's sister, Emily. However, despite his

---

[10] See E. T., *D. H. Lawrence: A Personal Record*, 84-85.
[11] Ernst Haeckel, *The Riddle of the Universe* (London: Watts, 1900), 228-29.
[12] See John Worthen, *D. H. Lawrence: The Early Years* (Cambridge: Cambridge University Press, 1991), 179-80.

original intention, Lawrence was unable to maintain this structure of two affined couples, or to endorse George Eliot's and Goethe's scientific viewpoint and social ideals associated with it. Cyril, who is Lawrence's alter ego, describes how "Emily was intensely serious, and generally succeeded in reducing me to the same state" (*WP*, 14). He does not acknowledge that they both have this effect on each other, because they are of a similar temperament: their affinity repels them from each other. By the end of 1909 Lawrence dispiritedly remarked in a letter to Blanche Jennings how he had married "Emily to a stranger and myself [Cyril] to nobody. Oh Lord – what a farce."[13]

In "A Modern Lover" Lawrence gives a comparable treatment of Cyril and Emily in the characters Cyril Mersham and Muriel, while directly invoking Goethe's affinities. Cyril returns from London to meet Muriel, and explains to her new lover that

> "we're discussing affinities, that ancient topic .... We agree so beastly well, we two. We always did. It's her fault. Does she treat you so badly?"

Cyril and Muriel's agreement on everything has forced them apart as lovers. Her new lover, Tom Vickers, is the opposite to Cyril, a man of "handsome, healthy animalism" (*LAH*, 39). Towards the end of *The White Peacock* Emily becomes engaged to Tom Renshaw who, like his namesake in "A Modern Lover", is "handsome" and "exceedingly manly" (*WP*, 308). With Tom, Emily has found her opposite, not her affinity, who can balance her excesses of emotion and self-consciousness. Opposition is the basis of sexual attraction in *The White Peacock*; Lawrence concentrates on sexual opposition in the triangular relationship between Lettie, George and Leslie Tempest, to break from the cultural inheritance of Eliot and Goethe.

From "affinities" to Schopenhauer's "Metaphysics of Love"

For George Eliot, as for Goethe, sexuality threatens the socially positive outcome of a couple's personal affinities. The danger of sexuality forces George Eliot and Goethe to abandon the framework of affinities for a tragic, mythical ending. In *Die Wahlverwandtschaften* Ottilie renounces her sexual affinity with Eduard and wills herself to

---

[13] *The Letters of D. H. Lawrence*, I, 141.

death. In her journal from 1854 George Eliot recalls defending against a German professor the plausibility of Ottilie's renunciation:

> This dénouement, he said, was "unvernünftig" [unreasonable]. So, I said, were dénouements in real life very frequently: Goethe had given the dénouement which would naturally follow from the characters of the respective actors.[14]

George Eliot distinguishes between "reason" and "real life" which is mysterious and irrational. The rationalism of Goethe's theory of affinities acknowledged the historical impact of the French Revolution by placing supposedly absolute moral principles in a relativizing, physical environment.[15] In Ottilie's death, though, Goethe restored the mystical power of religious piety and traditional morality. He was anxious that Enlightenment progress could threaten traditional morality; he puns *Scheidung* ("divorce") with *Scheidekünstler* ("analytical chemist").[16] Ottilie's renunciation of Eduard, and of her own life, signifies a condemnation of his divorce from Charlotte, but its motivation is alien to any scientific reasoning.

George Eliot shares Goethe's counter-tendency in her fiction. Despite her German-inspired adoption of free-thought, she retained a lingering Evangelicism from the mentor of her youth, Maria Lewis. Consequently, she found D. F. Strauss' empirical approach in *Leben Jesu* inadequate in describing a spiritual reality.[17] In *The Mill on the Floss* George Eliot re-enacts Goethe's own wavering between science and tragic myth. Maggie's renunciation is like Ottilie's. Maggie's self is divided between her intellectual and sexual desires, respectively for Philip and Stephen, which leaves her too weak to withstand the pressures of social duty. George Eliot resolves Maggie's predicament in the melodramatic ending where she finds reconciliation in the flood with Tom, who is the voice of order and duty.[18] The scene is at odds

---

[14] Rosemary Ashton, *George Eliot* (Oxford: Oxford University Press, 1983), 43.
[15] See T. J. Reed, *Goethe* (Oxford: Oxford University Press, 1984), 83-85.
[16] Goethe, *Gedenkausgabe*, IX, 42-43.
[17] See Ashton, *The German Idea*, 150; *George Eliot*, 20; *George Eliot: A Life* (London: Hamish Hamilton, 1996), 52.
[18] For a more extended analysis of the influence of *Die Wahverwandtschaften* on *The Mill on the Floss*, see Gerlinde Röder-Bolton, *George Eliot and Goethe: An Elective Affinity* (Amsterdam: Rodopi, 1988).

both with the patient objectivity of Goethe's narrative and his chemical observations, weighing the balance back to Christian tradition. George Eliot is following a Victorian trend; Matthew Arnold also regarded Ottilie's renunciation as morally important, interpreting it as Goethe's unambiguous denunciation of divorce as a threat to social order.[19]

George Eliot and Goethe suppress their characters' sexuality under a mythology of renunciation. Jessie Chambers recalls how on reading *The Mill on the Floss* Lawrence reacted against George Eliot's prioritization of intellectual over sexual affinity, which made possible her suppression of Maggie's sexuality:

> Lawrence adored *The Mill on the Floss*, but always declared that George Eliot had "gone and spoilt it half way through". He could not forgive the marriage of the vital Maggie Tulliver to the cripple Philip. He used to say: "It was wrong, wrong. She could never have made her do it." When, later on, we came to Schopenhauer's essay on *The Metaphysics of Love*, against the passage: "The third consideration is the *skeleton*, since it is the foundation of the type of the species. Next to old age and disease; nothing disgusts us so much as a deformed shape; even the most beautiful face cannot make amends for it." Lawrence wrote in the margin: "Maggie Tulliver and Philip."[20]

Lawrence stands in opposition to a whole critical tradition from the first reviewers of *The Mill on the Floss* to F. R. Leavis forty years later, who were disgusted by Maggie's rejection of Philip for the handsome but vacuous Stephen. I imagine that Lawrence thought her choice of Stephen was only poetic justice. According to Goethe's theory, Maggie's revulsion of Philip's deformity would have been overcome by their intellectual affinities; for Lawrence and Schopenhauer however, intellectual affinities between the sexes are insignificant when compared to sexual affinities.

In *The White Peacock* Alice's trivial quotation from Spinoza, "'Amor est titillatio' – 'Love is tickling'" (*WP*, 178), is borrowed from Schopenhauer's own withering reference to Spinoza's inadequate account of sex: "To amuse the reader ... Spinoza's definition deserves to be quoted because of its exuberant naïveté: *Amor est titillatio,*

---

[19] See James Simpson, *Matthew Arnold and Goethe* (London: The Modern Humanities Research Association, 1979), 124.
[20] E. T., *D. H. Lawrence: A Personal Record*, 97-98.

concomitante idea causae externae."[21] Encouraged by Schopenhauer, Lawrence imagined a sensuality in Maggie beyond George Eliot's creation of her; Chambers recalls him saying "that the smooth branches of the beech trees (which he especially admired) reminded him of Maggie Tulliver's arms".[22] He refers to Lettie's "white arms" in *The White Peacock* (302), suggesting that she is partly his recreation of George Eliot's Maggie.

Between 1906 and 1907 Lawrence read S. H. Dirks' translation of selected *Essays of Schopenhauer*,[23] including "The Metaphysics of Love". Lawrence's insertion of ideas from "The Metaphysics of Love" into *The White Peacock* has been examined by Worthen,[24] but here I want to look beyond the thematic to the formal influence of Schopenhauer on the novel, especially in terms of its tragic quality.

At the beginning of *Die Wahlverwandtschaften* Goethe included the paradoxical idea that opposites can have an affinity, as the Hauptmann explains:

> "Those natures which, when they meet, quickly lay hold on and mutually affect one another we call affined. This affinity is sufficiently striking in the case of alkalis and acids which, although they are mutually antithetical, and precisely because they are so, most decidedly seek and embrace one another, modify one another, and together form a new substance."

Charlotte comments that opposite qualities can make "eine innigere Vereinigung möglich"[25] ("a more intimate union possible"). Goethe's use of *innig* retains a chemical overtone, while being far more ambiguous in its psychological use, to imply a relationship which is anything between spiritually profound and sexually close.

---

[21] *Essays of Schopenhauer*, trans. and ed. S. H. Dircks (London: Walter Scott, 1897), 170.
[22] E. T., *D. H. Lawrence: A Personal Record*, 98.
[23] See Worthen, *D. H. Lawrence: The Early Years*, 157.
[24] *Ibid.*, 228.
[25] Goethe, *Gedenkausgabe*, IX, 42: "Diejenigen Naturen, die sich beim Zusammentreffen einander schnell ergreifen und wechselseitig bestimmen, nennen wir verwandt. An den Alkalien und Säuren, die, obgleich einander entgegengesetzt und vielleicht eben deswegen, weil sie einander entgegengesetzt sind, sich am entschiedensten suchen und fassen, sich modifizieren und zusammen einen neuen Körper bilden, ist diese Verwandtschaft auffallend genug."

As my earlier schematic description of the opening chapters of *Die Wahlverwandtschaften* indicates, however, Goethe tends to base his characters' affinities on similarity, which has its analogies in social relationships such as wealth, class and education. There is a conspicuous absence of sexual and socially subversive oppositions in the narrative. Schopenhauer by contrast explores this avenue thoroughly, using opposition as the basic principle of his "Metaphysics" of sexuality: "the two persons must neutralize each other, like acid and alkali to a neutral salt" to create biologically superior children who embody "the harmony concerning the individual and its perfection",[26] not the harmony of the lovers' souls.

In *The White Peacock* George and Lettie's first encounter follows Schopenhauer with striking faithfulness. Faults in Dircks' translation have been pointed out by critics, especially the replacement of *Geschlechtsliebe* ("sexual love") with mere "love".[27] In his treatment of Lettie and George, though, Lawrence uncannily reads the "sexual" back into the translation. Lettie, playing at the piano, is about to criticize George for his lack of artistic taste till she turns to look at him, struck into silence by his naked chest and arms. He looks "at her with glowing brown eyes, as if in hesitating challenge", and she answers "his challenge with a blue blaze of her eyes". One of Schopenhauer's examples is that since fair people "are a deviation from the type and almost constitute an abnormality",[28] they are attracted to dark people; according to Chambers, Lawrence "vehemently" agreed with this.[29] Schopenhauer's insight is the philosophical source of the drama of Lettie's blue eyes meeting George's brown ones; also, she is attracted to his brown skin and he finds her white skin desirable. Lawrence agrees with Schopenhauer's assertion that children inherit their mother's intellect and father's character, since Lettie's intellect is far superior to George's and her spiritual lightness contrasts with his sensual darkness.

Yet the sexual opposition between George and Lettie forces them apart from each other. After their intense eye contact she complains that

---

[26] Dircks, *Essays of Schopenhauer*, 188.
[27] See Worthen, *D. H. Lawrence: The Early Years*, 537; also Brunsdale, *The German Effect on D. H. Lawrence and His Works, 1885-1912*, 64.
[28] Dircks, *Essays of Schopenhauer*, 189.
[29] E. T., *D. H. Lawrence: A Personal Record*, 111.

"there's no change in your eyes when I look at you. I always think people who are worth much talk with their eyes .... Their eyes are so eloquent, and full of knowledge." (*WP*, 15)

At another point she asserts that "a few, – not you among them, – look me in the eyes for my thoughts. To you, I'm a fine specimen, strong! Pretty strong! You primitive man!" Of course, according to Schopenhauer, this is what a man who is in love should do! But Lettie marries Leslie instead; he shares more social affinities with her, being more "agreeable" (*WP*, 27, 21) than George. Even their names share an affinity, which George bitterly comments on.

The contradictory principles of similarity and opposition, of the social and sexual, the intellect and body, form the tragic conflict of *The White Peacock*. Lettie realizes that she and Leslie share no sexual affinity, that she cannot be "flesh of one flesh" with him. After he is crippled in a car accident, Leslie retains his hold on her by claiming their engagement to marry should not be reversed. By returning to her crippled lover Lettie re-enacts the scene in *The Mill on the Floss* that Lawrence could not accept. Instead of breaking from Leslie to unite with George, she remains true to the Victorian conventions; she dutifully sacrifices herself to her husband, and later also to her children. From Schopenhauer's ideas Lawrence developed an alternative mythology to George Eliot's and Goethe's, of the *Verneigung des Willens*, renunciation of the will.

Wagner, Hardy and Lawrence's transition to "pessimism"
Lawrence's most important English precursor in his literary appropriation of Schopenhauer was Thomas Hardy, especially in *Jude the Obscure* (1895). Jude and Arabella's first encounter foreshadows Lettie and George's at the piano in its foregrounding of their sexual attraction. Jude is daydreaming about his religious studies when Arabella throws a pig's penis at him; his offer to return it to her is "a dumb announcement of affinity *in posse*, between himself and her".[30] This affinity is purely sexual; Dennis Taylor has traced it back to Hardy's reading of Schopenhauer's *The World as Will and Idea*.[31] The split between Jude's sexual attraction to Arabella and spiritual affinity

---
[30] Thomas Hardy, *Jude the Obscure* (London: Penguin, 1998), 39.
[31] See notes to Hardy, *Jude the Obscure*, 419.

with Sue is central to the novel's tragedy. I have not found any commentary on the triangular relationship between Hardy, Schopenhauer and the young Lawrence, except in passing remarks by John Worthen and Mark Kinkead-Weekes.[32]

Hardy's example to Lawrence in his use of Schopenhauer is only rivalled by the German composer Richard Wagner. It cannot be argued that Schopenhauer actually caused these artists' pessimism, since this quality is latent in their early work. Here I shall outline how Schopenhauer's philosophy is used to legitimize their nihilism, enabling them to transform it from a theme into a *Weltanschauung* that gives formal order to their works, and demonstrate how in the process of composing *The White Peacock* Lawrence re-enacts Hardy's and Wagner's philosophical education through Schopenhauer.

Wagner read Schopenhauer's *Die Welt als Wille und Vorstellung* (1819) towards the end of composing *Die Walküre*, the second opera of *Der Ring des Nibelungen* (1876); he expressed the book's impact in the second half of the cycle, *Siegfried* and *Götterdämmerung*. Wagner's early operas were contradictory in their glorification of the hero's vitality, and his renunciation of life. For instance, Wagner uses the most powerful music to express Tannhäuser's debauchery in Venusberg, yet concludes the opera with his repentance and subsequent death. Wagner's initial libretto for the *Ring*, completed before the music was begun, described how "from the first sin a whole world of evil emerged, then collapses to the ground – to teach us the lesson that we must recognize evil, uproot it, and establish a more virtuous world in its place".[33] As Wagner himself explained in a letter to August Röckel in 1856, this first draft expresses his political idealism: the sin of capitalism is redeemed by Siegfried's martyrdom, while Brünnhilde celebrates the power of love over materialism.[34] There is a confusion about whether the hero affirms the purity of

---

[32] See Worthen, *D. H. Lawrence: The Early Years*, 174, 537. See also Kinkead-Weekes, Mark, *D. H. Lawrence: Triumph to Exile 1912-1922* (Cambridge: Cambridge University Press, 1996), 163.

[33] Richard Wagner, *Sämtliche Briefe* (Leipzig: Deutscher Verlag für Musik, 1967-), VIII, 153. "mit der Aufdeckung des ersten Unrechtes, aus dem eine ganze Welt des Unrechtes entsteht, die deshalb zu Grunde geht, um – uns eine Lehre zu geben, wie wir das Unrecht erkennen, seine Wurzel ausrotten und eine rechtliche Welt an ihrer Stelle gründen sollen."

[34] See Brian Magee, *The Philosophy of Schopenhauer* (Oxford: Clarendon Press, 1983), 340-46.

nature, as in Rousseau's sense of it, against a corrupt civilization, or whether nature is corrupt and must be overcome through death. Hardy's early novels, such as *Far from the Madding Crowd* (1874), share the idealism of early Wagner, in that the individual can overcome man's fallen state. Sergeant Troy is an expression of nature in its most vital, and destructive, form. He is countered by the resourceful Gabriel Oak who manages to cultivate the land against a harsh and indifferent nature. Although Oak does not redeem this fallen nature, which includes Troy's original sin, he sufficiently holds it in check to enjoy a harmonious existence with Bathsheba.[35] In his more humble way, then, Oak realizes the task that Wagner had first set Siegfried.

In the first versions of *The White Peacock* Lawrence shares Wagner and Hardy's pre-Schopenhauerian attitudes. We can see them most clearly in a surviving fragment, from between 1907 and 1908, which organizes details from Hardy's late novels into his attitudes of *Far from the Madding Crowd*. Michael Black sees George Saxton as a failed Gabriel Oak figure,[36] but in this earlier version of the novel George fits the role perfectly; Chambers disparagingly refers to him as a "simple, God-fearing yeoman".[37] He rescues Lettie from the scandal of having an illegitimate child by Leslie, who has abandoned her. In her pregnancy Lettie follows the harmonious seasons of nature, ripening like a fruit, while "this life, so gentle, quiet, retired, yet full of occupation, continued through September". After the birth of her child at New Year she feels outcast from society not nature, like the alienated Tess who suckles her child while harvesting. Yet through gentle support the "magnificent" George brings her back into society, and comforts her child who shares the solemn, staring eyes of Tess' Sorrow; he also saves Lettie and the child after her almost suicidal sleepwalk, like Jude's, over an iced pond. Finally, he carries her home after her confrontation with Leslie, enabling her to flourish in his pastoral environment as his "fat sorrow" (*WP*, 329, 344). George's ability to make nature whole, just as he is able to reintegrate Lettie into the social whole, is similar to Oak's relation to nature, and shares some

---

[35] See Ross C. Murfin, *Swinburne, Hardy, Lawrence and the Burden of Belief* (Chicago: University of Chicago Press, 1978), 105, 116.
[36] Michael Black, *D. H. Lawrence: The Early Fiction* (London: Macmillan, 1986), 47.
[37] E. T., *D. H. Lawrence: A Personal Record*, 118.

of the optimism of early Wagner.

It is impossible to judge how far Lawrence's intentions in this early draft succeeded, or failed, to achieve an aesthetic whole. Certainly, Wagner's visions in the earlier operas add up to a confusion of parts. The integrated form of *Far from the Madding Crowd* is only possible through limiting the catastrophes which are recuperated at the end. It is clear from the section "Studies in pessimism. Schopenhauer" in Hardy's *Literary Notebooks*, to which I shall be referring, that Schopenhauer contributed to his later tragedies.[38] The scenarios of these novels which interested Lawrence more deeply are far too devastating to be resolved; only Schopenhauer could provide a new means of reconciliation.

Wagner recalled that after reading Schopenhauer he was able to realize "the essence of the world itself, in all of its conceivable phases, ... and in its nothingness"[39] in the second half of the *Ring*. Schopenhauer had taught him that not only Siegfried, but also Brünnhilde and the Gods must all perish together, to confirm the ultimate *Nichtigkeit* of reality. Nietzsche exposes the political significance of Wagner's use of Schopenhauer. He labels Siegfried as "Den typischen Revolutionär" ("the typical revolutionary"), like Wagner in the failed 1848 German Revolution, who set about ousting all authoritarian gods and their dogmas. But then in the reactionary post-1848 political climate Wagner dealt with these aspirations through Schopenhauer, as Nietzsche explains:

> And he translated the *Ring* in a Schopenhauerian way. Everything goes wrong, everything goes to the ground, the new world is as bad as the old – *nothingness*, the Indian Circe beckons ... [40]

Lawrence was familiar with Schopenhauer's pessimism in the vocabulary of his educated social circle; May Holbrook's reminis-

---

[38] See T. J. Diffey, "Metaphysics and Aesthetics: A Case Study of Schopenhauer and Thomas Hardy" in *Schopenhauer, Philosophy, and the Arts*, ed. Dale Jacquette (Cambridge: Cambridge University Press, 1996).
[39] Wagner, *Sämtliche Briefe*, VIII, 153: "das Wesen der Welt selbst, in allen seinen nur erdenklichen Phasen, ... und in seiner Nichtigkeit."
[40] Friedrich Nietzsche, *Werke* (Berlin: Walter de Gruyter, 1967-), VI/1, 14-16: "Und er übersetze den 'Ring' in's Schopenhauerische. Alles läuft schief, Alles geht zu Grunde, die neue Welt ist so schlimm wie die alte: – das Nichts, die indische Circe winkt ...."

cences of his adolescence testify this:

> Bert began to change, and I asked him if College was doing it, or was it Schopenhauer?
> "Life," he said "and it gives me spiritual dyspepsia. It's right. You can have spiritual dyspepsia ...."[41]

Lawrence had probably read about pessimism in Dircks' translation of "The Emptiness of Existence" in *Essays of Schopenhauer*. Previous commentators on his reading of the *Essays* have tended to focus exclusively on "The Metaphysics of Love" because Jessie Chambers concentrated on this in her biography of his early years. Lawrence also had annotated this essay, but left "The Emptiness of Existence" unmarked. It has not been recognized that Chambers is biased towards the "Metaphysics" because Lawrence had used it to justify his attitudes towards her. Neither has it been recognized that Lawrence's annotations are implicated in this bias because they formed a dialogue between the two lovers, being addressed to Jessie who read the essay after Lawrence did; for example, Lawrence's first comment, "Qu'en pensez-vous?" in the margin of page 177, is a direct appeal to her, and indicates how she should attend to his later markings of passages. It is probable that Lawrence's reading of "The Emptiness of Existence" was more private but no less profound than his reading of the "Metaphysics".

The cyclical tragedy
We have seen how Goethe's affinities provided a theoretical model for George Eliot's style, in which her characters develop through interacting with each other. Through Schopenhauer's philosophy Wagner, Hardy and Lawrence turned Goethe and George Eliot's tragic alternative to affinities into their dominant style, where characters endlessly repeat their actions instead of developing through them. Schopenhauer replaces Goethe's *Entsagung* ("renunciation") of the individual's desires for social duty with his own expression *die Verneigung des Willens* ("the denial of the will") of the individual before the indifferent will of the universe. Schopenhauer turns Goethe's ethical imperative into a philosophical law that encompasses

---

[41] E. T., *D. H. Lawrence: A Personal Record*, 241.

the whole of nature.

Just as George Eliot's Realist style was not a viable option for Lawrence, neither could Wagner emulate Beethoven's analytical use of variation, a musical equivalent of Realism, as I explained in the Introduction. Adorno argues how in Beethoven's classical style ideas function as principles of pure becoming within the total structure, preserving their identity amid change; Beethoven's musical language is analogous to his society which cohered despite antagonisms within itself[42] – the dialectic between the whole and its individual parts which we see in George Eliot's novels. After the failed revolutions of 1848 Wagner found himself in a society whose alienated strata were comparable to the genre of opera he inherited, a conglomerate of arbitrary elements. He was unable to emulate Beethoven's mediation between individual and society; instead he alternated between a glorification of the individual's autonomy and its submergence in the totality of the *Volk*.[43] This situation is reflected in his contradictory celebration of desire and resignation in his operas.

Wagner structured his opera into discrete sections of myth, instead of following a linear development.[44] Under Schopenhauer's guidance he no longer wavered between sexuality and religion, but denied sexuality, in terms of *die Verneigung des Willens*. Adorno describes how this technique and belief are synthesized in Wagner's ordering principle of the *Leitmotiv*. In contrast to Beethoven's variations, musical phrases as *Leitmotive* are only repeated and intensified, but not developed. Beethoven's music is in a dialectical relation with time, as the melody develops while retaining its essential character. Wagner's music replaces a linear, progressive temporality with repetition, reifying its expression of feeling tautologically while the audience responds to it through habitual reflex.[45] Nietzsche incisively characterized this quality in Wagner's music: "he says something so often, until we get desperate, until we believe."[46] For example, we see most clearly in Siegfried's funeral march in *Götterdämmerung* how

---

[42] See Adorno, *In Search of Wagner*, 44.
[43] For instance, compare Richard Wagner's statements in *Gesammelte Schriften*, 14 vols (Berlin: Deutsches Verlagshaus, 1914), IV, 66-67 to those in III, 46-50.
[44] See *ibid.*, IV, 321.
[45] See Adorno, *In Search of Wagner*, 36-37.
[46] Nietzsche, *Werke*, VI/3, 8: "er sagt ein Ding so oft, bis man verzweifelt, bis man's glaubt."

Siegfried's melody, tending to develop through variation as in Beethoven's music, is held tightly in the grasp of the *Rheingold Motiv* which dominates the musical narrative and the audience's consciousness through being repeatedly intensified.

Although Hardy was able to order his characters' alienated, contradictory positions into what he called a "series of seemings", an open dialogue which could play these positions against each other,[47] his reading of Schopenhauer encouraged him, like Wagner, to realize their essential *Nichtigkeit*. Hardy notes from Schopenhauer that children are condemned to life, not death, in a vicious circle of suffering; he cites Schopenhauer's comparison between observing generations of suffering human beings and the repeated performances of a conjuror's tricks, whose familiarity no longer impresses the audience. The process is analogous to Schopenhauer's definition of tragedy, from which Hardy quotes: "Only when the intellect rises to the point where the vanity of all effort is manifest, & the will proceeds to an act of self-annulment, is the drama tragic in the true sense." From witnessing a series of God's repeated performances in His "conjurors [*sic*] booth"[48] (the world), Hardy's tragic characters and his readers realize that their individual wills are only manifestations of the whole world will, and that they are unable to escape from it. In Hardy's novels the narrative of linear progression is rejected, and a circularity emerges in its place.

We can trace this model of tragedy in Hardy and Schopenhauer's parallel use of the image of the wheel of Ixion. For Schopenhauer this image represents the unremitting rhythm of the individual enslaved to the will, destined always to suffer: "Thus lies the subject of willing constantly on the revolving wheel of Ixion, always drawing water in the sieve of the Danaids, and is the eternally thirsting Tantalus." Only in art can we transcend the will, where "we celebrate the Sabbath of the penal servitude of willing; the wheel of Ixion stands still".[49] In

---

[47] Hardy, *Jude the Obscure*, 3.
[48] Lennart A. Björk, *The Literary Notebooks of Thomas Hardy*, 2 vols (London: Macmillan, 1985), II, 29.
[49] Arthur Schopenhauer, *Sämtliche Werke*, 5 vols (Darmstadt: Wissenschaftliche Buchgesellschaft, 1968), I, 280: "So liegt das Subjekt des Wollens beständig auf dem drehenden Rade des Ixion, schöpft immer im Siebe der Danaiden, ist der ewig schmachtende Tantalus"; "wir feiern den Sabbath der Zuchthausarbeit des Wollens,

Hardy's *Tess of the D'Urbervilles* (1891) the wheel of Ixion becomes a metaphor for the inevitable cycle of fate in tragedy. Hardy describes how Tess' family suffer the "destiny" which they had inflicted on others "when they were among the Olympians of the country": "So do flux and reflux – the rhythm of change – alternate and persist in everything under the sky." The rhythm reaches its most excruciating pitch in the novel when Angel Clare finds Tess just after she has married Alec d'Urberville; her primal sighs sound like "a soul bound to some Ixionian wheel".[50] From this point, after expelling all her will in killing d'Urberville, Tess transcends it to accept her fate.

In *The White Peacock* Lawrence adopts Hardy's image of circularity both formally and thematically. Lawrence was familiar with Schopenhauer's image of circular entrapment; for instance, in "The Emptiness of Existence" life is compared to "a water-mill in that it is constantly changing",[51] while remaining the same in its lack of value. Lawrence borrows Hardy's image of the ensnared wild animal from *Jude the Obscure*, then transforms it to express the circular brutality of nature: a black cat's paws are caught in a trap when it had been about to use them to pounce upon a lapwing. Nature is a closed chain linking predator to prey. Lawrence's image of the cat contributes to the formal circularity of the novel by recurring as a motif. It is displaced onto Leslie after his crippling car accident, when Lettie's maid servant runs indoors, "like the frightened lapwing from the wounded cat". Lawrence uses the motif to relate the brutality of the will to the ideas of "The Metaphysics of Love". Lettie is repulsed by Leslie's physical condition after the accident, like the cat's mate who "shrugged his sleek shoulders, and walked away with high steps" on seeing her wounds. The theme of circularity is also in the image of Lettie and Cyril's father murmuring repeatedly to imaginary figures, "acting over again some part of his life"; Cyril is unaware of the poignant truth of his patronizing comment, "I don't mind your dreaming. But this is not the way to anywhere" (*WP*, 194, 12, 22-23).

The scenes of *The White Peacock* are developed around George and Lettie's encounters, in which they suggest their attraction to each other, but are unable to establish a satisfying relationship. During the

---

das Rad des Ixion steht still."
[50] Thomas Hardy, *Tess of the d'Urbervilles* (London: Penguin, 1991), 447-48, 486.
[51] Dircks, *Essays of Schopenhauer*, 61.

scene at the piano, when they recognize their sexual opposition, they look at each other silently, "with the blood beating madly in their necks" (*WP*, 30), then she leaves the room. Later, while he is gathering corn, she is attracted to the rhythm of his muscular body, but recoils from him when he digs a thorn from his hand. Lawrence plays with the image of the Fall where she offers him an apple, then hides it in her skirts, and throws it into the fire. After committing herself to Leslie, she visits George, looking "at him through a quiver of suppressed tears". Later, she refuses his proposal of marriage, and afterwards longs for him, singing Gretchen's "Meine Ruh ist hin" (*WP*, 138, 169), or "Gretchens Stube", as it is called in the First Part of Goethe's *Faust*. She suggests that they should live like larks, which he agrees with, but then she says that it would be impossible. When she is about to leave, she tells him that he has missed his opportunity to take her; he passionately kisses her, but she feels only weary. These scenes continue remorselessly over the course of the novel.

Schopenhauer argued that both intellect and sexuality are manifestations of the will, but at diametrically opposed levels. When they meet, as in the intellectual Lettie and the sensual George, or in Lettie's intellectual and sexual wills, the harmonious cycle of nature is corrupted; it continues, yet no longer self-grounded as an organic whole since different orders of the will remorselessly grind against each other. Goethe's pantheistic vision of the world of affinities has given way to a pessimistic one of discords. Suffering characterizes life in *The White Peacock*, whether it is the piglets eaten by the sow, or the newly hatched chicks who try to warm themselves and stumble into the open fireplace, or indeed, a person like Lettie whose will is divided between her body and mind, and can never be satisfied.

Lawrence specifically alludes to Schopenhauer to express the failure of his characters in the chapter "The Fascination of the Forbidden Apple". Lettie, "a seething confusion of emotion", wants to disrupt George's contentment with his life. She provokes him: "You, for instance – fancy *your* sacrificing yourself – for the next generation – that reminds you of Schopenhauer, doesn't it? – for the next generation, or love, or anything!" They find a dead wood-pigeon, which she interprets as having fought for a mate. She is torturing George about the pleasure the female must have felt in being fought over, and about her own pleasure in George's frustrated desire for her.

Then she rehearses George's burial by covering the bird with soil, softly intoning how it waited for death after losing the fight: "Don't you think life is very cruel, George: – and love the cruellest of all?" (*WP*, 210).

George's fate is like the wood-pigeon's, but ironically so is Lettie's, since she is forced to act out her Schopenhauerian diagnosis of him. In the chapter "The Dominant Motif of Suffering" Cyril moralizes on the subject of how in motherhood Lettie loses all sense of individuality:

> Having reached that point in a woman's career when most, perhaps all of the things in life seem worthless and insipid, she had determined to put up with it, to ignore her own self, to empty her own potentialities into the vessel of another or others, and to live her life at second hand. This peculiar abnegation of self is the resource of a woman for the escaping of her own development .... As a servant she is no longer responsible for herself, which would make her terrified and lonely. Service is light and easy. To be responsible for the good progress of one's life – is terrifying. It is the most insufferable form of loneliness, and the heaviest of responsibilities. (*WP*, 284)

Lettie has renounced her responsibility to herself in a passionless marriage and the children that it yields. She is entrapped in a Schopenhauerian dilemma: in her marriage to Leslie her intellect has dominated her sexual will to reproduce and rear offspring, and yet in these circumstances her intellect has only yielded her self-abnegation through serving the next generation.

In Schopenhauer's essay "The Emptiness of Existence", the terror that Lawrence describes comes from "constantly Becoming without Being", from the contrast between "the infiniteness of Time and Space as opposed to the finiteness of the individual in both". Lettie cannot accept the finite span of "her own development", so she renounces her development for a circular existence within the generations of her family. Christianity no longer consoles her, so she can only try to find "Being" in the next generation. Schopenhauer comments how people "attempt, when they are taking leave of life, to hand it over to someone else who will take their place". At most, the individual can only strive to reproduce itself. Schopenhauer attacks the Pantheist claim that life is "an end-in-itself": the process of Becoming only involves "hunger and the instinct of sex, helped perhaps a little by boredom". Life "passes by" while we are living. His only alternative advice to the Pantheists, and to Lawrence, is what Wagner and Hardy had learned from him: "It would be wisest to regard life as a *desengaño*, a delusion; that everything is intended to be so is sufficiently clear."[52] Lawrence's characters are forced into sharing this conclusion.

Yet Lawrence implies that Lettie should have been "responsible for herself" by pursuing her sexual desire for George, which points beyond Schopenhauer's own philosophy, towards Nietzsche. Contrary to Schopenhauer, Lawrence believes that the individual can fulfil the demands of their will; in *The White Peacock*, though, he is unable to envisage how this can be achieved by the characters.

Wagner's "Star of Eve"
Lawrence wrote the last parts of *The White Peacock*, alongside the first version of his second novel *The Trespasser*, in the spring of 1910. During this period he established the Wagnerian tragic vision that characterizes *The Trespasser*, visiting Covent Garden and sharing with Helen Corke his fascination with the composer. In the chapter "Pisgah" Lawrence quotes from *Tannhäuser*. Also, following from his emulation of Schopenhauer's cyclical vision of tragedy, he imitates Wagner's musical technique to express George and Lettie's suffering at their final meeting. I shall explore Lawrence's use of Wagner in greater depth during the next chapter, but this climactic scene of *The White Peacock* deserves a full examination itself. In this scene we see Lawrence emulate the expressiveness of Wagner's musical textures and incorporate Schopenhauer's "Metaphysic" into a *Motiv* drawn from *Tannhäuser* (1845). Simultaneously, however, Lawrence attempts to rebel against the pessimistic implications of this symbolic style; he refers to the characters of Wagner's scenario in implicit criticism of Lettie and George's actions.

In Lawrence's scene George visits Lettie one evening while her husband is away. George complains to her that his "marriage is more of a duel than a duet", and she attempts to avoid the subject of his frustration:

> She sang from Wagner. It was the music of resignation and despair.

---

[52] *Ibid.*, 54, 61, 56, 60.

She had not thought of it. All the time he listened he was thinking. The music stimulated his thoughts and illuminated the trend of his brooding. All the time he sat looking at her his eyes were dark with his thoughts. She finished the "Star of Eve" from "Tannhäuser" and came over to him. (*WP*, 301)

The "Star of Eve" aria, which occurs in second scene of the third Act of Wagner's opera, was popular among Lawrence's contemporaries, not least because its piano transcription by Liszt was so simple to play. Tannhäuser is loved by Elisabeth, but has left her to plead forgiveness for his sins from the Pope; all the pilgrims have returned from Rome except him, yet she steadfastly prays for his soul. Meanwhile Wolfram, who has always loved Elisabeth, sings to himself:

> O du mein holder Abendstern,
> wohl grüßt' ich immer dich so gern;
> vom Herzen, das sie nie verriet,
> grüße sie, wenn sie vorbei dir zieht,
> wenn sie entschwebt dem Tal der Erden,
> ein sel'ger Engel dort zu werden.
>
> O my fair evening star,
> I always gladly greeted you;
> from a heart that never betrayed her,
> greet her when she passes by you,
> when she soars above this earthly vale
> to become a blessed angel.
>
> *(He remains with his eyes turned to heaven, continuing to play his harp.)*[53]

What makes this passage from the opera so poignant is how, after Wolfram has stopped singing, the cellos replace his voice against the harp and chords of the bassoons, gradually turning what was such a simple harmony into something more uncertain and even strained. The cellos descend the chromatic scale and change conjunction with the sliding major/minor keys of the bassoons, whose thirds create a more insistent, pregnant effect. This section expresses Wolfram's unrequited love and introduces the tragic climax of the opera, his dialogue with

---

[53] Richard Wagner, *Tannhäuser* (London: John Calder, 1988), 87.

the unredeemed Tannhäuser. Lawrence emulates the emerging tension in Wagner's music. Lettie plays to George "the music of resignation and despair" ostensibly to make him "cheerful again". Her forceful self-repression is counterpointed by his gaining consciousness: the rhythm of words, "thought ... listened ... thinking ... stimulated ... thoughts ... illuminated ... brooding ... looking ... thoughts", follows the undulating rhythm of the music, while the reader is expected to play the familiar tune in his head. The apparent harmony between Lettie and George becomes discordant, and resists resolution.

The scene belongs to the "motivic" structure of the novel, of George and Lettie's frustrating and futile encounters, and we have reached the climactic point where they will either break out of the tragic cycle, or lapse into it permanently. From Wagner's song Lawrence appropriates the opposition of star and darkness to provide the counterpoint within his *Motiv*. It expresses Lettie and George's Schopenhauerian opposition of light and dark, the tragic mechanism that has attracted them to each other and forced them apart. Lettie's son has previously introduced the *Motiv* in his comment that her singing to George had sounded "quite small, as if it were nearly lost in the dark" (*WP*, 299). George tells her she is beautiful, at which she tells him he should be happy. He replies that he is in the grasp of the "lean arms" of "Tomorrow", alluding to his married life with Meg; she asserts that Tomorrow's arms "are white, like mine". He takes her casual statement and sharply questions it. She tries to avoid the bait, but he asserts that seeing her children had reminded him of "These lean arms of tomorrow's round me, and the white round you". She is moved, holding his hand, and he expresses his feelings through Wagner's song, recapitulating it:

> "I have needed you for a light. You will soon be the only light again.... And you know, I couldn't endure complete darkness, I couldn't. It's the solitariness." (*WP*, 302)

Yet while Lettie and George remain in this world of musical symbols they cannot hope to break out of the novel's Schopenhauerian "Metaphysic", because it determines their actions. In reaction to this impasse Lawrence, like Wagner, tries to counter the symbolic *Motiv* with the specific representation of Realist discourse. Adorno argues that in Wagner there can be an explosion of the individuality of each *Leitmotiv*, to resist the synthesis of its physical performance and the symbolism it is intended to express. Through his dramatic and richly coloured orchestration Wagner insists on the physicality of the *Motiv* as a concrete gesture of sound:

> Beneath the thin veil of continuous progress Wagner has fragmented the composition into allegorical leitmotivs juxtaposed like discrete objects. These resist the claims both of a totalizing musical form and of the aesthetic claims of "symbolism", in short, the entire tradition of German idealism.[54]

In Lawrence's scene the dramatic narrative of Lettie and George's actions vies with their symbolic meaning.

Earlier in the novel Lawrence had alluded to Wagner's opera in order to comment on Cyril's personality. He implicitly compared Cyril to Wolfram gazing upon the pilgrims as he sang "Star of Eve":

> I wished that in the wild valley where the cloud shadows were travelling like pilgrims, something would call me forth from my rooted loneliness. Through all the grandeur of the white and blue day, the poised cloud masses swung their slow flight, and left me unnoticed. (*WP*, 127)

The odd comparison of the cloud shadows to pilgrims links Cyril to Wolfram, and suggests that he shares Wolfram's loneliness and alienation from the events that he describes.

Again, in "Pisgah" Lawrence uses his allusion to *Tannhäuser* to comment on Lettie and George's personalities. In Lawrence's original manuscript, instead of calling the music from Wagner "Star of Eve", he accidentally referred to it as "Elisabeth's prayer" (*WP*, 445). The mistake suggests that Lawrence also found the opera useful in helping him to define Lettie's character, just as he had used Wolfram for Cyril. The image of Lettie singing "Elisabeth's prayer" to make George "cheerful again" would have been a startling description of her personality, especially where Elisabeth implores the Virgin Mary to accept her into heaven:

---

[54] Adorno, *In Search of Wagner*, 48.

> Wenn je in tör'gem Wahn befangen
> mein Herz sich abgewandt von dir,
> wenn je ein sündiges Verlangen,
> ein weltlich Sehnen keimt in mir:
> so rang ich unter tausend Schmerzen,
> daß ich es töt in meinem Herzen.[55]

> If ever, deluded by foolish illusions,
> my heart turned away from you,
> if ever a sinful desire
> or earthly longing stirred within me,
> I struggled with a thousand pangs
> to kill it in my heart.

Elisabeth ends in "andächtiger Entrücktheit" ("devout rapture"). It is probably the only possible kind of "rapture" that Lawrence imagined Lettie capable of. Elisabeth's resignation is unconvincing in *Tannhäuser*, since Wagner was yet to learn from Schopenhauer that his characters should completely renounce their desires. Tannhäuser expresses Wagner's eroticism, which almost overwhelms Elisabeth, and the audience, in Act II. The contradictory resignation and sexual desire in Elisabeth's character and the opera as a whole forms part of the subtext of Lawrence's Wagnerism. We are forced, then, to examine Lettie's motives: does she play the "Star of Eve" to console George, or to mock his persistence? Would she have played "Elisabeth's Prayer" to persuade George to be resigned, or to express her own repressed desire for him?

And so the musical spell is broken, since Lawrence has shattered the Wagnerian paradigm of the scene organized around a single "vorwaltende Hauptstimmung"[56] (dominant mood"). Instead he structures the scene around the characters' responses to each other, to return the reader to a reality of cause and effect, as in *Die Wahlverwandtschaften* and *Middlemarch*. Lawrence rebels against Wagner's symbolism, yet he is unable to commit himself to George Eliot's and Goethe's Realism. Wagner's individual musical ideas and Lawrence's characters can only insist on their own importance while

---

[55] Wagner, *Tannhäuser*, 86.
[56] Wagner, *Gesammelte Schriften*, III, 321.

remaining impotent in the musical, novelistic and social whole. As readers we can distance ourselves from Lettie and George to criticize their failings. But given the power of the Schopenhauerian metaphysic that determines their actions, and of the symbolic discourse that expresses this metaphysic, we are unable to envisage an alternative for them.

Wagner and Lawrence's dissonance

For Adorno, Wagner's music was both regressive in its use of the *Leitmotiv*, and progressive in the way that it departed from Beethoven's classical order of harmony into dissonance. Beethoven developed his musical themes in the sonata form by letting them diverge from the central triad of their key, into dominant and subdominant areas to create tension in the harmony. Adorno singles out moments when Wagner lets his ideas go, to abandon themselves into a primal dissonance outside the harmonic scheme, just as the individual can let himself go outside conventional authority, to assume the "character of sovereign subjectivity vis-à-vis the resolutions". In the dissonance of *Parsifal* (1882), for example in Act II where its hero cries out "Amfortas!" after Kundry's attempted seduction, Wagner breaks the "fulfilment promised in consonance", to explore "the poignant pain of non-fulfilment and the pleasure that lies in the tension".[57] It can be argued that Lawrence achieves a comparable effect in "Pisgah".

Helen Corke recalls that Lawrence's first "experience of Wagner's music had been a performance, in a Nottingham theatre, of *Tannhäuser*, when he reacted against the stridency of the Venusberg music".[58] The Venusberg music was one of Wagner's most radical, and dissonant, achievements. It was written while he was working on the later opera *Tristan und Isolde* (1865), whose instrumentation and harmonics it shares. Perhaps Lawrence's aversion to it is an example of how his reaction against other artists is coupled with a desire to confront and internalize their foreignness. After all, the dissonance of the Venusberg music is very reminiscent of the visionary scenes in *The White Peacock* where George and Lettie, Cyril and Emily let go of themselves in dance. These dances are probably the only way that

---

[57] See Adorno, *In Search of Wagner*, 62-70.
[58] See *Letters of D. H. Lawrence*, I, 99.

Lawrence could momentarily recreate George Eliot's utopian vision of two harmonious couples, as Cyril exclaims: "It was a tremendous, irresistible dancing. Emily and I must join, making an inner ring" (*WP*, 55). Mark Kinkead-Weekes perceives the visionary quality of the scenes: "For once George is on the move instead of sunk in lethargy and self-doubt; for once Cyril the narrator is jerked out of aestheticism; for once Lettie is no longer in control"; and for once Emily is not paralysed by self-consciousness. The characters transcend their limitations by transgressing their conventional relations with each other, just as Wagner's dissonant themes break from conventional tonal relations. Kinkead-Weekes describes how in *The White Peacock* "dancing becomes a way of breaking through 'character' and 'social relationship', to reveal something deeper".[59] In other words, Lawrence breaks out of the Realist discourse of traditional characterization, to express the erotic vitality of his characters.

Lawrence injects dissonance into Lettie and George's final encounter in "Pisgah". Although the corresponding scene in Wagner's opera, Tannhäuser's confrontation with Wolfram, is not dissonant, it abandons the initial musical argument with a new key area and thematic idea that threaten to disrupt the harmonic progression. Lawrence's characters act in a similar way: their *Motive* become antagonistic to express the Schopenhauerian alienation between their wills. Lettie runs her fingers through George's hair, telling him it is as thick as ever. At this point their *Motive* draw closest, yet instead of her remarking that he is also as physically attractive as ever, she introduces a separate *Motiv* by drawing back into her role as mother. She parts his hair with a comb to symbolize their estrangement from each other, and her resistance to his desire for them to let go of themselves. This gesture reverses the visionary dance scenes in which their hair was in bacchanalian disorder, his "glistening" and hers "wild about her face" (*WP*, 95). Against Lettie, George expands upon his "darkness" *Motiv*, that he could only give her warmth:

> "So you could do without me. But you were like the light to me, and otherwise it was dark and aimless. Aimlessness is horrible." (*WP*, 303)

---

[59] Mark Kinkead-Weekes, "D. H. Lawrence and the Dance", *The Journal of the D. H. Lawrence Society* (1992-1993), 46-47.

But as he becomes most forceful, she recoils, and speculates on what her daughter's opinion of his hair would be.

At the climax of Wagner's opera where Tannhäuser recounts the Pope's curse, the musical order threatens to dissolve into anarchy, since it has lost its central key and sustained thematic periods.[60] The corresponding dissonance between Lettie and George now reaches an excruciating, climactic pitch in this scene, threatening to break out of its "musical" order, and the social order of marital responsibility:

> "We can't go on like this, Lettie, can we?" he said softly.
> "Yes," she answered him, "Yes why not?"
> "It can't!" he said "It can't, I couldn't keep it up, Lettie."
> "But don't think about it," she answered. "Don't think of it."
> "I have to set my teeth with loneliness, Lettie," he said.
> "Hush!" she said "No! There are the children. Don't say anything – do not be serious, will you?"
> "No, there are the children," he replied, smiling dimly.
> "Yes! Hush now! Stand up and look what a fine parting I have made in your hair. Stand up, and see if my style becomes you."
> "It is no good Lettie," he said, "We can't go on." (*WP*, 303)

Lettie answers George's desperate pleas by complimenting him on his hair, which makes the narrative resemble musical bitonality, of two independent harmonic structures juxtaposed. Richard Strauss introduced this innovation in his opera *Elektra* (1909), which I shall compare later to Lawrence's style in *Sons and Lovers*. The dissonance continues to the end of the chapter. George insists that they must either make a life together or never see each other again, to which she assents, her voice "'muted' like a violin". He watches her "twisting the azurite jewels on her bosom, and pressing the blunt points into her flesh" (*WP*, 303).

Wagner achieves resolution in *Tannhäuser* when his hero dies, resigned and redeemed, beside Elisabeth's funeral bier. For George and Lettie there will be no resolution, not even in George's death which is later depicted with such uncompromising bitterness. On the other hand, Lawrence's dissonance is not radical enough to break out of the cycle of tragedy; similarly, Wagner's dissonance in *Parsifal* still only exploits the contrast with the harmonic triad. Their dissonance is

---

[60] See *Tannhäuser*, ed. John Nicholas John (London: John Calder, 1988), 49.

not expressive in an absolute way, as Schoenberg's is in his atonal works, but only in its remoteness from the consonance of tonality. By analogy, Lawrence only strains against bourgeois morality without breaking out of its boundaries. Both artists leave the tragic framework, and what Adorno calls the "immanent reality of bourgeois society", intact.[61] Lawrence forces George to act passively, to remain within the novel's Wagnerian parameters and the bourgeois values which entrap him.

The failure of Lawrence's "tragedy"
We see, then, isolated moments in *The White Peacock* where Lawrence affirms the vitality of his characters against their crippling circumstances. Lettie's contemplation of some snowdrops reflects the limits of Lawrence's achievement in this novel: "look at them – closed up, retreating, powerless. They belong to some knowledge we have lost, that I have lost, and that I need. I feel afraid. They seem like something in fate" (*WP*, 129). Lawrence is attempting to reclaim the lost "wisdom" of these snowdrops, against the social conventions that have repressed it. Like Lettie, he needs this wisdom yet is afraid to pursue it.

Lawrence valued Goethe and Eliot's use of affinity as motivation for his characters' actions, because it could liberate his characters from traditional morality. Yet Goethe and Eliot abandoned affinity when sexuality threatened to disrupt social affinity, and they fell back into a moralising tragedy. Schopenhauer developed affinity into a "Metaphysic" which centred upon sexuality, against George Eliot and Goethe's repression of it. And yet Schopenhauer could not offer anything more positive to Lawrence than Goethe and George Eliot's tragedies of renunciation because he could not affirm sexuality either.

George Eliot's apparent utopia of affinities at the end of *Middlemarch* is tinged with an underlying dissonance in the relationship between Lydgate and Rosamond that resembles Schopenhauer's "Metaphysic". In the "Finale" George Eliot mentions that Lydgate died at "only fifty",[62] exhausted, she implies, by his quarrels with Rosamond. The couple share more sexual opposition

---
[61] Adorno, *In Search of Wagner*, 68.
[62] George Eliot, *Middlemarch* (Oxford: Oxford University Press, 1986), 679.

than personal affinities; early in their marriage Lydgate reflects that "it seemed that she had no more identified herself with him than if they had been creatures of different species and opposing interests".[63] George Eliot would have agreed with the implications of Schopenhauer's "Metaphysic", that the failure of two individuals to realize their sexual opposition is not necessarily tragic. Instead it is a more tragic outcome when two people who are matched like Lydgate and Rosamond, or indeed Lettie and George, actually come together because they will spend the rest of their lives quarrelling while producing genetically superior children. This relationship results in self-abnegation, not fulfilment, because the sexual impulse is still alienated from the intellect.

In *The White Peacock* Lawrence partly subscribes to this conclusion. Lettie and Cyril's parents were attracted to each other through a sexual opposition, and yet it alienated them from each other. Lettie and George in turn have respectively internalized their parents' relationship in the alienation between their mind and body. Their minds repress their physical desires, and yet through this frustration they have developed a sensitivity to the beauty of life, as Lettie explains herself to George:

> You never grow up, like bulbs which spend all summer getting fat and fleshy but never wakening the germ of a flower. As for me, the flower is born in me, but it wants bringing forth. Things don't flower if they're overfed. You have to suffer before you blossom in this life. When death is just touching a plant, it forces it into a passion of flowering. You wonder how I have touched death. You don't know. There's always a sense of death in this home. I believe my mother hated my father before I was born. That was the death in her veins for me before I was born. It makes a difference. (*WP*, 28)

Perhaps Lawrence has borrowed the image of Bathsheba at the end of Hardy's *Far from the Madding Crowd*, in the quotation from Keats: "As though a rose could shut and be a bud again."[64] But Lettie's sense of genealogical fatality belongs more to *Jude the Obscure* and implies that, like Sue, she can never flower. At the same time, though, her self-alienation has given her the potentiality for passion, unlike the

---

[63] *Ibid.*, 487.
[64] Hardy, *Far from the Madding Crowd*, 463.

uncomplicated George who is only a "bulb". It is only after he has lost her to Leslie that he acquires her sensitivity. He tells Lettie that "you have awakened my life – I imagine things that I couldn't have done" (*WP*, 116), but towards the end of the novel he tells Cyril that "you and Lettie have made me self-conscious, and now I'm at a dead loss" (*WP*, 238). His frustration has given value to his desires, his lack of fulfilment has given him a sense of value to his life. Marriage to Lettie would not have provided him with a way forward, however, since they would only have repeated the mistake of her parents.

Perhaps the stray figure of the gamekeeper Annable suggests an alternative. He embodies the limits of Schopenhauer's answer to Goethe's denial of sexuality: his sexual opposition to his wife has only produced an innumerable mass of neglected and abused children; he rejects his intellect for his sexuality, but becomes nihilistic and alienated from society, committing suicide. When Emily and Lettie discuss his unfortunate marriage, Cyril concludes that "I suppose he did not know what he was doing any more than the rest of us". Yet Annable's unrepentant physicality and his dictum "Be a good animal, true to your animal instinct" (*WP*, 185, 147) fascinate Cyril and suggest an alternative to the novel's events that Lawrence is as yet unable to pursue.

To make *The White Peacock* tragic in the sense of his later novels, such as *Sons and Lovers* and *Women in Love*, Lawrence needs to envision moments of reconciliation in the ongoing conflict between his characters' intellect and sexuality. For Schopenhauer, sexual love reconciles the "individual and its perfection" only in the Platonic Idea of the conceived child. Lawrence is attempting to rewrite Schopenhauer's theory so that the tragedy lies not in George and Lettie's unborn children, but in their failure to give birth to themselves. Yet at this point Lawrence is unable to envisage the tragedy of their lost opportunity to break from the limits of their respective egos, to establish a creative conflict between each other's opposing qualities, so that as individuals they could achieve their own "perfection".

II
BETWEEN WAGNER AND NIETZSCHE:
THE TRESPASSER

Lawrence's main source for his second novel *The Trespasser* was in Helen Corke's diaries and conversations about her tragic affair with her music teacher Herbert Macartney. While completing the final revisions of his novel in February 1912, Lawrence described it to her as "a work of fiction on a frame of actual experience". He argued that it "should be a work of art" which could articulate the "original truth" of her past. Attempting to substantiate the link between "truth" and his "art", Lawrence offered her "my bit of a life philosophy": "Surely it has always been one of my tenets, that a truth, or a vital experience, is eternal, in so far as it is incorporated into one's being, and so is oneself" (Letters, I, 359-60). Lawrence believed then, that personal experience was essential for making "truth" "eternal" through art. When he began the novel as "The Saga of Siegmund" in the spring of 1910 he believed that music was the art medium which could express this truth. He told Helen Corke that he intended to create "a work of art that must be a saga since it cannot be a symphony".[1]

This combination of myth and music relates *The Trespasser* back to Wagnerian opera. In *The White Peacock* Lawrence was indebted to Wagner in his reaction against the objective, Realist tradition of George Eliot. In *The Trespasser* Lawrence uses Wagner's musical technique more extensively, not only in the structural principle of the *Leitmotiv*, but also at the level of language, of Wagner's principle of *Tonsprache* ("tone-speech"), which imitates the effects of music. Through Wagner, Lawrence attempts to express the "eternal" truth of Helen Corke's relationship with Macartney, but his technique fails to register the physical reality of their relationship, and leaves them powerless as characters in the novel. As we shall see, Lawrence will counter this Romantic tendency with the ideas of Nietzsche, but with mixed success.

---

[1] Helen Corke, *D. H. Lawrence: The Croydon Years* (Austin: University of Texas Press, 1965), 8.

Appropriating Wagner's musical technique

The origins of Lawrence's style in *The Trespasser* can be seen in two consecutive letters to Blanche Jennings dated 15 and 22 December 1908, just before he began his final revision of *The White Peacock*. In both letters he dismisses George Eliot's apparent objectivity which conceals the ethical assumptions of her "padding and moral reflection". His attitude reflects why he could not emulate Eliot and Goethe's Realism in *The White Peacock*. He observes that

> folks *will* want things intellectually done, so they take refuge in George Eliot. I am very fond of her, but I wish she'd take her specs off, and come down off the public platform. "I wouldn't mind if they spoke the truth, but they don't."

Lawrence is sceptical about the authenticity of Eliot's Realism, but he is uncertain about what constitutes the "truth". He admits that he cannot identify a "femme perdue", "as most men seem to be able to do". He does not understand everyday *"life"*, but a truth which transcends it: a *"Life"* of the soul: "No, I don't know much of *life* – but of *Life*. – I *do not* poke into peoples souls; peoples souls come flowing round me and touching me, and I feel them" (Letters, I, 101-102).

Lawrence is beginning to realize that music gives access to the *"Life"* which he believes he understands. Books on music, he maintains, can explain nothing: "the only way to learn about music is to listen to it, and think about it afterwards". His favourite composer is Wagner:

> Surely you know Wagner's operas – *Tannhäuser* and *Lohengrin*. They will run a knowledge of music into your blood better than any criticisms. We are withering nowadays under the barren warmth of other people's opinions, and second hand knowledge. It doesn't matter how little you *know*, so long as you are capable of feeling much, and giving indiscriminate sympathy.

Already Lawrence is distinguishing "feeling" from "knowledge", or "blood" from words, which anticipates his famous letter on the Italian "belief in the blood" in 1913. His notion of music is similar to Schopenhauer's which had inspired Wagner, as an independent form of life: "there isn't thought behind music, but the music is behind the thought, music behind the idea, music the first wild natural thing, and thought is the words writ to the music, the narrow row of words with little meanings" (Letters, I, 99-101). In contrast to Eliot, Wagner's music is identified with a "truth" of the "blood" and with *"Life"*.

In *The Trespasser* Lawrence envisages a *"Life"* for his two protagonists Siegmund and Helena, who are attempting to transcend the decay of their everyday *"life"*. Siegmund's *"life"* is described in the naturalist details of his home, "a dirty cloth, that had great brown stains betokening children", flies crawling over the food, a chipped cup with a stain "like the mark of a dirty mouth" (*T*, 50). This reality manifests itself in individual objects; it can only be transcended in a universalized, spiritual realm.

Lawrence uses Wagner's example to express Siegmund's transcendence of the everyday. Arriving on the Isle of Wight, Siegmund refers to Wagner as he transcends temporality: "How could it be Sunday! It was no time, it was Romance, going back to Tristan". Siegmund also alludes to *Die Walküre* when expressing how the island approaches *him*, in his transcendence of space: "In front, Sieglinde's island drew near, and nearer, creeping towards him, bringing him Helena" (*T*, 55-56). The world is only a projection of his desires.

Yet in expressing this transcendental *"Life"*, Lawrence's language fails in *The Trespasser*. With Wagner at the back of his mind, Lawrence had attempted to describe the experience of kissing to Blanche Jennings:

> I have kissed dozens of girls – on the cheek – never on the mouth – I could not. ... Like a positive electricity, a current of creative life runs through the two persons, and they are instinct with the same life force – the same vitality – the same I know not what – when they kiss on the mouth – when they kiss as lovers do. (Letters, I, 99)

"The same I know not what" betrays an embarassment over his lack of linguistic ability in expressing *"Life"*. The problem recurs in *The Trespasser* when Helena and Siegmund kiss:

> Suddenly she strained madly to him, and, drawing back her head, placed her lips on his, close, till at the mouth they seemed to melt and

fuse together. It was a long, supreme kiss, in which man and woman have one being, Two-in-one, the only Hermaphrodite. (*T*, 64)

The imagery of the characters "fusing" into a "Hermaphrodite" is more abstract than sensual. When Siegmund and Helena transcend their individuality into a oneness, the subject-object and signifier-signified relations collapse: language is abstracted from the tactile qualities of physical reality.

A similar effect occurs in Wagner's poetry, especially in *Tristan und Isolde*, for example where the lovers are teetering on the brink of consummation in Act II:

> Tristan: Ohne Gleiche!
> Isolde: Überreiche!
> Tristan: Überselig!
> Isolde: Ewig!
> Tristan: Ewig!
> Isolde: Ungeahnte, nie gekannte!
> Tristan: Überschwenglich hoch erhabne!
> Isolde: Freudejauchzen!
> Tristan: Lustentzücken![2]
>
> Tristan: Without equal!
> Isolde: Overflowing!
> Tristan: Overjoyed!
> Isolde: Eternal!
> Tristan: Eternal!
> Isolde: Unforeseen, never known!
> Tristan: Gushing, highly exalted!
> Isolde: Exhalted joy!
> Tristan: Joyful delight!

And so on. We can see in the original German that words have lost their semantic value, as those of similar meaning are fused together and piled on top of each other. Meanwhile, the singers merge into the orchestral texture, into the rhythm of the "yearning" *Motiv*. Language is imitating music, not representing but directly expressing the *Wille*, to use Schopenhauer's terms.

---

[2] Richard Wagner, *Tristan und Isolde* (London: John Calder, 1981), 67.

Wagner named his poetic technique *Tonsprache*, which he explains as the technical basis of his operas in Part III of *Oper und Drama* (1850-51). Through *Tonsprache* Wagner reconciled language with music to form a total vision of the world, the *Gesamtkunstwerk*. He argued that language did not originate in the rational "Verstand" ("understanding") of "wissenschaftliche Forschung" ("scientific knowledge"). Instead, it originated in the "Gefühl" ("feeling") of "das ursprünglichste Äußerungsorgan des inneren Menschen" ("the primal organ-of-utterance of the inner man"), where the speaker's emotion and utterance are immanently related in the "Stabreim". The consonants at the beginning and end of each word, the "tönende Laut" ("key sound") and "Mitlaut" ("consonant", or "end sound"), embody the "innere Gefühl" ("inner feeling") which is enunciated in the musical tone. They are regulated by the vowel between them, which converts their generalized "Gefühl" into "besondere Ausdrücke"[3] ("particular expressions"). Through repetition the consonants and vowels build up an emotional experience in the audience, similar to musical tones rhythmically repeated.

Lawrence could have learned about Wagner's poetic technique through Helen Corke, or by reading the criticism of the most important English Wagnerian at the turn of the century, Ernest Newman. In a letter to Blanche Jennings he mentions having "snatched at Ernest Newman" (Letters, I, 100), confident that she will approve of his choice. It is probable that Lawrence would have read either of Newman's monographs *A Study of Wagner* (1899) or *Wagner* (1904). *A Study of Wagner* gives critical analyses of all the operas and most of Wagner's writings, which could have provided Lawrence with a technical understanding of *Tonsprache*, or "Stabreim" as Newman referred to it.[4] Throughout *The Trespasser* Lawrence uses a form of *Tonsprache* to create a world which transcends the reality of cause and effect, of science, politics and history. Joseph Kestner compares Lawrence's style to Wagner's

---

[3] Richard Wagner, *Gesammelte Schriften und Dichtungen III*, 10 vols (Leipzig: E. W. Frisch, 1887-88), 137, 127, 91, 129-30.
[4] See Ernest Newman, *A Study of Wagner* (London: Bertram Dobell, 1899); *Wagner* (London: Bodley Head, 1904).

technique; my interpretation is greatly indebted to this paper, and seeks to elaborate on it.[5]

In Siegmund's first bathing scene *Tonsprache* is used to express his organic harmony with nature: "The wind nestled in to him, the sunshine came on his shoulders like warm breath." The harmony is expressed in the assonance of "wind", "in", "him", and the alliteration of "wind", "warm" and "sunshine", "shoulders". Then the harmony is disrupted by the spur of a rock catching Siegmund's leg:

> He glanced at himself, at his handsome, white maturity. As he looked he felt the insidious creeping of blood down his thigh, which was marked with a long red slash. Siegmund watched the blood travel over the bright skin. It wound itself redly round the rise of his knee.
> "That is I, that creeping red, and this whiteness I pride myself on is I, and my black hair, and my blue eyes are I. ...
> He glanced at his whole handsome maturity, the firm plating of his breasts, the full thighs, creatures proud in themselves. Only he was marred by the long scratch, which he regretted deeply. ...
> He wiped the blood from the wound. It was nothing. (*T*, 73-74)

Kestner argues that Lawrence uses *Tonsprache* to convey the tension of "handsome, white maturity", "whiteness" and "whole handsome maturity", against "blood", "long red slash", "redly round", "creeping red", "long raw scratch" and "regretted deeply". Yet Kestner does not recognize the tendency of *Tonsprache* to fuse objects into a non-physical, universalized ideal. The slash is recouped into the organic image of Siegmund's body: "Blood", "redly", "red", and "creeping red" harmonize with the "b", "r", "I" "ee" "d" "ea" sounds of "bright skin", "rise of his knee", "pride" and "creatures proud". Finally, consonance is achieved in "wiped the blood" with "wound", and Siegmund's body merges with the slash which had originally represented the threatening, objectified world. Through *Tonsprache* the Wagnerian singer merges into the fecund texture of the music, the individual into the *Wille*; Lawrence re-enacts Wagner's process of reconciliation through his own use of *Tonsprache*, till Siegmund complacently concludes, "It was nothing" (*T*, 73-74).

---

[5] See Joseph Kestner, "The Literary Wagnerism of D. H. Lawrence's *The Trespasser*", *Modern British Literature*, Part Fall (1977), II, 123-38.

At a structural level, the *Leitmotiv* reconciles constituent parts of *The Trespasser* into a totality, complementing the effect of *Tonsprache* on a larger scale. I have analysed this effect in *The White Peacock*. Newman's book *Wagner* could have helped Lawrence in his use of the *Leitmotiv* to order his work, through its analysis of the *Motiv* structures of Wagner's most important operas. Lawrence repeats scenes, dialogue and commentary till Helena and Siegmund's characters merge with each other. Adorno describes the basis of Wagner's use of the *Motiv* as the "ambiguity of musical meaning", which is echoed in his ambiguous characters such as Hagen, Kundry and Tristan. He argues that the *Motiv* structurally unifies the work through ambiguity: "the inexorable progression that fails to create any new quality and constantly flows into the already known ...."[6] Although Lawrence tries to establish a contrast between Helena and Siegmund, especially in their sexuality, at times their individual traits dissolve into each other, and into the totality of the novel's *Motive*.

Lawrence tries to characterize Siegmund as subjective and Helena as objective in their attitudes to reality, but he cannot sustain their difference while he is also conveying their transcendental oneness. At the beginning of the holiday Helena draws Siegmund to the edge of a cliff; he is afraid, but suggests they walk off it; she is shocked that he can "play with the idea of death" when they have the possibility of future fulfilment ahead of them. Later, though, she creeps towards the edge of a cliff; he stands back, "having too strong a sense of death", but she goes nearer to the edge: "What was Death to her, but one of her symbols, the death of which the sagas talk – something grand and sweeping and dark" (*T*, 61, 77). When there is the risk that they will be cut off from the incoming tide, he "hoped they were cut off, and hoped anxiously the way was clear" to the mainland; she is terrified of the brutality of the sea, but then comments "it might as well have been the sea as any other way, dear" (*T*, 83-84). Later, when he suggests they mount the cliffs again, she has become indifferent to the idea.

From Romanticism to Nietzsche
Lawrence, then, attempts to capture the "original truth" of Helen Corke's relationship with Macartney, not with a Realist discourse, but

---

[6] Adorno, *In Search of Wagner*, 43.

with one that is "incorporated into [Lawrence's] being" (Letters, I, 359). Lawrence tries to express this truth as something "eternal", as "Life" not "*life*", by concentrating on Helena and Siegmund's Romantic desire to transcend their individuality into the universal will. And yet, in their transcending "*life*", we lose the original truth of Helen Corke and Macartney's relationship as an actual event. The language cannot capture their physical experience, the *Motiv* structure leaves them dispossessed of individual intention. All that remains, as in the conclusion to Wagner's *Ring*, is *Nichtigkeit*. The reviewer in Katherine Mansfield's periodical *Rhythm* concentrated on this negative side of *The Trespasser*:

> the story simply doesn't matter; the characters don't even matter. What is important is the curious mood of passion exhibited by Siegmund and Helena on their holiday. (Letters, I, 507)

As early as 1909 Lawrence had complained to Jennings about the dangers of attempting to express "ecstasy" in art, that it "leads to so much vapour of words, till we are blind with coloured wordiness" (Letters, I, 107). In a letter to Helen Corke he observed that: "'We have broken down the bounds of the individual' – it is true – ... but with the bounds of the individual broken down, there is too deadly concentrated an intercourse not to be destructive". After first drafting the novel as "The Saga of Siegmund" Lawrence became aware of its excesses, of being "too chargé, too emotional", "fluid, luscious" (Letters, I, 239, 337, 351), especially in comparison to "Paul Morel". Yet during the final revising stage he felt that the novel was not "retrograde from the *White Peacock*", and that "it can't be anything else – it is itself" (Letters, I, 351, 358). Lawrence's ambivalent attachment to *The Trespasser* is echoed in his attitude to Wagner. As early as October 1909 he complained that "*Tristan* is long, feeble, a bit hysterical, without grip or force. I was frankly sick of it" (Letters, I, 140). On the other hand, his lingering fascination for Wagner was manifested throughout *The Trespasser* which he began the following year.

Lawrence could have been influenced by Ernest Newman's critical perspective on Wagner. In *A Study of Wagner* Newman is sceptical of *Tonsprache* as a poetic technique; he describes the section from *Tristan und Isolde* which I selected above as "admirably adapted for a musical setting, but ... no more poetry than an auctioneer's catalogue is poetry".[7] In both of his books Newman considers Wagner to be a great artist with a minor intellect – "a being of somewhat abnormal structure" – who was unable to recognize the otherness of the world at large: Wagner Romantically imagined his "personal struggles" were "the struggles of the whole modern world".[8] Newman is also sceptical of the claim that Schopenhauer influenced Wagner; he discounts the notion of transcending time and space as completely meaningless.[9]

Lawrence shares Newman's scepticism of Wagner. A large proportion of the references to Wagner in *The Trespasser* ironically point to the failure of Helena and Siegmund's transcendence of reality, and reveal the limits of Wagner in inspiring them to it. The unity of their experience is disrupted when Siegmund claims a Beethoven symphony as the musical equivalent of the sunset, while Helena chooses the Grail music in *Lohengrin*. Helena reveals her fanciful imagination in her comparison of the "rippling sunlight on the sea" to "the Rhine Maidens spreading their bright hair to sun", and in her speculation that the sea emerged when Wotan "knocks over the bowl, and flap – flap flap go the gasping fishes, pizzicato!" (*T*, 75, 84).

We see the failure of Lawrence's Wagnerian style to unite the lovers beyond their isolation from each other, geographically, and in terms of their personalities. Helena and Siegmund bathe in different areas by the coast but are united by the imagery of "green sap", "sunshine", "whiteness" and "birds", which conveys their experience. Helena swims in the water which is like "green-gold, glistening sap"; she is "a shadow cast by that fragment of sunshine", and her breast is "bright as the breast of a white bird". The transition to Siegmund is formed by her imagining him in the "sunshine, white and playing like a bird, shining like a vivid, restless speck of sunlight". He is in "a white cave welling with green water brilliant and full of life as mounting sap". Yet their geographical separateness prevents them

---

[7] Newman, *Study of Wagner*, 118.
[8] Newman, *Wagner*, 27, 3.
[9] See Newman, *Study of Wagner*, 32.

from understanding their shared experience: afterwards, she tries to express it, but

> he did not understand. He looked at her searchingly. She was white and still and inscrutable. ... He laughed again, not understanding, but feeling she meant love. (*T*, 87-90)

Their isolation from each other becomes the tragic mechanism of the novel, until they are left with nothing as individuals in the material, social world. They can only achieve Wagnerian transcendence in death, but Helena lacks even the courage to do this. Lawrence shares their failure, since his intention in writing the novel was to glorify their transcendence of everyday reality. He cannot affirm anything beyond their failure, except for a Schopenhauerian resignation. He has reached an impasse in his emulation of Wagner.

During the composition of *The Trespasser*, and throughout Lawrence's later career, Friedrich Nietzsche would inspire him to break from this impasse. Although Nietzsche's influence is one of the most widely discussed topics in criticism on Lawrence, it has yet to be treated in a satisfactory way. Unfortunately, we cannot be certain of the extent to which Lawrence understood Nietzsche's ideas. He could have borrowed from the Croydon library's selection of Nietzsche, which included *The Future of Human Institutions, Human, All-Too Human, The Dawn of Day, Joyful Wisdom, Thus Spake Zarathustra, Beyond Good and Evil, A Genealogy of Morals, The Case of Wagner, Twilight of the Gods* and *Will to Power*.[10] Nietzsche was also a subject of discussion in Lawrence's educated social circle. Edward Garnett, whom Lawrence first met in August 1911,[11] had written the essay "Nietzsche" as early as 1899; *The New Age*, which Lawrence subscribed to between 1908 and 1909, regularly featured articles on the philosopher.[12] Accordingly, Lawrence displays a wide range of Nietzschean ideas in his novels. Yet we have no proof that Lawrence

---

[10] See R. L. Drain, "Formative Influences on the Work of D. H. Lawrence" (Cambridge: Cambridge University, 1962); Worthen, *D. H. Lawrence: The Early Years*, 210.
[11] See Worthen, *D. H. Lawrence: The Early Years*, 320.
[12] See Edward Garnett, *Friday Nights* (London: Jonathan Cape, 1922), 3-12; Worthen, *D. H. Lawrence: The Early Years*, 210, 541.

read any of Nietzsche's works: he makes few specific references to Nietzsche, other than well-known slogans such as "will to power".[13] I shall try to avoid the two extreme solutions to this question of influence: the comparative which requires no evidence of a historical relationship, and the empirical which is based exclusively on biographical evidence. Instead, I shall integrate Lawrence's apparent Nietzscheanism into the texture of other German cultural issues which are treated in this chapter, and in my thesis.

I will examine how Nietzschean ideas function in *The Trespasser* in relation to those of Schopenhauer and Wagner, or to what Nietzsche referred to as "romantischen Pessimismus"[14] ("Romantic pessimism"). Nietzsche's philosophy can be characterized by how it emerges out of, and in reaction to, Schopenhauer and Wagner. His philosophical perspective was transformed in 1865 by his discovery of Schopenhauer's *Die Welt als Wille und Vorstellung*, where "every line cried renunciation, negation, resignation".[15] He described his relationship with Wagner as "my practical course in Schopenhauerian philosophy", and later reflected on himself as "the first to distil a sort of unity out of both".[16]

For Helen Corke, Nietzsche could not be separated from Wagner, since she was introduced to both of them during her relationship with Herbert Macartney in 1908.[17] In "The Cornwall Writing" and "To Siegmund's Violin", which Lawrence may have referred to in composing *The Trespasser*, she mentions the "copy of Nietzsche on the lid of the piano".[18] The coupling is evident in *The Trespasser*, where on the lovers' first evening together, Helena hands Siegmund "the Nietzsche I brought – –", then plays "fragments of Wagner on the

---

[13] Chambers, *D. H. Lawrence: A Personal Record*, 120.
[14] Friedrich Nietzsche, *Werke*, IV/3, 10.
[15] Dietrich Fischer-Dieskau, *Wagner und Nietzsche* (Stuttgart: Deutsche Verlags-Anstalt, 1974), 36: "jede Zeile, die Entsagung, Verneigung, Resignation schrie."
[16] Roger Hollinrake, *Nietzsche, Wagner, and the Philosophy of Pessimism* (London: George Allen and Unwin, 1982), 55, 71: "mein praktischer Kursus der Schopenhauerschen Philosophie"; "der Erste, der aus Beiden eine Art Einheit destillierte."
[17] See Helen Corke, *In Our Infancy* (Cambridge: University Press, 1975), 157.
[18] See A. R. Atkins, "Textual Influences on D. H. Lawrence's 'The Saga of Siegmund'", *D. H. Lawrence Review*, XXIV/1 (1992), 19.

piano" (*T*, 285, 66-67). In his essay Edward Garnett had described how Nietzsche began his career as "the follower of Wagner and Schopenhauer". In the article "Nietzsche the Olympian" from the 30 December 1909 issue of *The New Age*, Judah P. Benjamin declared that

> Schopenhauer was positive in his writing, negative in his philosophy. He renounced power; Nietzsche assumed it. Without Schopenhauer Nietzsche would have been impossible.[19]

A useful guide to focusing on particular Nietzschean issues in *The Trespasser* is its relationship to the plays of Gerhart Hauptmann. While composing the novel Lawrence read Hauptmann's *Einsame Menschen* (1891), *Die Versunkene Glocke* (1897) and *Elga* (1905). Although diverse in style, they are unified in their response to the ferment of artistic styles and cultural ideas of late nineteenth-century culture. In particular, Lawrence's references to these plays in his letters and *The Trespasser* all relate to the question of how to break from Schopenhauer and Wagner, especially through Nietzsche.

Cecil Byrne, Lawrence's alter ego, and Helena read *Einsame Menschen*, which dramatizes the attempt of two intellectuals, Johannes Vockerat and Anna Mahr, to establish a relationship without the issue of sexuality. Hauptmann seems to be influenced by *Menschliches, Allzu Menschliches*, where Nietzsche recapitulates Schopenhauer's "Metaphysik der Geschlechtsliebe", including how children internalize their parents' discords. Nietzsche attempts to solve the conflict of wills suggested in Schopenhauer's "Metaphysik" with "marriage considered in its higher conception, as the soul-friendship of two people of differing sex, as is hoped it will become in the future".[20] Johannes and Anna's relationship is destroyed by social convention, but Lawrence at least recognizes, in his sexual frustration with Helen Corke which is projected onto Siegmund, that the will cannot be repressed but must be channelled in a new direction. He wrote to her in June 1910, a month before reading the play, that

---

[19] Garnett, *Friday Nights*, 6; Orage, *The New Age*, 30 December 1909, 205.
[20] Nietzsche, *Werke*, IV/2, 286: "die Ehe in ihrer höheren Auffassung gedacht, als Seelenfreundschaft zweier Menschen verschiedenen Geschlechts, also so, wie sie von der Zukunft erhofft wird."

"gradually we shall exterminate the sexual part. Then there will be nothing, and we can part" (Letters, I, 164). *The Trespasser* takes the position of Nietzsche's later ideas, in trying to affirm the *Wille*, not to deny or transcend it.

Nietzsche's *grosser Mittag* versus Wagner's *Nacht*
In my discussion of Lawrence's Nietzscheanism in *The Trespasser* I follow Cecilia Björkén's approach by concentrating on *Die Geburt der Tragödie* and *Also Sprach Zarathustra*.[21] There is no evidence that Lawrence had read *Die Geburt der Tragödie*, which was only translated in 1909. Yet many English artists and writers had previously referred to its distinction between the Dionysian and Apollonian as confirmation of the uniqueness of their creativity.[22] In 1910 Lawrence mentions Ezra Pound's projected "account of the mystic cult of love – the dionysian rites, and so on" (Letters, I, 165). *Also Sprach Zarathustra* was perhaps the most famous and notorious of Nietzsche's works in England, having been first translated in the 1890s. Björkén shows how themes from these two works are manifested in *The Trespasser*, but I will focus on the specific cultural-historical question of how Lawrence attempts to emulate Nietzsche's break from Romanticism. The ideas in these two works relate closely to Schopenhauer and Wagner: *Die Geburt der Tragödie* applies a vitalistic revision of Schopenhauer's notions of the *Wille* and *Vorstellung* to Wagnerian opera; *Also Sprach Zarathustra* is a conscious attempt to overcome Schopenhauer and Wagner's pessimism. They are also central to the concerns of Hauptmann's plays *Die Versunkene Glocke* and *Elga*.

In *Die Geburt der Tragödie* Nietzsche borrowed Schopenhauer's insight that music expresses the primal *Wille*, unlike the other arts which represent the will as objectified reality. Nietzsche envisaged music as the *Dionysisch* spirit of tragedy, countered by the *Apollinisch* of visual art and poetry. In tragedy poetry and music are reconciled through myth. The Apollonian objectifies the tragic will,

---

[21] See Cecilia Björkén, *Into the Isle of Self: Nietzschean Patterns and Contrasts in D. H. Lawrence's* The Trespasser (Lund: Lund University Press, 1996).
[22] See David S. Thatcher, *Nietzsche in England* (Toronto: University of Toronto Press, 1970), 124-29, 140.

enabling the spectators to distance themselves from it; in the Dionysian ecstasy they identify with the will, the unremitting process of growth and destruction in nature, an "Urschmerz und Urwiederklang" ("primal pain and its primal echoing"). By following the dialogue between the Apollonian and Dionysian, the audience learns to affirm and survive the terror of the will:

> he who with a piercing glance has looked into the middle of the terrible destructive drives of so-called universal history, as well as the cruelty of nature, and who is in danger of longing for a Buddhistic negation of the will. Art saves him, and through art life saves him.[23]

While writing *Die Geburt der Tragödie* Nietzsche believed himself to be synthesising Schopenhauerian philosophy and Wagnerian opera. Yet soon after its publication he began to reject them. In *Menschliches, allzu Menschliches* he reflects on his past self-deceptions about Schopenhauer, and especially Wagner: "seemingly the all-conquering, in truth a decaying, despairing Romantic."[24]

The cultural ambiguity of *Die Geburt der Tragödie*, of whether it belongs to Romantic pessimism or to Nietzsche's anti-Romanticism, is reflected in *The Trespasser*. Contrary to *Die Geburt der Tragödie*, for Schopenhauer and Wagner art does not save man for nature, but enables him to transcend it and realize its *Nichtigkeit*. In *Tristan und Isolde*, after the dissonant, Dionysian ecstasy, the audience remains in what Nietzsche calls the "lethargisches Element" ("lethargic element") of the Dionysian:

> The world of the everyday and the world of Dionysian reality separate themselves from each other through this gulf of oblivion. But as soon as any everyday reality steps back into consciousness, it will be felt as

---

[23] Nietzsche, *Werke*, III/1, 40, 52: "der mit schneidigem Blicke mitten in das furchtbare Vernichtungstreiben der sogenannten Weltgeschichte, eben so wie in die Grausamkeit der Natur geschaut hat und in Gefahr ist, sich nach einer buddhaistischen Verneinung des Willens zu sehnen. Ihn rettet die Kunst, und durch die Kunst rettet ihn sich – das Leben."
[24] *Ibid.*, IV/2, 8; IV/3, 6: "scheinbar der Siegreichste, in Wahrheit ein morsch gewordener, verzweifelnder Romantiker."

such with repulsion; an ascetic will-negating mood is the fruit of these states.[25]

According to Nietzsche, the Apollonian saves us from denying the will: "it alone is able to turn these repulsive reflections on the dreadfulness and absurdity of existence into representations which may be lived with."[26] Nietzsche perceives this Apollonian redemption in *Tristan und Isolde*: the audience is saved through the representation of words and scenery from the "echo of countless cries of joy and sorrow" out of the "vast space of the world-night'", of the "Herzkammer des Weltwillens"[27] ("heart-chamber of the world-will"). Nietzsche denies that the most appropriate scenery is darkness to represent Tristan and Isolde's *Nacht*, and more crucially, he denies that in Isolde's *Liebestod* the words of the libretto fail to convey an Apollonian reality, because they are subsumed in the Dionysian texture of the music as *Tonsprache*.

In *The Trespasser* Lawrence struggles between the Romantic *lethargisches Element* of the Dionysian, and Nietzsche's affirmation of the return to reality. He plays objectified reality against the Dionysian effect of *Tonsprache*. Yet fundamentally, he fails to redeem reality through the tragic experience: as George Hyde points out,[28] there is no viable reality for Siegmund or Helena to return to. Consequently, Lawrence is unable to emulate Nietzsche's more coherent rejection of Romantic pessimism in *Also Sprach Zarathustra*; in *The Trespasser* his allusions to *Zarathustra* signify the reverse of Nietzsche's intentions. Roger Hollinrake has revealed how Nietzsche wrote *Also Sprach Zarathustra* partly in opposition to Wagner's pessimistic philosophy. The *Übermensch* is Nietzsche's

---

[25] *Ibid.*, III/1, 52: "So scheidet sich durch diese Kluft der Vergessenheit die Welt der alltäglichen und der dionysischen Wirklichkeit von einander ab. Sobald aber jene alltägliche Wirklichkeit wieder ins Bewusstsein tritt, wird sie mit Ekel als solche empfunden; eine asketische, willenverneinende Stimmung ist die Frucht jener Zustände."
[26] *Ibid.*, III/1, 53: "sie allein vermag jene Ekelgedanken über das Entsetzliche oder Absurde des Daseins in Vorstellungen umzubiegen, mit denen sich leben lässt."
[27] *Ibid.*, III/1, 131-32: "Wiederklang zahlloser Lust- und Weherufe aus dem, weiten Raum der Weltennacht."
[28] See G. M. Hyde, *D. H. Lawrence* (London: Macmillan, 1990), 29.

revision of Siegfried, and *ewige Wiederkehr* is his alternative to Schopenhauer and Wagner's pessimistic notion of cyclical time.

In *Also Sprach Zarathustra* Nietzsche's *grosser Mittag* opposes Wagner's *Nacht* from *Tristan und Isolde*. Where for Wagner *die Nacht* symbolizes the stasis of being and ultimately death, Nietzsche's "grosser Mittag" refers to the period of optimum growth, or *Selbst-Überwindung* towards the *Übermensch*, which Zarathustra anticipates at the end of the book:

> "Well now! The lion has come, my children are near, Zarathustra has become ripe, my hour has come: –
> This is my morning, my day begins: rise up now, rise up, great noon! –" [29]

Lawrence continuously describes the sunlight during Siegmund and Helena's ecstatic bathing scenes, but Siegmund only experiences a *grossen Mittag* at the end of their holiday. He resolutely lies in the sun, aware that they are due to leave, but stubbornly refusing to accept it: "Siegmund lay in the bright light, with his eyes closed, never moving. His face was inflamed, but fixed like a mask" (*T*, 149). Instead of dynamically overcoming himself, he denies his will to live. When he returns to his family and home, the sunburn has aged his face and weakened his power to master his situation; he feels helpless and commits suicide. He is destroyed by the Dionysian will in nature, and can only escape through death, not back to life.

Siegmund's failure to embrace the *grossen Mittag* is similar to Heinrich's failure in Hauptmann's *Die Versunkene Glocke*. Although Lawrence makes no direct reference to this play in *The Trespasser*, in 1910 he read it both in the original and in translation (Letters, I, 168). In the play, Heinrich the bell-founder leaves his wife for the elfin Rautendelein, no longer to make bells for the glory of the Church, but for the "Urmutter Sonne" ("mother sun"); he anticipates the sunlight descending to earth as the Redeemer. Then, out of guilt for his wife's death he pleads for God's pity, and rejects Rautendelein. Later, he attempts to return to Rautendelein, but she does not recognize him till

---

[29] Nietzsche, *Werke*, VI/1, 404: "Wohlan! Der Löwe kam, meine Kinder sind nahe, Zarathustra ward reif, meine Stunde kam: – Dies ist mein Morgen, mein Tag hebt an: herauf nun, herauf, du grosser Mittag! – "

he drinks the potion of death. He dies, kissing her while the sun ascends:

> Hoch oben: Sonnenglockenklang!
> Die Sonne ... Sonne kommt! – Die Nacht ist lang.
> *Morgenröte*[30].
> [High up: the ringing of the sun-bells!
> The sun ... the sun draws near! – The Night is long.
> *Dawn breaks.*]

Hauptmann has subsumed Nietzsche's symbolism into Wagner's, through Heinrich re-enacting Isolde's *Liebestod*: he can only affirm his religion of the sun through death; he falls into the *Nacht* like Isolde, while the sun rises. Similarly, Lawrence's Siegmund renounces life after his *grossen Mittag*.

Ewige Wiederkehr versus Schopenhauer's *Rad des Ixion*

Lawrence relates the failed *grossen Mittag* of Siegmund and Helena to his Romantically pessimistic reading of Nietzsche's *ewige Wiederkehr*. This concept can be understood as a reaction against Schopenhauer and Wagner, and as part of Nietzsche's whole philosophy, especially in relation to *Die Geburt der Tragödie*. As we saw in the previous chapter, Schopenhauer and Wagner dismissed the Enlightenment vision of linear time, where man progressively masters reality through science. In their notion of a cyclical time the individual is entrapped in the Ixonian wheel of his own will, or the operatic hero is in a *Motiv* structure which repeats itself till his death. Their notion of time follows from the *lethargisch* Dionysian. Nietzsche's Zarathustra called *ewige Wiederkehr* the "hochzeitlichen Ring der Ringe, – den Ring der Wiederkunft" ("wedding ring of rings – the ring of recurrence") which promises the eternity of "Lust"[31] ("joy"). Nietzsche is faithful to the Dionysian, and also to cyclical time, but he attempts to counter it with the individual impulse of the Apollonian. The result is not a synthesis of the individual and the whole of the universe, but an unresolved mediation between them. For Schopenhauer, the individual suffers eternally because he is alienated

---

[30] Gerhart Hauptmann, *Die Versunkene Glocke*, (Frankfurt am Main: Ullstein, 1959), 89, 144.
[31] Nietzsche, *Werke*, VI/1, 283.

from the will of the universe. For Nietzsche's Zarathustra, "alle Lust will – Ewigkeit!"[32] ("all joy wants – eternity!"): the individual is reconciled to the will, by facing its Dionysian creativity and destructiveness. In *Die Fröhliche Wissenschaft* Nietzsche describes *ewige Wiederkehr* as a moral imperative:

> the question in all and everything: "do you want this still once more and countless times more?" would lie as the greatest emphasis upon your actions. Or how well disposed towards yourself and towards life would you have to become to long for nothing more than this eternal confirmation and sealing?[33]

It is the individual's responsibility to make every action worth being repeated eternally.

In *The Trespasser*, because of the failure of the *grosses Mittag*, there can be no recurrence of *Lust*, only suffering. The characters cannot identify with the Dionysian will, but are destroyed by it. Half a year after the holiday, Helena contemplates with "peculiar joy" and "curious joy" the sunburns which recur every evening; she caresses them with her cheek and places her "mouth lovingly" (*T*, 43) on them. Cecil Byrne tries to encourage Helena out of her resignation, and into *ewige Wiederkehr*, with his irreverent suggestion that she apply some ointment to her burns. He echoes Zarathustra's animals that "Alles geht, Alles kommt zurück; ewig rollt das Rad des Seins. Alles stirbt, Alles blüht wieder auf, ewig läuft das Jahr des Seins."[34] He declares: "If you're alive you've got to live"; he claims she cannot deny this, "any more than a tree can help budding in April – it can't help itself, if it's alive; same with you". She retorts that she has stopped time, with her dead leaves still attached to her. Her room is sealed from outside reality, "foreign to the trams, and to the sound of London

---

[32] *Ibid.*, VI/1, 398.

[33] Nietzsche, *Werke*, V/2, 250: "die Frage bei Allem und Jedem ‚willst du diess noch einmal und noch unzählige Male?' würde als das grösste Schwergewicht auf deinem Handeln liegen! Oder wie müsstest du dir selber und dem Leben gut werden, um nach Nichts mehr zu verlangen, als nach dieser letzten ewigen Bestätigung und Besiegelung?"

[34] Nietzsche, *Werke*, VI/1, 268: "Everything goes, everything comes back; the wheel of existence rolls eternally. Everything dies, everything blossoms again; the year of existence runs on eternally."

traffic"; on the mantlepiece sits "a small soap-stone Buddha from China, grey, impassive, locked in his renunciation" (*T*, 45, 41-42).

At the end of the novel Helena tries to repeat her affair with Siegmund, this time with Byrne, like an operatic performance; she invites him to walk with her in the larch wood, which she had done with Siegmund a year before. Byrne resents her invitation, anxious that he is repeating Siegmund's fate: "He thought of Siegmund, and seemed to see him swinging down the steep bank out of the wood, exactly as he himself was doing at the moment, with Helena stepping carefully behind" (*T*, 227). He is conscious of the repetition, unlike Helena who lacks the consciousness to break out of it. He tries to make her aware, but fails:

> "History repeats itself," he remarked.
> "How?" she asked calmly. ...
> "I see no repetition," she added."No!" he exclaimed bitingly, "You are right." (*T*, 226)

Lawrence cannot directly affirm *ewige Wiederkehr* in his characters; he can only suggest how they fail to achieve it through his irony. He compares Helena to Hauptmann's Elga as an embodiment of *ewige Wiederkehr*. Siegmund comments to Helena: "You are not like other folk. 'Ihr Lascheks seid ein anderes Geschlecht'" (*T*, 131: "You Lascheks are another race"). He is quoting from Marina's judgement of Elga, which continues, "self-willed, light-hearted, treating everything as a game. – That is why you also lost everything."[35] Marina lives by the principle of self-renunciation and duty, but Elga follows only her desires. Lawrence's next reference to *Elga* comes from the same scene of the novel; Siegmund contemplates how Helena drives him both to life and death:

> He was thinking bitterly.
> She seemed to goad him deeper into life. He had a sense of despair, a preference for death. The German she read with him – she loved its loose and violent romance – came back to his mind: "Der

---

[35] Gerhart Hauptmann, *Sämtliche Werke*, 11 vols (Frankfurt am Main: Propyläen, 1962-63), I, 742: "eigenwillig, leichten Sinnes, immer bereit, alles aufs Spiel zu setzen. – Deshalb verlort ihr auch alles."

Tod geht immer zur Seite, fast sichtbarlich, und jagt einen immer tiefer ins Leben." (*T*, 131)

The second quotation is from Elga, that "death is always at one's side, almost visible, and drives one always deeper into life". In the play she continues, that instead of her awareness of death teaching her renunciation, "he taught me in a quite particular way to laugh at many different serious things of life".[36] She welcomes sorrow and loss as a part of life as a whole. Her older husband Starschenski cannot accept her affirmation of life and death. He wants to possess the joys of life permanently, especially her. When she has an affair with another man, he destroys her and his own home.

Lawrence's irony lies in Helena's inability to risk her social respectability, and her personal freedom, by committing herself to Siegmund. For Lawrence, Helen Corke was a failed Elga, as he wrote to her on 21 June 1910: "I would yield to you if you could lead me deeper into the tanglewood of life, by any path. But you never lead: you hunt from behind: 'jagt man tiefer ins Leben'" (Letters, I, 164). To "lead" means to have sex. His words sum up Byrne's relationship with Helena at the concluding impasse of the novel. Byrne is attracted to Helena because he believes that her experiences of death will give her a more vital attitude to life; on the contrary, though, she is languishing in nostalgia for death.

Although Lawrence has assimilated Nietzsche's ideas against Wagnerian Romanticism, his characters are still the protagonists of a Romantic tragedy. Like his alter ego Cecil Byrne, he advocates Nietzschean ideas while remaining fascinated by Wagner. At the end of the novel Byrne teaches Helena German so that she can "understand Wagner in his own language" (*T*, 228), and they compare two dogs to Fafner and Fasolt. Byrne attempts to interrupt Helena's Wagnerian *Motiv* of sunburns with his suggestion that they are beginning to fade, but fails. Wagner's influence over the novel as a whole has been too pervasive for Lawrence to overturn its effect through Byrne. Lawrence treats Siegmund's death with deflating irony, "a mesmeric performance, in which the agent trembled with

---

[36] *Ibid.*, I, 743: "Er lehrte mich auf eine ganz besondere Weise über vielerlei ernste Dinge des Lebens lachen."

convulsive sickness" (*T*, 204). Yet his tragedy is ultimately glorified: his wife survives it only because she cannot understand its profound meaning, and Helena respects his death by refusing to live.

The Trespasser, then, is caught in a similar impasse to *The White Peacock*: it is unable to envisage an affirmative existence for its characters in the material world. With Nietzsche, Lawrence has discovered a set of values that can achieve this, yet he is unable to enact them through his characters. In *Sons and Lovers* he will continue to struggle beyond this impasse, strengthened by his relationship with Frieda von Richtofen, and the Freudian-Nietzschean ideas of her lover, Otto Gross.

III
VERSIONS OF MODERNIST REALISM: *SONS AND LOVERS* AND *BUDDENBROOKS*

On 18 October 1910 Lawrence reported to Heinemann's editor Sidney Pawling that his new work in progress, "Paul Morel", was "a restrained, somewhat impersonal novel", compared to his previous novels. He suggested that its style followed from where *The Trespasser* had run "to seed in realism". In their interpretations of *Sons and Lovers*, critics have followed Lawrence's perception of his work at this early stage, "about one-eighth" (Letters, I, 184) into the first of four drafts. There has developed a tradition of discussing *Sons and Lovers* as a Realist novel which excludes the Romantic qualities of *The Trespasser*. Leavis almost dismisses *Sons and Lovers* for its adherence to the conventions of nineteenth-century Realism. Other critics, like Raymond Williams and Graham Holderness, instead have valued it for the adherence to Realism, comparing it to *The Rainbow* and *Women in Love* which slide into Modernist techniques. Kate Millett began a countertrend by exposing the lapses into subjectivity of Lawrence's supposedly omniscient narrator, which disrupt the Realist illusion. More recently, Michael Black has commented that "Realism" is an inadequate definition of the novel's style; he traces the development of its plot through a series of motifs, not historical events.[1]

The critical debate on *Sons and Lovers* parallels that on Thomas Mann's first novel, *Buddenbrooks*, published in 1901, which occupies a unique place in German literature, on the threshold of Modernism. So far we have seen how Lawrence imported German ideas and forms into his novels to reach beyond the terms of Victorian fiction. During the composition of *Sons and Lovers*, with his future wife Frieda, he left England for Germany, and from this point onwards began to inhabit German culture, not merely to insert its elements into the English tradition. Consequently it becomes imperative for us now to understand Lawrence's writing in comparison to contemporary

---

[1] See Michael Black, *D. H. Lawrence: Sons and Lovers* (Cambridge: Cambridge University Press, 1992) 42, 65-94.

developments in German culture, to evaluate him as a modern European writer.

In Germany *Buddenbrooks* has been the subject of continuous debate, and is a central case in the wider question of how to characterize the dominant trends in modern German culture. Lukács assumed that *Buddenbrooks* is a late example of nineteenth-century Realism, and compares it to Tolstoy's *War and Peace* in which "an individual's rise and decline was an organic part of social and historical rise and decline; it corresponded to objective reality". Yet he also recognizes that in *Buddenbrooks* Mann opposed contemporary capitalism with a nostalgic "former bourgeois-patrician past", through which he could only "criticize the capitalist system from the standpoint of a romantic anti-capitalist; a criticism therefore which inevitably lacked perspective". Mann's Romantic anti-capitalism fuelled his interest in Schopenhauer, Wagner and Nietzsche, all of whom Lukács associates with reactionary politics. Lukács maintains that the Realist narrative of *Buddenbrooks* holds Mann's forbears at a critical distance, and cites the episode where Thomas Buddenbrook is converted to Schopenhauer: "The bitterest opponent of Schopenhauer could not paint a better picture of the philosopher as the apostle of decadence." This "decadence", in Lukács' words, is only treated within the Realist paradigm of the individual's struggle to survive capitalist society.[2] Erich Heller, by contrast, regards the psychological decline of the Buddenbrooks, for which Mann had borrowed from Schopenhauer, as more important than economic history in determining the events of the novel.[3]

If we compare the debates on *Buddenbrooks* and *Sons and Lovers*, revealing how the two novels belong to a common cultural background, then we can also begin to locate the relationship between *Sons and Lovers* and German Modernism. The characters' renunciation of life in these novels can be traced back to the late Romantic tradition of Schopenhauer and Wagner. This tradition is countered with different forms of Realism: Mann contextualizes his

---

[2] Georg Lukács, *Essays on Thomas Mann* (London: Merlin Press, 1964), 79, 161, see also 22-25, 45.
[3] See Erich Heller, *Thomas Mann: The Ironic German* (New York: Paul P. Appel, 1973).

Romanticism in history, in terms of the characters' social relations, whereas Lawrence uses Freud to analyse Romanticism psychologically. Lawrence moves between two forms of Realism in his use of Freud. Just as Mann displays the historical circumstances of his characters' longing to transcend their individual suffering, Lawrence analyses this tendency in terms of the social developments of his characters. But under the influence of Frieda Weekley and her former lover Otto Gross, Lawrence reaches towards a more radical form of Realism. He identifies reality not merely in terms of social relations but also in the physical vitality of his characters, which empowers them to transform these relations.

Between Schopenhauer and Freud
Like *Buddenbrooks*, part of the narrative of *Sons and Lovers* follows social and economic history. The opening resembles *The Mill on the Floss* in its omniscient view of time and space. However, unlike *The White Peacock*, and George Eliot's novel, there is no personal voice communicating nostalgia, but an objective recording of economic transitions, from the pre-industrial community of "Hell Row" to "The Bottoms" whose inhabitants work in the financiers' large mines. The Morels belong to modern industrial society, and attempt to climb up its hierarchy. The Buddenbrooks belong to old patrician society, and are gradually superseded by the modern financiers who thrived during the period of late nineteenth-century industrialism. Yet about halfway through both novels the pace of the events slows down. Instead of loosely following historical patterns, time is measured by the characters' experiences. In *Buddenbrooks* this shift occurs when Thomas takes over the business; the novel becomes ambiguous about whether the fortunes of the business and family are subject to adverse historical circumstances, or to the decline of the protagonists' inner will. In *Sons and Lovers* the family's relation to its changing environment sets the pace of events, and then Paul's inner conflicts become the dramatic focus. The narratives of both novels become the mouthpieces of the characters' aspirations, reflections and fears, appearing to directly express their subjectivity. Michael Black comments that the second part of *Sons and Lovers* is "less impersonal" than the first, no longer objectifying events realistically,

"not more involved in what is related, but less able to stand outside and just see all round it."[4] Both Mann and Lawrence identify with their characters, while creating them.

Despite his original ambition to use restraint and impersonality, Lawrence abandoned "Paul Morel" immediately after his description of it to Pawling; on 11 February 1911 he declared that it "sticks where I left it four or five months ago, at the hundredth page".[5] John Worthen describes how the death of Lawrence's mother in the previous December fundamentally changed his intentions in "Paul Morel" to focus on the discords of the Morel marriage.[6] This shift is articulated in a letter from the same month to Rachel Annand Taylor where Lawrence sets up the opposition between his "clever, ironical delicately moulded" mother, and his father, "one of the sanguine temperament, warm and hearty, but unstable". He then tries to explain how his parents' subsequent conflict caused him to identify with his mother, in which they have "been like one" (Letters, I, 190). This letter anticipates Lawrence's description of the novel's plot to Edward Garnett almost two years later, a day after sending the completed final version to his new publisher Duckworth. Lawrence argued that the individual characters exist in a structural "form" derived from a psychological interpretation which departs from social circumstances. Although his summary has been used as the touchstone of Freudian readings of *Sons and Lovers*, its opening is interesting in how it also suggests an analysis that is not Freudian:

> It follows this idea: a woman of character and refinement goes into the lower class, and has no satisfaction in her own life. She has had a passion for her husband, so the children are born of passion, and have heaps of vitality. (Letters, I, 476-77)

The allusion has become vague, but we can still trace this analysis back to Lawrence's youthful reading of Schopenhauer's "Metaphysics of Love".

In *Buddenbrooks* Mann organizes the patterns of relationships according to Schopenhauer's ideas to represent the "Verfall einer

---

[4] Black, *D. H. Lawrence: Sons and Lovers*, 43.
[5] *Ibid.*, 230.
[6] See Worthen, *D. H. Lawrence: The Early Years*, 281-82.

Familie" ("decline of a family"), unlike Lawrence, who traces the regeneration of Lydia's burgher roots. Erich Heller cites Mann's reference to Schopenhauer in *Betrachtungen eines Unpolitischen* (1918) as confirmation of the philosopher's structural influence on *Buddenbrooks*. Thomas Buddenbrook enjoys a youthful love affair with an assistant at a flower shop, Anna, whose working-class vitality could have reinvigorated the family; when she pays her last respects to him after his death, she is "expecting, as usual".[7] He has to leave her for his business responsibilities, to make a good match with Gerda whose violin playing fascinates him, and who also has a large dowry. Their marriage is not fruitful, producing only the sickly Hanno who is too weak to face the challenges of bourgeois life; he dies of typhoid which, Mann writes, "quite simply, is a form of dissolution, the garment of death itself".[8]

The relationship between the Morels is analogous, not to Thomas and Gerda's, but to Lettie and George's in *The White Peacock*. The opposition between Gertrude and Walter is described in social terms: she is "of a good old burgher family" who had fallen into economic decline, while he is a working-class miner. Their class difference encompasses their opposing characteristics: Walter is "non-intellectual" and "so full of colour and animation", while "she loved ideas, and was considered very intellectual". According to Schopenhauer, children inherit these qualities respectively from the father and mother; the genetic difference between parents also provides the children with "heaps of vitality". Yet, as in the Schopenhauerian attraction between Lettie and George, Gertude and Walter are divided by their opposing qualities. When she tries to discuss a serious issue with him, "she saw him listen deferentially, but without understanding" (*SL*, 13, 17, 19).

In the third version of "Paul Morel", dated November 1911, Lawrence specifically referred to Schopenhauer's philosophy to explain the failure of Walter and Gertrude's relationship, and its effect on their children. Using imagery which is both scientific and

---

[7] Thomas Mann, *Gesammelte Werke*, 11 vols (Frankfurt am Main: Fischer, 1974), I, 689: "guter Hoffnung wie gewöhnlich."
[8] Mann, *Gesammelte Werke*, I, 753: "ganz einfach eine Form der Auflösung ist, das Gewand des Todes selbst."

poetically fanciful, Lawrence compares women to flowers who offer men the "sap of life":

> ‹And all they «wish» will to give the man, who can «lap up» select honey of beauty and store up wisdom from them, «to feed» for the next generation. «Mrs» Walter Morel had given his wife children, according to the doctrine of Schopenhauer. But he would not take from her, and help her to produce, the other finer products, blossoms of «beautiful» living «‹from› which she might make wisdom like honey, and dreams like worship. Therefore she refused him: also, fearfully, she combated him. She was too much of a woman, too much of the stuff of life, to despair for herself. She was still fast producing life, and religion of life for her children.» Therefore she nourished the souls of her unborn children on her own dissatisfaction. Her passionate yearning entered into her infants, poisoning, as it were, their naïve young spirits. She did not want children, after William. Annie she would «nearly» have preferred to die, rather than give birth again. But she waited as best she might for her third baby.›[9]

Lawrence replaces "wish" with "will" to reinforce his Schopenauerian argument. At first he imagines a "religion of life" for Mrs Morel in "producing" children instead of investing herself in her husband, which follows from Schopenhauer's conception of the individual subsuming itself in the will of the race. However, Lawrence later revises these lines to explain how the will destroys itself, how death is caused by conflict of the will in its various manifestations, between individuals and within themselves. Mrs Morel does not invest her "passionate yearning" in her husband, but poisons her children with it; in the lost hope of salvaging her individuality, she wishes they had not been born. The children will spend the vitality which she fed them by trying to return it to her, to redeem her frustrated yearnings, and themselves. If they fail, by breaking from her, they will experience the will to death, since they can only justify themselves through her. In accordance with this philosophical framework, the fourth version of "Paul Morel"

---

[9] D.H. Lawrence, *Sons and Lovers*, ed. Mark Schorer (Berkeley and London: University of California Press, 1977), "Paul Morel", Fragment 2, 32-33.

describes how the father's "will to live had gone" after he accidentally kills his son Arthur (*PM*, 126).

This passage reveals how Lawrence's Schopenhauerian ideas contribute to the form of *Sons and Lovers*. Yet he cut the passage out of *Sons and Lovers*, including its revisions, not just because, as John Worthen points out, it implies that Walter Morel is making love to his wife out of his respect for Schopenhauer,[10] but also because it suggests that Lawrence's characters are only puppets enacting his reading of the philosopher. In exploring the implications of Schopenhauer's model on the relationships between the parents and children, and the children's development into adulthood, Lawrence is already working beyond its limits and anticipating Freud's theory of developmental psychology. When Lawrence departs from Schopenhauer, he no longer glorifies the mother's heroic affirmation of life despite her oppressed state, but recognizes how she inadvertently destroys her children. His development from Schopenhauer to Freud is underpinned by a growing realization of the damage that his mother has inflicted on him.

According to Schopenhauer's pessimistic evolutionary model in "The Metaphysics of Love", the vitality of the parents' relationship should provide the child with a powerful intellect from its mother and will from its father. The child is more perfect than its parents, but at the same time more tragically self-divided. True to theory, Paul is divided between his intellect and the physical vitality he has inherited respectively from his mother and father. Thomas Buddenbrook denied his sexual desire for a physically vital wife; he sires a child who is not self-divided, but who has a powerful mind at the expense of physical strength. Though their problems are different, Hanno and Paul share similar symptoms because Paul denies his vitality while Hanno simply does not have any. Both have a tendency to depression, and renunciation through their genetic inheritances. Throughout his childhood, Hanno suffers from nightmares and weeps easily. Paul continually suffers from fits of depression. Despite the "great vitality in his young body", he is "rather a delicate boy, subject to bronchitis": "Usually he looked as if he saw things, was full of life, and warm; ... and then, when there was a clog in his soul's running,

---

[10] See Worthen, *D. H. Lawrence: The Early Years*, 574, 435.

his face went stupid and ugly" (*SL*, 90, 113). Since infancy both have understood death, having only just survived birth and childhood illnesses, which gives them a profounder consciousness than their peers have. At his christening Hanno stares at his relatives "with an almost precocious, probing gaze";[11] Gertrude notices in Paul "the peculiar knitting of the baby's brows, and the peculiar heaviness of its eyes, as if it were trying to understand something that was pain" (*SL*, 50).

Both Hanno and Paul's weaknesses are related to their attachment to their mother and alienation from the father. Hanno aspires to play music like his mother, and is unable to adapt himself to his father's mercantile values. Yet his relationships are only treated as symptomatic of his inner self. Compared to Hanno, Lawrence suggests that Paul's self-conflict is an internalization of his parents' conflict over the course of his development, which prefigures Freudian psychology. Even in his mother's womb, Paul is aware of the conflict between his parents, virtually witnessing Walter shut Gertrude out of the house. As a result of this, it is implied, Paul is born with "a peculiar pucker on the forehead, as if something had startled [his] tiny consciousness before birth" (*SL*, 45). Throughout his childhood he continues to sympathize with his mother, as is symbolized by her blood soaking into his scalp after Walter had injured her brow. Yet the narrative does not decide between a genetic and cultural explanation for the relationship between Paul's inner conflict and his attachment to his mother: whether his self-division is inherited, as Hanno's weakness certainly is, and has caused Paul to identify with the intellect of his mother, or if attachment to his mother and hatred towards his father causes him to reject his body for his mind. Until Paul heals the split, we cannot judge whether Lawrence is closer to Schopenhauer or Freud in his method of characterization. As we shall see, a Freudian analysis would encourage a Realism in *Sons and Lovers*, of how its characters develop through social relationships.

---

[11] Mann, *Gesammelte Werke*, I, 396: "mit einem beinahe altklug prüfenden Blinzeln."

Confronting death in the Wagnerian *Leitmotiv*

Following from Schopenhauer's theory of the individual's inability to break from the constraints of his genetic inheritance, Lawrence's and Mann's characters are unable to develop through interacting with their social environment. Without development, temporality no longer corresponds to what Lukács calls the "objective reality" of history, but to the characters' experience only. Time is cyclical, not linear, manifested in the symbolism of the recurring *Motiv*. Michael Black analyses the structure of *Sons and Lovers* in terms of its imagery, concentrating on the "great ramifying image cluster" of light.[12] Lawrence's use of imagery is indebted to the German Romantic tradition, particularly to Wagner.

Both Mann and Lawrence use Wagnerian imagery to express Schopenhauerian notions. Mann uses Wagnerian opera to structure *Buddenbrooks*; from first reading *Die Welt als Wille und Vorstellung*, he had recognized Schopenhauer's importance to Wagner. In "Leiden und Größe Richard Wagners" from 1933 he stresses "the connection between Wagner's work and this world-critical, world-ordering book, this cognitive poem and artistic metaphysic of drive and spirit, of will and contemplation – this miraculous edifice of ideas, at once ethical, pessimistic and musical, which exhibits such a profound historical and human affinity with the score of *Tristan*!".[13] In the scene where the charlatan Grünlich is exposed, Mann re-enacts part of Act II of *Die Walküre*. Consul Buddenbrook plays the role of Wotan who overrides his personal feelings of sympathy with his sense of duty. Buddenbrook leaves Grünlich at the mercy of his banker Kesselmeyer, like the unarmed Siegmund before Hunding. Buddenbrook's refusal to pay Kesselmeyer is similar to Wotan killing Hunding with a dismissive wave of the arm: "With a single motion of the hand he pushed away everything that lay in front of him, laid the pencil down with a jerk on the table and said: 'I declare that I am not

---

[12] Black, *D. H. Lawrence: Sons and Lovers*, 66, see also 65-94.
[13] Mann, *Gesammelte Werke*, IX, 397: "die Verbindung des Wagnerswerkes mit diesem weltkritisch-weltordnenden Buch, dieser Erkenntnis-Dichtung und Künstlermetaphysik von Trieb und Geist, Wille und Anschauung, diesem ethisch-pessimistisch-musikalischen Gedankenwunderbau, der so tiefe, epochale und menschliche Verwandtschaft aufweist mit der Tristanpartitur!"

willing in any way to occupy myself further with this affair.'"[14] The scene marks one of the events which cause the ultimate decline of the family, giving the inclusion of Wagner a poignant effect.

The image of the ash-tree in front of the Morels' house also has a Wagnerian symbolic value. In the mythology of the *Ring* Wotan breaks a branch from the ash-tree for his spear, representing the destruction of nature through civilization; the ash-tree is chopped into logs which fuel the destruction of Valhalla at the end of the opera cycle. In *Sons and Lovers* the ash-tree symbolizes fallen nature, including the discord between the Morels. The noise of the wind through the tree's branches heightens the children's terror while their parents argue:

> then the whole was drowned in a piercing medley of shrieks and cries from the great, wind-swept ash-tree .... There was a feeling of horror, a kind of bristling in the darkness, and a sense of blood. (*SL*, 84-85)

Lukács argues that Mann incorporates the decadence of Wagnerian opera, like Schopenhauer's, in a critical way. Mann exposes the ideological implications of the *Motiv* structure in Hanno's improvisation on the piano: "There was something brutal and monotonous, and at the same time something ascetic and religious, something like belief and self-abnegation in the fanatical cult of this nothing, this piece of melody, this short, childish harmonic invention of one and a half bars."[15] But Lukács is unaware that Mann is also characterizing his own Wagnerian *Improvisationen* in *Buddenbrooks*, which are ordered through the *Leitmotiv*. Reflecting on his composition of *Buddenbrooks* in his essay "Über die Kunst Richard Wagners", Mann acknowledged the influence of Wagner's epic style on him:

---

[14] *Ibid.*, I, 185: "Mit einer einzigen Handbewegung schob er alles weit von sich, was vor ihm lag, legte mit einem Ruck den Bleistift auf den Tisch und sagte: 'So erkläre ich, daß ich nicht willens bin, mich länger in irgendeiner Weise mit dieser Angelegenheit zu beschäftigen.'"

[15] *Ibid.*, I, 750: "Es lag etwas Brutales und Stumpfsinniges und zugleich etwas asketisch Religiöses, etwas wie Glaube und Selbstaufgabe in dem fanatischen Kultus dieses Nichts, dieses Stücks Melodie, dieser kurzen, kindischen, harmonischen Erfindung von anderthalb Takten."

Versions of Modernist Realism 83

The motif, the self-quotation, the symbolic formula, the verbal and significant reminiscence across long stretches, — these were epic devices which I had a feeling for, and were enchanting to me as such; ... really, it is not difficult to sense a hint of the spirit of the "Nibelungenringe" in my *Buddenbrooks*, that epic of generations linked together and interwoven by leitmotifs.[16]

The dominant *Motiv* in *Buddenbrooks* is that of decline, especially death; it is as repetitive and overwhelming as the *Rheingold Motiv* in *Götterdämmerung*. The events of decline are ritualistically transcribed in the family chronicle Hanno terminates with a double line and his own death. The narrative imitates the circular motif structure of the novel in its description of Hanno watching Ida Jungmann's departure from the household:

with the same brooding and introspective look, that his golden brown, blue shadowed eyes had on the body of his grandmother, at the death of his father, at the disintegration of the great household and so many lesser experiences of outward similarity .... Old Ida's departure in his view followed the other events of breakings up, closings, endings, disintegrations ... he was familiar with them all.[17]

Hanno is indifferent to decline because he is genetically destined to it. He watches it with "eigenartig goldbraunen Augen mit den bläulichen Schatten" ("strange, golden brown, blue shadowed eyes") and a "wehmütiger und ängstlicher" ("woebegone and anxious")

---

[16] *Ibid.*, X, 840: "Das Motiv, das Selbstzitat, die symbolische Formel, die wörtliche und bedeutsame Rückbeziehung über weite Strecken hin, – das waren epische Mittel nach meinem Empfinden, bezaubernd für mich eben als solche;... Wirklich ist es nicht schwer, in meinen 'Buddenbrooks', diesem epischen, von Leitmotiven verknüpften und durchwobenen Generationenzuge, vom Geiste des 'Nibelungenringes' einen Hauch zu verspüren."
[17] *Ibid.*, I, 699, 424: "mit demselben grüblerischen und nach innen gekehrten Blick, den seine goldbraunen, bläulich umschatteten Augen an der Leiche seiner Großmutter, beim Tode seines Vaters, bei der Auflösung der großen Haushalte und so manchem weniger äußerlichen Erlebnis ähnlicher Art angenommen hatten .... Der alten Ida Verabschiedung schloß sich in seiner Anschuung folgerichtig den anderen Vorgängen des Abbröckelns, des Endens, des Abschließens, der Zersetzung ... denen er beigewohnt hatte."

mouth,[18] which, like his headaches, have been inherited from his mother; he has also inherited his father's weak teeth. The teeth, headaches, mouth and blue-shadowed eyes are constantly repeated throughout the narrative as minor *Motive* which accompany the *Hauptmotiv* of death.

Paul as Siegfried

Lawrence incorporates Wagnerian imagery into a *motivisch* structure to narrate the dilemmas of Schopenhauerian self-alienation, between the body and intellect, life and death. One of his most important borrowings is from Wagner's idea of the hero, Siegfried. He had watched a performance of *Siegfried* on 13 November 1911, and reported to Louie Burrows that, although "it was good", it did not make "any terrific impression on me" (Letters, I, 327). In less than a week, however, Lawrence had contracted an almost fatal case of pneumonia which prepared the ground for his break with Louie Burrows and his teaching post in Croydon in the February of the following year. It also set him free to later marry Frieda Weekley and to develop his artistic maturity in the last drafts of *Sons and Lovers*. The Wagnerian nature of the hero, especially in his confrontation with death, is a central theme of *Sons and Lovers*.

Wagner's hero Siegfried suffers from a Schopenhauerian division; he has pure physical strength but no intellect. He kills a dragon, then wins Brünnhilde by penetrating her chamber of fire and kissing her back to life. As a woman, she compensates for his lack of intellect, as she reassures him:

> Was du nicht weißt,
> Weiß ich für dich[19]

> What you do not know,
> I know for you

The plot of *Siegfried* may hardly have impressed Lawrence, but he would have understood its significance in terms of Schopenhauerian thought, especially in its place within the whole cycle which he knew;

---

[18] *Ibid.*, I, 424.
[19] Richard Wagner, *Siegfried* (London: John Calder, 1984), 119.

he commented that *Siegfried* was "one of the *Ring* cycle that I had not heard" (Letters, I, 327). It is probable that he would have known the plot of the whole *Ring* through reading Ernest Newman, and through Helen Corke. She had seen the cycle in German, read Shaw's "The Perfect Wagnerite", and her lover played in the first violins for the *Ring* at Covent Garden in 1910.[20] The fate of Siegfried in *Götterdämmerung* could have impressed upon Lawrence the more complex situation of Wagner's hero. In *Götterdämmerung* Siegfried, unchanged by Brünnhilde's tuition, is destroyed through his lack of intellect by the conspiring Hagen. Siegfried's downfall, signifying the destruction of uncorrupted nature, confirms Wagner's philosophy of the ultimate *Nichtigkeit* of reality: Siegfried's funeral pyre purifies the ring of its curse, sets fire to the kingdom of the gods, and instigates the Rhine to flood and devastate civilization. Whether Lawrence ever saw *Götterdämmerung* or not, it is likely that he would have been aware of its plot, and its symbolic implications.

In *Sea and Sardinia* Lawrence recalls his past impressions of Fafner: "I have seen dragons in Wagner, at Covent Garden and at the Prinz-Regenten Theatre in Munich, and they were ridiculous" (*SS*, 190). It is possible, then, that Lawrence saw *Siegfried* for the second time in Munich in May or June 1912 while completing his revision of *Sons and Lovers*. Lawrence's fascination with the awakening scene between Siegfried and Brünnhilde was evident in the references he makes to it in *The Trespasser*. Siegmund imagines himself as Siegfried during the sunset which is "a splendid, flaming bridal chamber where he had come to Helena"; later the sunset is likened to "Brünnhilde ... sleeping" among the hills "in her large bright halo of fire" (*T*, 61, 106). The awakening scene symbolizes the reconciliation of man and woman, of intellect and body. It is opposed to the Schopenhauerian resignation of *Tristan und Isolde*, where the consummating kiss yields darkness, night and death. If Paul fails as the hero of *Sons and Lovers*, then he will confirm the pessimism of *Tristan* and *Götterdämmerung*. When he is unable to reconcile his intellect with his sexuality he tries to deny both by willing himself to unconsciousness and death.

---

[20] See Corke, *In Our Infancy*, 157.

When Gertrude has just died and lies "like a maiden asleep", Lawrence refers to the awakening scene of *Siegfried*. Later, Walter Morel sits on the couch afraid for the first time: "Morel had been a man without fear – simply nothing frightened him." Siegfried, too, has not known fear till he finds Brünnhilde. Paul tries to waken his mother through kissing her, but her lack of response only confirms his failure as a hero in the quest for sexual maturity:

> She was young again. Only the hair as it arched so beautifully from her temples was mixed with silver, and the two simple plaits that lay on her shoulders were filigrees of silver and brown. She would wake up. She would lift her eyelids. She was with him still. He bent and kissed her passionately. But there was coldness against his mouth. He bit his lip with horror. Looking at her, he felt he could never, never let her go. No! He stroked the hair from her temples. That too was cold. He saw the mouth so dumb and wondering at the hurt. Then he crouched on the floor, whispering to her: "Mother – Mother!" (*SL*, 443)

This passage echoes Siegfried's approach towards the sleeping Brünnhilde:

> O Mutter, Mutter!
> Dein mutiges Kind!
> Im Schlafe liegt eine Frau:
> die hat ihn das Fürchten gelehrt!
> Wie end ich die Furcht?
> Wie faß ich Mut?
> Das ich selbst erwache,
> muß die Maid ich erwechen![21]
>
> Oh mother! Mother!
> Your courageous child!
> A woman lies asleep:
> she has taught him how to fear!
> How can I stop the fear?
> How can I keep my courage?
> If I am to awaken myself,
> I must awaken the maid.

---

[21] Wagner, *Siegfried*, 118.

Like Lawrence, Wagner recognizes that the child's attachment to a maternal image is symptomatic of its immaturity. Siegfried cries out for his mother to protect him from his sexual anxiety, but he raises himself to sexual consciousness by awakening Brünnhilde through a kiss. Their consummation symbolizes the reconciliation of the male and female principles, of physicality and wisdom. In a disturbing reversal of Siegfried's achievement, Paul kisses Gertrude, imagining that their consummation will raise him to wholeness. Yet she does not waken, and he cries out to her, wanting her as his mother to protect him. He can only return to her through his own death; his attempt to overcome his death-wish forms the climax of the novel, and of his fate as its hero.

Paul's image as the hero of the novel is measured against Walter and William Morel. Walter's domestic activities are among the few happy times he has with his children; he is like a joyful Siegfried singing to the rhythm of forging Nothung:

> The only times when he entered again into the life of his own people was when he worked, and was happy at work .... He was a good workman, dexterous, and one who, when he was in a good humour, always sang. ... It was nice to see him run with a piece of red-hot iron into the scullery, crying:
> "Out of my road, out of my road!"
> Then he hammered the soft, red-glowing stuff on his iron goose, and made the shape he wanted .... He always sang when he mended his boots, because of the jolly sound of hammering. (*SL*, 88)

Gertude observes that Walter "*can't* understand rules and regulations" (*SL*, 112). He is the innocent hero like Siegfried; they are destroyed by events of which they have no understanding.

William, Paul's elder brother, inherits his father's Siegfried-like strength and his mother's Brünnhilde-like intellect. Yet his tragedy is that these qualities undermine each other. His physical abilities are greater than those of all other boys in the area: "All the things that men do – the decent things – William did. He could run like the wind". His heroic qualities are described on his first return from working in London, where his rise has been meteoric: "He was a fine fellow, big, straight, and fearless looking". Yet he is soon "losing himself", until he is exhausted and dies. London resembles the conspiratorial court of Gunther and Hagen, and William's lover, Louisa Lily Denys Western, is the false Gutrune. Paul regards William as the hero whose death he must learn from, comparing his dead body to a "monument". "William had been a prophet" about his lover's lack of faithfulness, but he is also a prophet of the fate of his generation, specifically of Paul's fate (*SL*, 70, 106, 116, 171).

As the hero of *Sons and Lovers* Paul's quest is to succeed where his Siegfried-like father and brother have failed. He must escape from the circularity of the novel's *Motiv* of the failed hero by breaking from its images of failed awakenings and the longing for sleep and death. His first important test is in the chapter ironically called "The Test on Miriam". In his relationship with Miriam he can only identify with his intellect, which confirms his Schopenhauerian self-division. When they have sex they are separate as individuals: he is only aware of her as "a woman", not "as a person". Before he makes love to her, in the twilight, he declares that "'I like the darkness,' ... 'I wish it were thicker – good, thick darkness.'" Afterwards he enters the darkness of "death" and "Being":

> ... he felt as if nothing mattered, as if his living were smeared away into the beyond, near and quite lovable. This strange, gentle reaching-out to death was new to him ....
>
> To him now life seemed a shadow, day a white shadow, night, and death, and stillness, and inaction, this seemed like *being*. To be alive, to be urgent, and insistent, that was *not-to-be*. The highest of all was, to melt out into the darkness and sway there, identified with the great Being ....
>
> "To be rid of our individuality, which is our will, which is our effort – to live effortless, a kind of conscious sleep – that is very beautiful, I think – that is our after-life – our immortality." (*SL*, 330-31)

Instead of reconciling Paul's mind and body, sex only relieves him of the tension between them. Similarly, Tristan and Isolde are only reconciled in the death of their desire for each other, without being transformed as individuals. Like Helena and Siegmund, Paul is stranded in what Nietzsche in *Die Geburt der Tragödie* called the *lethargisch* Dionysian state. His will is exhausted, and he is incapable of returning to the everyday reality of linear time, of entering *ewige Wiederkehr*. Although he usually blames Miriam's "soulfulness", her concentration on his thoughts, as the cause of his desire for death and "Being", she merely lets him indulge in his desire to relinquish his mind. Afterwards, she returns him to a reality of time and space; she urges them to return indoors because it is raining and her family is expecting them.

Like Hanno Buddenbrook, Paul is caught in a cyclical existence he cannot escape from because he is unaware of the causes of his entrapment. He is in the tragic situation of believing that he can redeem his brother's death, while adhering to a Schopenhauerian world view. After the "discussion of a book" with Miriam, he invokes the Schopenhauerian notion that *"one* isn't so very important", only the race as a whole is: William's death was "waste, no more" (*SL*, 193). Paul believes that he can redeem his brother's "waste" through his own survival, because of their shared genetic inheritance from their mother. Yet he is still following the notion that the race as a whole is important, not the individual. By implication, he is still glorifying Gertrude's role as the mother of her sons. For Lawrence to advance beyond the Romanticism in *Buddenbrooks*, Paul must survive by breaking from his mother's will. Freud has not proven essential in diagnosing Paul's problem, but Lawrence will be indebted to him in formulating a solution to it, and in systematically breaking from Schopenhauerian tragedy.

Unlike Hanno, Paul has the option of entering linear time to break from his circular existence, and of healing himself through erotic relationships, in particular with Clara Dawes. Paul's hope in eroticism is also different from Thomas Buddenbrook's declaration of love towards humanity after reading Schopenhauer; Thomas' love is Romantically transcendental because it is impossible to realize, but Paul's is focused on another individual.[22] In the relationship between Paul and Clara, Lawrence comes close to breaking the *Motiv* framework of sleeping maidens and darkness by combining it with a Realist discourse. Clara represents the sleeping Brünnhilde whom Paul must awaken to prove his manhood. When they discuss her marriage with Baxter Dawes, she explains that she married without

---

[22] See Heller, *Thomas Mann: The Ironic German*, 61-63.

thinking about it, that "I seem to have been asleep nearly all my life". Paul asks whether her husband ever woke her, and she replies "No – he never got there", by which she means he never got "At me. He never really mattered to me." The imagery echoes *Siegfried*, of the need for the man to somehow cross the wall of flames – or sexual difference – to reach the woman. Paul needs to understand Dawes' failure, which is similar to his father's with his mother, to succeed as a hero. He later explains to Miriam that Clara broke from her marriage because "she *had* to be awakened" (*SL*, 317-18, 361), and he understands that his role is to awaken her and waken himself into personal maturity.

Freud and Otto Gross' interpretations of tragedy

Lawrence's encounter with Frieda Weekley in March 1912 profoundly affected the composition of the final version of *Sons and Lovers* later in that year. Through Frieda, he would break from his past at every possible level: personally in his sexual relationship with her; geographically with their departure from England to Germany, then Italy; culturally through her background of German culture. Even more importantly, their relationship made possible Lawrence's development to artistic maturity in his greatest novels *The Rainbow* and *Women in Love*. In what remains of this chapter we shall see how Lawrence achieved this, at least in terms of German culture.

The most important cultural influence to which Frieda introduced Lawrence was that of the Austrian psychoanalyst Otto Gross, with whom she had a love affair between 1907 and 1908. Lawrence and Frieda's letters and memoirs vividly reveal their relationship, including the ideas she communicated to him throughout the composition of *Sons and Lovers* and beyond. Gross' letters to Frieda are also essential to our understanding of Lawrence's biography and artistic development. John Worthen argues that we can assume Lawrence read them because Frieda sent her husband some to explain her affair with Lawrence. Worthen sums up the significance of the letters as a struggle "to come to terms with the new and to escape the past": "they offered Lawrence the themes for his next eight years of writing; and (above all) they offered a way of thinking about Frieda."[23]

Gross attempted to combine Freud's ideas with Nietzsche's to produce a revolutionary philosophy, and through her relationship with Gross, Frieda suggested this philosophy to Lawrence. This includes Lawrence's modern sense of tragedy: instead of regarding tragedy as the failure of his characters to sustain a transcendence of the physical world, as in *The Trespasser*, Lawrence locates its processes in the Dionysian and libidinal experiences of his characters in *Sons and Lovers*.

Lawrence wrote to Louie Burrows on 3 March 1911, about two weeks before meeting Frieda:

> When I get sore, I always fly to the Greek tragedies: they make one feel sufficiently fatalistic. Im doing *Oedipus Tyrannus* just now – Sophocles .... These Greek tragedies make one quiet and indifferent. (Letters, I, 235)

The resignation of the individual before the will of the gods accorded with Schopenhauer's interpretation of tragedy. However, in Lawrence's letter to Louie Burrows on 1 April 1911 we can see his attitude beginning to shift. Reflecting on his sister's grief over the death of their mother, he retains the ideas of "fate" and "emptiness":

> Tragedy is like strong acid – it dissolves away all but the very gold of truth .... But I suppose it's fate. What life has set in progress, life can't arrest: There is nothing to do but ... to find in the emptiness a new presence.

But in the same letter, Lawrence anticipates his admiration for the Italian "belief in the blood" a few months after he completed *Sons and Lovers*, in contrast to Wagner's "fate" and "Nichtigkeit":

> I love Italian opera – it's so reckless. Damn Wagner, and his bellowings at Fate and death .... I like the Italians who run all on impulse, and don't care about their immortal souls, and don't worry about the ultimate. (Letters, I, 449)

---

[23] Worthen, *D. H. Lawrence: The Early Years*, 443-44.

Like Nietzsche in *Der Fall Wagner* (1888, *The Case of Wagner*), in this letter Lawrence chooses *Carmen* as one of his favourite opera after; he reverses his attitude to Wagner who, as he had previously advised Blanche Jennings, would "run a knowledge of music into your blood". It is probable that he had read *Der Fall Wagner* while writing *The Trespasser*.[24] He comments to Sallie Hopkin on 26 April that "*Oedipus* is the finest drama of *all* times. It is terrible in its accumulation – like a great big wave coming up – and then crash!" (Letters, I, 247-248). The "terrible" "crash" is the critical moment of tragedy, not the ensuing "emptiness". On the same day he writes to Ada that "life is full of wonder and surprise and mostly pain. But never mind, the tragic is most holding, the most vital thing in life" (Letters, I, 261). Lawrence is beginning to focus on the vitality of the individual hero in defiance of Wagner and Schopenhauer's inevitable "fate and death".

Through Frieda, Gross provided Lawrence with a Freudian and Nietzschean interpretation of *Oedipus Tyrannus*, and of the tragic element in *Sons and Lovers*. In *Die Traumdeutung* (1899, *The Interpretation of Dreams*) Freud redefined the significance of Greek tragedy, especially *Oedipus*. He denied that it expressed the powerlessness of the individual before the will of the gods. Instead, it depicts the conflict between the individual's consciousness and unconscious:

> King Oedipus, who slew his father Laïus and married his mother Jocasta, is merely our childhood wish-fulfilment. But, more fortunate than him, we have since managed, in so far as we have not become psychoneurotics, to detach our sexual stirrings from our mothers, to forget our jealousy of our fathers. Facing the person in whom every primal childhood wish has been fulfilled, we shudder back with the whole sum of repression, which those wishes have since then suffered within us.[25]

---

[24] *Ibid.*, 566.
[25] Siegmund Freud, *Gesammelte Werke*, 18 vols (Hamburg: Fischer, 1940-52), II and III, 269: "König Ödipus, der seinen Vater Laïos erschlagen und seine Mutter Jokaste geheiratet hat, ist nur die Wunscherfüllung unserer Kindheit. Aber glücklicher als er, ist es uns seitdem, insofern wir nicht Psychoneurotiker geworden sind, gelungen, unsere sexuellen Regungen von unseren Müttern abzulösen, unsere Eifersucht gegen unsere Vater zu vergessen. Vor der Person, an welcher sich jener urzeitliche

Frieda recalled that during her first meeting with Lawrence, they "talked about Oedipus and understanding leaped through our words".[26] While Lawrence was redrafting *Sons and Lovers* for the last time in September 1912, she wrote to Garnett that "L. quite missed the point in 'Paul Morel'. He really loved his mother more than any body, even with his other women, real love, sort of Oedipus" (Letters, I, 449). From Schopenhauer's notion of tragedy in which the individual faces the universal will, Lawrence moves closer to Freud's notion of the individual's consciousness facing his unconscious will. Paul is not cursed by his irreversible genealogy, but by his repressed sexual fixation upon his mother and aggression towards his father.

Freud's analysis of *Oedipus Tyrannus*, though, follows from the Aristotelian interpretation of catharsis: the spectators' unconscious desires are vicariously satisfied by Oedipus having acted them out, but then the terror of his punishment strengthens their consciousness in repressing their desires. Freud's analysis accords with his premise that consciousness must control the unconscious to restrain the individual within society's values. Following Nietzsche, Otto Gross instead believed that society must be transformed to encompass the individual's libidinal desires. In his book *Über psychopathische Minderwertigkeiten* (1909, *On Psychopathic Inferiors*), which he was perhaps planning during his affair with Frieda, he argued that Freud was continuing Nietzsche's work in revealing how the social majority repressed the individual's instincts.[27] Gross attempted to realize his synthesis of Freud and Nietzsche's ideas in his school of anarchists at Ascona; with the slogan *Nichts verdrängen!* ("repress nothing!"), they broke social conventions through experimentation in drugs and orgies.[28] His relationship with Frieda was part of this project, in which he envisaged her as the *übermenschlich*, *Weib der Zukunft* ("woman of the future").[29]

Kindheitswunsch erfüllt hat, schaudern wir zurück mit dem ganzen Betrag der Verdrängung, welche diese Wünsche in unserem Innern seither erlitten haben."
[26] Frieda Lawrence, *"Not I, But the Wind ..."* (London: Granada Publishing, 1983), 2.
[27] See Jennifer E. Michaels, *Anarchy and Eros* (New York: Peter Lang, 1983), 40.
[28] *Ibid.*, 39-40, 59, 25.
[29] John Turner, "The Otto Gross-Frieda Weekley Correspondence", *The D. H. Lawrence Review*, XXII/2 (1990), 198.

Gross suggested to Frieda a Nietzsche-Freudian understanding of tragedy:

> – you bring me the miracle, the unity of being in a joy – the Dionysiac, this is it – you bring me, that I don't have to be lonely anymore – As a boy I read and strangely felt as a phrase of destiny – it went "nam idem velle atque idem nolle" – "*to will the same thing in yes and no*" – I have waited *for you*, in order to find the truth in *it* – that this protracted longing and this great willing in an intoxication of the senses becomes life, is our love, Frieda – [30]

Following Nietzsche's *Die Geburt der Tragödie*, Gross envisaged the Dionysian as a combination of "Freude" and "lange Sehnsucht", of joy and pain, "Ja und Nein". He realized this truth through his relationship with Frieda: the erotic experience, the discharge of the libido into the Other, is "das Dionysische". The Apollonian is Freud's analytical process which objectifies this experience, and places it with the past. In tandem with his sexual encounters with Frieda, Gross was also undergoing self-analysis. He reported to her: "I have spoken face to face with all the ghosts from my evil childhood and all my evil hours ... since then I am able to look *everything* in the eye".[31] Yet for Gross, analysis does not enable the subject to sublimate his repressed desires, but to release them in a sexual relationship.

Gross recognized the tragic struggle between life and death within himself, of "how strangely within the inner soul the future clashes with the past, longing with weakness".[32] From Nietzsche, Gross valued decadence in the process of growth, as he explained to Frieda:

---

[30] *The D. H. Lawrence Review*, XXII/2, 212: "– Du bringst mir ja das Wunderbare, das Einssein in Einer Freude – das Dionysische, das ist es – Du bringst mir, dass ich nicht mehr einsam sein muss – Als Bub hab ich gelesen und seltsam wie ein Schicksalswort empfunden – es heisst 'nam idem velle atque idem nolle' – '*Dasselbe wollen im Ja und Nein*' – ich hab' *auf Dich* gewartet, um *Das* zu finden – dass diese lange Sehnsucht und dieses grosse Wollen in einem Rausch der Sinne Leben wird, ist *unsere* Liebe, Frieda – "

[31] *Ibid.*, 209-210: "ich mit allen den Gespenstern aus meiner bösen Kindheit und allen meinen bösen Stunden von Angesicht zu Angesicht geredet habe ... seither vermag ich *Allem* in's Auge zu schauen."

[32] *Ibid.*, 211: "wie sich doch sonderbar im Seeleninnern die Zukunft mit Vergangenem, die Sehnsucht mit der Schwäche kreuzt."

"You know my belief, that it is always only out of *decadence* that a *new harmony* of life creates itself – and that the wonderful age which we are in has just been determined as *the Epoch of Decadence* to the womb of the great future."[33]

Similarly, Lawrence integrates Paul's will to death into the Dionysian cycle of nature. Every assertion by Paul, every success, is accompanied by a shadow of death and failure. After his painting wins first prize, his first major success as an artist, he argues with his mother about the irrelevance of happiness:

> "But I want you to be happy," she said, pathetically.
> "Eh my dear – say rather you want me to live."
> Mrs Morel felt as if her heart would break for him. At this rate, she knew he would not live. He had that poignant carelessness about himself, his own suffering, his own life, which is a form of slow suicide. (*SL*, 300)

This exchange is extremely complex: Lydia realizes that Paul's relationship with Miriam is making him unhappy and is also destroying him; she wants him to return to her to revive his childlike happiness with her. Yet "happiness" with his mother would also destroy him, which is why "to live" is his alternative to it, even if his life with Miriam is a futile situation. Paul's tragic quality is that, despite affirming "life" over happiness, he cannot realize a way of actually living. The distinction has been made though, and he strives towards life.

Lawrence perceived his early years with Frieda and his final version of *Sons and Lovers* as a form of tragedy in Gross' terms. Although they were "bogged in tragedy from England" (Letters, I, 438), of her abandoned husband and children, Lawrence realized that his "tragedy" with Frieda was exclusively between them. He explained to Edward Garnett on 29 June 1912:

---

[33] *Ibid.*, 212: "Du kennst ja meinen Glauben, dass immer nur aus einer *Decadence* sich eine *neue Harmonie* des Lebens erschafft – und dass die wunderbare Zeit, in der wir sind, gerade *als die Decadenceepoche* zum Mutterschooss der grossen Zukunft bestimmt ist."

Oh no – the great war is waged in this little flat on the Isarthal, just as much as anywhere else. In fact, I don't think the *real* tragedy is in dying, or in the perversity of affairs, like the woman one loves being the wife of another man – like the last act of *Tristan*. I think the real tragedy is in the inner war which is raged between people who love each other, a war out of which comes knowledge and – (Letters, I, 419)

Lawrence's idea of tragedy, which he defines in opposition to *Tristan und Isolde*, bears a great resemblance to Nietzsche's in *Die Geburt der Tragödie*. His reduction of Wagner to naturalism, "in the perversity of affairs", echoes Nietzsche in *Der Fall Wagner*, that Wagner's heroines are frustrated "New Women" like Emma Bovary.[34] While writing *The Trespasser* Lawrence identified Nietzsche's ideas in *Die Geburt der Tragödie* with Wagner's late Romanticism; now he recognizes the opposition between Nietzsche and Wagner, which Nietzsche had only perceived later in his career. For Lawrence, "*real* tragedy" is not in "dying", as Schopenhauer and Wagner believed. It is in the "inner war" between two people, encompassing death and life, and yielding a "knowledge" which will enable the protagonists to survive. Repudiating his earlier Schopenhauerian attitude, Lawrence now asserts that "tragedy ought really to be a great kick at misery", and that *Sons and Lovers* is "a great tragedy ... the tragedy of thousands of young men in England" (Letters, I, 459, 477).

Lawrence and Mann's Realism
In the Nietzsche-Freudian tragic vision of *Sons and Lovers* Paul inhabits a Dionysian symbolic existence, and Apollonian Realist one. To break into *ewige Wiederkehr* Paul must mediate between cyclical and linear time, the unconscious and conscious, his sexuality and intellect. He must not merely attempt to transcend reality into the universal, as Helena and Siegmund did in *The Trespasser*, but transform himself in the universal and then return to reality. Paul's "universal", "unconscious" "will" is grounded in his relationships with others, which Lawrence expresses through a Realist discourse. The discussion of *Sons and Lovers* has come full-circle: Lawrence has

---

[34] See Nietzsche, *Werke*, VIII, 31.

developed from his late Romantic inheritance of Schopenhauer and Wagner, to acquire a Modernist form of Realism through Nietzsche and Freud. His synthesis of these ideas reaches beyond the debate over the Realism or anti-Realism of *Sons and Lovers*: the novel's Realism evolves out of the Romantic tradition.

During Lettie and George's final meeting in *The White Peacock* Lawrence imitated Wagner's music in structure and style, while also anticipating a break from Wagner's symbolism. One of Wagner's most progressive achievements had been to undermine the symbolic power of his *Motive* by bringing attention to their physical quality as sound. This process counters symbolism with a Realism of the sound as individual melodic phrases. By analogy, we saw how Lettie and George appear as realistic characters whose apparently individual intentions are determined by the *Motive* that organize the novel as a whole. At the same time, though, Wagner anticipated the Modernist style of Schoenberg in a dissonance which breaks through the harmonic structures of tonality that give meaning to the *Motive*. In *The White Peacock* the tension between Lettie and George almost liberates them from the novel's *Motive*, and the social values signified by them. These alternative styles correspond respectively to Freud's notion of tragedy in which the audience objectifies the characters as individuals enslaved to their unconscious will, and Gross' Nietzschean tragedy in which the characters are liberated through their unconscious impulses. As Modernist novels, *Sons and Lovers* may be compared to *Buddenbrooks* in terms of how they enact these alternative responses to the Romantic tradition.

First, both Lawrence and Mann bring attention to the *Leitmotiv* structure of their novels, to show how their characters' intentions are entrapped within it. Mann reverts back to a nineteenth-century form of Realism that contextualizes the circular existence of his characters in history. For Hanno, "one does not believe in Monday, when he is to hear *Lohengrin* on Sunday evening"; Wagner cannot be reconciled with the harsh reality of school, which the narrator recognizes, is "ein Staat im Staate" [35] ("a state among states"). Mann attempts to historicize his *Motive* to expose their decadent effect on the

---

[35] Mann, *Gesammelte Werke*, I, 701, 722: "Man glaubt an keinen Montag, wenn man am Sonntag-abend den ‹Lohengrin› hören soll."

characters. Thomas' chain-smoking is a *Motiv* which soothes him of reality: he confesses to his doctor, "one is so frightfully alone ... I smoke".[36] The *Motiv* of weak teeth becomes absurd in its effect on the characters. The narrator explains that Hanno's "teeth affected not only his spirits but also the functioning of all his other organs".[37] Thomas' death from a broken crown is tragicomic, as the town's citizens wonder to themselves: "a person doesn't die of that! ... Whoever heard of the like?"[38]

Mann demonstrates how the Buddenbrooks' journal, as a *Motiv* structure which ritually commemorates their lives, develops the power to affect their fate. Consul Johann enters the details of his family's history, including their insurance policies, while interspersing it with prayers to God in "an expression of earnest, almost suffering piety".[39] His entrepreneurial father has no interest in the book. Later, Tony is inspired by it to marry Grünlich, despite being revolted by him. She admires its "almost religious observation of facts" which confirms that her relatives are all "God's will and work, wonderfully guiding the destinies of the family". Acknowledging herself as "a link in a chain", "she was filled with reverence for herself"[40] and records her engagement to Grünlich in the journal. Her notion of herself as a "Glied" in the family's line encourages her to deny "conceptions of free will and self-development". She regards herself with "fatalistischen Gleichmut" ("fatalistic indifference"), believing that "any characteristic, no matter of what kind, was regarded as an heirloom, a family tradition, which one must at all times respect".[41] Afterwards, she enjoys her divorce suit as a momentous occasion in

---

[36] *Ibid.*, I, 651: "Man ist so fürchterlich allein ... Ich rauche."
[37] *Ibid.*, I, 514: "Zahnbeschwerden nicht nur seine Gemütstimmung, sondem auch die Funktionen einzelner Organe."
[38] *Ibid.*, I, 688: "daran starb man doch nicht! ...War dergleichen erhört?"
[39] *Ibid.*, I, 53: "einen ernsten und vor Andacht beinahe leidenden Ausdruck."
[40] *Ibid.*, I, 160-61: "fast religiösen Achtung vor Tatsachen"; "Gottes Wille und Werke, der die Geschicke der Familie wunderbar gelenkt"; "ein Glied in einer Kette"; "erfurcht vor sich selbst erföllte sie."
[41] *Ibid.*, I, 205: "Begriffen des freien Willens und der Selbstbestimmung"; "jede Eigenschaft, gleichviel welcher Art, ein Erbstück, eine Familientradition bedeute und folglich etwas Ehrwürdiges sei, wovor man in jedem Falle Respekt haben müsse."

the family's history; she is "emsig und stolz"[42] ("industrious and proud") when entering it into the chronicle.

Adorno argued that in Wagner's fragmentation of his *motivisch* order, the individual *Motiv* can only insist on its own importance while remaining impotent in the musical whole. By analogy, Mann can only reveal how insignificant his characters are within history: he cannot rescue them from it. The circular and linear forms of reality in *Buddenbrooks* do not interact with each other: Hanno has no consciousness of his historical circumstances, playing with his toys while Bismarck unifies Germany; when Frankfurt capitulates to Bismarck, Thomas loses twenty thousand thaler, and can only conclude that "Nichts fügte sich mehr! Nichts ging mehr nach seinem Willen!"[43] (Nothing went right anymore! Nothing happened according to his will!") The Buddenbrooks are unable to save themselves through confronting the fate of their class in history.

In *Sons and Lovers* Lawrence foregrounds how Paul's psychological condition is expressed by the novel's *Motive*. Paul recognizes that his identification with his mother is forcing upon him "the bitter peace of resignation", to entrap him within a cyclical existence. "Things were going in a circle", because he cannot love another woman while she is alive:

> His life wanted to free itself of her. It was like a circle where life turned back on itself, and got no further. She bore him, loved him, kept him, and his love turned back into her, so that he could not be free to go forward with his own life, really love another woman. (*SL*, 389)

These insights on the source of Paul's aimlessness confirm Lawrence's advance from Schopenhauer's explanation of the divided individual, to Freud's on the individual who is fixated on one of his parents. Freud's theory locates the individual's lack of self-integration not in his or her genealogy, which Schopenhauer does, but in childhood experiences which lead up to maturity. Paul's condition is a product of his childhood development, of his family relationships. His cyclically futile existence has emerged from the linear developments

---

[42] *Ibid.*, I, 234.
[43] *Ibid.*, I, 435.

of his past. Hanno watched the spiralling decline of his family uncritically, because he had genetically inherited its decline and had no resource with which to break from it. Paul's consciousness sets him apart from the Buddenbrooks, and enables him to survive.

Transforming or transcending reality?
These passages characterizing Paul's "circular" fate are analogous to how Freud interpreted Oedipus' tragedy, as something for the reader to observe, and distance himself from. Yet *Sons and Lovers* is not merely an Aristotelian, Realist tragedy, but a Nietzschean one which attempts to express directly Paul's Dionysian impulses, to transform his Apollonian reality. In this sense, Lawrence's novel reaches beyond the achievements of *Buddenbrooks*.

Adorno describes how Wagner lets his *Motive* "go", to abandon themselves into a primal dissonance which undermines the harmonic scheme. Similarly, Lawrence lets his characters "go" into an erotic dissonance with each other, to undermine the social customs that they inhabit. According to Adorno, Wagner breaks the "fulfilment promised in consonance" to explore "the poignant pain of non-fulfilment and the pleasure that lies in the tension".[44] Nietzsche understands *Dissonanz* in *Die Geburt der Tragödie* as "Das Dionysische, mit seiner selbst am Schmerz percipirten Urlust".[45] Dissonance rejects the classical laws of harmony, of distinct major and minor keys. Gross would have identified this dissonance with the libidinal impulse, which rejects the laws of society. Yet there is still the danger of merely transcending society, as in *The Trespasser*, not changing it.

Lawrence would have been familiar with the dissonance of modern music since watching Strauss' *Elektra* in 1910. This opera extensively applies atonality and bitonality, especially in Klytämnestra's dream scene, to convey her paranoia that her body is rotting from the sin of Agamemnon's murder. The libretto of Hugo von Hofmannsthal complements the music with its Nietzschean vision of the violence of ancient Greece, and its exploration of conflict

---

[44] Adorno, *In Search of Wagner*, 62-70.
[45] Nietzsche, *Werke*, III/1, 148: "The Dionysian, with its primal joy experienced in pain itself".

within the characters, including Klytämnestra; its treatment of Elektra is indebted to Freud's case study of Anna O.[46] Compared to Freud's notion of tragedy which distances the audience from the protagonist, Strauss and Hofmannsthal intended their audience to become embroiled in the dissonant, Dionysian power of their opera. Although the dissonance of *Elektra* is concentrated on vengeance, Lawrence associates its dissonance with eroticism; he reported to Jessie Chambers that *Elektra* had almost inspired him to make love to Alice Dax the morning after (Letters, I, 157).

Lawrence attempts to create a comparable dissonant effect in Paul's relationship with Clara by countering this Dionysian side with the Apollonian, by placing their relationship in a social context. Clara is described in terms of her social and economic relationships, of her status as a separated wife and sweated labourer. Paul observes her simultaneously as a worker and as an object of desire: "She was making an elastic stocking of heliotrope silk, turning the spiral-machine with slow, balanced regularity, occasionally bending down to see her work, or to adjust the needles: then her magnificent neck, with its down and fine pencils of hair shone white against the lavender, lustrous silk" (*SL*, 307). She bends her "magnificent neck" to her work, and her "pencils of hair" mirror the needles; in the presence of her beauty the "heliotrope silk" looks "lavender, lustrous". Her social identity counters Paul's desire to transcend material reality with her when they make love.

In the first love scene by the river they manage to balance material reality with its transcendence:

> Her mouth was offered him, and her throat, her eyes were half shut, her breast was tilted as if it asked for him. He flashed with a small laugh, shut his eyes, and met her in a long, whole kiss. Her mouth fused with his; their bodies were sealed and annealed. It was some minutes before they withdrew. They were standing beside the public path. (*SL*, 353)

While merging together, the lovers are still objectifying each other as distinct physical beings. As in *The Trespasser* Lawrence expresses

---

[46] See Richard Strauss and Hugo von Hofmannsthal, *Salome/Elektra* (London: John Calder, 1988).

their transcendental oneness in the *Tonsprache* of the language, of "fused with his" and "sealed and annealed", yet its effect is countered by the vivid descriptions of their eyes and movements. Paul and Clara's transcendence is measured in time by the length of each sentence and is located in a specific place which registers that they belong to a society whose conventions they are momentarily defying.

Paul and Clara venture further, anxious not to return by the pathway, manoeuvring past the water which has flooded it, past the watching fishermen, until:

> He sank his mouth on her throat, where he felt her heavy pulse beat under his lips. Everything was perfectly still. There was nothing in the afternoon but themselves.

The presence of a social reality becomes vaguer while their sexual experience intensifies. Yet they are aware of the cows grazing nearby, and soon return "back at the ordinary level" (*SL*, 355-56) above the grove. He cleans their boots and washes his hands in preparation for their return to society. The more intense their feelings are, the weaker Lawrence's references to society become. He is straining against his Realist discourse to make their Dionysian impulses the dominant subject of the scene, to give them a revolutionary force. Like Gross, Lawrence's intention is not to transcend society, but to transform it, by liberating the characters through their sexual impulses.

In the scene between Paul and Clara in a field at night, Lawrence expresses a dissonance which "lets go" of the *Motive* of darkness. The Dionysian and unconscious inhabit the darkness which no longer signifies death, but the processes of life and death. Darkness is occupied by lovers: "The night contained them." The landscape around Paul is "curving and strong with life in the dark". Clara is "a strong, strange, wild life, that breathed with his in the darkness through this hour"; her eyes are "dark and shining and strange, life wild at the source staring into his life, stranger to him, yet meeting him" (*SL*, 398).

While Lawrence drives further into the Dionysian, in the scene between Paul and Clara he fails to balance it with an Apollonian, Realist discourse. The stars are the universal will, while the grass and birdsong are representations of the environment in which Paul and Clara have sex:

> It was all so much bigger than themselves, that he was hushed. They had met, and included in their meeting the thrust of the manifold grass stems, the cry of the peewit, the wheel of the stars.

Yet the represented world, including Clara, is desocialized and without any tactile reality of its own. Clara is not satisfied or "awakened" because, as when Paul was with Miriam, the experience does not involve her personally:

> It was something that happened because of her, but it was not her. They were scarcely any nearer each other. It was as if they had been blind agents of a great force.

They "know their own nothingness" (*SL*, 398-99), but not each other as individuals. Their love-making has lapsed into the *lethargisch* Dionysian. When Lawrence explores the Dionysian most intensely, the Apollonian is obliterated. Paul and Clara have transcended their individuality only to experience nothingness, not to transform themselves as individuals.

This problem is shared by Gross in his letters to Frieda, and Lawrence may have been able to objectify it when reading them. Gross' letters are characterized by expressions of passionate extremes, emphasized by underlinings, including multiple ones. His visionary style anticipates the Expressionist poetry of Georg Heym and Georg Trakl. Gross is not conveying an objective reality to Frieda; he is attempting to directly express his Dionysian passion to her in his language, to overcome the reality of her marriage that separates them from each other. Unfortunately, his language often collapses into meaningless histrionics. Freud was critical of this quality in Gross' writing and thought, especially in *Das Freud'sche Ideogenitätsmoment* (1907), which Gross sent to Frieda. Freud diagnosed Gross' personal sensationalism as the cause of his excess of superlatives in his writing.[47]

---

[47] *The D. H. Lawrence Review*, XXII/2, 147.

John Turner perceives a form of essentialism in Gross' language which denies "relations of power, property, class, finance, and labor" for an "area of experience that seemed most inward, most 'personal,' most 'natural': human sexuality". Turner relates Gross' "idealism of desire"[48] to his failures in acknowledging the otherness of his sexual partners. Frieda had criticized him: "why do I have to then, poor soul that I am, be a *'type'*, do let me be a living individual and not a dead type."[49]

Unlike Gross, Lawrence is aware of the problem of his style, and dramatizes it in the novel through Paul. He is unable to acknowledge Clara's otherness because he is still fixated on his mother, unable to resolve his mind and body. Clara had initiated their lovemaking to help him forget his mother, to "soothe him into forgetfulness" (*SL*, 397). Lawrence projects his failings onto Paul, which perhaps explains his outburst "I *loathe* Paul Morel" (Letters, I, 427), on beginning the final revision in July 1912.

In the failure to transform himself through his erotic relationship with Clara, Paul lapses back into the Romanticism of Wagner. After the death of his mother, Paul feels "there was nothing left". He enters the *lethargisch* Dionysian state; he transcends material reality and moves towards death, where "things had lost their reality", and "the realest thing was the thick darkness at night." His "will" persuades him to either paint or have children to continue his mother's existence, not for him to live as an individual (*SL*, 454-55). After rejecting Miriam's offer of marriage he is completely alone:

> Everywhere the vastness and terror of the immense night which is roused and stirred for a brief while by the day, but which returns, and will remain at last eternal, holding everything in its silence and its living gloom. There was no Time, only Space. (*SL*, 464)

The last sentence echoes Wagner's *Parsifal*, where Gurnemanz leads Parsifal to the castle of the Grail, and comments that "zum Raum wird hier die Zeit"[50] ("time here becomes space"). Lawrence may have

---

[48] *Ibid.*, 148.
[49] *Ibid.*, 216: "warum muss ich denn, ich Unglückswurm ein *'Typus'* sein, lass mich doch ein lebendiges Individuum sein und kein toter Typus."
[50] Richard Wagner, *Parsifal* (London: John Calder, 1986), 96.

picked up the line from *A Study of Wagner*, where Ernest Newman criticizes it as an extreme form of Wagner's idealism.[51] The line describes how the universal will swallows up Paul as an individual, like the rest of Lawrence's description which describes a temporal circularity, an "immense night" whose "return" is "eternal".

Yet transcendence in *Sons and Lovers* is interrupted by time, and the material reality of Paul's "body, his chest that leaned against the stile, his hands on the wooden bar". His body is only "one tiny upright speck of flesh" pressed into "extinction" by "the immense dark silence". Paul has acknowledged the Dionysian will of the universe while affirming his individuality, to enter the realm of *ewige Wiederkehr*. He re-enacts the scene with his dead mother when he had tried to awaken her. He wants to touch her: "'Mother!' he whimpered, 'mother!'" But this time he is faithful to Siegfried's example, by courageously walking forward, not to a sleeping maiden, but to "the faintly humming, glowing town" (*SL*, 464), the only source of light in the darkness.

Paul's body is only "one tiny speck" in the "immense night" (*SL*, 464), but this is enough to ensure his existence. He survives, then, because he has been created at a different historical moment to Hanno Buddenbrook. Against Romantic pessimism, Mann realistically depicts a history his characters are alienated from, and are unable to re-enter. His Realism cannot reverse their fate, but only explain it. The reality of Paul's history, of his family and of his environment, is inscribed upon his body. Through his body's desires he is able to "make history", which Lawrence believed himself to be doing with Frieda (Letters, I, 390). The body is the foundation of Lawrence's Modernist Realism. Yet Paul's survival is only suggested, not confirmed. His failures reflect Lawrence's awareness of the limited achievements of Frieda's previous lover Otto Gross in affirming individuality through sexuality.

In *Sons and Lovers* Lawrence has achieved a partial solution to the dilemmas of *The White Peacock* and *The Trespasser*, that is, between his characters' entrapment in social convention and their futile longing to transcend it. But this polarity will remain problematic for Lawrence. He cannot resolve his characters with society, since it

---

[51] See Newman, *A Study of Wagner*, 356.

would demand either the transformation of society according to the individual's needs, or the assimilation of the individual into society's laws. He can only juxtapose the two against each other, with varying outcomes. In *The Rainbow* he emulates Gross' aspiration to transform society through the individual. Lawrence's characters liberate themselves from society to be fulfilled, yet at other times transcend it into their own nothingness.

IV
UNITY AND FRAGMENTATION IN *THE RAINBOW*

While composing the first version of *The Rainbow* from March to June 1913 as "The Sisters", Lawrence commented that "it's like a novel in a foreign language I don't know very well – I can only just make out what it is about" (Letters, I, 544). The "foreignness" of *The Rainbow* was partly due to the experiences of Germany that he was bringing to bear on his fiction: his relationship with Frieda, his encounters with her relatives, his review of Thomas Mann's work, his exposure to the paintings of the Blaue Reiter, and his wider reading of Goethe, Novalis and Nietzsche. In order to understand the German influences upon *The Rainbow*, it is worth looking first at Lawrence's developments during this period of the early drafts, before he embarked on the final version of the novel in December 1914.

Transition in "The Prussian Officer"
Before he completed "The Sisters" Lawrence wrote the short story "The Prussian Officer" (1914) which reveals his stylistic development at this crucial moment. In this story he develops the style he had used to depict Paul and Clara's sexual encounters in *Sons and Lovers*. We saw in the previous chapter how Lawrence's struggle in that novel against the Romantic tradition of Wagner was comparable to Thomas Mann in *Buddenbrooks*. Lawrence's development in "The Prussian Officer" is worth comparing to another contemporary artist, Arnold Schoenberg, in his transition from Romanticism to the Expressionism of his monodrama *Erwartung* (1909).

The images at the beginning of "The Prussian Officer" appear to create distinct characters within a realistic prose; they convey the soldier's "warm, full nature" and "dark, unthinking eyes", for example, in contrast to the officer's "light blue eyes that were always flashing with cold fire" (*PO*, 2-4). Yet the oxymoronic image of "cold fire" threatens to disrupt the reality constructed from the officer and soldier's opposition to each other as individuals. This effect is foregrounded at the opening of the story. The soldier suffers from the "suffocating heat" of the valley, despite identifying himself with it; he longs for the "snow gleaming" on the mountain peaks beyond, and for the coldness of the officer's presence. This contradiction disrupts the *Motiv* structure of heat and cold: the straps of the soldier's knapsack no longer burn his shoulders, "but seemed to give off a cold, prickly sensation"; although he feels numb, there is a "tight, hot place in his chest", and yet "he walked almost lightly" (*PO*, 1).

While the *Motive* shift in their meaning, they no longer provide a framework for the narrative's unity. Here Lawrence has employed Wagner's *Leitmotiv* technique, not to create a totalizing work of art, but to break up the unity of the narrative. In 1909 Schoenberg reflected how "first I became a Wagnerian – then further development came quite fast". His debt to Wagner parallels Lawrence's. In early works, such as *Pelleas und Melisande* (1902-1903), Schoenberg had used *Motive* to structure increasingly diverse thematic material. Then Wagner's "short motives, with their possibility of changing the composition as quickly and as often as the least detail of mood requires",[1] were incorporated into *Erwartung*. In the ostinato sections of *Erwartung* Schoenberg compresses the repetition of *Motive* into localized passages of a few seconds. The ostinati include "substitute" tones that undermine the hierarchy of distinct tonal regions through the instruments oscillating a half-step above or below the natural tones of the scale. Like Lawrence's condensed, ambivalent imagery, the ostinati imitate the accumulating pressure of a repressed force, which pushes towards an extreme tension of contradictory emotions and sensations.

Throughout "The Prussian Officer" Lawrence constructs "ostinato" passages based on the contrasting images of the soldier's warmth and officer's coolness. Like Schoenberg's disruption of the tonal framework through dissonant tones, Lawrence destabilizes the reality of his narrative, and the individuality of his characters, through overlapping the images with each other. The soldier acts "like a warm flame" upon the officer. When the soldier spills wine, the officer observes with his "eyes, bluey like fire", how "the red gushed out". He attempts to obliterate the soldier's otherness by hitting him, only

---

[1] Arnold Schönberg, *Gesammelte Schriften* (Frankfurt am Main: Fischer, 1976-), I, 157: "Erst wurde ich Wagnerianer – dann kam die weitere Entwicklung ziemlich rasch"; "kurzen Motive, mit ihrer Möglichkeit, den Satz so rasch und so oft zu wenden, als es das kleinste Stimmungsdetail erfordert."

to watch "the black eyes flare up into his own, like a blaze when straw is thrown on a fire". The officer feels a "hot flame ... in his blood", and his "heart runs hot". He strikes the soldier for the satisfaction of seeing "the blood on his mouth", which imitates the spilling of red wine. In the next scene the officer also spills wine while pouring it into a glass. The *Motive* of warmth associated with the soldier have penetrated the officer, who feels both "the intense gratification of his passion", and an "agony breaking down of something inside him" into a "chaos of sensations" only resisted by his "rigid will" (*PO*, 3, 4-7, 8).

The soldier quenches the dissonance by killing the officer, and "here his own life also ended". The crucial issue at this point of the story is whether the soldier will free himself from his individual existence only to die, as the heroes and heroines of Wagner's tragic operas do, or whether he will be ultimately renewed as an individual:

> But now he had got beyond himself. He had never been here before. Was it life, or not-life?

His experiences echo Paul Morel's lapse from "time" into "space" at the end of *Sons and Lovers*: "everything slid away into space"; "the darkness fell like a shutter, and the night was whole" (*PO*, 15, 18-19). Lawrence refers back to Wagner's reconciliation of the musical dissonance in *Tristan und Isolde* through death in the universal darkness of *die Nacht*. For Schoenberg there can be no reconciliation in *die Nacht*: he sets the word *Nacht* in the libretto of *Erwartung* to a dissonant, low-pitched ostinato alternating between two notes.

Yet in "The Prussian Officer" the "unknown" is also "the darkened open beyond, where each thing existed alone". This darkness is a space in which individual beings are free of each other. The soldier's consciousness disintegrates into separate parts, until "they would all fall, fall through the everlasting lapse of space" (*PO*, 18, 20). It is ambiguous whether the fragments of his self retain their autonomy, or whether they dissolve into the universal, "everlasting" "space". Schoenberg ends *Erwartung* in a comparable way. Instead of following Wagner's conclusion with the traditional resolution of tonality of *Tristan und Isolde*, each group of instruments in *Erwartung* moves up and down the chromatic scale to saturate the musical space, expressing the woman's madness; they do not provide a homogeneous sound because they move at different speeds, insisting on their individual sonority within the diverse musical texture.

Lawrence still tries to suggest a possible existence beyond death for the soldier, whose body looked "as if at every moment it must rouse into life again, so young and unused, from a slumber" (*PO*, 21). Yet Lawrence's soldier is not positively transformed by the loss of his self, to a new self that is liberated from the oppressive social duties enforced upon him by the officer. As for Siegmund in *The Trespasser*, "darkness" is literally a Romantic death, not a momentary loss of consciousness from which he is reborn as an individual. Lawrence's struggle against Romanticism in "The Prussian Officer", then, is only a partial success.

Lawrence and Der Blaue Reiter
The parallels between "The Prussian Officer" and *Erwartung* can be traced back to Lawrence's exposure to the Expressionist movement in Munich. Jack Stewart places Lawrence's style in the context of German Expressionist art, but Mark Kinkead-Weekes is more sceptical, pointing to Lawrence's self-distancing from the Münchener Sezession in his essay "Christs in Tyrol" of 1913, written while gathering stories for *The Prussian Officer* collection.[2] Yet if we compare this essay to its revised version as "The Crucifix across the Mountains" published in the collection *Twilight in Italy* of 1916, then we can see how Lawrence's attitude to Expressionist art developed over the crucial, intervening years between their composition.

In "Christs in Tyrol" Lawrence recounts his impressions of the roadside crucifixes on the journey from Bavaria, over the Brenner Pass, into Italy in August 1912. Lawrence observes that the crucifixes of the Bavarian peasants "seemed to me to be real. In front of me hung a Bavarian peasant." The religious power of the crucifix transforms the peasant's own suffering into "the distinctness of an eternal thing, so that he can go further, leaving it" (*TI*, 43-44). The artists to whom Lawrence refers as the "Munich Secession", by

---

[2] See Jack Stewart, *The Vital Art of D. H. Lawrence: Vision and Expression* (Carbondale: Southern Illinois University Press, 1999); Kinkead-Weekes, *D. H. Lawrence: Triumph to Exile*, 40.

contrast, distort reality to force the spectator to experience pain or joy for their own sake:

> I, who see a tragedy in every cow, began by suffering from the Secession pictures in Munich. All these new paintings seemed so shrill and restless. Those that were meant for joy shrieked and pranced for joy, and sorrow was a sensation to be relished, curiously; as if we were epicures in suffering, keen on a new flavour. (*TI*, 43)

It is doubtful that Lawrence is referring to the Münchener Sezession here, which had lapsed into the dominant naturalist mode of the Munich artistic establishment since the 1890s. Nor is he referring to the Expressionist art of Die Brücke, which he only saw at the Munich Glaspalast in the summer of 1913, a year after the first draft of "Christs in Tyrol". Kinkead-Weekes identifies Lawrence's Munich Secession with the Blaue Reiter, whose most prominent members were the Expressionist artists Wassily Kandinsky and Franz Marc. The second, and last, of their exhibitions in Munich had ended in April 1912, a month before Lawrence first arrived in Bavaria; on the other hand, it is highly probable that Lawrence was at least aware of the art of the Blaue Reiter, if only through Edgar Jaffe's painting by Marc. The Blaue Reiter continued to be a focus of Munich's cultural life since Kandinsky had published the second edition of *Über das Geistige in der Kunst* in April 1912, and a third edition later in the year; the first editions of the Almanac *Der Blaue Reiter* and *Klänge* came out in May.

The ideas of Kandinsky and Marc can be traced in Lawrence's revision of "Christs in Tyrol" as "The Crucifix across the Mountains" of 1915. Lawrence excludes his earlier criticism of Munich art, but implicitly incorporates it into his revised argument. He is more critical of the peasant artist, recognizing in him the limitations of the soldier in "The Prussian Officer", who was also a peasant from the Bavarian Alps. Like the soldier, the peasant artist lives in a "heat of physical experience" which becomes "at length a bondage, at last a crucifixion", "driving him mad, because he cannot escape". Both the soldier and peasant long for the snow of the Alps, "brilliant with timeless immunity from the flux and warmth of life" (*TI*, 92-93). Through his religion the peasant is reconciled to the world outside: all of his actions, "whether it is the mowing with the scythe on the hill-slopes, or ... drinking in the Gasthaus, or making love, ... or walking in the strange, dark, subject-procession to bless the fields", are part of his religion. The static expression of the Christ articulates the peasant's existence, where

> there is no flux nor hope nor becoming, all is once and for all. The issue is timeless and changeless... Hence the strange beauty and finality and isolation of the Bavarian peasant. (*TI*, 94-95)

Through death, the soldier has achieved this "eternal" "isolation", where there is no "hope".

Lawrence reinterprets the distorted-looking Christs closer to the Austrian border in terms of "the influence of the educated world". Here the crucifixes are "new, they are painted white, they are larger, more obtrusive. They are expressions of a later, newer phase, more introspective and self-conscious." Lawrence believes that the sculptor "is an artist, trained and conscious, probably working in Vienna. He is consciously trying to convey a *feeling*, he is no longer striving awkwardly to render a truth, a religious fact." "Death is the complete disillusionment" (*TI*, 96), not the transcendence of material suffering. The religion of Lawrence's "Viennese artist" does not encompass his dislocated, modern existence; his "religious truth" only consists of specific "feelings", like the "sensations" depicted by the Munich Expressionists. His art resembles that of Kandinsky and Marc in its struggle to reconcile disconnected sensations into a religious *Weltanschauung*.

Like Lawrence, Marc and Kandinsky were fascinated by Bavarian religious art and imitated the tradition of painting on glass and mirrors. Kandinsky abstracted the forms of *Komposition VI* (1913) from his glass paintings of nudes, the Ark, animals, floods and palm trees, into a "mighty collapse in objective terms". He described the resulting portrayal of a Biblical Deluge as "a hymn of that new creation that follows upon the destruction of the world".[3] Kandinsky

---

[3] Felix Thürlemann, *Kandinsky über Kandinsky* (Bern: Benteli, 1986), 224: "großer, objektiv wirkender Untergang"; "ein Hymnus der neuen Entstehung, die dem Untergang folgt."

and Marc believed that the new creation of the "Epoche des Grossen Geistigen"[4] ("Great Epoch of the Spiritual") would emerge when through abstraction they could reconcile the diverse material world into a religious oneness, as the Bavarian peasant unifies his limited world in his art.

During the process of writing the earlier drafts of *The Rainbow* up to early 1914, Lawrence appears to have identified the style of *Sons and Lovers* with that of German Expressionist art. He declares that he will no longer write "in that hard, violent style full of sensation and presentation", "accumulating objects in the powerful light of emotion, and making a scene of them", as he had done in *Sons and Lovers*. Yet his criticism that "in *Sons and Lovers* it feels as if there were nothing *behind* all those happenings as if there were no "Hinterland der Seele" only intensely felt fugitive things" (Letters, II, 132, 142, 151), parallels Kandinsky's prioritization of the "inneren Inhaltes" ("inner content") over the "äußere Ausdruck" ("outer expression").[5]

For Kandinsky and Lawrence the "inner", or "Hinterland der Seele", evoked a religious wholeness which they inherited from Romantics such as Wagner, and prophesized for the future. Ironically, the greatness of Lawrence, Kandinsky and Marc lies in their failure to achieve this reconciliation; it is in the tension they share between expressing the physicality of feelings, while struggling to impose meaning upon them as parts of a symbolic whole. But there remains the danger of success by idealising feelings into a totality, as we see in Wagner.

From the *Rheintöchter* to the modern world
Michael Bell argues that in *The Rainbow* "'myth', far from being a static and alternative vision to modernity, is a dynamic and interactive potentiality within it". He maintains that Lawrence interacts his mythology with the temporality of a realist novel, mediating between simple and complex sensibilities, to stress "the multilayered simultaneity of these orders of sensibility within a culture or an

---

[4] *Der Blaue Reiter*, eds Wassily Kandinsky and Franz Marc (Munich: R. Piper, 1965), 313.
[5] *Ibid.*, 237.

individual".[6] Lawrence's characters are forced into the disintegration and relentless becoming of modern society, upon which they struggle to impose a religious significance. His symbolic language is confronted by a discourse of social reality, which fragments his symbolism, but also infuses it with a dynamism to create new meanings according to its dramatic context.

The imagery in *The Rainbow* contains within itself a force that stimulates the development of the characters. This force lies in the diverse cultural meanings of Lawrence's symbolism: on one side light expresses the process of life towards greater consciousness, which is comparable to Goethe's imagery in *Faust*; against Goethe, Lawrence alludes to Schopenhauer's notion of the primal *Wille*, as expressed in a Wagnerian imagery of darkness. Tom and Lydia's relationship is driven by the conflict between these two extremes, through which they develop their consciousness of the outside world while realizing their primal desires. In Will, Lawrence evokes the Romanticism of Novalis, a contemporary of Goethe who inspired Wagner's use of darkness. In Will's relationship with Anna, and later in Ursula's experiences, Lawrence arranges his oppositions in a series of dialogues between interpretations of Nietzsche's philosophy, which were prominent in German culture immediately before the First World War. Anna and Will play out debates among the Expressionists: she resembles Gross' *freie Geist* in her affirmation of female sexuality, and an accompanying stress on the physicality of the individual's relation to the world; against her, Will enacts the Romantic Nietzscheanism of Marc, which is directed towards a religious idealism of unity. Ursula conflates these positions in her struggle against Skrebensky, Winifred and the young Tom Brangwen, who evoke Max Weber and Thomas Mann's use of Nietzsche in terms of conscious power over the body and social disorder. In Ursula Lawrence asserts an Expressionist ideology against German liberal imperialism, and yet in her career as a teacher he echoes Weber and Mann's ideas, revealing his scepticism of Expressionist utopianism in modern society.

---

[6] Michael Bell, *D. H. Lawrence: Language and Being* (Cambridge: Cambridge University Press, 1991), 84.

Finally, these various threads in the novel are drawn together in Ursula's later experiences. This closing section, and the novel as a whole, can be compared to the achievements of Kandinsky and Marc's paintings. In these German cultural terms, the novel's success hinges on whether Lawrence lapses into a religious wholeness that does not correspond to Ursula's experiences, or he incorporates the disintegrative processes that have stimulated her development as an individual.

As in *Sons and Lovers* Lawrence structures *The Rainbow* with Wagner's Romantic imagery from the *Ring*. Wagnerian mythology had become the source of a pseudo-religion in Europe, especially in Germany, and Lawrence grapples with this religious tendency in his novel. His penultimate title for *The Rainbow* was "The Wedding Ring", which is ambiguous about whether the novel depicts the *Fluch* ("curse") of modern capitalism as Wagner's *Ring* does, or of traditional marital relationships. *The Rainbow* deviates from Wagner under the pressure of the characters' developments as individuals out of traditional social values, into the modern world.

The beginning of *The Rainbow* at Marsh Farm echoes the extended undulation of the opening E flat chord of *Das Rheingold*, whose timeless lack of harmonic progression portrays the current of the Rhine. Like the Bavarian peasants of *Twilight in Italy*, the Brangwen men follow the cycle of seasons, in complete harmony with nature: "they took the udder of the cows, the cows yielded milk and pulse against the hands of the men, the pulse of the blood of the teats of the cows beat into the pulse of the hands of the men." The Brangwens belong to the age of the *Rheintöchter* who play together while protecting the Rheingold. Unlike Wagner though, Lawrence's vision already carries a potential dynamic duality within itself, since the women look out towards "the far-off world of cities and governments ... where men moved dominant and creative, having turned their back on the pulsing heat of creation, and with this behind them, were set out to discover what was beyond, to enlarge their own scope and range and freedom" (*R*, 10-11).

This potential dynamic will enable the members of the community to respond to the onset of modern society. Wagner symbolized the rise of capitalism in the entry of Alberich, who renounces his love for the *Rheintöchter* and steals the gold for power over Nibelheim. Lawrence describes the transformation of Ilkeston into an industrial town: a canal is built through Marsh Farm to the newly opened collieries which spread around the other side of the farm, followed by the arrival of the Midland railway. The sound of engines disturbs the Brangwens in the rhythm of their work, making them "strangers in their own place" (*R*, 14). Lawrence represents the political development of modern society in the arrival of Lydia Lensky, wife of an aristocratic radical in the suppressed Polish Revolution of 1863. As we have seen already in Chapter 1, it was the failure of the 1848 Revolutions throughout Europe that had originally inspired Wagner's allegory in the *Ring*.

A crucial issue throughout the whole of *The Rainbow* is how Lawrence's treatment of this process of disintegration compares to Wagner's treatment of it in the *Ring*: whether Lawrence will attempt to reconcile the disintegration of experience into nothingness, as he has done in his previous novels, or whether he will embrace disintegration as a potentiality from which to imagine new experiences. The change of the title from "The Wedding Ring" to *The Rainbow* signifies a more positive vision. It relates back to the ending of *Das Rheingold* when the Rainbow Bridge stretches between Valhalla and Nibelheim below, reconciling the gods with mortals. The rainbow confirms the Gods' rule over the world below and, for Lawrence, a religious meaning in society. Unlike Wagner who uses the *Ring Motiv* as the single unifying element of his operatic cycle, Lawrence will play with the images of the ring and rainbow. The dialogue between these *Motive* creates new signification which reaches beyond Wagner's nihilism. George Hyde observes that the romantic and religious quality of the opening, an "'overture' to Lawrence's Wagnerian music-drama", gives way to "a world in which *dialogue*, heteroglossia, supplants the monologic Scriptural word".[7]

Between Schopenhauer's *Wille* and Goethe's *Morphologie*
Related to Lawrence's revision of the *Ring* mythology is his treatment of the contrasting imagery of light and darkness that Wagner used to express his Schopenhauerian vision in *Tristan und Isolde*. In the

---

[7] Hyde, *D. H. Lawrence*, 43.

"Study of Thomas Hardy", begun in September 1914, Lawrence revealed his continuing fascination with Schopenhauer. He diagnoses Hardy's Schopenhauerian pessimism which, as we noted earlier, had inspired his own use of the philosopher in *The White Peacock*. Lawrence focuses on Hardy's image of Egdon Heath from *The Return of the Native*:

> Here is the deep, black source from whence all these little contents of lives are drawn. And the contents of the small lives are spilled and wasted.

The Heath is analogous to Schopenhauer's *Wille*, and to Lawrence's images of darkness in *Sons and Lovers*. It is the "mystery" of Lawrence's religious vision: "It cannot be futile, for it is eternal. What is futile is the purpose of man" (*Hardy*, 25).

Yet against Schopenhauer, Lawrence also glorifies the emergence of individuals from the "great Mass":

> It seems as though one of the conditions of life is, that life shall continuously and progressively differentiate itself, almost as if this differentiation were a Purpose. Life starts crude and unspecified, a great Mass. And it proceeds to evolve out of that mass ever more distinct and definite particular forms, an ever-multiplying number of separate species and orders, as if it were working always to the production of the infinite number of perfect individuals, the individual so thorough that he should have nothing in common with any other individual. (*Hardy*, 42)

The process of "Differentiation" is the individual's development into self-consciousness, to achieve an awareness of his difference to the world outside. This development into "perfect individuals" is the equivalent on a generalized scale to Goethe's theory of the *Morphologie* of organisms into beings that are "vollkommen", as he explained in "Die Absicht ist eingeleitet" ("The Objective is introduced") from 1807:

> Each living thing is not a singularity, but a multiplicity; in so far as it appears to us as an individual, still it remains a collection of living,

independent beings, which in idea and in conception are the same or similar, and can become different or dissimilar.

The more imperfect a creature is, then the more these parts are the same or similar, and the more they are identical with the whole. The more perfect the creature becomes, then the more diverse its parts become. In the former case, the parts as a whole are more or less the same, in this case they are dissimilar.[8]

Goethe identifies the mechanisms within this process as the "two great driving wheels of nature: the concept of polarity and of intensification ... all is in continuous attraction and repulsion, this in ever-striving ascent".[9] Lawrence also describes "the great male and female duality and unity", the creative polarity of nature, which "has become extended and intensified, what was one great mass of individual constituency has stirred and resolved itself into many smaller, characteristic parts, what was an utter, infinite neutrality has become evolved into still rudimentary, but positive, orders and species" (*Hardy*, 54, 42-43).

The parallels with Goethe can be traced back to Lawrence's contact with Frieda's sister Else, to whom he originally dedicated *The Rainbow* with "zur Else" in Gothic script. Else had a love affair with Otto Gross, but unlike Frieda, rejected him for the intellectual world of Heidelberg. It was the centre of middle-class liberal opposition to the politically dominant Wilhelmine Berlin, in comparison to Munich as the bohemian, socialist centre of opposition. Else had studied for her doctorate under the sociologist and philosopher Max Weber, who gave her a permanent place to teach Political Economy in Heidelberg. While married to Edgar Jaffe, who was a close friend of Weber, Else

---

[8] Johann Wolfgang von Goethe, *Werke*, 14 vols (Hamburg: Christian Wegner Verlag, 1948-60), XIII, 56: "Jedes Lebendige ist kein Einzelnes, sondern eine Mehrheit; selbst insofern es uns als Individuum erscheint, bleibt es doch eine Versammlung von lebendigen selbständigen Wesen, die der Idee, der Anlage nach gleich oder ähnlich, ungleich oder unähnlich werden können....

Je unvollkommener das Geschöpf ist, desto mehr sind diese Teile einander gleich oder ähnlich, und desto mehr gleichen sie dem Ganzen. Je vollkommner das Geschöpf wird, desto unähnlicher werden die Teile einander. In jenem Falle ist das Ganze den Teilen mehr oder weniger gleich, in diesem das Ganze den Teilen unähnlich."

[9] *Ibid.*, 48: "zwei großen Triebräder aller Natur: der Begriff von Polarität und von Steigerung ... jene ist in immerwährenden Anziehen und Abstoßen, diese in immerstrebendem Aufsteigen."

had a long-term affair with Weber's brother, Alfred.[10] All three men represented the progressive side of the Verein für Sozialpolitik, which researched social and political issues for liberal reform.[11] Lawrence never met Max Weber, but developed a friendship with Alfred, using his flat at Icking, a village south of Munich, from June to early August 1912; he also spent a week with Alfred at Heidelberg in the summer of 1914. Lawrence occasionally stayed with Edgar Jaffe at Irschenhausen in 1912, and at Lerici in 1913.[12]

Goethe was extremely important to the Jaffes and Webers, as the archetypal figure of German liberal culture.[13] In the characters Professor Sartorius and Louise in *Mr Noon* Lawrence focuses on Alfred and Else's preoccupation with Goethe, including a discussion of the *Urfaust*. In one scene Lawrence even comically refers to Goethe's scientific theories: Gilbert Noon, alias Lawrence, argues that Goethe's lyrics are "cold, less than human, nasty and functional, scientific in the worst sense" (*MN*, 230), provoking Sartorius and Louise to leave in disgust. The Heidelberg intellectual community was concerned with reviving Enlightenment culture in Germany, after the excesses of Positivism in the nineteenth century. Goethe's *Lebensphilosophie* focused on the individual's *Bildung* through its *Morphologie*. Alfred Weber perceived in this philosophy an alternative to Positivism and industrial values which had dissected the individual into a *Gestalt*, in the laboratory and the factory.[14]

The *Farbenlehre* ("Theory of Colours") which Goethe developed in opposition to Newton's quantification of nature was central to his *Lebensphilosophie*. It provided, together with his morphological precepts, the basis for a whole metaphysic of nature's increasing enlightenment, in which each part differentiates itself through polarity and progressive intensification, catching the light of consciousness. Goethe applies this metaphysic throughout both parts of *Faust*. Light is consistently associated with God, from the "Paradieseshelle" of the "Prolog im Himmel", to Faust's longing for "das liebe

---

[10] See Green, *The von Richtofen Sisters*, 16, 23, 129.
[11] See Wolfgang J. Mommsen and Jürgen Osterhammel, *Max Weber and His Contemporaries* (Hemel Hempstead: Allen and Unwin, 1987), 88.
[12] See Kinkead-Weekes, *D. H. Lawrence: Triumph to Exile*, 19, 39, 98.
[13] See Green, *The von Richtofen Sisters*, 18.
[14] See Mommsen and Osterhammel, *Max Weber and His Contemporaries*, 3, 95.

Himmelslicht".[15] In Part II Faust achieves redemption through his consistent pursuit of light. He vows to:

> Verfolge froh mein innerliches Licht, ...
> Das Helle vor mir, Finsternis im Rücken.[16]
>
> Gladly pursue my inner light, ...
> The light before me, darkness behind.

After death, Faust is transformed into Doctor Marianus, ascending towards the "ewig helle" ("eternal light"), "Strahlenreiche" ("radiant realm")[17] of heaven. This light signifies Faust's renunciation of his individuality and reconciliation with God, beyond a world of many colours. Following Goethe's *Morphologie*, the extreme stage of individualization coincides with a disintegration of the self, which can only be recuperated in the light of the Creator. Lawrence's concerns focus on this paradox of Goethean, and Weberian, liberal ideology: the sovereignty of the individual, who is nevertheless subsumed in religious and social conventions.

In the "Study of Thomas Hardy" Lawrence follows the symbolism of *Faust II*, if only to criticize its implications. He argues that since the advent of Christianity "there has been the striving for the Light, and the escape from the Flesh, from the Body, the Object", towards individualization and knowledge, which form a "great, white, uninterrupted Light, infinite and eternal". Within this light "wonderful, distinct individuals, like angels, move about, each one being himself, perfect as a complete melody or a pure colour" (*Hardy*, 82, 125, 43). Lawrence and Goethe's "perfect" individual, then, is only a bodiless ideal.

Marc and Kandinsky used Goethe's ideas on colour to develop their formal vocabulary of its associative values.[18] In the Almanac *Der Blaue Reiter* Kandinsky identifies the evolving spiritual impulse

---

[15] Goethe, *Gedenkausgabe*, V, 149, 156.
[16] *Ibid.*, 357.
[17] *Ibid.*, 524.
[18] See Magdalena Dabrowski, *Kandinsky Compositions* (New York: Museum of Modern Art, 1995), 18-19; Claus Pese, *Franz Marc: Life and Work* (Stuttgart: Belser, 1990), 113.

with white light: "This white ray leads to evolution, to elevation. Behind matter, within matter, the creative spirit is hidden." [19] Kandinsky's "spiritual epoch" would be realized when his colourful forms disappeared to leave only a white canvas, which resembles Lawrence's description of Turner's art, "consummate with the Light" of "the perfect marriage in the spirit". Turner's white is a "blazing and timeless silence" (*Hardy*, 86), like Kandinsky's white, "*a great silence*, which for us is absolute ... stretching away to infinity". Yet, unlike Kandinsky, Lawrence rejects this purity of light. For Kandinsky, this triumph of the spirit in light "*is a silence that is not dead, but full of possibilities*".[20] By contrast, Turner's white cuts Lawrence "off from my future, from aspiration," until he remembers the physical reality of "my own knees and my own breast" (*Hardy*, 87).

Lawrence's imagery in *The Rainbow* oscillates between light and darkness, and between Goethe and Schopenhauer's metaphysics. Tom is continuously touched by the light of the outside world: he loves anybody "who could convey enlightenment to him through feeling", and "his eyes filled with a strained, almost suffering light" when he listens to poetry; even a drunken encounter with a prostitute causes "a strained light" in his eyes. Tom's first impression of Lydia echoes the moment when Tristan and Isolde face each other after drinking the love potion at the end of Act I, as embodiments of the Schopenhauerian *Wille*, independent of their social backgrounds: "'That's her,' he said involuntarily." Tom is inert, unable "to think or to speak, nor make any sound or sign, nor change his fixed motion" (*R*, 17, 21, 29); Wagner also directed Tristan and Isolde to look at each other, "seized with shuddering, gaze with deepest emotion, but fixed expressions, into one another's eyes".[21] Like them, Tom stares into the darkness, towards Lydia who is "dressed in black", with a "black coat" and "black bonnet". Yet he also sees "her face clearly, as if by a light in the air". Lawrence waits till the next chapter before

---

[19] *Der Blaue Reiter*, 132: "Dieser weiße Strahl führt zur Evolution, zur Erhöhung. So ist hinter der Materie, in der Materie der schaffende Geist verborgen."
[20] Wassily Kandinsky, *Über das Geistige in der Kunst* (Bern: Benteli, 1973), 96: "*ein großes Schweigen, welches für uns absolut ist ... ins Unendliche gehende*"; "*ist ein Schweigen, welches nicht tot ist, sondern voll Möglichkeiten.*"
[21] Wagner, *Tristan und Isolde*, 61.

describing Lydia's perception of Tom at this moment, to confirm their otherness. There we learn that Tom "was the man who had come nearest to her for her awakening", which is a reversal of Isolde's experience with Tristan. After her exile and the death of her husband, she had lived "passive, dark, always in shadow", in a "dark religion", until moved by the "white" "light" of the dawn and the "brilliant stars" (*R*, 29, 49, 52, 53).

Because Lawrence's symbolism is contradictory, it is unable to signify an expression on its own: it requires a reference point of material reality. On the other hand, the discourse of representation does not function independently of the symbolism, and Lawrence plays between the notions of "reality" and "unreality", and between the preservation and loss of individuality. Tom's material circumstances are both "the mean enclosure of reality" and "the commonplace unreality". He aspires towards Lydia who inhabits "a far world, the fragile reality", and a "world that was beyond reality" (*R*, 26-27, 30). While reality is dynamic, so is the nature of individuality in its process of development. Tom remains passive to form a connection with Lydia: "He submitted to that which was happening to him, letting go of his will, suffering the loss of himself, … like a creature evolving to a new birth." Lydia must "acquiesce" to his presence, despite her conscious anxiety to "defend herself against it, for it was a destruction". Yet Tom actively holds on to "the will to surety" in his aspiration for her, and she establishes "a common will with him" (*R*, 38-40, 43-44).

The Rainbow shares the "Schoenbergian" qualities of "The Prussian Officer". Images of darkness and light are juxtaposed in dissonant "ostinato" sections, for example in the marriage proposal scene. Lydia fears Tom as "this invasion from the night"; then she kisses him with "her dark face", turning his face "very white" and making "something break in his brain, and it was darkness over him for a few minutes" (*R*, 44). Together they are "involved in the same oblivion, the fecund darkness", and then,

> He returned gradually, but newly created, as after a gestation, a new birth, in the womb of darkness. Aërial and light everything was, new as a morning, fresh and newly begun. Like a dawn the newness and the

bliss filled in. And she sat utterly still with him, as if in the same. (*R*, 45)

Their merging into the "infinite" "darkness" with each other lasts for only a few minutes, until they are "reborn" to the "light" of their individuality. As in Paul and Clara's first love scene by the river in *Sons and Lovers*, Lawrence counterpoints symbolic language with realistic: Tom muses how "the strange, inviolable completeness of the two of them made him feel as sure and as stable as God. Amused, he wondered what the vicar would say if he knew" (*R*, 46). Unlike for Paul and Clara, and the soldier in "The Prussian Officer", the entry into darkness is part of a process that transforms Tom and Lydia and awakens them to the light of a new existence.

By developing beyond *Sons and Lovers* and "The Prussian Officer", Lawrence has enabled Tom and Lydia to break free from the constrictions of material reality, into a symbolic reality from which they can return, to transform both "realities" while manoeuvring between them. Yet Tom must forsake the idyllic world of his ancestors, and reconcile himself to the frustration of "his innate desire to find in a woman the embodiment of all his inarticulate, powerful religious impulses". The Romantic symbolism which articulates his "religion" is checked by other symbolic frameworks, and by temporal reality. His religious consummation with Lydia is never completely fulfilled: "Such intimacy of embrace, and such utter foreignness of contact! It was unbearable" (*R*, 21, 48). Their social backgrounds are too different for them to achieve a state of religious unity: Tom is an English farmer, attached to the land where animals are fellow labourers; Lydia is a Polish aristocrat, for whom labourers are as cattle.

Yet Lawrence still attempts to envisage in their relationship a redemption of the "Fluch" of modern life that Wagner symbolized in the image of the "ring". Her "wedding-ring" represents her past existence, which he must overcome: "It excluded him: it was a closed circle. It bound her life, the wedding-ring, it stood for her life in which he could have no part. Nevertheless, beyond all this, there was herself and himself which should meet." They can only meet as opposing poles which form an open "arch", or rainbow. In their last described encounter they realign "the broken end of the arch" to enter "another circle of existence", and meet "to the span of the heavens" (*R*, 39, 91, 89).

Despite the dynamic relation between Lawrence's symbolism and realistic style, there are still dangers in Tom and Lydia's scenes of an idealized, religious language that denies the dissonance between the characters. John Worthen points out that phrases such as "it was the transfiguration, the glorification, the admission", belong to "a language of miracle and mystery", and are detached from the dynamics of Tom and Lydia's relationship.[22] The symbolic imagery functions independently of the action, regressing to the late romanticism of Wagner's *Tristan und Isolde*. Nevertheless, even this consummation is only momentary. The modern, industrial world later destroys Tom: the canal bursts, and after he struggles through the flood, "a great wonder of anguish went over him, then the blackness covered him entirely" (*R*, 229), returning him to the Marsh, the home of his ancestors.

Will Brangwen and the Romanticism of Novalis

In the next generation of Brangwens Lawrence maintains the conflict between his characters' individualization, and their need for religious wholeness. Carrying over his use of Schopenhauer's "Metaphysik der Geschlechtsliebe" from *Sons and Lovers*, Lawrence shows how the conflict between Tom and Lydia is internalized by Anna, and then multiplied in her relationship with Will. Anna has inherited her mother's remoteness, remaining aloof from the pettiness of the dame's school, but she also emulates her stepfather's oneness with his natural environment. Will works as a draughtsman in a lace factory, like his father whose "hand swung naturally in big, bold lines, rather lax", but was confined to "the tiny squares of his paper, counting and plotting and niggling"; Will's mother regularly goes to church, and is tormented by her husband's insistence that "you've got to go on by yourself, if it's only to perdition" (*R*, 15, 132). Will has inherited his father's experience of industrial alienation and his mother's longing for spiritual wholeness.

---

[22] John Worthen, *D. H. Lawrence and the Idea of the Novel* (London: Macmillan, 1979), 67-68.

This Schopenhauerian process of disintegration constitutes Wagner's "Fluch" in the *Ring*, and Lawrence's curse of the "wedding ring" in *The Rainbow*. In *Tristan und Isolde* Wagner appropriated a language of night and darkness from the late eighteenth-century poet Novalis to suggest an escape from disintegration through death. In Will Brangwen Lawrence also explores this path. However, he understands Anna and Will's relationship in terms of Goethe's "Morphologie", as well as in the Schopenhauerian conflict within the "Wille". Anna "Victrix", heroic like Siegfried ("Joyful victory"), will confront the "Fluch" by acknowledging the contradictory "light" and "darkness" within herself, as opposed to Will who seeks reconciliation in darkness.

Will's interest in Romanticism is part of the English Gothic Revival of the nineteenth century, in which writers such as John Ruskin argued for a return to medieval values of craftsmanship and community, against the encroaching tide of industrialization. But Will is also interested in the German Gothic, such as Bamberg Cathedral, and Lawrence draws on German Romanticism in his treatment of Will. In 1913 Lawrence compared his friend Henry Savage to Novalis: "I am by nature active, I think. I suppose you are something of a sensuous mystic – like Novalis. I feel myself the appeal of 'magic' in verse – but I like things to be very human" (Letters, II, 34). Like Lawrence's Novalis, Will is a "sensuous mystic" whose religion centres on his relationship with Anna. Lawrence specifically mentions the "hymns" to Savage, which is probably a reference to Novalis' most famous work, the *Hymnen an die Nacht* (1800, *Hymns to the Night*). The narrator of this series of poems mourns the death of his beloved, and longs to die, to be reunited with her in the "Nacht". Aware of Goethe's contemporary research into colour, Novalis begins by substituting the dark "Nacht" for Goethe's "Morphologie" of

> Das allerfreuliche Licht –
> Mit seinen Strahlen und Wogen
> Seinen Farben[23]

> The most pleasant light –

---

[23] Novalis, *Schriften*, 4 vols (Stuttgart: W. Kohlhammer, 1960-75), I, 130.

> With its beams and waves
> of its colours

In his own pastiche of the *Hymnen*, Lawrence is tracing back the roots of the Romantic culture that he partly inherited from Wagner. Lawrence examines the genealogy of Wagner's notion of a "verflucht" modern world, in an attempt to overcome it.

In the first weeks of his marriage Will enters the "inexhaustible, unchanging, unexhausted" "eternal being" and "unawakened sleep of all wakefulness" (*R*, 135) with Anna. His state of being is comparable to Novalis' description of death as an "unergründliche", "zeitlos" "Nacht" of "Schlummer ewig" and "unerschöpflicher Traum" ("unfathomable", "timeless night" of "eternal slumber" and "inexhaustible dream").[24] Will's relationship with Anna is a part of his religion. During his religious contemplation, "his mind he let sleep", to experience "a dark, nameless emotion, the emotion of the great mysteries of passion" (*R*, 160, 147). Similarly, the narrator of the *Hymnen* aspires to the "heiligen, unaussprechlichen / Geheimnissvollen Nacht" ("holy, inexpressible / Mysterious night")[25] where his dead beloved exists, with God.

Anna's battles with Will provide a criticism of Novalis, and more broadly, of Lawrence's Romantic inheritance. She resembles Lawrence's self-characterization in his letter to Henry Savage as "active" and "very human". She enacts his advice to Savage a few days later, on the value of children; through affirming the creative "life" of her body in childbirth she struggles against Will's darkness.

Unlike Tom Brangwen, for whom "reality" changed according to his circumstances, Will regards his existence with Anna as "a world to him within a chaos: a reality, an order, an absolute, within a meaningless confusion". He believes that she is "forfeiting the reality, the one reality, for all that was shallow and worthless", when she returns to "the outside world" (*R*, 190-91, 140). Given Will's inability to manoeuvre between religious and temporal states of being, a violent conflict develops between him and Anna. In the opposition between his darkness and her light, there is no common ground

---

[24] *Ibid.*, 134, 136.
[25] *Ibid.*, I, 130.

between them where they can negotiate a truce. Tom and Lydia had shared the light and darkness between them to sustain a relationship of balanced contradiction and reconciliation, but for Anna and Will there is no reconciliation. Where Will's "darkness" threatens to subdue and obliterate Anna's "light", Lawrence turns Novalis' Romantic imagery of darkness into something that is predatory in its longing for death. The narrator of the "Hymnen" wants to enter the "Nacht" of death where his beloved is, to possess her:

> Wir sinken auf der Nacht Altar
> Auf weiche Lager –
> Die Hülle fällt
> Und angezündet von den warmen Druck
> Entglüht des süßen Opfers
> Reine Glut.[26]

> We sink on the night altar
> On soft bed –
> The garment drops
> And lit from the warm pressure
> Glowing of the sweet sacrifices'
> Pure embers.

In Will and Anna's relationship Lawrence draws attention to the aggression implicit in this Romanticism. As they gather the sheaves before their marriage, Will attempts to capture Anna's light through his darkness. When he approaches her, "walking shadowily", "she turned away towards the moon, which seemed glowingly to uncover her bosom every time she faced it"; again, he is "coming shadowy", and "she turned away", walking "between the moon and his shadowy figure". He reaches further into the darkness, trying to take her with him, "nearer and nearer to the shadowy trees, threading his sheaves with hers". To capture her he comes into the light, "with a moonlit, shadowy face that frightened her" (*R*, 114-15). Later in the novel at Lincoln Cathedral Anna's soul is like the dead lover of the *Hymnen*, "carried forward to the altar, to the threshold of Eternity", but she resists, deciding that "the altar was barren, its lights gone out. God

---

[26] *Ibid.*, 132.

burned no more in that bush. It was dead matter lying there" (*R*, 188-89).

In this scene the conflict between Anna and Will demonstrates the limitations in the modern world of both the Gothic Revival and German Romanticism. Will achieves his "consummation" in "timeless ecstasy":

> Spanned round with the rainbow, the jewelled gloom folded music upon silence, light upon darkness, fecundity upon death, as a seed folds leaf upon leaf and silence upon the root and the flower, hushing up the secret of all between its parts, the death out of which it fell, the life into which it has dropped, the immortality it involves, and the death it will embrace again.

The cathedral, with its rainbow-arch encompassing all processes of life, resembles Lawrence's religious vision of Tom and Lydia's last described encounter. The "jewelled gloom" echoes Novalis' religious vision of all life being contained within the "Nacht". Novalis directly addresses life:

> Die Farbe der Nacht –
> Sie trägt dich mütterlich
> Und ihr verdankst du
> All deine Herrlichkeit.
> Du verflögst
> In dir selbst
> In endlosen Raum
> Zergingst du,
> Wenn sie dich nicht hielte – [27]

> The colour of the night –
> It carries you motherly
> And you owe it
> All of your glory.
> You vanished
> In yourself
> In endless space
> You dissolved,

---

[27] *Ibid.*, 138.

When it did not hold you –

Lawrence emulates Novalis' vision of the "Nacht", only to challenge it through Anna. She remembers the stars in the sky beyond the cathedral, and draws attention to "the wicked, odd little faces carved in stone", with "separate wills, separate motions, separate knowledge, which rippled back in defiance at the tide" (*R*, 189). In other words, she affirms the modern fragmentation that has liberated her as an individual from religious convention.

Compared to Tom and Lydia, in Will and Anna's relationship we see a greater tension between the Enlightenment individualism of Goethe, and the Romantic pessimism of Novalis, Schopenhauer and Wagner. The secular and religious, rational and irrational, have become polarized from each other, and reflect the deepening *Fluch* of modern experience. In the relationships between his characters Lawrence demonstrates how this conflict is destructive but also creative in its extremes, and once again, this leads us to Nietzsche.

The Nietzschean dialogue
In *Sons and Lovers* Lawrence responded to Otto Gross' reading of Nietzsche in conjunction with Freud to affirm the liberation of the individual's unconscious energies. In *The Rainbow* this dialogue widens out to such diverse figures as Marc, Max Weber and Thomas Mann, who used Nietzsche for diverse ideological ends.[28] Marc saw in Nietzsche a spiritual transcendence which could be realized in the First World War; Weber used the philosopher to assert a liberal imperialism of national power; Mann valued Nietzsche for his consciousness of the "Dekadenz" of his age.

Lawrence personifies these different readings in his characters. In Will he combines the Romanticism of Novalis with a Nietzschean aggressiveness to evoke Marc's Expressionist vision of the war. Against Will, Anna embodies Gross' stress on the body against Marc's idealism. Later, we shall see Ursula incorporate these two positions against Skrebensky's Weberian dedication to social duty, then against Mann's consciousness of bodily and social corruption in

---

[28] See Steven E. Ashheim, *The Nietzsche Legacy in Germany 1890-1990* (Berkeley: University of California Press, 1992).

Winifred and the younger Tom Brangwen's coal mines. Running through this analysis is the theme of unity and disintegration, first of Anna's personal wholeness in her body against Will's longing for an absolute unity. Then Ursula's personal and religious wholeness confronts Skrebensky, Winifred and Tom Brangwen's inner disintegration and dependence on the social totality. *The Rainbow* forms a series of dialogues between these different elements of German culture, within the Expressionist movement of Gross and Marc, and between the political radicalism of Gross and the conservative liberalism of Mann and Weber. Over the course of these dialogues Lawrence reveals his sympathy with Gross' philosophy and politics, but he also acknowledges the value of Marc, Mann and Weber's ideas, giving a relentless dynamism to *The Rainbow* in its diverse styles and ideologies

Anna and Will's conflict reflects debates on the philosopher in Expressionist circles, in particular between the psychological, or Freudian, Nietzscheanism of Otto Gross, and the romantic, spiritual Nietzscheanism of Ludwig Rubiner in *Die Aktion*. Throughout 1913 Gross contributed articles to this Expressionist periodical, including "Zur Überwindung der kulturellen Krise" ("Towards the Overcoming of the Cultural Crisis"). In this article, Gross proclaimed an imminent "Umwertung aller Werte" ("revaluation of all values") ignited by the "thoughts of Nietzsche on the background of the soul and with the discovery of the so-called psychoanalytic technique by S. Freud". From exploring the unconscious and reaching self-knowledge, Gross argued, "is a new ethic born", which is the "preparation for Revolution". Gross envisaged that through liberating the unconscious, the individual becomes a Nietzschean "freie Geist"[29] ("free spirit"), and society as a whole can be set free.

Like Freud who restricted the psychoanalyst's vocation to professional medicine, Rubiner argued that Gross was wrong to derive his revaluation of values from science. For Rubiner, Nietzsche's significance lay not in harmonizing man's consciousness with his

---

[29] Otto Gross, *Von geschlechtlicher Not zur sozialen Katastrophe* (Berlin: Nautilus, 2000), 59, 63: "Gedanken Nietzsches über die Hintergründe der Seele und mit der Entdeckung der sogennanten psychoanalytischen Technik durch S. Freud"; "ist eine neue Ethik geboren"; "Vorarbeit der Revolution."

unconscious desires, but in the transcendence of physical desire through the *Wille zur Macht*, into a spiritual realm.[30] This idealism connects Rubiner's ideas to Marc, and also to Lawrence's Will Brangwen in its religious sense of unity. During the First World War Marc reflected that "*very* early on I felt that man was "ugly" the animal seemed to me more beautiful, purer; but even in that I discovered so much against feeling and uglier, that my presentations instinctively [(]out of inner necessity) became more and more schematic and abstract".[31] For Marc, this process of abstraction from nature was historically realized through the war: "Bloodshed is preferable to eternal lying; the war is just as much an atonement as it is a self-created sacrifice to which Europe submitted in order to become 'pure' within itself."[32] In his last literary work, "Die 100 Aphorismen. Das zweite Gesicht", Marc argued that the war was a realization of Nietzsche's ideas: "Nietzsche has laid his powerful mine, the concept of the will to power. It ignited terribly in the great war. When it ends, the tension of that thought will also come to an end .... *From the will to power, the will to form will arise.*"[33] Through the *Wille zur Macht* "form" would be transformed from the human to the abstract, as in the painting *Kampfende Formen* (*Fighting Forms*, 1914), until the form itself would disappear, as in the genocide of war: "There is only one blessing and redemption: death. The destruction of the form, by which the soul becomes free."[34]

---

[30] See Seth Taylor, *Left-Wing Nietzscheans: The Politics of German Expressionism* (Berlin: Walter de Gruyter, 1990), 100-101.

[31] Franz Marc, *Briefe aus dem Feld* (Berlin: Rembrandt, 1948), 65: "Ich empfand schon *sehr* früh den Menschen als 'häßlich'; das Tier schien mir schöner, reiner; aber auch an ihm entdeckte ich so viel gefühlwidriges u. häßliches, sodaß meine Darstellungen instinktiv, [(]aus einem inneren Zwang) immer schematischer, abstrakter wurden."

[32] *Ibid.*, 60: "lieber Blut als ewig schwindeln; der Krieg ist ebenso sehr Sühne als selbstgewolltes Opfer, dem sich Europa unterworfen hat um »in's Reine« zu kommen mit sich."

[33] Franz Marc, *Schriften* (Cologne: Dumont, 1978), 193: "Nietzsche hat seine gewaltige Mine gelegt, den Gedanken vom Willen zur Macht. Sie zündete furchtbar im großen Kriege. Mit seinem Ende wird auch die Spannung jenes Gedankens ihr Ende haben. ... *Aus dem Willen zur Macht wird der Wille zur Form entspringen.*"

[34] Marc, *Briefe aus dem Feld*, 81: "Es gibt nur einen Segen u. Erlösung: den Tod; die Zerstörung der Form, damit die Seele frei wird."

Lawrence was aware of this attitude among Germans, describing them as "full of the altar-fire of sacrifice to the war" (Letters, II, 221). His treatment of Will accords with Marc and Rubiner's romantic notion of Nietzsche. In his affirmation of the body, Gross invokes Nietzsche against this process of the abstraction of material reality, and Lawrence expresses this perspective through Anna.

Lawrence concentrates on Will and Anna's *Willen zur Macht* to express their conflict. Will tries to dominate Anna through "his power persisting on her", and through "trying to force his will upon her". His romantic darkness gains a Nietzschean aggressiveness when Anna frustrates his desire for oneness with her. He becomes a "vast, hideous darkness" with "incalculable dark rages, when a blackness filled him" (*R*, 168, 172, 194). The dissonance between Anna and Will corresponds to Lawrence's conception of the *Wille zur Macht* in describing the Ajanta Frescoes in a letter from 25 December 1915:

> I *loved* them: the pure fulfilment – the pure simplicity – the complete, almost perfect relations between the men and the women .... That which we call passion is a very one-sided thing, based chiefly on hatred and Wille zur Macht. There is no Will to Power here – it is so lovely – in these frescoes. (*TI*, 488-89)

The perfect mating of male and female is impossible for Anna and Will, instead the dissonance between them defines their individual wills, locked in a contest for power.

In Anna, Lawrence deploys the Nietzschean concepts which he had absorbed since composing *The Trespasser* into a powerful metaphysic to sweep away his lingering sympathies with German Romanticism, and the Nietzschean Romanticism held by Marc. In the second chapter we saw the relationship between Nietzsche's ideas of the *Wille zur Macht* and *ewige Wiederkehr*: the Schopenhauerian pessimism of eternal suffering is transformed into eternal joy through the individual subject affirming each moment as if it were to be eternally repeated. As in *The Trespasser*, though, Lawrence still isolates these concepts from each other in the "Study of Thomas Hardy". He describes male desire as served by the female in the following terms:

It is a powerful stimulant to him, the female administered to him. He feels full of blood, he works the earth like a Lord. And it is to this state Nietzsche aspires in his "Wille zur Macht". (*Hardy*, 103)

Here is the "friction" between male and the female as the "unknown". The *Wille zur macht* is no longer identified with the conscious will of the individual, but with Freud's libido, as in Gross' interpretation of it. In comparison to this passion of individuals, however, Lawrence sees "the Ewige Wiederkehr" as a reconciliation of the male-female duality into a "pure symbolic solution". This notion is more similar to Schopenhauer's reconciliation of individual elements into the mass of the *Wille*, than to Nietzsche's *ewige Wiederkehr*. Lawrence finds in Botticelli's paintings an alternative to this notion of *ewige Wiederkehr*: "each cycle is different. There is no real recurrence", only "different cycles of joy, different moments of embrace, different forms of dancing round, all contained in one picture, without solution. He has not solved it yet" (*Hardy*, 72). Ironically, despite rejecting his own interpretation of *ewige Wiederkehr*, Lawrence's description of these paintings approaches Nietzsche's conception of it as actions which are physically distinct from each other, while being recurrences of the *Wille zur Macht*. In these Nietzschean terms, Anna enacts "different cycles of action" which repeat each other, while shaping their particularity through the individual motions of her *Wille zur Macht*.

During her pregnancy, Anna articulates her *Wille zur Macht* against Will through her Dionysian dance, "lifting her knees and her hands in a slow, rhythmic exulting ... in the pride of her bigness ... to the unseen Creator who had chosen her, to Whom she belonged". She dances to Will's "nullification" and "non-existence" (*R*, 170-71). Lawrence had described Nietzsche's "Dionysian ecstasy" in similar terms in *Twilight in Italy*, as "the triumphal affirmation of life over death, immortality through procreation" (*TI*, 200). In Lawrence's understanding of the Dionysian, he resolves Nietzsche's *Wille zur Macht* and *ewige Wiederkehr*: Anna asserts her will through procreation, which establishes her immortality before her Creator, in an eternal recurrence. She symbolizes this recurrence in the Dionysian rhythm of her dance.

Yet in his persistent longing for Romantic oneness, Will oppresses Anna "under the silent grip of his physical will. He wanted her in his power". He fears that without her, he would "fall through endless space, into the bottomless pit, always falling, will-less, helpless, non-existent ..." (*R*, 172, 175). Similarly, Novalis' narrator cannot survive without his beloved, being "Einsam, wie noch kein Einsamer war, von unsäglicher Angst getrieben, Kraftlos, nur ein Gedanken des Elends noch" ("alone, as if one could not be more lonely, driven by unspeakable anxiety, powerless, with only thoughts of distress"). He lets go of his individual self for the "Nacht", to be reunited with her:

> Und mit einemmale riß das Band der Geburt, des Lichtes Fessel – Hin floh die irrdische Herrlichkeit und meine Trauer mit ihr. Zusammen floß die Wehmuth in eine neue unergründliche Welt. Die Nachtbegeisterung, Schlummer des Himmels kamst über mich.[35]

> And ripped the umbilical cord, the light's fetter – the delusive splendour and my sorrow fled with it. Together flowed the melancholy in a new unearthly world. Enthusiasm for the night, heaven's slumber came over me.

Anna instead forces Will to sleep alone at night, so that he "lay alone through the white sleep, his will unchanged, unchanged, still tense, fixed in its grip", until he also resigns himself, feeling "an infinite relief to drown, a relief, a great, great relief". Will lets go, not to be reunited with Anna, but to be "born for a second time, born at last unto himself", with "an absolute self, as well as a relative self" (*R*, 175-77).

Yet in his treatment of Anna, Lawrence reveals his ambivalence towards Gross' ideas. Perhaps we can understand Lawrence's attitude to Gross from a passage in *Twilight in Italy*, where he simultaneously identifies himself with Gross, and regards him as a father-figure. In "The Return Journey", which describes Lawrence's travels through Zurich in September 1913, he refers to Gross as "a doctor from Graz who was always wandering about". Lawrence pretends that he is Gross in claiming that he is from Graz, "walking for my pleasure

---

[35] Novalis, *Schriften*, I, 134.

through the countries of Europe" (*TI*, 208-209). At the same time, though, by alleging that his father is a doctor from Graz, Lawrence insinuates that Gross is also his father. Gross is represented both as Lawrence's imagined father, and as the wandering son. Lawrence's relationship with Gross is deeply ambivalent: he is the man whom Frieda married after rejecting Gross, and yet he has had to compete with Gross as her image of the ideal lover. Frieda's relationship with Gross later inspired her to leave her husband for Lawrence; also, in liberating Frieda sexually, Gross has liberated Lawrence in his marriage with her. Lawrence has both triumphed over Gross as Frieda's husband and yet owes his marriage with her, and his own fulfilment, to Gross. This complex, Oedipal, relationship with Gross incites Lawrence to both emulate and rebel against his ideas, as is revealed more explicitly in *Mr Noon*.

Anna "Victrix" has broken Will's scriptural law, like Siegfried who broke Wotan's spear. She represents the possibility of cleansing a *verfluchtet* world, but not through uniting with her opposite as Siegfried did in his subsequent relationship with Brünnhilde, and as Paul Morel attempted with Clara Dawes. Instead she approaches Gross' celebration of Frieda as the female "Übermensch" of a new social order, and his assertion in his essay for *Die Aktion* that "The coming revolution is the revolution for the mother's law." In another essay, "Ludwig Rubiners 'Psychoanalyse'" Gross argued that the revolution would "bind together woman and freedom and spirit". The woman would become a "freie Geist" in "freien Liebe"[36] ("free love"). Lawrence does not give this significance to Anna, since in overcoming the curse of the "wedding ring" she affirms marriage in modern society, instead of discrediting it. Her freedom still exists within the bounds of marriage. Lawrence does not take sexuality as far as Gross does, as the exclusive basis for a new social value, but places it alongside Will's scriptural law. Although Lawrence emulates Gross' eroticism here, as we shall see, he has reservations about Gross' political programme.

---

[36] Gross, *Von geschlechtlicher Not zur sozialen Katastrophe*, 62-63: "Die kommende Revolution ist die Revolution fürs Mutterrecht"; "Frau und Freiheit und Geist in eins zussammenfaßt."

Will resembles the defeated spirit of Alberich, who waits for his child Hagen to fulfil the *Fluch* of the *Ring*. Will waits for Ursula "to come to consciousness .... his heart waited in darkness. His hour would come" (*R*, 194). In Lawrence's playful treatment of Wagner's symbolism, Will is opposed to the original curse of modernization, which Ursula will overcome through his, and Anna's, influence. Despite Anna's victory, Will's Romantic Nietzscheanism continues to exert a powerful influence upon the later sections of the novel.

Ursula versus Anton Skrebensky, and the Protestant ethic
So far, then, we have seen the dialogue within Lawrence's imagery, with Goethe's light on one side, and the Romantic pessimism of Schopenhauer, Wagner and Novalis' darkness on the other. This dialogue has developed a contemporary cultural significance in the relationship between Will and Anna. Lawrence has introduced Nietzsche into the dialogue, with Will's darkness expressing the transcendence of Marc's war idealism, and Ursula's light and darkness evoking Gross' eroticism. In Ursula's development Lawrence synthesizes elements from this dialogue to form another one between left-wing Expressionism and the liberal, bourgeois culture of Max Weber and Thomas Mann.

Ursula internalizes the conflicts between her parents, re-enacting their battles throughout her childhood. This process further defines her individuality, to the point that her self threatens to disintegrate. Will's "sense of the eternal and immortal" enables her to avoid "the cruelty and ugliness always imminent", in "the week-days". Yet his occasional violence also belongs to the outside world. Then, on reaching adulthood she believes that "the Sunday world was not real, or at least, not actual. And one lived by action". In her failure to reconcile these two worlds, she feels "soulless, uncreated, unformed" (*R*, 255, 252, 263, 268). Her first lover, Skrebensky represents an extreme example of Goethe's "Morphologie". His individuality has disintegrated his being, leaving him torn between his sexuality and his social self as a representative of civilization in the army. He is struck by another man's "worship of the woman in Ursula, a worship of body and soul together", which makes her "feel the richness of her own life"; Skrebensky "never loved, never worshipped, only just physically wanted her" (*R*, 294).

Like the other characters whom Ursula will meet, Skrebensky embodies some of the cultural positions of Else Jaffe's intellectual circle. Lawrence was continuously exposed to its ideas throughout his stays at Munich, commenting in a letter of 20 August 1913 that "we sit by lamplight and drink beer, and hear Edgar on Modern Capitalism. Why was I born?" During a week-long stay at Heidelberg in 1914, Alfred Weber took Lawrence under his wing:

> Exhibitions in Bern – and now I am with Prof Weber in Heidelberg hearing the latest in German philosophy and political economy. I am like a little half fledged bird opening my beak *very* wide to gulp down the fat phrases. But it is all very interesting. (Letters, II, 63, 186)

It is likely that much of this recent "German philosophy and political economy" derived from the research of Alfred's more famous brother, Max Weber. Since childhood, Alfred and his brother Max had a close and often tense relationship; the difference in their attitudes can be seen in their shared opposition to Wilhelmine bureaucracy, with Alfred being concerned about social issues such as workers' rights while Max focused on the power of the Reich.[37]

Lawrence's characterization of Skrebensky echoes Max Weber's answer to the inadequacies of Goethe's liberal thought in Germany's industrial culture. Differing from Alfred, Max believed that Goethe's *Lebensphilosophie* of *Bildung* could not provide the individual with the means to integrate his personality within itself, and in society. He interpreted the endings of *Wilhelm Meisters Lehrjahre*, the *Wanderjahre* and *Faust II* as arguments that the individual must define his *Personalität* not through his life experiences, which threaten to disintegrate his self, but through reducing and disciplining his self for *Dienst* and *Hingabe* to the Protestant ethic of work. Weber was critical of the Protestant ethic, but at the same time submitted to its imperatives in his lifestyle.

---

[37] See Mommsen and Osterhammel, *Max Weber and His Contemporaries*, 88-100.

Lawrence first explored Max Weber's ideas in the short story "The Mortal Coil" (1917) which he composed in October 1913, a couple of months after his conversations with Edgar Jaffe, and set in Germany. A lieutenant, Baron von Friedeburg, becomes suicidal at the prospect of losing his commission in the army, since "apart from the social fabric he belonged to, he felt himself nothing, a cipher". He confides to his mistress that "My career *is* my life," and that his "*self*" is defined by his uniform (*EMyE*, 174-75, 177). In his characterization of Skrebensky Lawrence transports von Friedeburg to England.

Weber revealed the Nietzschean qualities of his political philosophy in his Inaugural Address at Freiburg, "Der Nationalstaat und die Volkswirtschaftspolitik" ("The Nation State and the Political Economy", 1895), which has been interpreted as the merging of German liberalism with nationalism into liberal imperialism. He focused on the *Wille zur Macht* in terms of the "*Machtkämpfe*" ("*power* struggle") of economic development and "*Machtinteressen*" ("*power* interests") of the nation. They form an *ewige Wiederkehr* in terms of the "*ewigen Kampf um die Erhaltung und Emporzüchtung unserer nationalen Art*" ("*eternal struggle* for the preservation and improved breeding of our national species"), towards a nation of *Übermenschen*. The individual would develop his *Personalität* in service to the nation, for the "*Resonanz der Weltmachtstellung*"[38] ("*resonance of a position of world power*") in colonization.

Skrebensky makes similar arguments about the necessity of the imperial cause at Khartoum: "You want to have room to live in: and somebody has to make room." His argument rests on "the nation" as the ultimate principle; he concludes that "you wouldn't be yourself, if there were no nation". His identity is centred on his duty to it: "I belong to the nation and must do my duty by the nation". At church he listens "to the sermon, to the voice of law and order"; the nation is the object of his religious worship, where "the whole mattered – but the unit, the person, had no importance, except as he represented the Whole" (*R*, 288-89, 302-304). Skrebensky's religious "duty" to the "nation" mirrors Max Weber's description of the Protestant ethic of "Dienst" to one's "Beruf" and nation. Like Goethe's process of

---

[38] Max Weber, *Gesammelte Politische Schriften* (Tübingen: J. C. B. Mohr, 1958), 14, 23.

morphology which results in the fragmentation of the individual until his reconciliation with God, or Marc's vision of nature disintegrating into abstraction and forming a spiritual unity, Skrebensky's self can only find unity in the totality of the nation. Lawrence is arguing against Weber's philosophy when Ursula concludes that Skrebensky is "nothing"; he retorts that she is a "romanticist", which she agrees with: "Yes I am. I want to be romantic" (*R*, 288-89). She has inherited the unity within herself from her parents' differing senses of religion, which both exclude the Protestant ethic.

Weber was opposed to Otto Gross' interpretation of Nietzsche. He explained to Edgar Jaffe that he had rejected Gross' article for the *Archiv für Sozialwissenschaft* in 1907, because Gross used biology as the basis of his *Umwertung aller Werte*.[39] Weber instead valued the individual's *Wille zur Macht* in service to the power of the nation, which Marc did in the First World War. Lawrence expresses his aversion to Weber's form of the *Wille zur Macht* from February 1915: "The great serpent to destroy is the Will to Power: the desire for one man to have some dominion over his fellow men" (Letters, II, 272). Following his interpretation of the *Wille zur Macht* in the "Study of Thomas Hardy", though, Lawrence acknowledges that an individual's dominion over others can only be countered through it, as a sexual power. At her Uncle Fred's wedding party, Ursula opposes Skrebensky's desire to take her in the "power of his will": "It was his will and her will locked in a trance of motion, two wills locked in one motion, yet never fusing, never yielding one to the other" (*R*, 295).

Ursula overwhelms Skrebensky through the power of her sexuality to affirm a "romantic", religious sense of herself as a whole person. Meanwhile, the symbolism of Wagner and Novalis loses its meaning in the disintegration of "reality". Ursula and Skrebensky follow the bank of the canal, which marks the division of the town into the "black agitation of colliery and railway" with "the round white dot of the clock on the tower" at its top, against the colourful landscape on the other side. In her white dress, Ursula is like the white dot of the church tower's clock; her religious quality is now a light within the darkness of everyday reality, which Skrebensky

---

[39] See Taylor, *Left-Wing Nietzscheans*, 96.

embodies. Yet with her contrasting black hair she also incorporates the darkness, like a hound

> ready to hurl itself after a nameless quarry, into the dark. And she was the quarry, and she was also the hound. The darkness was passionate and breathing with immense, unperceived heaving. It was waiting to receive her in her flight. (*R*, 295)

In this scene Lawrence sets Gross' affirmation of sexuality aggressively against the social values of the Weber circle. Especially after his arrest in November 1913 on the orders of his father, Gross had become increasingly militant in his notion of "Revolution", up to his involvement in the Vienna Revolution in 1917.[40] Yet in Ursula's later experiences Lawrence diverges from Gross' erotic utopianism. She does not emerge from her battle with Skrebensky unscathed, since the symbolism, and the unity of herself that it signifies, fragments while she attempts to affirm her inner wholeness. In the following scenes, too, we see her compromised by the *Fluch* of modern, disintegrated experience that she asserts herself against. In this process Lawrence qualifies his opposition to Weberian liberalism, and distances himself from Gross' ideal of *Liebe*.

Der Tod in Venedig and the mining industry

In Ursula's next series of adventures Lawrence continues his dialogue with German liberal culture; he places Weberian ideas alongside the fiction of Thomas Mann, while sustaining the thread of Nietzschean philosophy. In his review "German Books: Thomas Mann" (1913) Lawrence denounced *Der Tod in Venedig* (*Death in Venice*, 1912) to the point of portraying it as a negative image of his own art. In his treatment of Ursula and Winifred's lesbian affair Lawrence parodies Mann's novel; he continues to borrow from Mann's imagery in his description of a coal mine, which is also the site of a Weberian vision of capitalist alienation. Lawrence then elaborates his marriage of Weber and Mann's ideas in Ursula's career as a school teacher, further to redefine her relation to modern civilization.

---

[40] See Green, *The von Richtofen Sisters*, 67, 70-71.

In *Betrachtungen eines Unpolitischen*, written during the First World War, Mann recognized his shared insight with contemporary sociologists such as Max Weber: "the modern capitalist businessman, the bourgeois with his *ascetic* idea of duty in a calling, was the creation of the Protestant ethic, of Puritanism and Calvinism".[41] Mann and Weber demystified the Protestant ethic in bourgeois culture while acknowledging that they were unable to liberate themselves from its strictures. Weber concluded his analysis in *Die protestantische Ethik und der Geist des Kapitalismus* (*The Protestant Ethic and the Spirit of Capitalism*, 1904-5): "The puritan wanted to be a man of calling, – we *must* be it."[42] (This work will be discussed in greater depth in the next chapter.) Harvey Goldman analyses Gustav von Aschenbach in *Der Tod in Venedig* as Mann's depiction of an artist who adheres to the Protestant ethic in his struggle to bring order to his art, tragically to become alienated from sensual experience of reality.[43]

In his review of *Der Tod in Venedig* Lawrence conflated Mann with his fictional bourgeois artist Gustav von Aschenbach. Lawrence perceived the failings of the Protestant ethic, and the Nietzschean ideas associated with its modern practice, both in Aschenbach and in the style Mann uses to depict him. While Lawrence countered Paul's tendency to death with an erotic vitality in *Sons and Lovers*, Mann encouraged his reader's awareness of the characters' death wish in *Buddenbrooks*, so that it could be understood and overcome. In these novels, as in *The Rainbow* and *Der Tod in Venedig*, Lawrence asserts the Nietzschean *Wille zur Macht* as a sexual power, whereas for Mann it is a conscious power to master the body's corruption.

Der Tod in Venedig describes the obsession of an ageing writer, Aschenbach, with a beautiful boy called Tadzio. They share an "uneasiness and overstimulated curiosity" for each other: "But sometimes [Aschenbach] looked up, and their eyes would meet. They

---

[41] Mann, *Gesammelte Werke*, XII, 145: "der modern-kapitalistische Erwerbsmensch, der Bourgeois mit seiner *asketischen* Idee der Berufspflicht sei ein Geschöpf protestantischer Ethik, des Puritanismus und Kalvinismus."
[42] Max Weber, *Gesammelte Aufsätze zur Religionssoziologie*, 2 vols (Tübingen: J. C. B. Mohr, 1947), I, 203: "Der Puritaner wollte Berufsmensch sein, – wir *müssen* es sein."
[43] See Harvey Goldman, *Max Weber and Thomas Mann: Calling and the Shaping of the Self* (Berkeley: University of California Press, 1988), 173-75, 187, 202.

would both be deeply serious when this happened."[44] In a parallel scenario, Ursula develops with Winifred an "unspoken intimacy that sometimes connects two people who may never even make each other's acquaintance", until they become "aware of each other, almost to the exclusion of everything else". Ursula becomes obsessed in her frustrated, secret, desire to see Winifred, to a comical extreme: "Miss Inger was to take the swimming class. Then Ursula trembled and was dazed with passion. Her hopes were soon to be realized. She would see Miss Inger in her bathing dress" (*R*, 312-13). Aschenbach's desires threaten to become ridiculous also. When Tadzio smiles at him, he collapses on a park seat, confusedly whispering, "impossible here, absurd, depraved, ludicrous and sacred nevertheless, still worthy of honour even here: 'I love you!'".[45] Both Ursula and Aschenbach perceive their distant objects of desire as abstract ideals, not human beings. For Ursula, Winifred's "whole body was defined, firm and magnificent" (*R*, 314), and Aschenbach feels awe before the aesthetic perfection of Tadzio's body: "What discipline, what precision of thought was expressed in that outstretched, youthfully perfect physique!"[46]

In his playful allusion to *Der Tod in Venedig*, Lawrence foregrounds the qualities he had perceived in his review of the novel: "It is absolutely, almost intentionally, unwholesome. The man is sick, body and soul .... It portrays one man, one sick vision" (*IR*, 211). Lawrence is unambiguously displaying this "unwholesomeness" in *The Rainbow* to demonstrate its wider implications, from the individual's sexuality to society at large. Lawrence suggests Ursula and Winifred's perversity in phrases such as "hot delight", "subtly-intimate teacher", "deliciously, yet with a craving of unsatisfaction", the "delicious privacy", their "delicious afternoons", and so on. He even borrows the turgid atmosphere of Mann's Venice, "a moist, warm, cloudy day" (*R*, 312-14), when Ursula and Winifred go

---

[44] Mann, *Gesammelte Werke*, VIII, 496-97: "Unruhe und überreizte Neugier"; "Zuweilen aber auch blickte [Aschenbach] auf, und ihre Blicke trafen sich. Sie waren beide tiefernst, wenn das geschah."
[45] *Ibid.*, 498: "unmöglich hier, absurd, verworfen, lächerlich und heilig doch, ehrwürdig auch hier noch: 'Ich liebe dich!'."
[46] *Ibid.*, 490: "Welche eine Zucht, welche Präzision des Gedankens war ausgedrückt in diesem gestreckten und jugendlich vollkommenen Leibe!"

swimming. Sharing the theme of homosexual desire with Mann, Lawrence suggests the narcissism and fetishism of a relationship which lacks the otherness of a heterosexual relationship. Ursula is fascinated by individual parts of Winifred's body: "how straight and fine was her back, how strong her loins, how clean and free her limbs! ... Ah, the beauty of the firm, white, cool flesh! Ah, the wonderful firm limbs". Ursula becomes mesmerized by the sensations of parts of her own body, enjoying the rain on her "flushed, hot limbs, startling, delicious", and receiving "the stream of it upon her breasts and her belly and her limbs" (*R*, 312-13, 316). Aschenbach also dissects Tadzio's body: "the sun gleamed in the down on his upper spine, the subtle outlining of his ribs and the symmetry of his breast stood out through the scanty covering of his torso".[47]

Eventually, as in the processes of Goethe's "Morphologie" and Marc's abstraction, from this "great attack of disintegration", Ursula and Winifred begin to merge with each other, "to fuse into one, inseparable". Then Ursula rebels against Winifred – "A heavy, clogged sense of deadness began to gather over her" – while with Winifred, whom she perceives as "ugly, clayey", "she wanted some fine intensity, instead of this heavy cleaving of moist clay, that cleaves because it has no light of its own" (*R*, 319, 316). Aschenbach responds to the "still und riechend" ("stagnant and foul") air of Venice in the opposite way to Ursula, since the prospect of returning to his solitude as a writer "filled him with such repugnance that his face twisted into an expression of physical nausea".[48] He loses himself in his obsession with Tadzio, wishing that everyone else in Venice would die to leave them alone together; he dreams of orgies in which he devours the diseased and rotting flesh of animals and drinks the blood of fellow revellers.

Lawrence explores the social implications of Mann's novel in his description of Ursula's uncle Tom Brangwen, who manages a local coal mine. Lawrence quotes from *Der Tod in Venedig*, in his own

---

[47] *Ibid.*, 490: "die Sonne erleuchtete den Flaum des oberen Rückgrates, die feine Zeichnung der Rippen, das Gleichmaß der Brust traten durch die knappe Umhüllung des Rumpfes hervor."
[48] *Ibid.*, 502, 515: "widerte ihn in solchem Maße, daß sein Gesicht sich zum Ausdruck physischer Übelkeit verzerrte."

translation, of "the amiable bearing in the empty and severe service of form" that is necessary for "the elegant self-control that hides from the eyes of the world to the last moment the inner undermining, the biological decay" (*IR*, 209). In *The Rainbow* industrial society is ordered under an analogous principle to the "form" of Mann's style: the mine is "a monstrous mechanism that held all matter, living or dead, in its service," its adjacent town is "a moment of chaos perpetuated, persisting, chaos fixed and rigid" (*R*, 325, 321). Lawrence argues that Mann relishes the gruesome details of Aschenbach's inner decay because he shares it, despite trying logically to distance himself from it. Similarly, Tom and Winifred are "cynically reviling the monstrous state and yet adhering to it ... in spite of his criticism and condemnation, he still wanted the great machine .... when the machine caught him up, was he free from the hatred of himself, could he act wholly, without cynicism and unreality" (*R*, 324-25). Lawrence observes that Mann's style leaves the individual to "ferment and become rotten" within himself, until he is "like an exhausted organism on which a parasite has fed itself strong" (*IR*, 209). Both Winifred and Tom are exhausted within themselves: she feels that Ursula's rejection of her "seemed like the end of her life"; he is also "at the end of his desires", having reached "a stability of nullification" (*R*, 319).

In his review Lawrence asserted that "Germany is being voiced, or partly so" in its "conventions and arbitrary rules of conduct" (*IR*, 211) through Mann. Lawrence wrote the review at Irschenhausen in May 1913, a month after first meeting Edgar Jaffe and Alfred Weber; together with Else, they could have provided Lawrence with brief descriptions of Mann's biography, and of *Buddenbrooks* and *Königliche Hoheit*. Certainly, in his treatment of Tom Brangwen, Winifred and the mine, Lawrence synthesizes his attitude to Mann with his newly acquired awareness of German social and political philosophy. The pit has become the object of worship under the Protestant ethic, to which the men must adapt themselves, "sold to their job": "One man or another, it doesn't matter all the world. The pit matters." The pit is also the religion that Tom and Winifred serve: only "when he was serving the machine ... was he free from the hatred of himself, could he act wholly"; only "in its service, did she achieve her consummation and her perfect unison, her immortality" (*R*, 323-25).

In contrast to Tom and Winifred, Ursula embodies "the fulsomeness of life" which Lawrence had claimed as his subject and form, in opposition to Mann who lacks "the rhythm of a living thing". Lawrence implicitly denied that his own art belongs to Aschenbach's Nietzschean conception as a "heroism ... of weakness", yet the "unexpectedness" that he sees in life necessarily includes its possible "disordered corruption" (*IR*, 209, 211-12). As we saw in the previous chapter, both Mann and Lawrence were concerned with the corruption of life, following from their interest in Schopenhauer and Wagner's pessimism. Partly through Otto Gross' example Lawrence emulated Nietzsche's acknowledgement of "Dekadenz" for the prospect of further growth. Yet through this process Lawrence breaks from Gross' eroticism.

Ursula has almost accepted Wagner's *Fluch* of modern capitalism, only to reject the mines, but she must repeatedly confront corruption in the capitalist society that she wishes to enter. The school where she teaches is part of the economic and social system to which the mine and industrial town belong. The world of the school is under the same curse as Wagner's *Ring*, where Alberich had renounced love for power: Ursula "dreamed how she would make the little, ugly children love her" (*R*, 341), yet after teaching, she realizes that "in school, it was power and power alone that mattered". This difference reveals Lawrence's break from Gross' commitment to free love, to accept the necessity of the social mechanisms of power. Martin Green points to the political limitations of Gross' anarchism, as revealed in his arguments with the socialist leader Gustav Landauer:

> Landauer's anarchism was more a matter of practical politics, of some buildable ideal state, and he could not accord so much primacy to personal emotional freedom. Gross' matriarchal revolution would have led to no state at all. All compulsions to work and to sublimate one's energies would be removed.[49]

---

[49] Green, *The von Richtofen Sisters*, 63.

Ursula faces the corrupted nature Mann depicted in *Der Tod in Venedig*: "The air of hostility and disintegration, of wills working in antagonistic subordination, was hideous." Like Mann facing his corrupt subject matter, and Weber's sense of the individual in society, she must impose her will on the chaos of pupils through "an application of a system of laws", and "put away her personal self, become an instrument, an abstraction, working upon a certain material". Ursula emulates the aim of every teacher she knows, "to bring the will of the children into accordance with his own will" (*R*, 355-56).

Lawrence's depiction of Ursula's *Wille zur Macht* here resembles Max Weber's and Mann's, not Gross' Nietzscheanism. Instead of attempting to escape from the *Fluch* of modern society as Wagner did in *Götterdämmerung*, and as Gross is doing, Ursula must enter this decadent world of "reality" "because nothing was ever fulfilled, she found, except in the hard, limited reality". As in Tom and Lydia's relationship "reality" is dynamic. The mining town had seemed to Ursula "just unreal, just unreal", and when she enters the school for the first time "all seemed unreal", but only because "there was no reality in herself, the reality was all outside of her, and she must apply herself to it" (*R*, 341, 321, 343, 341).

Lawrence's complex use of Nietzsche, then, includes Gross' assertion of the body's desires, but also Weber and Mann's stress on conscious power. Ursula affirms the romantic, religious unity of herself against the alienation of modern society, but she has the courage to internalize this alienation and develop her consciousness as an individual, as in Goethe's *Morphologie*. Lawrence's rejection of any single metaphysical position confirms the dynamic of his vision, unlike Marc's vision of the disintegration of material reality into a spiritual unity.

Ursula's rainbow

In the final section of the novel – Ursula's studies at university, her second affair with Skrebensky and her concluding vision of the rainbow – Lawrence recapitulates all of the preceding themes of the novel. He reincorporates the German influences which have contributed to it, from Goethe and Novalis to the Blaue Reiter.

First, Lawrence returns to Goethe's *Faust I* in Ursula's rejection of academic knowledge. Her desire "to hear the echo of learning pulsing back to the source of mystery" (*R*, 404) is similar to Faust's aspiration to know "was die Welt / Im Innersten zusammenhält" ("how the world / is inwardly held together").[50] Goethe and Lawrence suggest that the "light" of knowledge can guide their protagonists towards fulfilment. Faust wants to follow the course of the sun, "ihr ew'ges Licht zu trinken" ("to drink its eternal light"),[51] to view the fields, valleys, mountains, rivers, bays and sea, the world in its entirety. Passing "away into an intensely gleaming light of knowledge", Ursula believes she has perceived the world in the detail of a "plant-animal lying shadowy in a boundless light" (*R*, 408-409) of her microscope.

Yet Ursula rejects the "inner circle of light" of "man's completest consciousness", which has become "the security of blinding light", "wherein the trains rushed and the factories ground out their machine-produce and the plants and animals worked by the light of science and knowledge" (*R*, 405). In his despair, Faust also laments that

> Geheimnisvoll am lichten Tag
> Läßt sich Natur des Schleiers nicht berauben[52]

> Mysterious in the bright day
> Nature does not let its veils be stolen

Both of them envisage an alternative to knowledge in eroticism. Ursula leaves her microscope to meet Skrebensky, with whom she exists "in the sensual subconscious"; Faust demands from Mephistopheles "Tiefen der Sinnlichkeit" ("depths of sensuality").[53]

Sexual adventure for Faust is his only alternative to nihilism, to spurn the "holden Erdensonne" ("beloved earth's sun"), and to enter the "dunkeln Höhle" ("dark abyss") of "Nichts" ("nothingness")[54] through suicide. Unlike Goethe, Lawrence's Romantic heritage from

---

[50] Goethe, *Gedenkausgabe*, V, 155-56.
[51] *Ibid.*, 176.
[52] *Ibid.*, 164.
[53] *Ibid.*, 195.
[54] *Ibid.*, 165.

Novalis and Wagner still suggests a religious, transcendental existence through eroticism. For Ursula, the darkness beyond is inhabited by "grey shadow-shapes of wild beasts" and "dark shadow-shapes of the angels" which promise death, or redemption. She anticipates sex with Skrebensky as "their final entry into the source of creation". The language depicting their encounters is a more extreme form of that which Lawrence used for Paul and Clara, in its exclusion of material reality: "they were one stream, one dark fecundity, ... one fecund nucleus of the fluid darkness ... the light of consciousness gone, then the darkness reigned" (*R*, 406, 417, 414). Lawrence defines their relationship as the exclusive "reality", against civilization: "All the time, they themselves were reality, all outside was tribute to them", in contrast to the "dutiful, rumbling, sluggish turmoil of unreality" of the world; "they alone inhabited the world of reality. All the rest lived on a lower sphere" (*R*, 421-22).

At this point of the novel Lawrence abandons his dialogue, between darkness and light, transcendental and material "realities", the universal and the particular, for the romantic impasse of *Sons and Lovers* and "The Prussian Officer". Words such as "darkness" and "reality" are repeated like Wagnerian *Motive*, not to explore their various meanings within different contexts as Schoenberg does, but to repeat the context until the words appear to have a singular, intrinsic meaning. Recognizing how the language is detached from its context in the characters as individuals, John Worthen concludes that "the earlier part of the novel created its visionary experience through our sense of lives led and feelings lived. This later part is much more propagandist for its experience."[55]

Yet the ambivalence of Ursula and Skrebensky's condition returns. Lawrence expresses it paradoxically: "in her, the antagonism to the social imposition was for the time complete and final". Ursula breaks from the "reality" of the darkness through affirming her "self". In her epiphany at the microscope, she had realized that "self was oneness with the infinite" (*R*, 417, 409). This idea echoes Goethe's vision at the end of *Faust II*, when his hero dies, to be reconciled with the light of God.

---

[55] Worthen, *D. H. Lawrence and the Idea of the Novel*, 72.

Ursula's self belongs alternately either to the light of knowledge, or to the darkness of her sexuality. One excludes the other. In the process of fragmentation, there is no dialogical relation between darkness and light, and consequently they have become severed from the dynamic of Ursula's developing character. Yet in their isolation from each other, the images appear to express unconditionally her state of being, since there is no dissonance between them. The disintegration within Ursula's self appears as a resolution: she is either conscious or unconscious, there is no tension between the two states. This problematic situation threatens to undermine the signifying power of Lawrence's climactic symbol, Ursula's rainbow, since its promise of resolution does not correspond to Ursula's disintegrated state of being. Diane S. Bonds observes that "the authority of the organic metaphor" of the rainbow which claims to "unite signifier and signified", "is undermined by the way in which the text questions the conception of the self implied by that metaphor".[56] Is the rainbow a symbol of Ursula's fulfilment, or is it an ideal that is imposed upon her character?

Ursula's vision of the rainbow is worth comparing to those of the German artists who have contributed to the novel as a whole. The two contrasting treatments of the rainbow in German culture are in Goethe's enlightened affirmation, and Wagner's nihilism. At the beginning of *Faust II*, through awakening to a rainbow, Faust recognizes that "Am farbigen Abglanz haben wir das Leben" ("On a coloured mirror we have life").[57] The contradictory strains of his personality which caused the tragedy of the *Erster Teil* will be reconciled into the pure light of heaven. In Wagner's *Ring* reconciliation between man and God is no longer possible, except through death. The rainbow bridge, from the "Morgens Scheine" ("morning light") to when "Abendlich strahlt der Sonne Auge" ("the sun's eye radiates at evening"), only offers Wotan a temporary haven at Valhalla, from the "Bang' und Graun" ("terror and dread") of "die Nacht".[58] Darkness and nothingness inevitably come in *Götter-*

---

[56] Diane S. Bonds, *Language and the Self in D. H. Lawrence* (Ann Arbor: UMI Research Press, 1987), 62.
[57] Goethe, *Gedenkausgabe*, V, 294.
[58] Richard Wagner, *Das Rheingold* (London: John Calder, 1985), 91.

dämmerung. Both artists order their art around a religious sense of unity, Goethe to the light of God, Wagner to the darkness. In Ursula's fascination for science and her relationship with Skrebensky she alternately inhabits these two visions. The question is whether she can inhabit them simultaneously, and embrace the dynamic process of fragmentation within her state of religious wholeness.

Through entering the "darkness" with Skrebensky, Ursula has broken the "Fluch" of the "wedding ring"; she has emptied its symbolic power, and rejected the social conventions attached to it. The "wedding ring for a shilling" (*R*, 420) that she wears at a hotel is only a respectable cipher for her anti-social desires. Yet Skrebensky buys her an emerald ring, and wants them to be married and to participate in the colonial life of India. The final sequence of events in the novel which lead to the rainbow is triggered by her ultimate rebellion against marriage.

As Lawrence's narrative enters his contemporary history and verges on the future, his imagery resonates with the recent, prophetic art of Kandinsky and Marc. First, Lawrence's treatment of the horses which confront Ursula has been related to Marc's treatment of the same theme. Kinkead-Weekes asserts boldly that "as Lawrence walked through farmland at ploughing time, the great horses, the animal-of-oneself, and the looming Post-Impressionist horses he had seen in *Blaue Reiter* pictures in Munich, began to fuse in his imagination", and he conceived the scene in *The Rainbow*. Kinkead-Weekes also discloses, though, that "we do not know which *Blaue Reiter* painting by Franz Marc hung on Edgar Jaffe's wall".[59]

Notwithstanding, Marc's *Die großen blauen Pferde* (Plate 1, *The large blue Horses*) is most like Lawrence's horses in the final chapter. They are "a dark, heavy, powerfully heavy knot": "their haunches, so rounded, so massive, pressing, pressing, pressing to burst the grip upon their breasts, pressing forever till they went mad, running against the walls of time, and never bursting free" (*R*, 451-52). The energy of Marc's horses is contained within the knotted curves of their overlapping bodies. In his colour symbolism, Marc believed that

---

[59] Kinkead-Weekes, *D. H. Lawrence: Triumph to Exile*, 207, 804.

"*Blue* is the *male* principle, austere and spiritual".[60] His horses are trying to break into the spiritual, whitish blue sky above them. They press against the red, green and yellow landscape; they are unable to burst free because their heavy, dark blue runs into the blue of the landscape on the left and right edges of the canvas, and their black-green manes mirror the leaves at the bottom. Similarly, Lawrence's horses aspire beyond their natural environment with their "bluish, incandescent flash of the hoof-iron, large as a halo of lightning round the knotted darkness of the flanks". Marc's horses can only rub their dark flanks against the white tree-trunks, whose vertical lines lead beyond, towards the sky. Similarly, Lawrence's horses cannot direct their energy upwards; "loosening their knot, stirring, trying to realise" only disperses their energy, until they are a "huddled group ... almost pathetic, now" (*R*, 452, 454).

If we relate the "darkness" of Lawrence's horses to Ursula's sexuality then her escape from them, "spent ... like a stone, unconscious, unchanging, unchangeable, whilst everything rolled by in transience", indicates her transcendence "from her body, from all the vast encumbrance of the world that was in contact with her". The material world is "all unreal ... an unreality", and Skrebensky had never become finally real": "The kernel was the only reality: the rest was cast off into oblivion" (*R*, 456). She re-enacts Faust's redemption, as the penitent Gretchen observes it:

> Sieh, wie er jedem Erdenbande,
> Der alten Hülle sich ertrafft[61]
>
> See, how he breaks from every earthly bond
> Of the old exterior

Ursula's future lover, who "would come out of Eternity to which she herself belonged", refers back to her Goethean epiphany at her microscope, and echoes the reunion of Faust and Gretchen in heaven as Doctor Marianus and Una Poenitentium.

---

[60] Armin Zweite, *Der Blaue Reiter im Lenbachhaus, Munich* (Munich: Prestel, 1989), 66: "*Blaue* ist das *männliche* Prinzip, herb und geistig."
[61] Goethe, *Gedenkausgabe*, V, 525.

Faust's ascendance to heaven prefigures Ursula's vision of people "rising to the light and the wind and the clean rain of heaven" of the rainbow which "was arched in their blood and would quiver to life in their spirit". In turn, this image corresponds to Marc's *Turm der blauen Pferde* (*Tower of Blue Horses*, Plate 2). The horses' areas of deep and whitish blue form a linear rhythm that points towards the overarching rainbow of the spiritual realm. The rainbow encompasses the horses, resolving their contrasting patches of orange, yellow, red and green into its spectrum. Even the green and red landscape reaches towards the rainbow, like Ursula's vision of "the world built up in a living fabric of Truth, fitting to the over-arching heaven" (*R*, 459).

Lawrence and Marc's rainbows belong to a tradition of German idealism in which the individual elements of material reality are transcended for a spiritual oneness. We have already seen the historical dangers of this idealism, especially in Marc's involvement in the First World War. But an alternative reading of Ursula's rainbow is possible. While the dissonance of Ursula's past experiences with Skrebensky and Winifred at college and at school continues to reverberate, the final rainbow takes its place alongside, not above, Tom, Lydia, Will and Anna's rainbows. It is a vision of one of the characters at a particular moment of their development that is determined by historical circumstances. No single rainbow has authority over the novel as a whole; as Leavis observed, "no real conclusion of the book, only a breaking-off is possible".[62]

Perhaps in the end *The Rainbow* is closer to Kandinsky's paintings than to Marc's. Kandinsky avoids structural hierarchy, giving the individual elements equal pictorial value, unlike Marc in *Turm der blauen Pferde*. Despite the idealism of Kandinsky's aesthetic theory, his art, like Lawrence's, draws upon a cosmopolitan diversity of influences. In *Komposition IV* (Plate 3) the colours of the unobtrusive rainbow bridge are repeated over the whole canvas, in the skyscape at the top right corner, in the mountains over the lower half, and even in the fighting cossacks at the top left corner. The diversity of individual forms is unified by various "rainbows". The black lines are not merely negative in their contrast to the colour. As the fortress and cossacks' lances in the centre they cut through the colour to

---

[62] Leavis, *D. H. Lawrence: Novelist*, 169.

disperse the forms on either side, and free the picture from a central focal point. Other lines also give form and material substance to the rainbows as mountains and human figures. As in Lawrence's novel, darkness and light are in a creative conflict.

Kandinsky's *Bild mit schwarzen Bogen* (*Picture with Black Arches*, Plate 4), painted a year later, perhaps reaches beyond *The Rainbow* to anticipate the anarchy and freedom of characters' experience in *Women in Love*. The rainbow has exploded into black arches and dispersed patches of colour. The colours are like disconnected sensations which the lines attempt and fail to unify. The arches jar with the colours, while struggling to hold them in place. Some patches float independently of the arches, none are encapsulated by them; the arches even lack unity among themselves in their arhythmical distribution and various shapes.

Lawrence and Kandinsky, as participating outsiders, shared a cultural diversity that resisted being fixed into ideals. On the outbreak of war, despite retaining his belief in the spiritual epoch, Kandinsky wrote to Marc: "I thought that the clearing of ground for building the future would take a different form. The price for this kind of cleansing is appalling."[63]

The development of Lawrence's characters towards fulfilment as conscious individuals in modern society, and as unconsciously passionate lovers, is driven by conflict throughout *The Rainbow*. Goethe's "Morphologie" towards the light of consciousness competes with Novalis, Schopenhauer and Wagner's stress on a primal darkness. Lawrence uses Nietzsche's philosophy as an arena of competing ideologies, from Weber and Mann's conscious control over disruptive social and erotic impulses, to Gross' identification with these impulses. This conflict sustains the vitality of Lawrence's religious vision in the novel, as reflected in his subversive application of Wagner's mythology from the *Ring*.

In Lawrence's novel and Kandinsky's paintings the religious imagery of arches and rainbows both succeeds and fails to unify the diverse characters and forms, and avoids the idealism of Goethe,

---

[63] Wassily Kandinsky and Franz Marc, *Briefwechsel* (Munich: R. Piper, 1983), 265: "Ich dachte, daß für den Bau der Zukunft der Platz auf eine andere Art gesäubert wird. Der Preis dieser Art Säuberung ist entsetzlich."

Marc and Germany at war. Ursula's discovery of "a new knowledge of Eternity in the flux of Time" (*R*, 456) in her rainbow confirms and contradicts the rainbows of her ancestors. Among the flaws of Lawrence's religious vision, resonates the artistic achievement of his novel.

Figure 1: Franz Marc, Die großen blauen Pferde (1911).

Figure 2: Franz Marc, Turm der blauen Pferde (1911)

Figure 3: Wassily Kandinsky, Komposition IV (1911).

Figure 4: Wassily Kandinsky, Bild mit schwarzen Bogen (1912).

V
MYTH AND HISTORY IN
WOMEN IN LOVE

In 1917 Lawrence reflected on *The Rainbow* as a pre-war work: "But alas, in the world of Europe I see no Rainbow." He characterized *Women in Love* as "purely destructive – not like the *Rainbow*, destructive-consummating" (Letters, III, 142-43). In his Foreword to *Women in Love* Lawrence described how the novel "took its final shape in the midst of the period of war, though it does not concern the war itself ... the bitterness of the war may be taken for granted in the characters" (*WL*, 485). In the last Chapter I argued that Ursula's vision of her rainbow was idealistic; Lawrence indicates that *Women in Love* is without such visions, or "consummations". In this text the characters do not transcend the bitterness of their historical circumstances.

In 1955 Leavis had asserted that *Women in Love* touches on "the whole pulse of social England".[1] But during his composition of the novel in 1916 in Cornwall, Lawrence declared his estrangement from humanity, and that he was only "writing, to the unseen witnesses" (Letters, II, 602). As Kinkead-Weekes observes, Lawrence was "an alien and exile in his own land"[2] after the suppression of *The Rainbow* in late 1915, when he had hoped "to change my public" (Letters, II, 429) and emigrate to America. His arrival in Cornwall in February 1916 also confirmed the failure of his projected "revolution" of English society with Bertrand Russell. The circumstances of Russell's break would inspire his denunciation fifty years later of Lawrence as a proto-fascist obsessed with a mythology of "blood",[3] to the exclusion of any social reality.

Writing of this controversy, John Worthen traces the ambivalent relationship between the characters in *Women in Love* and the society they inhabit. He observes that "the Crich family is a mythic analogue, not a historical reality" because Lawrence's account of its mining

---
[1] Leavis, *D. H. Lawrence: Novelist*, 207.
[2] Kinkead-Weekes, *D. H. Lawrence: Triumph to Exile*, 286.
[3] See Russell, *The Autobiography of Bertrand Russell*, II, 22.

firm seems untouched by contemporary social unrest in the mining industry. Like Leavis, Worthen's criterion for appraising *Women in Love* as "a significant novel" is in whether "it succeeds in having a relation with the world outside it". But given Lawrence's alienation from the nation at war, Worthen suggests, the novel suffers from a social nihilism and consequent antisocial idealism: "it transmutes social reality into the play of heightened consciousness, and says that *that* is our true world." Worthen counters his own criticism by defending *Women in Love* as "a novel which also creates worlds of other people and other attachments".[4] In other words, it imagines an alternative social reality of a higher "consciousness" in which readers can liberate themselves from their own social restrictions.

Worthen is trying to impose a positive significance onto Lawrence's nihilistic sentiment in 1916 that "one must forget, only forget, turn one's eye from the world ... having another world, a world as yet uncreated" (Letters, II, 593). Without a discourse of specific historical references these "other people and other attachments" exist in an ideal and mythical world, not in "the world outside". The mass carnage of the war was only possible through an idealism that disavowed the suffering of individuals on the battlefield. By attempting to create an alternative world of social harmony at the end of *The Rainbow*, Lawrence mirrored the patriotic, anti-individualistic idealism of his own world at war. Only through submitting to history by faithfully recording its grim details of genocide can he and his characters begin to overcome and survive its processes of self-reification. In this chapter I will examine how Lawrence records the events of the First World War in *Women in Love*, and assess whether he empowers the reader to understand and learn from this historical trauma.

In *Women in Love* Lawrence addresses the problems that arose from his use of symbolic language towards the end of *The Rainbow*. Diane S. Bonds comments that "verbal repetition in *Women in Love* becomes the means by which the novel makes the reader aware of the differential nature of knowledge of language, of the contextuality of words".[5] The "differential" quality of symbolic language corresponds

---

[4] Worthen, *D. H. Lawrence and the Idea of the Novel*, 99-100, 103-104.
[5] Bonds, *Language and the Self in D. H. Lawrence*, 93.

to what I characterized as Lawrence's "dissonance" in the previous chapter. As in Schoenberg's musical language, Lawrence repeats words, not to naturalize their meaning as Wagner does, but to reveal their different possible meanings by shifting their context.

At a thematic level, this "differential" quality takes the form of Lawrence's experimental combination of myth and history, in which characters' actions and experiences symbolize the events of his era. Lawrence's mythical scenarios can only have a relation to the dynamic of history if their symbolic language has a differential value based on its context in the characters' actions.

In his treatment of the novel's characters Lawrence also parodies the *leitmotivisch* repetition of symbols, to express a character's problematic relation to his environment. The reader is alienated by the remorseless intensity of Lawrence's repetition in the descriptions of Gerald's management of the mines and his destructive relationship with Gudrun. John N. Swift, to whom I shall refer later, has analysed these cases in terms of Freudian theory, but I shall broaden my analysis to Germany's industry and participation in the war, which are part of the historical foundations of *Women in Love*.

Gerald and the rise of modern Germany
Worthen focuses his analysis of *Women in Love* on the description of the mine owner Gerald Crich in "The Industrial Magnate". Worthen considers this chapter as "not an objective social reality but a facet of consciousness", which is "more concerned with myth than with history".[6] Graham Holderness presses Worthen's argument further, that Lawrence's "ideology" in *Women in Love* rejects the working-class movement. Holderness contends that the play *Touch and Go* (1918) "utterly exposes the false autonomy of the novel's historical images" by treating this subject in a "realist style" of confrontations between the miners and owner.[7] Yet in opposing objective reality and consciousness, history and myth, I would argue that Worthen and Holderness have missed the complexity of Lawrence's language which enables these perspectives to interact with each other.

---

[6] Worthen, *D. H. Lawrence and the Idea of the Novel*, 99.
[7] Graham Holderness, *D. H. Lawrence: History, Ideology and Fiction* (Dublin: Gill and Macmillan Humanities Press, 1982), 211-13.

In his examination of the social context of modern English literature, Malcolm Bradbury has argued that the cultural and economic synthesis of tradition and progress in England encouraged the continuation of the English social novel in Forster and Waugh, and, it could be argued, in Lawrence's *Sons and Lovers*. The social novel assumed a common literary language and the conventions of realism, while the *avant-garde* trends of artistic self-consciousness and extremism were reactions to a greater social and economic alienation on the continent.[8] In *Women in Love*, I shall argue, Lawrence draws on this alienation in Germany through allusions and isolated references, to substantiate his Modernist vision of the First World War. Compared to the realistic descriptions of English mining life in *Sons and Lovers*, in the Modernist realism of *Women in Love* Lawrence uses the mining industry as an emblem of social, economic and political modernization.

As we have seen in the previous chapter, Lawrence's German acquaintances, Alfred Weber, Edgar and Else Jaffe, discussed sociology and economics with him before the war. They continue to be a source for his analysis of modernization in *Women in Love*. Lawrence met the economist John Maynard Keynes in March 1915 through Bertrand Russell. Keynes traced the war back to Europe's economic instability resulting from Germany's industrialization in *The Economic Consequences of the Peace* (1919).

Lawrence's treatment of Gerald Crich is coloured by the history of modern Germany and by cultural ideas circulating around the Weberian circle of intellectuals. Lawrence scatters associations throughout the novel that link Gerald to Germany, including his education at the universities of Bonn, Berlin and Frankfurt. Gudrun compares him to Bismarck:

> He would be a Napoleon of peace, or a Bismarck .... She had read Bismarck's letters, and had been deeply moved by them. And Gerald would be freer, more dauntless than Bismarck. (*WL*, 417-18)

---

[8] See Malcolm Bradbury, *The Social Context of Modern English Literature* (Oxford: Basil Blackwell, 1971), 21-24, 27.

In what follows I will compare Gerald's management of the mines to Bismarck's rule over Germany, to the modernization of the mining industry in Germany, and to the capitalist ideology of the Protestant ethic that Max Weber had analysed.

Gerald's management of the mines bears many analogies with Bismarck's rule in Germany. Both men attempt to bring unity and coherence to concerns whose parts "were ready to go asunder in terrible disintegration". Before Unification the German Confederation had been organized at the Congress of Vienna as a buffer zone against France to secure the Imperial order of Europe, with monarchs regaining their power in each state. The liberal attempt to unify Germany in 1848 shared Thomas Crich's dilemma between democracy and authority, "trapped between two half-truths, and broken" (*WL*, 221, 226). The liberal members of the short-lived Frankfurt Parliament wanted to establish Germany as a democratic nation, and yet were dependent on the princes and their armies against the radicals who represented the urban workers.[9] Thomas Crich shares this dilemma; he wants to be "one and equal with all men", but uses the army to maintain his authority when they riot against him.

In rejecting the "democratic-equality problem" for "position and authority" (*WL*, 227) Gerald echoes Bismarck's "Machtpolitik", as famously expressed in 1862: "Germany does not look upon Prussia's liberalism but its power ... not through speeches and majority decisions will the great questions of the day be decided – that was the great mistake of 1848 and 1849 – but through iron and blood."[10] For Bismarck, the German nation was defined by the military power of Prussia, not by a politics of liberalism and democracy. In *Movements in European History* (1921), written from 1918 to 1919, Lawrence describes how Bismarck achieved his power and unified Germany through military successes (*MEH*, 248). This militarism later spilled

---

[9] See William Carr, *A History of Germany 1815-1990* (London: Edward Arnold, 1991), 55.

[10] Otto von Bismarck, *Werke in Auswahl*, 8 vols (Stuttgart: W. Kohlhammer, 1962-83), VIII, 3: "Nicht auf Preußens Liberalismus sieht Deutschland, sondern auf seine Macht ... nicht durch Reden und Majoritätsbeschlüsse werden die großen Fragen der Zeit entschieden – das ist der große Fehler von 1848 und 1849 gewesen – sondern durch Eisen und Blut."

over into the First World War, just as Gerald's violent assertion of power leads to his destructive relationship with Gudrun.

Under Bismarck, Germans identified their nation state with its meteoric rise in industrial, as well as military, power. It is likely that Lawrence agreed with Frieda's comment to Edward Marsh on the outbreak of war, that German militarism had originated in its "mechanical ideal" (Letters, II, 215). Gerald's management of his father's business mirrors the development of coal mining in Germany between Unification and the First World War. Compared to the gradual development of British industry since the late eighteenth century, over the course of forty years the mining and other heavy industries transformed Germany into the world's second largest economy with extraordinary speed. While British exports between 1889 and 1910 increased by 105%, German exports increased by 181%.[11] For Keynes, Germany's dominance in Europe lay in its coal mining, having increased its output from 30 million tons in 1871 to 190 million tons by 1913.[12] This increase was possible through the technological developments originating in Germany of mechanized hammer-drills and electric pumps,[13] which made possible the digging of deeper mines in Germany. Gerald also introduces "an enormous electric plant ... both for lighting and for haulage underground, and for power", and "great iron men, as the machines were called", to overcome the problem of reaching the coal:

> There was plenty of coal. The old workings could not get at it, that was all. Then break the neck of the old workings. (*WL*, 230, 223)

Holderness has located a similar history to the Crich family's mines in the Barber-Walker family of Nottingham.[14] But Gerald's project to organize the mines rationally is especially reminiscent of German, rather than English, industrialization at the turn of the

---

[11] See Dietrich Orlow, *A History of Modern Germany: 1870 to Present* (New Jersey: Prentice-Hall, 1987), 88.

[12] See John Maynard Keynes, *The Collected Writings of John Maynard Keynes*, 30 vols (London: Macmillan, 1971-89), II, 9.

[13] See Thomas Nipperdey, *Deutsche Geschichte 1866-1918*, 2 vols (Munich: C. H. Beck, 1990), I, 227.

[14] See Holderness, *D. H. Lawrence: History, Ideology and Fiction*, 209-11.

twentieth century. In Germany, industrial works were three to four times larger than in England to accommodate a rationalized, integrated production which enabled greater efficiency and higher output.[15] These works were organized into huge cartels that monopolized political as well as economic power, and which were particularly hostile to the Social Democrat Party who represented the workers' interests. Like the cartels which demanded a more precise organization of personnel centralized around the managing director,[16] Gerald finds "educated and expert men" as "efficient substitutes" for "the old grey managers". He organizes the mines from the "butty system" controlled by the miners into a "wonderful and delicate system" centralized upon himself as "the God of the Machine" (*WL*, 231, 228).

In the context of Germany, Lawrence's analysis of Gerald's industry is also directly applicable to the nation as a whole. Keynes describes how "Germany transformed herself into a vast and complicated industrial machine", around which the rest of Europe was "organised socially and economically as to secure the maximum accumulation of capital". The First World War, he argues, erupted from the instability of "complicated and artificial organisation" and of relations between "labouring and capitalist classes".[17] In his depiction of Gerald's system Lawrence has developed a metaphor for these highly organized, but volatile economic conditions.

Gerald and modern German culture
Worthen's and Holderness' criticisms that Lawrence's portrayal of the miners' obedience to the industrial system substitutes myth and ideology for history and reality would still follow from my contextualization in German history. After all, there was even more social unrest among the mining communities in Germany than in Britain.[18] Yet in the German context that I have outlined Lawrence's analysis moves from empirical history to social theory, not to myth, as

---

[15] See Nipperdey, *Deutsche Geschichte*, I, 229-30.
[16] See Eda Sagarra, *A Social History of Germany 1648-1914* (London: Methuen, 1979), 301. Also see Nipperdey, *Deutsche Geschichte*, I, 243.
[17] Keynes, *The Collected Writings*, II, 7, 11, 15.
[18] See Sagarra, *A Social History of Germany*, 361.

it appears in an English context to Worthen and Holderness. In his depiction of Gerald's mines Lawrence invokes the sociological analysis of Max Weber, and more broadly the ideas of Goethe and Nietzsche, to outline the cultural traditions that he identified in Germany's military aggression.

Lawrence's description of the ideology that drives Gerald and his workers particularly reflects ideas from Max Weber's *Die protestantische Ethik und der Geist des Kapitalismus*. Gerald is directly linked to Weberian thought in his study of "all kinds of sociological ideas, and ideas of reform" in Germany. Weber argued that the Protestant ethic of work and productivity, as opposed to Catholic charity, provided a catalyst for the development of capitalism in northern Europe. Under Gerald's father the miners worked in what Weber calls a system of *Traditionalismus* ("traditionalism"), which was based on the following philosophy: "a person does not 'by nature' wish to earn money and more money, but simply to live, to live as he is accustomed to live and to acquire as much as is necessary for this."[19] In terms of Weber's analysis, Gerald establishes his capitalist principles into an "immense cosmos": "It imposes the norms of industry and commerce upon the individual, in so far as he is entangled in the interrelation between markets."[20] The miners' widows are forced to pay for their coal, and the miners for their expenses. Weber describes how the Protestant capitalist forced his workers to labour harder by paying them less, through which he promoted the value of their work, not the enjoyment of their earnings. The capitalist focused on the "most pressing task, the destruction of uninhibited, instinctual pleasure in life" of the workers; this task included "the most important method of asceticism, to bring *order* to their lifestyle."[21] Gerald reduces the miners into "mere mechanical

---

[19] Weber, *Gesammelte Aufsätze zur Religionssoziologie*, I, 44: "der Mensch will »von Natur« nicht Geld und mehr Geld verdienen, sondern einfach leben, so leben wie er zu leben gewohnt ist und soviel erwerben, wie dazu erforderlich ist."

[20] *Ibid.*, 37: "ungeheuer Kosmos"; "Er zwingt dem einzelnen, soweit er in den Zusammenhang des Marktes verflochten ist, die Normen seines wirtschaftlichen Handelns auf."

[21] *Ibid.*, 117-18: "Vernichtung der Unbefangenheit des triebhaften Lebensgenusses die dringendste Aufgabe"; "*Ordnung* in die Lebensführung derer [...] zu bringen, das *wichtigste Mittel* der Askese."

instruments" who have "to work hard, much harder than before, the work was terrible and heart-rending in its mechanicalness" (*WL*, 230). The miners' adaptation to their economic function is analogous to the situation under Protestantism, according to Weber, where "the estimation of fulfilling one's duty within worldly callings" was the "highest content that moral self-affirmation could take".[22] According to Gerald,

> every man was fit for his own little bit of a task – let him do that, and then please himself. The unifying principle was the work in hand. Only work, the business of production, held men together. It was mechanical, but then society *was* a mechanism. Apart from work they were isolated, free to do as they liked.

Gudrun compares his idea to the German system: "Then we shan't have names any more – we shall be like the Germans, nothing but Herr Obermeister and Herr Untermeister" (*WL*, 102).

Through identifying with their *Beruf* the miners lose all "joy" and "hope", but find "a further satisfaction":

> The men were satisfied to belong to the great and wonderful machine, even whilst it destroyed them. It was what they wanted, it was the highest that man had produced, the most wonderful and superhuman. (*WL*, 230-31)

Weber analysed how the valuing of work was first of all utilitarian, in that it was useful to man, but became the "Zweck seines Lebens" ("purpose of his life"), transcendental and irrational, an ideal irrespective of its material benefits to him.[23] Ursula comments that Gerald is devoted to "making all kinds of latest improvements" to his family home. He confesses to Birkin that he only follows "the plausible ethics of productivity": "I suppose I live to work, to produce something, in so far as I am a purposive being. Apart from that, I live because I am living" (*WL*, 48, 56).

---

[22] *Ibid.*, 69: "die Schätzung der Pflichterfüllung innerhalb der weltlichen Berufe"; "höchsten Inhaltes, den die sittliche Selbstbetätigung überhaupt annehmen könne."
[23] *Ibid.*, 35-36.

Weber analysed the "'Rationalisierungen' der mystischen Kontemplation" ("'rationalization' of mystical contemplation") under Protestantism: the religious framework falls away in the individual's consciousness: "He 'gets nothing' out of his wealth for himself, – other than: the irrational sense of a 'job well done'."[24] Profit is the means of measuring the success of work, and becomes a transcendental value, an ideal. Gerald is not concerned with making money to enjoy, rather "his will was now, to take the coal out of the earth, profitably. The profit was merely the condition of victory, but the victory itself lay in the feat achieved". He imposes a religious value upon profit in the system he has created for the miners: "Gerald was their high priest, he represented the religion they really felt" (*WL*, 224, 230-31). Under Protestantism, compared to the Catholic cycle of individual acts of sin, repentance, atonement, release and renewed sin, there was a systematic method of rational conduct to free man from the power of irrational impulses and from his dependence on nature.[25] Gerald imposes this system on the miners.

In the previous chapter I connected the influence of Weberian ideas on Lawrence to wider elements of German culture; here, once again, Lawrence responds to Goethe and Nietzsche alongside Weber. Goethe is part of Gerald's middle-class education, and is discussed by him with the German professor at Hohenhausen. In particular, Goethe's classicism is implicated in Gerald's aspiration towards a "new and terrible purity" (*WL*, 231). The word "purity" echoes Lawrence's dismissive attitude to Goethe in a letter to Thomas Dunlop in 1916:

> You were very miserable. But whatever possessed you to quote Goethe and "Reinheit"? What does one mean by Reinheit? Purity lies in pure fulfilment, I should say. All suppression and abnegation seem to me dirty and unclean. (Letters, II, 511)

In "The Crown" Lawrence opposes the "flesh of darkness" of the lion to "the white light, the Mind" of the unicorn, whom we may implicitly associate with Goethe as "Mr Purity" (*RDP*, 253). Like the image of

---

[24] *Ibid.*,11, 55: "Er 'hat nichts' von seinem Reichtum für seine Person, – außer: der irrationalen Empfindung guter 'Berufserfüllung'."
[25] *Ibid.*, 115-17.

light in *The Rainbow*, the source of Lawrence's Goethean *Reinheit* is the final scene of *Faust II*. The choir of angels bears Faust's body away from Mephistopheles, to where "Luft ist gereinigt" ("Air is purified"). Faust is transformed into Doctor Marianus, "in der höchsten, reinlichsten Zelle" ("in the highest, purest cell"), from which he addresses the Virgin Mary, "rein im schönsten Sinn" ("pure in the most beautiful sense").[26]

In *Die protestantische Ethik* Max Weber found in this part of *Faust II* the message "that the limitation to specialized work, with the sacrifice of the Faustian universality of mankind, which it demands, is a precondition of valuable work in the modern world; hence "deeds" and "renunciation" inevitably condition each other today".[27] In other words, Faust's *Reinheit* consists of renouncing his various desires and limiting himself to the *Reinheit* of a Protestant God. Gerald, as priest and God, creates a pure system by repressing the individuality of the miners. He is "translating the mystic word harmony", which is associated with Goethe's classicism, "into the practical word organisation" (*WL*, 227). In *The Rainbow* Lawrence used the symbolism of light from the ending of *Faust II* to express his characters' rational consciousness; similarly, Gerald is described in terms of light whenever he forces his rational organization upon nature, such as his horse, or his workers, or Gudrun.

Alongside Goethe, Nietzsche was important to Weber, and Lawrence approached them together. Lawrence saw England in terms of the traditionalist Christianity of Thomas Crich, the "great christian-democratic principle". By contrast, Germany was "the Lucifer, the Satan, who has reacted directly against this principle" (Letters, II, 604). In his 1913 review "Georgian Poetry" Lawrence singled out Nietzsche as "demolishing ... the Christian religion as it stood" (*IR*, 201). Gerald shares Germany's, and in particular Nietzsche's, overturning of traditional political and religious values, as perceived by Lawrence. Gudrun's comparison of Gerald to Bismarck in

---

[26] Goethe, *Gedenkausgabe*, V, 516, 522-23.
[27] *Ibid.*, 203: "Daß die Beschränkung auf Facharbeit, mit dem Verzicht auf die faustische Allseitigkeit des Menschentums, welchen sie bedingt, in der heutigen Welt Voraussetzung wertvollen Handelns überhaupt ist, daß also 'Tat' und 'Entsagung' einander heute unabwendbar bedingen."

revolutionising industry is expressed in terms of the "Wille zur Macht": "Gerald, with his force of will and his power for comprehending the actual world, should be set to solve the problems of the day, the problem of industrialism in the modern world" (*WL*, 417).

In Nietzschean terms, Gerald identifies with the "Wille zur Macht". Lawrence compresses a Weberian interpretation of Nietzsche and Goethe into his description of Gerald's direction of the mines:

> There were two opposites, his will and the resistant Matter of the earth. And between these he could establish the very expression of his will, the incarnation of his power, a great and perfect machine, a system, an activity of pure order, pure mechanical, repetition ad infinitum, hence eternal and infinite. (*WL*, 228)

Gerald expresses his "Wille zur Macht" through his impact upon the outside world, to "reduce it to his will". In a similar context, Ursula refers to his forceful control over his horse beside a passing train as "a lust for bullying – a real Wille zur Macht – so base, so petty" (*WL*, 227, 150). Gerald's Goethean purity is achieved through his "Wille zur Macht" compelling all forms of nature into an ideal economic system. In its purity, Gerald's will transcends the physical circumstances in which it had originally defined itself, like Weber's Protestant ethic, to become self-perpetuating. The "eternal and infinite" mechanized repetition of Gerald's will is an ideal – or perverse – form of Nietzsche's "ewige Wiederkehr".

In answer to Worthen and Holderness, then, Lawrence's references to Nietzsche return us to the historical moment of the war. In Britain, and in Germany itself, the "Wille zur Macht" was identified as the founding principle of the German nation, from its unification to its involvement in the First World War.[28] In *Fighting a Philosophy* of 1915 William Archer argued that "it is the philosophy of Nietzsche that we are fighting", because "wherever his ideas are clear, definite and easily translated into action, they are aggressively inhuman". Lawrence's depiction of the "Wille zur Macht" in Gerald accords with Archer's, and with those of many other writers,

---

[28] See Steven G. Aschheim, *The Nietzsche Legacy in Germany*, 130.

including Thomas Hardy. When he describes Gerald's will as a transcendental ideal of aggression, Lawrence also echoes the British linking of militarism with German idealism, as in the purity and light of *Faust II*. Archer refers to Nietzsche as "a terminal flower in the tree of idealistic thought";[29] after *Also Sprach Zarathustra*, Goethe's *Faust* was the most common book carried into the trenches by German soldiers.[30] Finally, as we saw in the previous chapter, Weber appealed to Nietzsche in his vision of an expansionist Germany in his "Freiburger Antrittsrede", and maintained this position in his support of the war.[31]

A psychoanalysis of the war
Gerald's character, then, is a collage of historical and cultural references, not an ahistorical myth. In the treatment of Gerald, Lawrence alludes to the events of Bismarck's rule and industrialization, the sociology of Weber, and the culture of Goethe and Nietzsche, in order to capture these contributory factors to the First World War. Of course, Gerald does not exclusively symbolize Lawrence's notion of Germany, but nonetheless these parts of his character contribute to his tragic fate which in turn allegorizes the war. Through personifying history and culture in a character, Lawrence can examine them at a dramatic, psychological level.

For his psychological analysis of Gerald, Lawrence is indebted to Freud. Lawrence follows from the Modernist realism of *Sons and Lovers* in which he had analysed Paul's relationship with his mother to explain his romantic longing for death. Lawrence's understanding of Freud was enriched during this period by his association with the founders of psychoanalysis in Britain. In 1914 he first met Ernest Jones, the first British doctor to practise psychoanalysis, and the leader of the British Psychoanalytic Movement. In the same year he also became acquainted with Barbara Low, who was to publish *Psychoanalysis: A Brief Outline of the Freudian Theory* in 1920.

---

[29] Peter Edgerly Firchow, *The Death of the German Cousin* (London: Associated University Press, 1986), 161-62.
[30] See Ashheim, *The Nietzsche Legacy in Germany*, 134.
[31] See Wolfgang J. Mommsen, *Max Weber and German Politics 1890-1920* (Chicago: University of Chicago Press, 1984), 190.

Most important, he developed a strong friendship with Barbara's sister Edith and brother-in-law Dr David Eder, with whom he would continue to exchange ideas into the Twenties.[32] David Eder practised psychoanalysis, and had delivered the first paper on it to the British Medical Association in 1911, during which, allegedly, the whole audience walked out.[33] John Middleton Murry recalls Lawrence's discussions on Freud with Eder in 1914.[34] In my comparison of *Women in Love* to Freudian theory I will refer to Freud's works that were published in German before Lawrence's completion of his novel, and to Barbara Low's book on psychoanalysis.

During Thomas Crich's protracted death, Mrs Crich asks Gerald if he is "letting it make you hysterical". Her notion of hysteria is not of an isolated reaction to a specific event but of a personality condition, as defined by Freud; she remarks to Gerald, "You're hysterical, always were" (*WL*, 327). Mrs Crich also indicates that his hysteria is not physically induced – Gerald is physically powerful – but psychologically, from his need to be "important".

In *Studien über Hysterie* (*Studies on Hysteria* 1893-95) Freud commented that neuroses are often wrongly identified as cases of hysteria.[35] Gerald's hysteria is, more accurately, an obsessional neurosis about being important in the firm, and about his fear of death. In "Bemerkungen über einen Fall von Zwangneurose" ("Notes upon a Case of Obsessional Neurosis", 1908) Freud describes how obsessional neurotics believe in their own omnipotence. From the anxiety of doubting their power, they overcompensate by compulsively proving their ability to achieve something.[36] To counter his anxiety about death, Gerald compulsively strives for power over the mines. John N. Swift has described how in *Women in Love* Lawrence's repetitive imagery severs words from their reference, to

---

[32] See Kinkead-Weekes, *D. H. Lawrence: Triumph to Exile*, 788-89.
[33] See J. B. Hobman, *David Eder: Memoirs of a Modern Pioneer* (London: Victor Gollancz, 1945), 88.
[34] See John Middleton Murry, *Between Two Worlds: An Autobiography* (London: Jonathan Cape, 1935), 287.
[35] See Freud, *Gesammelte Werke*, I, 256.
[36] *Ibid.*, VII, 450, 457.

express the characters' repetition of senseless actions.[37] Here I want to show how Lawrence diagnoses this symptom in Gerald, and in European nations at war.

In "Drei Abhandlungen zur Sexualtheorie" ("Three Essays on the Theory of Sexuality", 1905) Freud remarks on the "increased *pertinacity* or *susceptibility to fixation*" in people who later develop into neurotics or perverts".[38] When Gerald sees his own name on the coal wagons "he had a vision of power ... his power ramified" (*WL*, 327). The miners are "subjugate to his will", and the coal seams are

> subject to the will of man. The will of man was the determining factor .... His mind was obedient to serve his will. Man's will was the absolute, the only absolute. (*WL*, 222-23)

Power and will are tautological; their signification depends on an accumulated effect of repetition. Lawrence is deliberately imitating the Wagnerian *Leitmotiv* structure where the symbols become detached from any representational context. He expresses Gerald's compulsive behaviour and neurotic detachment from reality. In "Formulierungen über die zwei Prinzipien des psychischen Geschehens" ("Formulations on the two Principles of Mental Functioning", 1911) Freud observes that "every neurosis has as its result, and probably therefore as its purpose, a forcing of the patient out of real life, an alienating of him from reality".[39] After inheriting all power on his father's death, Gerald is "faced with the ultimate experience of his own nothingness". His eyes are "only bubbles of darkness", his mind is "like a bubble floating in the darkness", and he fears that he will "break down and be a purely meaningless babble lapping round a darkness" (*WL*, 337, 232).

In "The Crown" (1925) Lawrence argued that "all absolutes are prison-walls": "our will-to-live contains a germ of suicide." "Falling into final egoism", "the power of the Will" achieves "final

---

[37] See *The Challenge of D. H. Lawrence*, eds Michael Squires and Keith Cushman (Wisconsin: University of Wisconsin Press, 1990), 122-23.
[38] Freud, *Gesammelte Werke*, V, 144: "erhöhte *Haftbarkeit* oder *Fixierbarkeit*."
[39] *Ibid.*, VIII, 230: "jede Neurose die Folge, also wahrscheinlich die Tendenz habe, den Kranken aus dem realen Leben herauszudrängen, ihn der Wirklichkeit zu entfremden."

consummation" in death (*RDP*, 287-89). Gerald's will and power become inert through their self-sustained meaning, and eventually his egoism collapses into a romantic nothingness. Nietzsche's "Wille zur Macht" was intended to answer Schopenhauer and Wagner's escapism from the modern world. Yet as a transcendental ideal, the will conquers otherness. It can only be fulfilled in nothingness, or mass carnage, when the individual will universalizes itself and disintegrates, because it lacks anything outside to define itself against. Gerald's conscious will has dominated outside reality and his inner unconscious, leaving him alienated from them, as in Freud's definition of a neurosis.

Gerald's mining system is both perfect, and a "pure organic disintegration and mechanical organisation ... the first and finest state of chaos" (*WL*, 231). Gerald's neurosis is a result of his repressed unconscious. Lawrence defined hysteria in his essay "On Human Destiny" (1924): "The emotions that have not the approval and inspiration of the mind are just hysterics" (*RDP*, 205). According to Freud in "Bruchstück einer Hysterie-Analyse" ("Fragment of an Analysis of a Case of Hysteria, 1905"), hysterics suffer from repression caused by "psychical trauma" and "conflict of emotions".[40] In "Die Verdrängung" ("Repression", 1915) and "Das Unbewusste" ("The Unconscious", 1915) Freud explains that an obsession is the result of a failed repression that prevents any discharge of unconscious desires; they fuel the neurotic's anxiety.[41] Lawrence suggests that Gerald has repressed his childhood murder of his brother, and perhaps also his conflicting love and hatred towards his father.

In *Women in Love* this theme of repression shifts to the socio-economic realm. In *Psychoanalysis: A Brief Account of the Freudian Theory* Barbara Low describes how Freud attributes the increased cases of neuroses and hysteria to the increasing speed of progress in civilization; the sublimation process in individuals is under more pressure, forcing them to repress their needs.[42] When Gerald claims

---

[40] *Ibid.*, V, 182: "psychische Trauma"; "Konflikt der Affekte."
[41] *Ibid.*, X, 256, 285.
[42] See Barbara Low, *Psychoanalysis: A Brief Account of Freudian Theory* (London: Allen and Unwin, 1920), 35-36.

that individuality is maintained outside the "mechanism" of a society based on work, Ursula is sceptical: "But won't it be rather difficult to arrange the two halves?" He answers that "they arrange themselves naturally – we see it now, everywhere" (*WL*, 103), but the chaos of individual miners threatens to disrupt his system, like the unconscious against his consciousness.

Socially and psychologically, Gerald is in an analogous position to Germany on the eve of war. In *Movements in European History* Lawrence describes this situation:

> the German Empire and the Kingdom of Prussia were reckoned the most powerful state organisations in Europe .... And yet labour organisation and socialist influence were perhaps stronger among the German people than anywhere. The state was keenly divided against itself .... in Germany as in Russia, the working people were most united, most ready to strike against war-lords and military dominion. (*MEH*, 251)

The increasingly ruthless state authorities encouraged nationalist fever to reduce the power of socialism and bring domestic stability to Germany, until it spilled over into war. A political truce was called on the outbreak of war for national unity, but by 1916 social polarity was more extreme than ever, until the collapse of Germany in 1918.[43] Lawrence symbolizes this repression of the working classes by the political elite in Gerald's repression of his unconscious needs. Gerald looks to Gudrun to unify his disintegrating personality, but like Germany which looked for unity in the war only to be ruined through it, he is ultimately destroyed by her. The two lovers play out these large-scale historical conflicts, between capital and labour during the First World War. They share the contradiction of a systematic order built on chaos, which fuels their relationship. Gudrun closes herself off from the outside world by objectifying it as distinct from herself, as in Freud's notion of the neurosis. Ursula observes how she "finished life off so thoroughly, she made things so ugly and so final". Like Gerald, Gudrun's individual will threatens to cave in from the pressure of the chaos outside, and from within her unconscious. Despite wishing the crowds observing the wedding party were

---

[43] See Carr, *A History of Germany*, 174, 182-83, 193, 201, 206, 212, 221.

"annihilated, cleared away, so that the world was left clear for her", she enjoys mixing with the miners, who live in "the voluptuous resonance of darkness", with "a secret sense of power, and of inexpressible destructiveness, and of fatal half-heartedness, a sort of rottenness in the will" (*WL*, 263, 13, 115, 118). These miners belong to the history which Worthen and Holderness had accused Lawrence of excluding from the novel. As individuals the miners constitute the chaos upon which Gerald has ordered his system, and Gudrun enacts this chaos upon him.

Gudrun is attracted to Gerald's "Wille zur Macht" against the outer chaos. She watches him controlling his horse beside a passing train, "his will bright and unstained", and the blood trickles down the sides of the horse while he digs his heels into it. In response "she turned white", losing consciousness, then wakens to her individuality, "separate, ... hard and cold and indifferent". While sketching beside Willey Water, Gudrun observes Gerald's "white loins", "the whiteness he seemed to enclose", his "glistening, whitish hair": "Gerald was her escape from the heavy slough of the pale, underworld, automatic colliers – he started out from the mud" (*WL*, 112, 119-20). Her fascination with his beauty is expressed in *Leitmotive* of light which are opposed to the earth and blood that give substance to his power and beauty, and which express the repression of their unconscious desires.

In the chapter "Rabbit" Lawrence places Gerald and Gudrun's relationship in the context of the war. George Hyde demonstrates how the multi-lingual discussion of the Crichs' pet rabbit, Bismarck, forms "a sort of hypnotic rhapsody of power, the struggle for power in Europe but also the power game that is under way between Gudrun and Gerald".[44] The play of words veers between historical accuracy and linguistic anarchy. Gerald's young sister Winifred describes the rabbit as "almost as big as a lion .... He's a real king, he really is", and Gudrun continues the game by chanting, "Bismarck is a mystery, Bismarck, c'est un mystère, der Bismarck, er ist ein Wunder". The French mistress corrects them, "Doch ist er nicht ein König. Beesmarck, he was not a king, Winifred, as you have said. He was only – il n'était que chancelier" (*WL*, 237-38). The descriptive

---

[44] Hyde, *D. H. Lawrence*, 60.

narrative shares the confusion between historical fact and hyperbole of the characters' speech.

Lawrence describes how the rabbit, "inconceivably powerful and explosive", "exploded in a wild rush around the hutch". The imagery suggests the violence of war and the rhythm of the machine: "Round and round the court it went, as if shot from a gun, round and round like a furry meteorite, in a tense hard circle that seemed to bind their brains" (*WL*, 240-41, 243). The rabbit enacts Gerald and Gudrun's unconscious energies, erupting while still enslaved to an obsessional neurosis of meaninglessly repeated actions. The rabbit's actions also resemble the futile, repetitive symptoms of hysteria that Freud identified in *Studien über Hysterie*, including stammering and clacking.[45]

Gudrun and Gerald's corresponding hysteria is so intense that they border on insanity in their complete estrangement from reality, and the lost hierarchy between their consciousness and unconscious. The language expressing their feelings appears to tear itself from all historical and representational references, but as George Hyde observes,[46] its hysterical repetition of images mimics the dislocation from reality of war hysteria. Lawrence uses the *Leitmotiv*, with its alienation from temporal reality, to express how Gerald and Gudrun are alienated from the sensual needs of their bodies. Images are chaotically repeated and juxtaposed with each other, mirroring Gerald and Gudrun's hysterical gestures to each other. Whiteness, which has developed associations with Gerald's rational order, clashes with images of darkness and blood. Trying to control the rabbit, Gerald feels a "white-edged wrath", and strikes the animal "swift as lightning". Hearing the rabbit's scream in its fear of death, Gudrun's eyes turn "black as night in her pallid face", and she stares at Gerald with "strange, darkened eyes, strained with underworld knowledge ... like a soft recipient of his magical, hideous white fire".

Conscious order and unconscious desire are married to each other, while the brutal conflict between them persists. Gerald and Gudrun share a "mocking, white-cruel recognition", both fascinated by the scratches upon their skin from the rabbit's claws. Gerald's forearm is

---

[45] See Freud, *Gesammelte Werke*, I, 147-48.
[46] See Hyde, *D. H. Lawrence*, 61.

"white and hard and torn in red gashes", and she has "a deep score down the silken white flesh". The imagery, expressing their "abhorrent", "vindictive" and "sinister" feelings towards each other, reaches beyond rational signification: "The long,shallow red rip seemed torn across his own brain, tearing the surface of his ultimate consciousness, letting through the forever unconscious, unthinkable red ether of the beyond, the obscene beyond" (WL, 241-42). Consciousness and unconscious are indistinguishable; the lightness of skin and deep red of blood are juxtaposed. The imagery, in contrast to the mechanical expressions of Gerald's ordering of the mines, is chaotic, and through its disorder Lawrence eloquently conveys the historical moment of the First World War.

Freud and Nietzsche's "child"
In Gerald and Gudrun's relationship, then, Lawrence has used the conditions of obsessional neurosis and hysteria as metaphors for war hysteria. The cause of Gerald and Gudrun's neuroses, a repression of unconscious drives that prohibits their discharge, is analogous to the nations at war, in particular Germany whose political elite had repressed the needs of its working classes. Each nation hoped that war could unite its classes, but as we see in the chaos between conscious and unconscious impulses in "Rabbit", through the war German society disintegrated into anarchy.

Lawrence uses Freud to diagnose the problems of his era, and to suggest a cure for them. The cure lies, for Lawrence, in negotiating between conscious and unconscious impulses, not letting one dominate over the other. Lawrence continues to emulate Otto Gross' synthesis of Nietzsche and Freud for an "alternative world", as Worthen puts it, to those of Gerald and Gudrun, and of Europe at war.

While completing *The Rainbow* in spring 1915 Lawrence mentioned that he wanted to rewrite "Le Gai Savoir", his name for "Study of Thomas Hardy" (Letters, II, 295). This allusion to Nietzsche's *Die Fröhliche Wissenschaft* marks the beginning of Lawrence's composition of "The Crown", a series of philosophical essays which anticipate his developments in *Women in Love*. In April Lawrence referred to his new philosophy as "Morgenrot", after Nietzsche's book *Morgenröte* which prefigured the revolutionary ideas of *Also Sprach Zarathustra* (Letters, II, 315, 317). In *Women in Love* Lawrence combines Nietzsche's ideas with those learnt from the English Freudians. He attempts to reconcile the Freudian unconscious with the Nietzschean *Wille* in his image of the child.

Nietzsche's *Kind* ("child") symbolizes the Übermensch in *Also Sprach Zarathustra*. Nietzsche describes how the *Geist* will become a camel, then a lion, and finally a child: "The child is innocence and forgetfulness, a new beginning, a game, a self-rotating wheel, a first movement, a sacredly uttered yes."[47] Given the omnipresence of the *Wille* in Nietzsche's philosophy, the child's innocence is created only through the *Wille*: "if there is innocence in my knowledge, it occurs because the will to begetting is in it."[48] Nietzsche also implies that the body's impulses constitute the human *Wille*; following the child's assertion "I am body and soul", the man says "I am body, completely and nothing besides; and the soul is only a word for something in the body".[49] In Nietzsche's child, the will and unconscious desire are united, yet we see Lawrence struggle to reconcile them with each other.

Lawrence reveals his ambivalence in two crucial letters written on 19 February 1916 to S. S. Koteliansky and Bertrand Russell, which give different interpretations of Nietzsche's *Kind*. Lawrence explains to Koteliansky:

> I understand Nietzsche's child. But it isn't a child that will represent the third stage: not innocent unconscious: but the maximum of fearless adult consciousness, that has the courage even to submit to the unconsciousness of itself. (Letters, II, 546)

Lawrence's understanding is faithful to the subtleties of Nietzsche's conception of the *Kind*: "In order for the creator to be a child, to be newly born, he must also be willing to be the mother and to

---

[47] Nietzsche, *Werke*, VI 1, 27: "Unschuld ist das Kind und Vergessen, ein Neubeginnen, ein Spiel, ein aus sich rollendes Rad, eine erste Bewegung, ein heiliges Ja-sagen."
[48] *Ibid.*, 107: "wenn Unschuld in meiner Erkenntnis ist, so geschieht dies, weil Wille zur Zeugung in ihr ist."
[49] *Ibid.*, 35: "Leib bin ich und Seele"; "Leib bin ich ganz und gar, und nichts außerdem; und Seele ist nur ein Wort für ein Etwas am Leibe."

experience the pain of the mother."[50] The child is conscious of itself, having given birth to its own innocent creativity; it is both free of conventions and responsible for its actions.

Yet in the letter to Russell, instead of this dialectic between conscious and unconscious, Lawrence portrays the child as unconscious, anti-social and irrational:

> You said in your letters on education that you didn't set much count by the unconscious. That is sheer perversity. The whole of the consciousness and the conscious content is old hat – the mill-stone round your neck.
> Do cut it – cut your will and leave your old self behind ....
> Do stop working and writing altogether and become a creature instead of a mechanical instrument. Do clear out of the whole social ship.... Do for heavens sake be a baby, and not a savant any more. (Letters, II, 546-47)

Here Lawrence displays the ideology of the blood and irrationality, which would inspire Russell's later condemnation of him as a fascist. Lawrence opposes the "will", which is social and only "mechanical", with the "unconscious" of a baby or animal. Certainly, the context here is different from the letter to Koteliansky, in that Lawrence is raging against Russell's exclusive dependence on consciousness and rationality. But Ursula's rejection of the light of civilization for the darkness with Skrebensky in *The Rainbow*, and Paul Morel's struggle against the darkness in the last chapter of *Sons and Lovers*, are previous instances in Lawrence's writing of the rejection of consciousness for the unconscious, not of their interaction with each other. This problem resurfaces in the composition of *Women in Love*, a symptom Lawrence's complete sense of alienation from European civilization.

In "Das Unbewusste" Freud defined the unconscious as the "inherited mental formations" and the elements of the psyche which were "discarded during childhood development as unserviceable".[51] In

---

[50] *Ibid.*, 107: "Daß der Schaffende selber das Kind sei, das neu geboren werde, dazu muß er auch die Gebärerin sein wollen und der Schmerz der Gebärin."
[51] Freud, *Gesammelte Werke*, X, 294: "ererbte psychische Bildungen"; "während der Kindheitsentwicklung als unbrauchbar Beseitigte."

the context of his developmental theory, Freud's *Kind* is the unconscious of childhood complexes and instincts which affect adult behaviour, in defiance of conscious repression. The child unconsciously pursues the *Lustprinzip* ("pleasure principle"), while oblivious of the reality principle.[52] Under the influence of Nietzsche, Otto Gross had opposed Freud's insistence on unconscious impulses being sublimated by consciousness to accord with the reality principle of civilization. Gross wanted to change civilization to give voice to the unconscious, and Lawrence accords with him in his appeal to Russell to "clear out of the whole social ship". Yet Lawrence identifies the will, including the "Wille zur Macht", with consciousness, which ironically leaves his Nietzschean child as a rejection of Nietzsche's philosophy.

While composing *Women in Love* Lawrence struggled between opposing Nietzsche and Freud to each other, and combining them. In the chapter "Class-room", Rupert Birkin attacks Hermione Roddice during a discussion about education. Birkin recapitulates Lawrence's outburst against Russell's will and consciousness: "You've got that mirror, your own fixed will, your immortal understanding, your own tight conscious world, and there's nothing beyond it." Birkin's alternative, like Lawrence's, lies exclusively in the unconscious, from Russell's "social ship" into the "deluge": "In the blood, ... when the mind and the known world is drowned in darkness. – Everything must go – there must be the deluge" (*WL*, 42-43). In the version of this scene in *The First 'Women in Love'*, written between April and November 1916, Birkin is "like a boy who has broken something and is wickedly pleased" (*FWL*, 35). In other words, he is the Nietzschean child who has broken Hermione's rational consciousness. In the final version of *Women in Love*, though, Lawrence is more sceptical towards Birkin whom he describes as "fixed and unreal", and "sounded as if he were addressing a meeting" (*WL*, 44). Lawrence is also sceptical of his own glorification of the unconscious.

Again, in the "Prologue" which was edited out of the final version of *Women in Love*, Lawrence opposes will and desire at a metaphysical level when he describes Birkin's attempt to love Hermione: "

---

[52] *Ibid.*, 286.

He might will it, he might act according to his will, but he did not bring to pass that which he willed. A man cannot create desire in himself, nor cease at will from desiring. Desire, in any shape or form, is primal, whereas the will is secondary, derived. The will can destroy, but it cannot create. (*WL*, 510)

Zarathustra's "ardent creative will"[53] is denied by Lawrence, who is implicitly opposing consciousness and unconscious. However, when Lawrence returns to this dilemma towards the end of *Women in Love*, he removes all metaphysical significance. On Gerald's attachment to Gudrun, Lawrence comments that "however he might mentally *will* to be immune and self-complete, the desire for this state was lacking, and he could not create it". At this point of the novel Gerald also feels a "blind, incontinent desire" to kill Gudrun, while "his consciousness was gone into his wrists, into his hands". His consciousness, associated with the will, is consonant with his desire. Yet he is also in "a state of rigid unconsciousness", attempting to avoid "the solid darkness confronting him" of the night and from within himself (*WL*, 445, 462, 467). In *Women in Love* Lawrence attempts to combine consciousness and unconscious in dynamic ways, according to the circumstances of his characters.

Lawrence understood the dangers of the purely unconscious child. After all, Freud characterizes the Oedipal child as incestuous and murderous. Similarly, Nietzsche described how the *Kind* emerges from the *Löwe* ("lion"): "it wants to capture freedom and be master of its own wilderness."[54] The lion, as the destructive principle which makes possible the creation of new values, is bound up with the other militaristic images that became so evocative during World War I, in Zarathustra's call to his "Brüder im Kriege" ("brothers in war"), and in his orders to them: "You should seek your enemy, you should wage your war, for your opinions!"[55] This destructiveness inspired many German soldiers and repulsed English writers. Lawrence described Germany as the "purely destructive" "child of Europe" (Letters, II, 425) in late 1915.

---

[53] Nietzsche, *Werke*, VI 1, 107: "inbrünstiger Schaffens-Wille."
[54] *Ibid.*, 25-26: "Freiheit will er sich erbeuten und Herr sein in seiner eignen Wüste."
[55] *Ibid.*, 54: "Euren Feind sollt ihr suchen, euren Krieg sollt ihr führen, und für eure Gedanken!"

Lawrence registers the ambivalent nature of the unconscious in *Women in Love*. Mrs Kirk, who had been Gerald's nanny, describes him as "wilful, masterful", "a proper demon, ay, at six months old". She describes his childhood impulses as aggressive and tyrannical, demanding everything he wants. The wish to "drag the kitten about with a string round its neck" even prefigures Gerald's treatment of his horse in front of a passing train. Yet Mrs Kirk's attempt to instil the rule of the "reality principle" upon Gerald is treated unsympathetically, especially in her repetitive reminiscence of how "I pinched his little bottom for him" (*WL*, 212-13). Her repetitive punishment foreshadows his later obsessional behaviour.

Lawrence had discussed with Barbara Low the Freudian significance given to supposedly accidental actions. In a letter from 1915 he suggests giving her a box to protect her from bees, then challenges her, "Now find Freud in *that*" (Letters, II, 306). In *Women in Love* Lawrence follows Freud's examination of how unconscious impulses can affect conscious intentions in *Zur Psychopathologie des Alltagslebens*, translated as *The Psychopathology of Everyday Life* in 1914. After reluctantly participating in a discussion of the individual's responsibility for fighting in national conflicts, then "thinking about race or national death", Birkin unintentionally empties his glass of champagne before the toast is made. He decides he has acted "accidentally on purpose", in repudiation of "toasts, and footmen, and assemblies, and mankind altogether, in most of its aspects" (*WL*, 30). The train of associations reveals the subversive meaning of his act.

Birkin's unconscious liberates him, whereas Gerald is cursed by the trauma of accidentally shooting his brother during childhood. Gerald's unintentional act of murder mirrors a case in Freud's book, of a man who accidentally shot himself while playing with a revolver which he thought was unloaded. Freud judged the case as an unconscious attempt of suicide.[56] Gerald's fratricide also refers back to Freud's description of sibling rivalry in *Die Traumdeutung*, which includes the case of a little girl who tried to strangle an infant. Freud concluded that "children at that time of life are capable of jealousy of

---

[56] Freud, *Gesammelte Werke*, IV, 202-203.

any degree of intensity and obliviousness".[57] This observation leads into his outline of the Oedipus Complex.

Ursula speculates whether Gerald had "an unconscious will" or "primitive desire" (*WL*, 49) to kill his brother. Her diagnosis conflates Lawrence's opposed terms will, and unconscious and desire. She also touches on the confused levels of Gerald's personality which will attract him to Gudrun. The question that Lawrence raises in *Women in Love* is of the possible relationships between unconscious and consciousness, not of the choice between them. The "fearless adult consciousness" of the child that Lawrence describes to Koteliansky must take responsibility for the destructive impulses of its unconscious. I shall now examine whether Birkin and Ursula succeed or fail to achieve this mediation between the different levels of their personalities.

Ursula and Birkin's battles and negotiations
Lawrence describes Birkin's relationship with Ursula as "a fight to the death between them – or to a new life" (*WL*, 143). They face the challenge of surviving the conflict within their relationship, to give birth to themselves as Lawrence's symbolic child whose consciousness has the courage to submit to its unconscious needs. At the beginning of the novel Birkin and Ursula stand at each extreme: he is over-conscious in his idealized, Goethean attraction to Gerald; she longs to sink into oblivion of the world. Through their arguments they struggle towards each other's position, to reconcile the extremes within themselves.

Birkin is associated with the rationalism of his university at Heidelberg, where the Weberian circle of intellectuals was located. He shares Gudrun's ambivalent fascination with Gerald. Besides his relationship with Ursula, he wants a "Blutbrüderschaft" with Gerald, an "*additional* perfect relationship between man and man", as he explains: "We will swear to stand by each other – be true to each other – ultimately – infallibly – given to each other, organically – without possibility of taking back." Blutbrüderschaft, with its associations of medieval knights, and of German soldiers in the war,

---

[57] *Ibid.*, II and III, 257: "Der Eifersucht sind Kinder um diese Lebenszeit in aller Stärke und Deutlichkeit fähig."

reflects an ideal vision of united men, while its absolute, mystical terms deny social difference. Birkin responds to Gerald's glorification of productivity with "I rather hate you", but he longs to transcend his personal contempt for Gerald. Like Gudrun, he feels a "curious desire" for Gerald's idealized "northern kind of beauty, like light refracted from snow – and a beautiful plastic form" (*WL*, 352, 207, 56, 272-73). In his attraction to Gerald, Birkin is implicated in Lawrence's diagnosis of the war in terms of Gerald.

Ursula responds to Birkin with the unconscious desire that Lawrence had suggested to Russell. Waiting for Birkin, she implicitly compares her work to Gerald's "ewige Wiederkehr" of will, in her "barren routine" of "another school-week … absolved within my own will". She would prefer to "die than live mechanically a life that is a repetition of repetitions". "Death is a great consumption, a consummating experience", a romantic escape into "unconsciousness" and "sleep" "within the darkness" of the "unknown". She echoes the final lines of Isolde's climactic "Liebestod" which glorify death: "unbewußt – / höchste Lust!" ("unconscious – / highest joy!"). [58] When Birkin arrives, "she seemed transfigured with light" from him, yet his face "seemed to gleam with a whiteness almost phosphorescent" from his illness. After he has left, she hates him as "a beam of light that did not only destroy her, but denied her altogether" (*WL*, 191-92, 194). For now, as opposites they are alienated from each other.

Throughout *Women in Love* Ursula and Birkin attempt to establish a fulfilling relationship. In this endeavour they are also attempting to reach beyond Ursula's situation at the end of *The Rainbow*. During the early parts of *Women in Love* she often regresses to her epiphany in the previous novel, when she imagined herself "unconscious on a bed of the stream, like a stone, unconscious, unchanging, unchangeable, whilst everything rolled by in transience" (*R*, 454). In *Women in Love* she believes that "she herself was real, and only herself – just like a rock in a wash of flood-water. The rest was all nothingness." Her *repudiation* of others alternates with a desire for "pure love, only pure love". Birkin identifies this condition with the idealism of war, as I did in the conclusion to the previous

---

[58] Wagner, *Tristan und Isolde*, 117.

chapter; he comments that people "distil themselves into nitroglycerine, all the lot of them, out of very love. – It's the lie that kills." His solution is to embrace the destruction of humanity, because "the reality would be untouched. Nay, it would be better" (*WL*, 244, 127). But he is only reproducing the nihilism underlying his, and Ursula's, frustrated idealism.

To distance himself from Ursula's Romanticism, Birkin identifies with the will as consciousness. He constantly uses the word "pure", with its Goethean associations, to define his ideal relationship of "two pure beings ... singling away into purity and clear being ....The man is pure man, the woman pure woman, ... only the pure duality of polarisation .... The man has his pure freedom, the woman hers". Birkin's image of his ideal relationship with Ursula, "as the stars balance each other", resembles that of Faust and Gretchen at the end of Goethe's play, transformed into spirits in "höhern Sphären" ("higher spheres").[59] Ursula responds accordingly, "But why drag in the stars!". The terms of Birkin's relationship with Ursula mirror the Blutbrüderschaft that he wants with Gerald. He warns Ursula: "if you enter into a pure unison, it is irrevocable, and it is never pure till it is irrevocable." Yet his idealism is betrayed by his unconscious desires. He wonders if he aspires to "only an idea", or to "a profound yearning" which he feels is incongruent with his desire for "sensual fulfilment" (*WL*, 199-201, 148, 152, 252).

Birkin begins his last encounter with Ursula before their marriage with a gift that reconciles the images of ring and rainbow from the previous novel: three rings of opal, sapphire and topaz.[60] Almost immediately, though, "it was a crisis of war between them". Criticising his lingering attachment to Hermione, Ursula quotes back at Birkin his earlier Goethean, idealist propositions to her:

> You purity-monger! It *stinks*, your truth and your purity. It stinks of the offal you feed on...

After she walks away, Birkin becomes like a child:

---

[59] Goethe, *Gedenkausgabe*, V, 525.
[60] See P. T. Whelan, *D. H. Lawrence: Myth and Metaphysics in* The Rainbow *and* Women in Love (Ann Arbor: UMI Research Press, 1988), 73.

> The terrible knot of consciousness that had persisted there like an obsession was broken, gone, his life was dissolved in darkness over his limbs and his body. But there was a point of anxiety in his heart now. He wanted her to come back. He breathed lightly and regularly like an infant, that breathes innocently, beyond the touch of responsibility.

Despite his dependence on Ursula, like a child on its mother, Birkin has not simply regressed to unconsciousness, but feels "all his body awake with a simple, glimmering awareness ... like a thing that is born" (*WL*, 306-12). He has developed a new awareness of his unconscious, bodily desires. The questions remain though, whether as children Birkin and Ursula can survive the world they have been born into, and whether they can redeem the failures of *The Rainbow*.

As "one of the Sons of God from the Beginning" (*WL*, 133) Birkin fulfils Ursula's prophecy at the end of *The Rainbow*, of finding "a man created by God ... from the Infinite". Yet the final line of *The Rainbow*, which envisaged "the world built up in a living fabric of Truth, fitting to the over-arching heaven" (*R*, 457, 459), cannot be answered. In *The First 'Women in Love'* Birkin echoed this vision; he believed that in Italy or California he and Ursula could be "quite safe in a Paradise of Truth" (*FWL*, 332). Yet in the final version of the novel his options are drastically reduced to "somewhere where one needn't wear much clothes – none even". When he suggests they "wander away from the world's somewhere, into our own nowhere", Ursula is sceptical, replying "that while we are only people, we've got to take the world that's given – because there isn't any other" (*WL*, 315-16).

Their powerlessness as isolated lovers in a world bent on destruction is confirmed, not overcome, when their love is consummated:

> With perfect fine finger-tips of reality she would touch the reality in him, the suave, pure, untranslatable reality of his loins of darkness. To touch, mindlessly in darkness to come in pure touching upon the living reality of him, his suave perfect loins and thighs of darkness, this was her sustaining anticipation. (*WL*, 320)

Lawrence repeatedly combines the words "darkness" and "reality", such as "dark reality", as he had in Ursula's last futile encounters with Skrebensky. Like the repetition of Gerald's will and power, the *Leitmotive* are tautological, detached from the physical reality which they are intended to transform. The marriage of Birkin's idealism and Ursula's romantic longing for unconsciousness in the pure darkness can only beget death, not the child. The repetition of the word "living" in and around this passage does not obscure the lurking presence of death. The failure of this scene to be convincing, despite its insistence on reality, is confirmed when Birkin drives his car like an "Egyptian Pharaoh", while his arms are "rounded and living like those of a Greek" (*WL*, 318-20) on the steering-wheel.

Lawrence's child, then, fails as an alternative to contemporary history. Ursula and Birkin lapse into unconsciousness, as they escape from history instead of confronting the world with their conscious thoughts and unconscious desires. Ultimately, they repeat Ursula's denial of history at the end of *The Rainbow*.

Lawrence's differential language
Yet *Women in Love* is not a failure because it registers the tragic limits of its vision, which *The Rainbow* failed to do at its close. Lawrence encourages the reader to examine the relative value of each couple's relationship by using similar imagery for both of them. Lawrence recapitulates the imagery of "Excurse" in the following chapter to express Gerald and Gudrun's "consummation". After his father's death, Gerald wanders through the "utterly dark night" with "great gaps in his consciousness" like Birkin as a child, except that Gerald is obsessed with death. Gudrun idealizes Gerald's "pure beauty", just as Ursula idealizes Birkin's "perfect loins and thighs". Yet Gerald does not romantically die to be reborn as a child, but pours "his pent-up darkness and corrosive death" into Gudrun, and vampirically feeds on the warmth and strength of her body: "Like a child at the breast, he cleaved intensely to her, and she could not put him away" (*WL*, 338-39, 343-45).

This scene is part of a dense web of images stretching across the novel. "Destroyed into perfect consciousness ... with dark, wide eyes looking into the darkness", Gudrun is conscious of all her past, including previously repressed memories. While travelling through Europe, Birkin and Ursula are "conscious only of this pure trajectory through the surpassing darkness"; staring into the darkness like Gudrun, Ursula enters "the great chasm of memory", from her earliest childhood (*WL*, 345, 388, 390). Yet Gudrun is entrapped within the consciousness of her past, while Ursula rehearses her memories to give significance to her future.

By using similar imagery in disparate situations, Lawrence is drawing attention to the limits of what it can express, and foregrounding the significance of the novel's dramatic context. This quality relativizes the significance of "Excurse", encouraging the reader to distance himself from, and judge the value of, Ursula and Birkin's relationship. The two pairs of lovers can only be distinguished from each other by their actions, not by a symbolism which supposedly expresses their deepest experiences. Through this technique Lawrence brings a critical self-consciousness to his romantic inheritance. Unlike Wagner's *Leitmotiv* technique where symbols reify themselves independently of their dramatic context, in *Women in Love* symbolism and realism, or myth and history, are intertwined and interdependent.

Gudrun and Gerald's war

Compared to the momentary triumphs of Birkin and Ursula's relationship, there is no possible mediation for Gerald and Gudrun between consciousness and unconscious, only a dominance of one over the other. Their relationship is an "ewige Wiederkehr" of competing wills: "always it was this eternal see-saw, one destroyed that the other might exist, one ratified because the other was nulled". When Gudrun's "overbearing *will*" repudiates Gerald's "power over her" he is overcome by a Wagnerian "darkness ... great waves of darkness ... great tides of darkness ... the darkness lifting and plunging ... purely unconscious ... all but unconscious". He can only revive by destroying her in his embrace, through which she achieves a consummation: "'Shall I die, shall I die?' she repeated to herself." But unlike Gerald, she has the power to return to her individual self. Inspired by the snow of the Alps, she feels "übermenschlich – more than human". She recognizes the materialistic impurity, and banality, of the "ewige Wiederkehr" of Gerald's "Wille zur Macht" in the mining industry: "These men, with their eternal jobs – and their eternal mills of God that keep on grinding at nothing! It is too boring, just boring .... Let them become instruments, pure machines, pure wills that work like clock-work, in perpetual repetition" (*WL*, 443-45, 394, 463-64, 466).

In "The Crown" Lawrence had explored the romantic, Wagnerian implications of the "Wille zur Macht", that to have sex is to "quickly die, to have all power, all life at once ... my will fuses down, I melt out and am gone into the eternal darkness, the primal creative darkness reigns ...". Although a positive process, there is the danger that after the extreme of having all power, one cannot recover from its loss. Lawrence describes *Tristan und Isolde* in the essay "Love" (1917) as "the lovers that top the summit of pride" (*RDP*, 266, 10), which can only be consummated in death. The power of Gerald and Gudrun's wills can only be exhausted and consummated in unconsciousness and death.

The German artist Loerke acts as a catalyst in the development of their relationship to its tragic end. He has been linked to the Deutsches Werkbund, a movement founded in 1907 which anticipated the Bauhaus project of reconciling art with industry. In December 1916 Lawrence mentioned to Mark Gertler that Loerke was based on "a german, who did these big reliefs for great, fine factories in Cologne" (Letters, III, 46). Loerke mentions constructing a factory frieze in Cologne where the Werkbund had organized their most important exhibition in 1914, and he lives in Dresden, home of the Werkbund's original headquarters. Loerke and Gerald have much in common because they are from shared historical sources. Lawrence would probably have learned most about the Werkbund through the Jaffes and Webers, especially since Alfred Weber was to join it immediately after the war. The Verein für Sozialpolitik shared many of the Werkbund's principles, especially of reconciling industry and German culture in terms of the Protestant ethic of work.[61]

Like Gerald, Loerke serves the Protestant ethic. He declares that "art should interpret industry, as art once interpreted religion", and

---

[61] See Frederic J. Schwartz, *The Werkbund: Design Theory and Mass Culture before the First World War* (London: Yale University Press, 1996), 75-79.

complains that the ugliness of factories "ruins the work", despite machinery and labour being "extremely, maddeningly beautiful". Walter Gropius, a member of the Werkbund and the most advanced German architect at this time, was a Jew like Loerke. He anticipated Loerke's desire to build "beautiful machine-houses" (*WL*, 424) by advocating that factories should be like palaces dedicated to labour, to give the worker a sense of his value in the industrial system. Despite acknowledging the oppression inherent in labour, Gropius believed that factory architecture could inspire an idealism of work, and more crucially, avoid a revolution.[62]

Gropius and Loerke acknowledge the contradictions between the ideal of productivity, and the disintegrated reality of alienated labour. Birkin observes that Loerke is "further on than we are. He hates the ideal more acutely. He *hates* the ideal utterly, yet it still dominates him." Loerke does not idealize the Protestant ethic: it is not the "Wille zur Macht" that Gerald glorifies, but always work in which he is often subservient: "Nothing but work! ... serving a machine, or enjoying the motion of a machine." He has "worked as the world works", stamping clay bottles in a factory to survive as Gerald's miners do. Like them, he is fascinated by a "grotesque, ... mechanical motion ..., a confusion in nature". He has internalized the violence of the machine in terms of the Protestant ethic; while describing how he beat his model, "he was thinking over the work, his work, the all-important to him". The rhythms of his body follow the machine, which is barren in its "religious" detachment from nature. He comments that women older than eighteen years "are no good to me, for my work" (*WL*, 428, 424-25, 448, 433).

Where Gerald processes nature into a commodity, Loerke processes it into art. Loerke's formalized sculpture of a horse is analogous to Gerald's forcing of his horse against a passing train to discipline it. In turning the horse and girl into art, Loerke has dissected them from reality; he argues that his sculpture is "a work of art, it is a picture of nothing, of absolutely nothing". Where work entraps Gerald, it liberates Loerke through transforming nature into an objectified, mechanical ideal: "He existed a pure, unconnected will, stoical and momentous. There was only his work" (*WL*, 430, 427).

---

[62] *Ibid.*, 55.

Gudrun realizes that Gerald cannot break from the ideal of "oneness with the ultimate purpose", whereas Loerke is "detached from everything". Lacking Gerald's "masterful will or physical strength", his power is "subtle and adjusts itself". With "an unbroken will reacting against her unbroken will", he can explore with detachment Gudrun's "inner darkness" and "critical consciousness, that saw the world distorted, horrific". Lawrence relates Gudrun and Loerke's art to Goethe's detached classicism: "It was a sentimental delight to reconstruct the world of Goethe at Weimar, or of Schiller and poverty and faithful love …" (*WL*, 451-53).

By contrast, Gerald has fallen from the egoism of his "Wille zur Macht", to a romantic, Wagnerian longing for unconsciousness. He suffers from "a flaw in his will", and like Tristan "mit blutender Wunde" ("with bleeding wound"),[63] he bears a "wound, this strange, infinitely-sensitive opening of his soul, where he was exposed, like an open flower, to all the universe, and in which he was given to his complement". Gerald imagines the "perfect voluptuous fulfilment" of killing Gudrun, "then he would have her finally and for ever" (*WL*, 446, 480). He brutally twists Tristan's assurance to Isolde that death could make their oneness eternal:

> Was stürbe dem Tod,
> als was uns stört,
> was Tristan wehrt,
> Isolde immer zu lieben,
> ewig ihr nur zu leben?[64]

> What could death kill,
> but what disturbs us,
> what hinders Tristan,
> to love Isolde forever,
> to always live for her?

Gerald also resembles Siegfried who is betrayed by Gutrune, or Gudrun. Lawrence juxtaposes imagery of Wagner and Nietzsche in his treatment of Gerald's fate, to conclude his analysis of the war.

---

[63] Wagner, *Tristan und Isolde*, 109.
[64] *Ibid.*, 82.

Myth and History

Gerald's death scene imitates *Tristan und Isolde* while, like "Rabbit", signifying the historical context of the First World War. His approach to Loerke and Gudrun resembles a military ambush; Loerke appears to him "distinct and objective, as if seen through field glasses". Loerke provides a multi-lingual speech mimicking the warring sides, in English, French and German. In contrast to "Rabbit", which imitated the hysteria at the outbreak of war, Loerke's hyperbole is sarcastic, signifying the lost idealism of both sides as the war dragged on. After Gerald punches him, he responds, "demoniacal with satire", "Vive le héros, vive – ". Gerald's attempt to kill Gudrun combines a romantic *Liebestod* with contradictory violence:

> And her throat was beautifully, so beautifully soft .... What bliss! Oh what bliss, at last, what satisfaction, at last! The pure zest of satisfaction filled his soul. He was watching the unconsciousness come into her swollen face, watching her eyes roll back. How ugly she was! What a fulfilment, what a satisfaction! How good this was, oh how good it was, what a god-given-gratification, at last!

The transcendental effect of repeated *Leitmotive* is disrupted by the dissonant physical details of Gudrun's strangled face. Gerald's estrangement from reality and his own death are confirmed in his attempt to kill Gudrun. She "violently struggles in a frenzy of delight", consenting to her own romantic death, reaching the "zenith" of unconsciousness, "softer, appeased".

Loerke interrupts the Wagnerian climax with "Quand vous aurez fini – ", which echoes the French response to the Germans' persistent attempt to execute the Schlieffen Plan after years of trench warfare. Gerald releases Gudrun. Then, like Tristan in Act III, and the German army's stalemate after the offensives at the Marne and Ypres, he feels

> weak, but he did not want to rest, he wanted to go on and on, to the end .... So he drifted on and on, unconscious and weak, not thinking of anything, so long as he could keep in action.

He continues walking through the snow till, like Tristan, "he went to sleep" (*WL*, 470-72, 474), and dies.

The Kaiser's "Ich habe es nicht gewollt"

After he releases Gudrun, Gerald utters "the last confession of disgust in his soul": "I didn't want it, really." The significance of this phrase is revealed when Birkin visits his corpse:

> "I didn't want it to be like this – I didn't want it to be like this," he cried to himself.
> Ursula could but think of the Kaiser's: "Ich habe es nicht gewollt." She looked almost with horror on Birkin. (*WL*, 472, 479)

The quotation is from a manifesto issued by Kaiser Wilhelm II on the first anniversary of the outbreak of war in 1915. Lawrence placed the quotation halfway through *The First 'Women in Love'* but here it is at the end, more conspicuous in being repeated, to sum up the novel as a whole.

In his manifesto Wilhelm provides a model for Gerald's tragic fate in his idealistic imposition of social unity through war. Kaiser Wilhelm declares that

> an unprecedented bloodshed occurred in Europe and the world. Before God and history my conscience is clear. I did not want the war.[65]

Like Gerald's purity in the face of everything he violates, including the horse which he masters while its flanks bleed from his spurs, the Kaiser asserts that his conscience is *rein*, despite the "unerhört blutige Zeit". In spite of his apparent repulsion before the war, Kaiser Wilhelm glorifies how it has brought unity to Germany, "of the silenced political debate, old enemies began to understand and recognize that the spirit of true community fulfilled all national comrades". Also, the war encouraged economic unity: "State and communities, agriculture, the flow of trade, and industry, science and technology competed in easing the needs of war."[66] Gerald strives for

---

[65] *Berliner Tageblatt*, 3 August 1915, 2: "Eine unerhört blutige Zeit kam über Europa und die Welt. Vor Gott und der Geschichte ist mein Gewissen rein. Ich habe den Krieg nicht gewollt."

[66] *Ibid.*, 2: "der politische Meinungsstreit verstummte, alte Gegner fingen an, sich zu verstehen und zu achten, der Geist treuer Gemeinschaft erfüllte alle Volksgenossen." "Staat und Gemeinden, Landwirtschaft, Gewerbefleiss und Handel, Wissenschaft und Technik wetteiferten, die Kriegsnöte zu lindern."

this unity in his mines, and is drawn into his war with Gudrun in an attempt to enforce it within himself.

Birkin is also implicated in this situation. His love for Gerald belongs to the idealism of the First World War, as in his reminiscence of when Gerald had expressed love for him:

> If he had kept true to that clasp, death would not have mattered. Those who die, and dying still can love, still believe, do not die. They live still in the beloved. Gerald might still have been living in the spirit with Birkin, even after death. He might have lived with his friend, a further life. (*WL*, 480)

Birkin still believes in a Brüderschaft despite its denial of a material reality of conflict between individuals, and of death. As Kaiser Wilhelm notes, people from different classes united for the sake of their "Brüder im Felde" ("brothers in the field").[67] Despite being repelled by Gerald's frozen "carcass", Birkin feels as if he "were freezing too, freezing from the inside ... [his] heart began to freeze, his blood was turning to ice-water" (*WL*, 477). The repetition of "freezing" expresses Birkin's compulsion towards the white purity of Gerald, made literal in his frozen state.

Birkin's need for this Brüderschaft with Gerald, an "eternal union with a man" (*WL*, 481), lies at the heart of an unanswered dilemma in *Women in Love*. He needs Gerald as a footing in the economic and social world to counter the romantic escapism of his relationship with Ursula. We have seen how Birkin's "consummation" with Ursula failed as a viable alternative to social relations based on competition and violence. Birkin longs for Gerald to make him powerful in this world, but Gerald can only draw him back into its death processes, since their relationship is based on an idealism that denies its conflicts.

Lawrence does not envisage an alternative to Gerald and Birkin's relationship, but the "purely destructive" achievement of *Women in Love* exposes the limitations of the "worlds" that it creates. It is not "a barren tragedy, barren, barren", as Gudrun believes, but contains the seed of Lawrence's child who can take a conscious responsibility for

---

[67] *Ibid.*, 2.

his unconscious impulses. Perhaps though, as Birkin insists to Ursula, this child will only grow "after us, not out of us" (*WL*, 476, 173).

VI
REWRITING *WILHELM MEISTERS LEHRJAHRE* IN *THE LOST GIRL*

Since its publication in 1920, *The Lost Girl* has been evaluated – positively and negatively – within the parameters of Realism.[1] F. R. Leavis judged parts of it as superior to Dickens and Bennett, but found "no compelling total significance in control"[2] in its structure. John Worthen reads it as an attempted "'popular' novel", whose low sales were due to its unconvincing characters and plot developments.[3] George Hyde, though, has shifted the debate on the failings of *The Lost Girl* as a Realist novel by showing how Lawrence subverts the Realist genre. Hyde argues that the novel's structural dislocations and unstable narrative voice deliberately upset the construction of reality, as practised by Bennett in *Anna of Five Towns*.[4]

In *The Lost Girl* the interaction between Woodhouse's bourgeois society and the counter-culture of the foreign performing troupe reproduces a popular trope in the Realist novel. Lawrence had read Dickens' *Hard Times* (1854) which places the utilitarianism of Thomas Gradgrind against a circus community, and George Moore's *A Mummer's Wife* (1885) in which the heroine abandons her family drapery business to marry an actor and join his troupe.[5] One of the earliest, and most seminal, examples of this trope is in Goethe's *Wilhelm Meisters Lehrjahre*, where the hero joins, then abandons, a group of performers.

Social debates on the *Wilhelm Meister* novels
Goethe's *Wilhelm Meister* novels, like his *Faust*, express the development of his politics and art over most of his career. Throughout these novels Goethe attempted to mediate between the

---

[1] See R. P. Draper, *D. H. Lawrence: The Critical Heritage* (London: Routledge and Kegan Paul, 1970), 146-54.
[2] Leavis, *D. H. Lawrence: Novelist*, 34.
[3] See Worthen, *D. H. Lawrence and the Idea of the Novel*, 105-17.
[4] See Hyde, *D. H. Lawrence*, 76-87.
[5] See Christopher Heywood, "D. H. Lawrence's *The Lost Girl* and its Antecedents by George Moore and Arnold Bennett", in *D. H. Lawrence: Critical Assessments*, eds David Ellis and Ornella de Zordo, 4 vols (Mountfield: Helm Information, 1992), II, 402-404.

individual's *Bildung* ("formation") of his all-round potentialities, and his social duty to specialize in work. Goethe began composing *Wilhelm Meisters theatralische Sendung*, his first draft of the *Lehrjahre*, in 1776. Through Wilhelm's collaboration with a lower-class troupe of performers, Goethe imagined a cultural role for the middle class in Germany. In 1786 Goethe left Wilhelm as the reluctant leading actor of the troupe, to symbolize the collaboration of the middle and working classes as the cultural power in Germany. Goethe began the novel again in 1794 while consciously pledging loyalty to the Weimar monarchy in opposition to the Terror in France. Reflecting Goethe's rejection of the French Revolution, Wilhelm abandons the performing troupe for the aristocratic *Turmgesellschaft* ("Society of the Tower"). Wilhelm's *Bildung*, in which he develops his qualities in relation to others, is forced into *Entsagung* ("renunciation"). Nicholas Boyle defines the *Entsagung* of the subject's liberty before traditional authority as Goethe's precondition for the individual to belong to society. Through *Entsagung* Goethe rejected the Girondin *Declaration* during the French Revolution of the individual's political autonomy before the state.[6] Between 1821 and 1829 Goethe composed *Wilhelm Meisters Wanderjahre*, subtitled *Die Entsagenden*. Here Wilhelm renounces his freedom from bourgeois life by dedicating himself to the profession of surgery.

The *Wilhelm Meister* novels are crucial in the development of the Realist novel, and of bourgeois culture in Germany. According to Georg Lukàcs, the *Lehrjahre* reveals the contradiction of the humanistic ideal of individual fulfilment in the economic alienation of bourgeois society, which is central to the Realist genre.[7] Alfred Weber, who researched the standard of life for workers under the demands of large scale industry, identified Wilhelm and the troupe with the liberal ideal of the individual's all-round self-realization through creativity. He believed that the Girondin ideal rejected by Goethe was still possible in Germany's industrial society. In his work with his brother, Max Weber concentrated on how to optimize worker productivity for the power of the Reich.[8] As we saw in the previous

---

[6] See Nicholas Boyle, *Goethe: The Poet and the Age* (Oxford: Oxford University Press, 2000), II, 324-26.
[7] *Ibid.*, 56, 62.
[8] See Mommsen and Osterhammel, *Max Weber and His Contemporaries*, 90-92, 95.

chapter, in *Die protestantische Ethik und der Geist des Kapitalismus* Max Weber valued Wilhelm's choice of specialized profession in the *Wanderjahre*, like the *Entsagung* of Faust's creative potentialities in the final scene of the play.[9]

In *Mr Noon*, written immediately after *The Lost Girl*, Gilbert Noon argues about Goethe with Alfred Weber as "Professor Sartorius". It is probable that Lawrence was aware of the political questions at stake for the German middle class in the *Wilhelm Meister* novels. In *Studies in Classic American Literature*, begun in 1917, Lawrence examined the contrasting worlds of American civilization and the character of Natty Bumppo in James Fenimore Cooper's Leatherstocking novels. Lawrence's analysis seems to borrow from German philosophical terms, of the social "Ideal" of love and democracy, which he connects to Cooper's Protestant ethic of "MY WORK". The *Studies* even echo Max Weber's analysis of the Protestant ethic in the case of Benjamin Franklin's philosophy of double bookkeeping; Lawrence introduces his analysis of American capitalism with Franklin, whose God is "The heavenly storekeeper", and whose notion of freedom is work (*Studies*, 52-53, 21, 29).

Although Lawrence diagnosed many harmful ideals in modern society, in Goethe he found an ideal of social conformity. In the essays "Education of the People", written immediately after the First World War, he criticizes modern society's "production of social units: dangerless beings, ideal creatures", and its exclusion of the "individual" who is "a menace to society". In particular, he sees the oppression of social duty over individual freedom in the soldiers who served their country in the war: "The whole world screams *Ich Dien*. Heaven knows *what* it serves!" (*RDP*, 114, 88). *Dienst* ("duty") had been a central concept of Max Weber's Protestant ethic, which he had identified in Goethe.

In a letter from 30 October 1919 Lawrence describes reading Thomas De Quincey's *Works*: "I can go on reading and reading him. I laughed over 'Goethe' yesterday. I like him [*sic*] De Quincey because he also dislikes such people as Plato and Goethe, whom I dislike" (Letters, III, 407). In his two essays on Goethe, De Quincey concentrated on *Wilhelm Meisters Lehrjahre*, criticizing its moral

---

[9] See Weber, *Gesammelte Aufsätze zur Religionssoziologie*, I, 203.

laxity: "'Wilhelm Meister' is at open war, not with decorum and good taste merely, but with moral purity and the dignity of human nature."[10] Despite readers from Thomas Carlyle to Max Weber voicing the same opinion,[11] Lawrence admired De Quincey's irreverence in contrast to the Victorians' deference for Goethe. Lawrence was opposed to Goethe as an upholder of "moral purity" in bourgeois society, just as he would criticize the "purity and high-mindedness" (*LG*, 36) of Woodhouse in *The Lost Girl*.

It is possible that Lawrence was aware of Goethe's first ending in *Wilhelm Meisters theatralische Sendung*. In *Mr Noon* he describes Alfred Weber and Else Jaffe's characters arguing over the ownership of the *Urfaust* manuscript which had been found in 1887; this controversy of ownership was more intense in the case of the *Theatralische Sendung*, which was only discovered in 1910. In *The Lost Girl* Lawrence emulates the ending of the *Theatralische Sendung* through Alvina's marriage to a member of the theatrical troupe, Ciccio. Unlike Alfred Weber, though, Lawrence does not believe that Alvina can pursue her *Bildung* in industrial society. Lawrence shares Max Weber's social pessimism, but not his advocacy of *Entsagung*.

In *The Lost Girl* Lawrence counters Goethe with a Romantic style that bears comparison to Novalis. Lawrence echoes Novalis' retort against the *Lehrjahre* in *Heinrich von Ofterdingen*, which foregrounds the subjectivity of characters and their ability to create their own reality. Partly inspired by Nietzsche and Freud, Lawrence's Romanticism is manifested in Alvina's anti-social, sexual energies which power her *Bildung* beyond her social constrictions. Yet Lawrence is conscious of the limitations of Romanticism as a counter to Realism; in *Sea and Sardinia*, written immediately after *The Lost Girl*, he derides the "romantic-classic" elements of *Wilhelm Meister*, from which Novalis had developed his vision. In *The Lost Girl* Lawrence plays with the Realist genre alongside his Romanticism to overcome the inadequacy of both in isolation from each other, and to point towards the political vision of his late novels.

---

[10] Thomas De Quincey, 15 vols (Edinburgh: Adam and Charles Black, 1862-71), XV, 173.
[11] See C. F. Harrold, *Carlyle and German Thought* (New Haven: Yale University Press, 1978), 46; Arthur Mitzman, *The Iron Cage: An Historical Interpretation of Max Weber* (New York: Alfred A. Knopf, 1970), 55.

Wilhelm's performing troupe and the Natcha-Kee-Tawaras

The Lost Girl, then, shares the dilemma of the *Wilhelm Meister* novels, and of the Realist genre, between individual fulfilment and its *Entsagung* for social duty. From childhood Wilhelm Meister lives in his imagination with his stage set, and in adulthood he envisages the theatre as an alternative to bourgeois life. In the *Lehrjahre* he argues with his friend Werner, who tends "to consider his businesses as elevating the soul", [12] in accordance with the Protestant ethic. Similarly, *The Lost Girl* focuses on Alvina Houghton's life-struggle to avoid becoming one of Woodhouse's "old maids", "the famous sexless Workers of our ant-industrial society". Lawrence satirizes Werner's position in his treatment of Alvina's father, James Houghton, through such enterprises as an exclusive hotel for a non-existent upper-class clientele: "So he soared to serene heights, and his Private Hotel seemed a celestial injunction, an erection on a higher plane" (*LG*, 2, 56). James gradually wastes away in his pursuit of a reified wealth, like Werner who has become "a hard-working hypochondriac"[13] by the end of the *Lehrjahre*.

Wilhelm and Alvina join lower-class performers to become "déclassés". Wilhelm declares to his troupe that "We have nothing but ourselves".[14] Neither troupe performs high drama: Wilhelm's includes acrobats, jugglers and tightrope walkers; Alvina's "Natcha-Kee-Tawaras" yodel and impersonate Red Indians. Wilhelm's troupe and Alvina's Tawaras proclaim themselves as independent nations. In the *Lehrjahre* the performers agree to follow a democratically elected director who is assisted by a senate, like the American Constitution. On joining the Natcha-Kee-Tawaras, Alvina recites "the strict rules of the tribe":

> We are one tribe, one nation, …
> No nation do we know but the nation of the Hirondelles…

The Tawaras convert the proceedings into a carnival by repeating the laws in a "ragged chant of strong male voices, resonant and gay with

---

[12] Goethe, *Gedenkausgabe*, VII, 41: "an seine Geschäfte mit Erhebung der Seele zu denken."
[13] *Ibid.*, 536: "ein arbeitsamer Hypochondrist."
[14] *Ibid.*, 227: "Wir haben nichts als uns selbst."

mockery", and concluding with a tarantella. George Hyde observes how the multilingualism and theatricality of the Tawaras are subversive in an anxiously xenophobic England on the brink of a European war. After the proceedings Madame Rochard, alias Kishwégin, alludes to the dangers of the troupe's playfulness: "And now, children, unless the Sheffield policemen will knock at our door, we must retire to our wigwams all – " (*LG*, 199, 83, 201).

Unlike Lawrence, Goethe mocks Wilhelm's "Republik": "The time passed by unnoticed during this play, and because they had spent it so pleasantly, they really believed that something useful had been done, and that through this new form [of government] new prospects for the national stage had been opened up."[15] Goethe inserted this sentence into the *Lehrjahre*; in the *Theatralische Sendung* the moral character of the performers is treated more ambiguously. When the *Republik* is devastated by soldiers, the performers exile Wilhelm as their failed leader, and refuse to take any responsibility upon themselves. This event precipitates Wilhelm's rejection of them in the *Lehrjahre*, but in the *Theatralische Sendung* he questions his own behaviour and joins them in his project to establish a *väterlandische Bühne* in capitalist Germany.

When the Tawaras are spied on by detectives on suspicion of being "immoral foreigners" Alvina begins to feel excluded from them, and the historical events of the First World War scatter them across Europe. Lawrence resists the closure of the *Lehrjahre* where Wilhelm rejects the performers for middle-class society. But neither can he emulate the ongoing *Bildung* of the "Theatralische Sendung". In his venture into the theatre James Houghton embodies Goethe's idealistic marriage of the performers with middle class values. Miss Pinnegar argues that show business is "all against his better nature", but Alvina answers that "father was a showman even in the shop" (*LG*, 245, 170). Although Alvina supports James' venture, and follows him, it eventually destroys him; as members of the middle class, neither of them can adapt themselves to the Tawaras' lifestyle. Alvina can only commit herself to them through her sexuality in her relationship with Ciccio.

---

[15] *Ibid.*, 231: "Die Zeit ging unvermerkt unter diesem Spiele vorüber, und weil man sie angenehm zubrachte, glaubte man auch wirklich etwas Nützliches getan und durch die neue Form eine neue Aussicht für die vaterländische Bühne eröffnet zu haben."

Consequently, Alvina's rejection of the Tawaras for a career in medicine has a different significance from Wilhelm's parallel choice in the *Wanderjahre*. Jarno, who had advised Wilhelm to abandon Mignon and the troupe in the *Lehrjahre*, attempts to reconcile a *vielseitige Bildung* ("many-sided education") with the need for *Einsigkeiten* ("specialization"): "in the thing that one does well, one sees the metaphor of everything that is done well."[16] He recommends the profession of surgery to Wilhelm, through which he can be reconciled to the processes of nature: "through competent treatment, nature is easily restored".[17]

"Speaking at random" (*LG*, 28), Alvina declares that she will become a maternity nurse: unlike Wilhelm, she only wants to avoid the *Entsagung* of an "old maid". As David Lodge observes, her random choice exposes the arbitrariness of a specialized vocation in an alienated society,[18] instead of the meaningfulness that Wilhelm tries to discover in it. Later, when she tells her superior, Doctor Mitchell, "you have lived for your work", he corrects her: "I have lived for others, for my patients." But we see that he has only worked to acquire power over others; he regresses into "a hysterical little boy under the great, authoritative man" (*LG*, 261, 271) on her rejection of his marriage proposal. In Alvina's rejection of Dr. Mitchell and of her own career as a nurse, Lawrence dismisses the significance of Wilhelm's medical profession in the *Wanderjahre*.

The Lost Girl shares the narrative intrusions and shifting perspectives of the *Theatralische Sendung*, unlike the omniscient narrator of the *Lehrjahre*. Both Hyde and Lodge ascribe these qualities to a "crisis of subject" which opens up a "carnivalesque" range of values.[19] Narrative intrusions in the *Theatralische Sendung*, such as "glaub' ich" ("I believe")[20] and its apologies to "unsere Leser" ("our reader"), encourage our awareness of the construction of reality in the novel. Goethe's narrator swings between mocking Wilhelm, and identifying with him; Boyle observes that these "uneasy

---

[16] Goethe, *Gedenkausgabe*, VIII, 43: "in dem einen, was er recht tut, sieht er das Gleichnis von allem, was recht getan wird."
[17] *Ibid.*, 305. "durch einsichtige Behandlung stelle sich die Natur leicht wieder her."
[18] See David Lodge, *After Bakhtin* (London: Routledge, 1990), 74.
[19] Hyde, *D. H. Lawrence*, 81; see Lodge, *After Bakhtin*, 73-74.
[20] Goethe, *Gedenkausgabe*, VIII, 546, 808.

moments" betray "an increasing awareness on Goethe's part that there is no logic to his story", or to his use of Realism.[21] In the *Lehrjahre* Goethe overcame this problem by means of a measured, transparent prose which objectifies Wilhelm in relation to his circumstances.[22] As in the *Theatralische Sendung*, Lawrence breaks the illusion of reality in the narrator's comments to the reader, which anticipate the hectoring against the "gentle reader" in *Mr Noon* and *Aaron's Rod*. Through these gestures in *The Lost Girl* Lawrence defers his solution to Goethe's dilemma between *Bildung* and *Entsagung*.

Alvina and Heinrich von Ofterdingen

Lawrence attempts to counter Goethe's objective discourse, and the bourgeois conventions of post-war England, by articulating Alvina's subjectivity. Through her subjectivity she is able to create her own reality and *Bildung*. Placed against the tradition of *Bildungsromane* in German literature which have attempted to rewrite the *Lehrjahre*, *The Lost Girl* resembles most closely *Heinrich von Ofterdingen* by Novalis. Their affinity partly derives from Lawrence's earlier debt to Novalis in *The Rainbow,* which emulated the images of darkness in *Hymnen an die Nacht* as an alternative to Goethe's light imagery in *Faust*.

In what he described as his "Übergangs Jahre" ("transition years"), *Heinrich von Ofterdingen*, Novalis attempted to envisage an alternative to the ending of the *Lehrjahre*. He explained to Ludwig Tieck in 1800: "I see so clearly the great art, with which poetry in Meister is destroyed through itself – and while poetry is wrecked in the background, economy does well, secure on firm ground with its friends."[23] In *Heinrich von Ofterdingen*, left incomplete at his death in 1800, Novalis defined the break between Romanticism and the classicism of Goethe and Schiller. The novel reverses Goethe's revisions of the *Theatralische Sendung*, as Lawrence does in *The Lost*

---

[21] Nicholas Boyle, *Goethe: The Poet and the Age* (Oxford: Oxford University Press, 1991), I, 370.
[22] See Hans Reiss, *Goethe's Novels* (London: Macmillan, 1969), 93.
[23] Novalis, *Schriften*, IV, 281, 323. "ich sehe so deutlich die große Kunst, mit der die Poësie durch sich selbst im Meister vernichtet wird – und während sie im Hintergrund scheitert, die Oeconomie sicher auf festen Grund und Boden mit ihren Freunden sich gütlich thut."

Girl. One of the most visionary episodes of Novalis' novel, set in a mine, is comparable to Alvina's experience in her father's mine. The comparison with Novalis points to how Lawrence rejects the Realist tradition in his response to Goethe's *Lehrjahre*, to organize his novel around the characters' perceptions of reality.

Hyde shows how Lawrence transforms Bennett's objective description of a mine in *Anna of the Five Towns* "into a drama of consciousness" experienced by Alvina.[24] Both Lawrence and Novalis associate the mines with terror and desire: Alvina is "frightened, but fascinated" by "the crannied, underworld darkness"; Heinrich enters the "schauerlichen Tiefen" ("appalling depths"), and "dunkeln, wunderbaren Kammern" ("dark, wonderful chambers").[25] These impressions reach beyond material reality: Alvina senses "something forever unknowable and inadmissible, something that belonged purely to the underground"; Novalis' miner also experiences a "complete satisfaction of an innate wish ... a closer relation to our mysterious existence".[26] "Melting out ... her mind dissolved", Alvina feels "as if she were in her tomb forever, like the dead and everlasting Egyptians" (*LG*, 47). The mine is also a timeless space for Heinrich: "like long years, lay the mere past hours behind him, and he believed that he had never thought or felt otherwise."[27]

In the Realism of the *Lehrjahre*, the narrative voice consistently objectifies Wilhelm with a detached irony generated by the incongruity between his expectations and the events he experiences. John Neubauer contrasts Goethe's omniscient narrator with Novalis' who identifies with the protagonist's perception of reality.[28] According to Paul Böckmann, Novalis portrays encounters between characters' consciousnesses, instead of Goethe's encounters between characters and their circumstances. Novalis foregrounds the

---

[24] Hyde, *D. H. Lawrence*, 84.
[25] Novalis, *Schriften*, I, 246, 241.
[26] *Ibid.*, 242: "volle Befriedigung eines angebornen Wunsches ... ein näheres Verhältniß zu unserm geheimen Daseyn."
[27] *Ibid.*, 263: "Wie lange Jahre lagen die eben vergangenen Stunden hinter ihm, und er glaubte nie anders gedacht und empfunden zu haben."
[28] See John Neubauer, *Novalis* (Boston: Twayne Publishers, 1980), 135.

characters' subjectivity to reveal their construction of reality, "as an exploration of self-awareness and its relation to the world".[29]

Heinrich and Alvina imagine a subjective, alternative world in order to reappraise material reality. Novalis describes how the miner "climbs with renewed joy in life out of the dark tombs every day. Only he knows the charms of light and rest, the benevolence of free air and the panorama around".[30] Alvina has a comparable revelation on leaving the mines: "strange beautiful elevations of houses and trees, and depressions of fields and roads, all golden and floating like atmospheric majolica. Never had the common ugliness of Woodhouse seemed so entrancing." Yet while her perspective coincides with the narrator's, Alvina confirms the material conditions of industrial society: "truly nothing could be more hideous than Woodhouse, as the miners had built it and disposed it" (*LG*, 47-48).

In his sustained Realism Lawrence diverges from Novalis. Like Lawrence, Novalis is repulsed by everyday life; his mine is "far from the restless tumult of the day".[31] Yet Novalis' mine provides the precious metals and jewels to dedicate to God; in his mine one can religiously transcend the material world to be ultimately reconciled to its hardships. Instead of gold, Lawrence's mine only contains the "yellow-flecked coal" whose pollution exacerbates the "conventional ugliness" of Woodhouse. In his essay "Die Christenheit oder Europa" of 1799, Novalis had called for a medieval Catholicism to overcome the individual's alienation in capitalist society. In *The Lost Girl* Lawrence rejects Christianity for eroticism. Alvina's sexuality does not enable her to transcend or be reconciled to her material life, but drives her to rebel against it.

The images of "dark, fluid presences in the thick atmosphere", "the draughts of the darkness", "the bubbling-up of the under-darkness" (*LG*, 47-48), simultaneously belong to Lawrence's Romantic inheritance, and to Alvina's subjectivity. Yet Roger Fowler

---

[29] See Paul Böckmann, "Der Roman der Transzendentalpoesie in der Romantik", in *Geschichte, Deutung, Kritik*, eds Maria Bindschedler and Paul Zinsli (Berlin: Francke Verlag, 1969), 179: "als eine Erforschung des Ich-Bewußtseins und seines Weltverhältnisses." See also 165.

[30] Novalis, *Schriften*, I, 292: "steigt jeden Tag mit verjüngter Lebensfreude aus den dunkeln Grüften seines Berufs. Nur Er kennt die Reize des Lichts und der Ruhe, die Wohlthätigkeit der freyen Luft und Aussicht um sich her."

[31] *Ibid.*, 245: "entfernt von dem unruhigen Tumult des Tages."

argues that "Alvina's consciousness is subordinated to authorial ideology" in this scene, since the language is not particular to her, but echoes Gudrun's fantasies about miners in *Women in Love*. Fowler describes this language as "Lawrencian":

> A reader is unlikely to experience it as just one voice among others in a polyvocal text. It is the dominant, already charged with authorial values which obstruct the individualization of Alvina.[32]

According to Fowler, the Lawrentian discourse is monological, and imposes itself upon the characters instead of describing them.

Fowler's diagnosis of Lawrence has been applied by German critics to Novalis. Novalis initially interpreted all of the characters of the *Lehrjahre* as "the same individual in variations. Natalie – the beautiful soul", and later expanded this connection between two characters to all of them.[33] Gerhard Schulz characterizes Novalis' idea that "all people are variations of a complete individual"[34] as a rejection of Goethe's individualized characters; Novalis creates an ideal reality in which "The personal reality is only an expression of part of an ideal personality".[35] Schulz implies that each individual is part of Novalis' religious ideal or, to use Fowler's words, "authorial ideology".

Yet Lawrence's technique of characterization in *The Lost Girl* cannot be dismissed as the expression of authorial ideology. As I have argued throughout my thesis, the Lawrenctian discourse is eclectic, combining a diversity of cultural traditions and ideologies. The miners speak in a Romantically "dark, fluid viscous voice", yet Lawrence quotes the Midlands dialect of their speech. Lawrence's Romanticism is unstable in its diversity; it shares the miners' "force of darkness which had no master and no control", and which will "cause the superimposed day-order to fall" (*LG*, 47-48).

---

[32] Roger Fowler, "*The Lost Girl*: Discourse and Focalization", in *D. H. Lawrence: Critical Assessments*, II, 442-44.
[33] Novalis, *Schriften*, II, 561: "Desselbe Individuum in Variationen. Natalie – die schöne Seele." Cf. *Schriften*, III, 312.
[34] *Ibid.*, 564: "Alle Menschen sind Variationen Eines vollständigen Individuums."
[35] Gerhard Schulz, "Die Poetik des Romans bei Novalis", in *Deutsche Romantheorien*, ed. Reinhold Grimm (Frankfurt am Main: Athenäum Verlag, 1968), 92: "Die personelle Wirklichkeit ist nur Teilausdruck einer idealen Persönlichkeit."

Alvina's subjectivity is not part of a religious ideal that unifies the novel, but is fuelled by her sexuality. The concreteness of her physical drives sustains her against the social conventions that unify the Realism of the novel. While Novalis' miner worships the crucifix underground, Alvina has come to a realization:

> The puerile world went on crying out for a new Jesus, another Saviour from the sky, another heavenly superman. When what was wanted was a Dark Master from the underworld. (*LG*, 48)

This passage introduces the reader to Nietzsche and Freud, whose ideas inspire Lawrence to overcome the limits of Romanticism and Realism by juxtaposing them in an unstable and potentially revolutionary way. Lawrence rejects the idealism of Nietzsche's "heavenly superman" for an *Übermensch* whose *Wille* is directed towards a Freudian notion of the libido, not power.

As a Romantic who uses the modern ideas of Nietzsche and Freud, Lawrence reaches beyond the idealism of Novalis as an alternative to Goethe. In Zuleima, a vagrant Middle-Eastern princess, Novalis attempted to recreate Mignon, Goethe's personification of a pre-Romantic escapism in the *Wilhelm Meister* novels. In *The Lost Girl* Lawrence creates his own Mignon in the Italian Ciccio, whom Alvina falls in love with. In Ciccio Lawrence uses his Romanticism, alongside Nietzsche and Freud, to overcome the limitations of Goethe's Mignon as a symbol of political freedom.

Ciccio and Mignon

In *Sea and Sardinia* Lawrence compares the island's landscape to the mainland: "Italian landscape is really eighteenth-century landscape, to be represented in that romantic-classic manner which makes everything rather marvellous and very topical: aqueducts, and ruins upon sugar-loaf mountains, and craggy ravines and Wilhelm Meister water-falls: all up and down" (*SS*, 72). In this passage Lawrence is alluding to "Mignons Lied" in Goethe's novel: "Es stürzt der Fels und über ihn die Flut" (The rock plunges, and over it the tide").[36] After singing, Mignon asks Wilhelm if he knows this land, which he presumes is Italy. She pleads with him to take her to Italy, but when

---

[36] Goethe, *Gedenkausgabe*, VII, 155.

he asks if she has been there, she is silent. This ambiguity reflects how Goethe wrote the nostalgic "Mignons Lied" before he had travelled to Italy; he imagined the country as a place where all of Wilhelm's problems in native Germany could be left behind. Goethe's objective prose in the *Lehrjahre* is only interrupted by these passages of lyrical poetry from Mignon, and her secret father the harpist, whose unrestrained subjectivity expresses longing for an alternative world. They personify Wilhelm's utopian quest in the *Theatralische Sendung*, which he abandons in the *Lehrjahre*.

Lukàcs describes these characters as "the highest poetic personifications of Romanticism", but as hopeless against the "prose of capitalism" in the novel. He dismisses Novalis' attempt to realize the triumph of Mignon's Romantic spirit in *Heinrich von Ofterdingen* as mere escapism from a capitalist reality.[37] Lawrence was fascinated by "Mignons Lied", quoting its first line in his reminiscences of Italy during the autumn of 1914 at Chesham: "Kennst du das Land, wo die Citronen blühen? Yes, so do I. But now I hear the rain-water trickling animatedly into the green and rotten water-butt" (Letters, II, 217). He too was aware of its escapism, in this case from the weather in England.

At the close of *Twilight in Italy* Lawrence quotes this line again in his description of crossing the St Gotthard Pass to Italian speaking Switzerland in 1913: "so sunny, with feathery trees and deep black shadows. It reminded me of Goethe, of the Romantic period: 'Kennst du das Land, wo die Citronen blühen?'" (*TI*, 221). His tone is nostalgic, evoking Lake Garda as described in "The Lemon Gardens". In this essay he observed that "the Lago di Garda cannot afford to grow its lemons much longer" because they are produced more cheaply in Sicily. The owner of the lemon gardens longs for the material wealth of the north; Lawrence reluctantly concurs with him, that "it is better to go forward into error than to stay fixed inextricably in the past" (*LG*, 130, 132). Lawrence is conscious of how Mignon's Romanticism fails to correspond to the reality of Italy, where the lemon gardens are abandoned because of their lack of profit.

In *The Lost Girl* Ciccio is Lawrence's Mignon, the Italian who lures Alvina away from the social alienation of the north. During her

---

[37] Lukàcs, *Goethe and His Age*, 58-59.

engagement to Dr Mitchell, Ciccio calls to her, "Yes, come with me, Allaye. You come with me to Italy", echoing Mignon's call to Wilhelm:

> Dahin! Dahin
> Geht unser Weg; Gebieter, laß uns ziehn![38]

> There! There
> Go our way; master, let us go!

In the *Lehrjahre* Goethe only includes "Mignons Lied" in Wilhelm's inadequate translation in German: "The childlike innocence of the expression disappeared where the broken speech was smoothed over and disjointed parts held together."[39] Mignon's song exists outside the German language, and in her silence she exists outside German conventions and laws. Ciccio also lacks speech:

> For him, it was not quite natural to express himself in speech. Gesture and grimace were instantaneous, and spoke worlds of things, if you would but accept them. (*LG*, 138)

Alvina is fascinated by his physical presence, as Wilhelm is by Mignon: "This form impressed Wilhelm very deeply; he kept on looking at her, silenced and oblivious of the present in his contemplation."[40]

Ciccio shares Mignon's Romantic mystery, but also has a tactile immediacy that she lacks. Accompanied by her zither, Mignon's voice is "geheimnisvoll und bedächtig" ("mysterious and measured"), and then expresses an "unwiderstehliche Sehnsucht" ("irresistible longing").[41] With his mandolin, Ciccio plays to Alvina Neapolitan songs "in a soft, yearning voice" like Mignon's, then "a clamorous, animal sort of yearning" accompanied by a "slightly distorted look of overwhelming yearning, yearning heavy and unbearable" (*LG*, 277,

---

[38] Goethe, *Gedenkausgabe*, VII, 155.
[39] *Ibid.*, 156: "Die kindliche Unschuld des Ausdrucks verschwand, indem die gebrochene Sprache übereinstimmend, und das Unzusammenhängende verbunden ward."
[40] *Ibid.*, 105: "Diese Gestalt prägte sich Wilhelmen sehr tief ein; er sah sie noch immer an, schwieg und vergaß der Gegenwärtigen über seinen Betrachtungen."
[41] *Ibid.*, 156.

281). Unlike Mignon's song, whose original version in Italian exists outside Goethe's text, Lawrence quotes Ciccio's Neapolitan songs in their original form; the unfamiliar sounds of the language are Romantically evocative and historically authentic at the same time. Ciccio's nostalgia for his homeland, shared by Mignon, is countered by bitter memories of its poverty which drove him to England.

The social reality of Italy is imprinted on Ciccio's physical presence, whereas the image of Mignon is incompatible with Goethe's direct experience of Italy. Immediately after abandoning *Wilhelm Meisters Theatralische Sendung*, Goethe fled from his onerous duties for the Weimar Court to Italy in 1786. Like Lawrence, after crossing the Alps he found "interest in life again": "the sun is bright and hot, and one can believe again in a God." He admired the Italians for their political system: "the people feel that they always come first". Yet he criticized their lack of "inner need", for instance in their neglect of Palladio's architecture in Vicenza.[42] Lawrence's famous letter on the Italians' "belief in the blood" ("I want that liberty, I want that woman, I want that pound of peaches" (Letters, I, 503-504), is anticipated by Goethe, but with crucial reservations:

> I don't know what else to say about the nation, except that they are children of nature who, under the magnificence and dignity of religion and the arts, are not a hair different from how they would be in caves and forests. What all foreigners notice, and what today makes the whole city talk, but only talk, are the murders that commonly occur.[43]

Goethe's interest in the historical Italy became centred on its classical aesthetic, whose order would be crucial to all of his later works, including the *Lehrjahre*.[44] In the *Lehrjahre* Mignon wastes away from the cold of the north, until her heart stops during

---

[42] Goethe, *Gedenkausgabe*, XI, 27, 28, 54, 57: "wieder Interesse an der Welt"; "die Sonne scheint heiß, und man glaubt wieder einmal an einen Gott."; "Das Volk fühlt sich immer vor"; "inneres Bedürfnis."
[43] *Ibid.*, 156: "Von der Nation wüßte ich nichts weiter zu sagen, als daß es Naturmenschen sind, die unter Pracht und Würde der Religion und der Künste nicht ein Haar anders sind, als sie in Höhlen und Wäldern auch sein würden. Was allen Fremden auffällt und was heute wieder die ganze Stadt reden, aber auch nur reden macht, sind die Totschläge, die gewöhnlich vorkommen."
[44] See Boyle, *Goethe: The Poet and the Age*, I, 652-53.

Wilhelm's betrothal to the practical, matronly Therese. By prosaically locating the details of her origins in Milan, Goethe also used Realism to weaken Mignon's Romantic power, which had evoked the mythical paradise of Italy.[45]

Lawrence attempts to sustain Ciccio's Romantic mystery alongside a physical and historical reality that can empower him to provide a practical alternative in Italy to Woodhouse. He foregrounds Ciccio's violence as "powerful, mysterious, horrible in the pitch dark" (*LG*, 202). Goethe accentuated Mignon's enigmatic quality by leaving her gender ambiguous; from referring to her in the neutral case as "das Kind" ("the child"), he oscillates between personal pronouns "es" ("it") and "sie" ("she"), and between possessive pronouns "sein" ("his" / "its") and "ihr" ("her").[46] Lawrence evokes a Romantic delicacy in Ciccio, like Goethe created in Mignon, by describing his "rather small and effeminately-shod feet", and clasp which is "almost like a child's touch". Lawrence plays with these incongruities, for instance where Alvina perceives in Ciccio's eyes "something fathomless, deepening black and abysmal, but somehow sweet to her" (*LG*, 137, 127, 211).

Bildung as the unconscious and will

Lawrence is attempting to retain a Romantic alternative in the modern world. In accordance with his development since *Sons and Lovers*, he uses Freudian and Nietzschean ideas to give his Romanticism a physical vitality, and to define his notion of *Bildung*. In this period, after *Women in Love* and the First World War, Lawrence was attempting to formulate his notion of the unconscious by opposing it to the ideal. We have already seen forms of idealism in Lawrence, from Ursula's vision of the rainbow to Gerald and Gudrun's repressed personalities. His research into idealism became focused on the relation between unconscious and will. Immediately before *The Lost Girl* Lawrence wrote *Psychoanalysis and the Unconscious* which attempts to clarify his distinction between different levels of the unconsciousness, and their relation to the will. He interprets the Freudian unconscious as the repressed "human consciousness which ... recoils back into the affective regions and acts there as a secret

---

[45] *Ibid.*, II, 387.
[46] Goethe, *Gedenkausgabe*, VII, 105.

agent, unconfessed, unadmitted, potent, and usually destructive" (*PUFU*, 13) upon the body. Alvina's mother suffers from a "nervous heart-disease" (*LG*, 4) in her frustrating marriage, and Alvina is threatened by these symptoms at the prospect of becoming an "old maid". Lawrence shows how these women must renounce their *Bildung* as rounded human beings, including their physical desires, to fit into bourgeois society.

In *Psychoanalysis and the Unconscious* Lawrence identifies an idealism within the Freudian unconscious, which is "the motivizing of the great affective sources by means of ideas mentally derived". Lawrence identifies this idealism with the materialism of industrialized capitalism: "Ideal and material are identical. The ideal is but the god in the machine – the little, fixed, machine-principle which works the human psyche automatically" (*PUFU*, 14).

His insight into idealism and materialism as products of the same historical conditions prepares his case against Goethe's ending to the *Lehrjahre*. After Wilhelm renounces his acting career, the style of the novel changes from a series of adventures to dialogues in which he decides his purpose in life with the members of the *Turmgesellschaft*. These dialogues form what Boyle describes as "the realm of reason and the meaning-bestowing moral ideal"[47] upon Wilhelm's former rebelliousness. They function in an analogous way to how Lawrence regarded the Freudian unconscious of ideas as intervening in the release of the body's desires. Despite Wilhelm's impatient request to the *Turmgesellschaft*, "do not read to me from these wonderful words anymore",[48] it guides him towards Nathalie, who believes "it is better to err through rules, than to err when the capriciousness of our nature drives us to and fro".[49] Goethe rationalizes Wilhelm's previous adventures when the Society reveals that it had arranged them as part of Wilhelm's "apprenticeship" to adulthood. Meanwhile, Mignon's silence of longing forms the exception among all of these negotiations.

---

[47] Boyle, *Goethe: The Poet and the Age*, I, 424.
[48] Goethe, *Gedenkausgabe*, VII, 590: "lesen Sie mir von diesen wunderlichen Worten nicht mehr."
[49] *Ibid.*, 566: "es sei besser nach Regeln zu irren, als zu irren, wenn uns die Willkür unserer Natur hin und her treibt."

Freud and Goethe's idealism demands the *Entsagung* of the body's *Bildung*. Lawrence demands a rejection of the Freudian "unconscious which is the inverted reflection of our ideal consciousness" for "the true unconscious, where our life bubbles up in us, prior to any mentality" (*LG*, 205-207). This unconscious is a network of nerve "circuits" throughout the body, beginning with the infant's polarity of the solar plexus and lumbar ganglion, which multiplies throughout the development to adulthood. Lawrence then attempts to formulate a relationship between the desires of the body and a Nietzschean will, between the unconscious and consciousness, as he had done in *Women in Love*.

In *Psychoanalysis and the Unconscious* the will can relate to the unconscious in both a negative and positive way. It is like Schopenhauer and Nietzsche's description of *Wille* as the intrinsic force within an organism; a "blind will" emerges from the lumbar ganglion as the infant asserts its difference from the world outside. The will is not opposed to the unconscious, but is "the great *voluntary* centre of the unconscious flashing into action". Borrowing Nietzsche's combination of terms, Lawrence argues that "the will is the power" "against the exaggeration of any one particular circuit of polarity"; it ensures that all circuits of the body balance each other. Yet there is the danger "that the will shall identify itself with the mind and become an instrument of the mind" (*LG*, 221, 247-48); as "mental consciousness" the will and mind become detached from the body's other circuits, and gradually dominate them. The Freudian unconscious, then, involves this "ideal" partnership of the will and mind over the body's "affective sources"; Lawrence's alternative is a will whose power can regulate the spontaneity of all the body's "true unconscious". This balance between the will and unconscious in the body constitutes Lawrence's notion of *Bildung*, which he attempts to realize in Alvina.

In *The Lost Girl* Lawrence attempts to illustrate these distinctions between different manifestations of the unconscious and the will in Alvina's experiences. The Freudian ideal unconscious and will are products of the materialism of society. Unlike a "vast stratum of inferiors" who "submit" to Dr Mitchell's social authority, Alvina "obstinately set her will" (*LG*, 257, 267) against him; her instinctual will conquers his mental will, and reduces him to helplessness.

Through his will, Ciccio has the power to transform Alvina's life. The mere *Sehnsucht* of Mignon could not incite Wilhelm to realize his unconscious desires; it could only make him recognize his frustration in his *Entsagung*.

Yet the problems that Lawrence had encountered in *Women in Love*, of a balanced relation between the individual's will and conscious desires, recur in *The Lost Girl*. Alvina's *Bildung* consists of her "true unconscious" which is not regulated by her own will, but by Ciccio's. His "strange mesmeric power" leaves her "powerless", "submissive", "will-less" (*LG*, 287-88). She must renounce her will to realize her *Bildung*. Hilary Simpson recognizes this problem in *The Lost Girl*. She acknowledges Lawrence's rejection of Realist social analysis to overcome the pessimism of the genre, but connects his alternative with his "insistent emphasis on submission and passivity" in women. For Simpson, his lack of "genuine concern with the socio-economic causes of the so-called 'women surplus'" prevents Alvina from achieving "a successful career or a conversion to feminism" in this society.[50]

While subjected to Ciccio's "dark nature" and "blood", "Alvina saw nothing of all these complexities". In the novel's confrontation between Romanticism and social Realism, though, he does not conceal the power relations between Alvina and Ciccio,. Like the Italians in *Twilight in Italy* who abandoned their lemon gardens for the industrialized north, Ciccio wants to exploit the wealth and social status of "his well-to-do, Anglicised cousin". When Alvina admits that she has no money left for him, he strips her of her social superiority through raping her, with the power of his will over her body: "recklessly, he had his will of her ... leaving her stark, with nothing, nothing of herself – nothing." Afterwards, she breaks the "trance of obstinacy" of her conscious will, to wash the dishes and accept her "desire to fall at his feet". Later, Lawrence reveals how Ciccio's will derives its power from Italian social conventions, as "now it was *his* will which counted. Alvina, as his wife, must submit" (*LG*, 289, 233-34). These conventions and Ciccio's will are tautological, each justifying the other. Alvina is freed from bourgeois

---

[50] Hilary Simpson, *D. H. Lawrence and Feminism* (London: Croom Helm, 1982), 78, 75.

society, only to renounce her conscious self for another set of social duties.

There is the danger that Alvina will be a victim of circumstances like Mignon, silent under the pressure of her longings. In glorifying Alvina's unconscious desires, Lawrence turns them into a self-validating ideal which demands as much *Entsagung* as Goethe's ideal of social duty. But Lawrence does not attempt to resolve the Romantic inner existence of his characters with the social reality outside. This issue dominates all of Lawrence's novels: his characters attempt to choose between unconscious desire and social duty, but are destroyed by what they reject; they can only survive if they accept the burden of both of these irreconcilable demands. Goethe's Wilhelm Meister rejects desire for duty, and in the final section of *The Lost Girl* Lawrence attempts to provide Alvina with an alternative to Wilhelm's choice.

The escape to *Mignons Land*

Ciccio personifies the Italy to which he and Alvina escape, from the alienated capitalism of the north. In the region around Naples Goethe had speculated that his completion of *Wilhelm Meisters Theatralische Sendung* could "communicate in the last books something of this heavenly air".[51] Perhaps he had conceived an ending in Italy where Mignon, and Wilhelm's theatrical career, could flourish. Of course, the *Lehrjahre* concludes in the north, but in *The Lost Girl* Lawrence attempts to realize what Goethe had momentarily imagined doing.

In *The Lost Girl* the train journey to Naples includes the Romantic landscapes that Lawrence had found in Goethe, "round bays and between dark rocks and under castles, a night-time fairy-land" (*LG*, 299). In *Sea and Sardinia* Lawrence found Sardinia's "unremarkable ridges of moor-like hills" a relief from the "Wilhelm Meister water-falls" of the rest of Italy:

> Lovely space about one, and travelling distances – nothing finished, nothing final. It is like liberty itself, after the peaky confinement of Sicily. Room – give me room – give me room for my spirit: and you can have all the toppling crags of romance. (*SS*, 72)

---

[51] Goethe, *Gedenkausgabe*, XI, 238: "von dieser Himmelsluft den letzten Büchern etwas mitteilen."

In his description of Sicily, Lawrence discounts Goethe's Romanticism as merely fanciful, and ultimately as restrictive as the social reality of the north. Sardinia's landscape symbolizes the openness necessary for the fulfilment of one's *Bildung*. The Abruzzian landscape of Ciccio's home shares Sicily's confined "romance", despite a broad valley: "From the terrace of the highroad the valley spread over, with all its jumble of hills, and two rivers, set in the walls of the mountains, a wide space, but imprisoned" (*LG*, 327).

The valley symbolizes Alvina's new existence, sexually and socially. When she first entered it, she felt that "she had gone out of the world, over the border, into some place of mystery". Like Ciccio's subjection of Alvina in sex, the landscape provides her with a Romantic transcendence of her former identity: "the mysterious influence of the mountains and valleys themselves ... seemed always to be annihilating the Englishwoman." Yet the valley is imprisoned by the mountains, and Alvina is confined within a male society "threatening her with surveillance and subjection" (*LG*, 306, 329), with its "oriental idea of women". Ciccio merges with the landscape as a power to make her unconscious, but not to fulfil her. Instead, her instinctive will must repudiate him:

> She felt the strange terror and loneliness of his passion. And she wished she could lie down there by that town gate, in the sun, and swoon forever unconscious. Living was almost too great a demand for her .... There was nothing for her but to yield, yield, yield. And yet she could not sink to earth. (*LG*, 321)

The independent will of the child within her womb strengthens her against Ciccio's will.

Simpson believes that Alvina can only assert herself through consciousness,[52] yet for Lawrence only the unconscious can yield freedom. Goethe, and Max Weber, believed the individual can only find fulfilment through *Entsagung* to the social demands of capitalism, and to the authority of imperial rule. In Italy Lawrence rejects capitalist society for a feudal one which denies the possibility of the individual's *Bildung*. As in *Women in Love*, he tries to imagine

---

[52] See Simpson, *D. H. Lawrence and Feminism*, 77.

for his characters an existence beyond materialism and reason, but in doing so he only creates an ideal which denies the historical reality which he is attempting to transform. Even Alvina's physical desires become an ideal which restricts her *Bildung*. Lawrence reaches beyond the ideological restrictions of Goethe's Realism only by regressing to an earlier ideology, as Novalis had done. When he reintroduces Realism through his characterization of Ciccio and Italian society, Lawrence only exposes the limitations of his alternative to the genre.

Lawrence acknowledges these problems by showing how Alvina and Ciccio are still subject to the pressures of European history. Ciccio is called up for the First World War and leaves Alvina to an uncertain future alone, as she ponders, "Was she to bear a hopeless child?" (*LG*, 338). Yet Lawrence does not seal the novel from hope, as Goethe had closed *Wilhelm Meisters Theatralische Sendung* with the materialistic and rational certainty of the *Lehrjahre*. Alvina convinces Ciccio that he will return, posing the question of whether, when Lawrence was writing their story in 1920, they would have resumed their lives together in Italy. At the same time, Lawrence leaves open the political question of whether an alternative to bourgeois society is possible after the war. In searching for this alternative he will occasionally answer the dilemma of the individual's relation to society by abolishing individual rights, as right-wing politicians would do throughout Europe. But he will also attempt to envisage a world that Mignon had longed for, and that Alvina had struggled to find.

VII
A REFLECTION ON PAST INFLUENCES:
MR NOON

After his escape from England midway through *Mr Noon*, Gilbert Noon surveys the open panorama of the "rolling plains of Germany". In southern Bavaria where "the sense of space was an intoxication for him", he discovers a world of possibilities that had eluded Alvina in Italy. He gazes north to "the massive lands of Germany" and "subarctic whiteness" of Scandinavia, east to Austria and "the vast spaces of Russia", south to "magical Italy", but away from "the islands of the west":

> And he became unEnglished. His tight and exclusive nationality seemed to break down in his heart. He loved the world in its multiplicity, not in its horrible oneness, uniformity, homogeneity. He loved the rich and free variegation of Europe, the manyness.

Gilbert is "unEnglished" in a Germany whose "glamorous vast multiplicity" (*MN*, 97, 107-108) forms a microcosm of Europe and the world beyond.

Gilbert's view of the landscape symbolizes Germany's influence over Lawrence's vision throughout his lifetime, such as in *Essays of Schopenhauer*, Wagner at Covent Garden, Nietzsche at Croydon Library, and the escape from England with Frieda. In the process of representing his earlier attitudes, in *Mr Noon* Lawrence reveals their significance for the post-war period of his writing. While Gilbert reenacts Lawrence's first, glorious impressions of Germany in 1912, Lawrence alludes to it as the "disreputable land" (*MN*, 99) of 1920. Lawrence and Gilbert have escaped to Germany, but Lawrence now longs to escape from it after experiencing its middle-class culture and the First World War. In mining *Mr Noon* for details of Lawrence's life, Worthen and Kinkead-Weekes have attempted to counter the distorting effect of his hindsight in the novel,[1] but conversely this hindsight reveals to us Lawrence's attitudes after the war.

---

[1] See Worthen, *D. H. Lawrence: The Early Years*, 382; Kinkead-Weekes, *D. H. Lawrence: Triumph to Exile*, 18-19.

Although Lawrence had not visited Germany since 1913, immediately after the war he and Frieda monitored its events and she visited her family in Baden-Baden. Despite lacking direct experience of the situation, he would have been aware of how the defeat of the monarchy in war, and of the radical Left in revolution, had left Germany in a crisis over its politics, culture, economy and society. This crisis paralleled Lawrence's own artistic crisis after *Women in Love*, and he responds to both in *Mr Noon* by examining the ways they intersect: in the German influence upon his development as a novelist.

Following *The Lost Girl*, Lawrence continues his dialogue with Goethe, this time concentrating on *Faust*. In the last chapter we saw how he opposed Goethe's ideal of *Entsagung* with his own ideal of eroticism. *Mr Noon* continues this struggle by tracing the development of Lawrence's thought from the influences of Goethe through to Schopenhauer, Nietzsche and Otto Gross. Lawrence recognizes how his development, that made *The Rainbow* and *Women in Love* possible, is bound to the Romantic idealism of Wagner. Wagner and Gross had provided an escape from war, only to reinforce the nationalistic escapism that fuelled the war, from the political reality of individuals in society and on the battlefield. Consequently, it becomes apparent in *Mr Noon* that Gross and Wagner shared with German militarism an idealism that negated the individual.

These insights are left exposed as contradictions in *Mr Noon*, since Lawrence left it incomplete as a first draft. *Mr Noon* leaves these contradictions in their barest form, and gives us the opportunity to examine some of the constituent ideas of his work. He uses clichés about Germany as pawns for his ideas – the Faustian hero, the Wagnerian lovers and heroines, the theorising intellectuals, the forests of tribal savages and Teutonic gods, the authoritarian soldiers and public officials – but he juxtaposes them in loose and ironic ways to articulate his unique vision.

Gilbert Noon as Faust

In Part I of *Mr Noon* Lawrence parodies the events of Goethe's *Faust I* and uses the play's themes to give unity to the whole of the novel. Lawrence drops clues as to his literary debt by mentioning Gilbert's "lifted, Mephistophelian brows", and that "Mephistopheles himself, in a good-natured mood, could not have been more fascinating" (*MN*, 24, 9) than Gilbert is when lecturing to the Woodhouse Literary Society. Gilbert is not Mephistopheles, but like Faust is driven by Mephistopheles in his consciousness. Gilbert's attempt to seduce Emmie parallels Faust's approach to Gretchen: he arranges to meet Emmie in her father's greenhouse, while Faust and Gretchen consummate their relationship in a *Gartenhäuschen* ("garden-house"). On finding Gilbert and Emmie together, her father Alfred calls her a whore and curses her, as the righteous and possessive Valentin does with his sister Gretchen. Faust stabs and murders Valentin, whereas Gilbert threatens to kill Alfred but falls into a gooseberry bush with him.

In *Mr Noon* Lawrence continues the dialogue with Goethe from *The Lost Girl*, and returns to his specific use of *Faust* in *The Rainbow*, now with a greater awareness of Goethe's significance in contemporary Germany. Composed between 1769 and 1808, in tandem with *Wilhelm Meisters theatralische Sendung* and *Lehrjahre*, *Faust I* shares their historical concerns. In the *Lehrjahre* Goethe had supplanted the political idealism of the *Theatralische Sendung* and French Revolution with the ideal of *Entsagung* ("renunciation") of individual liberty before social duty. In *The Lost Girl* Lawrence attempted to manoeuvre beyond these two apparently opposed positions, and he repeats this project in *Mr Noon*.

Nicholas Boyle interprets *Faust I* as a criticism of the philosophical idealism that Goethe had associated with the French Revolution and the *Theatralische Sendung*. The old order of Papacy and Empire was on the brink of collapse, and Faust articulates the revolutionary ideology of the autonomous individual who gives expression to new social and economic forms.[2] In the Chapter on *The Rainbow* I outlined how the two parts of *Faust* express the idealism of Goethe's *Morphologie* in Faust's developing individuality which becomes abstracted into an ideal, to be redeemed in the oneness of God. In political terms, while the individualism of the *Theatralische Sendung* was renounced for social duty in the *Lehrjahre*, Faust renounced his individual striving in Part II for reconciliation with God, and traditional authority.

---

[2] See Boyle, *Goethe: The Poet and the Age*, II, 768.

For Lawrence during this period, the political ideal of liberal democracy was equivalent to social conformity. In the essay "Democracy" (1919) Lawrence branded democracy as "the worst of ideals" because it reduces individuals to "The Law of the Average", defined by the "state" or "nation" which uses it as an abstract principle to wage war. In his dialogue with *Faust*, Lawrence is attempting to formulate a "democracy" for the individual, not as a mere member of society, but as an "inscrutable and incarnate Mystery" (*RDP*, 63, 66, 78).

In the closing chapters of *The Rainbow* Ursula emulated Faust by renouncing the materiality of her body, and of history, as an "unreality". Her vision of a social and religious oneness encompassed by the rainbow was, if distantly, related to the idealism of war which promised a spiritual transcendence on the battlefield. Leading up to this conclusion, Ursula's intellect and body had become dislocated, no longer developing in tandem but to the exclusion of each other as singular ideals. In *The Lost Girl* Lawrence attempted to balance Alvina's intellectual and physical needs, but towards the end of the novel he prioritized her body over her mind, which weakened her ability to fulfil herself. In *Mr Noon* Lawrence attempts to liberate Gilbert as an individual with diverse needs. Gilbert experiences the dilemma of Faust and Ursula, and Lawrence attempts to mark out a solution to it.

In his admission that his lectures are "a pack of lies" (*MN*, 12), Gilbert echoes Faust and Ursula's dismissal of academic study, and of traditional values. All three abandon their university careers to establish their own value systems in their sensual experiences. In the supremacy of his ego Faust experienced the world, but only as an object of enjoyment from which he was alienated. When Faust identified himself with the creative power of the Erdgeist, it answered that

> Du gleichst dem Geist, den du begreifst,
> Nicht mir![3]

> You resemble the spirit you can grasp,
> Not me!

---

[3] Goethe, *Gedenkausgabe*, VII, 159.

Faust only understood the *Geist* that appeared as Mephistopheles, who would enable him to impose his subjectivity upon the world. Like Ursula who "was a traveller on the face of the earth" (*R*, 387), Gilbert has unwittingly emulated Faust's pact with Mephistopheles to resist pleading "Verweile doch! Du bist so schön!" ("Linger on, you are so beautiful!")[4] to any of the experiences that are offered to him. Faust, Ursula and Gilbert want to prove the inadequacy of their experiences in comparison to their ideals.[5] They apply the values of their idealism against a material reality that includes Gretchen, Emmie and Anton Skrebensky.

Gilbert rejects life for mathematics and art, because he can objectify them: "Life is incompatible with perfection, or with infinity, or with eternity. You've got to turn to mathematics, or to art." Gilbert's acquaintance, Patty, recognizes the link between his contempt for "life" and women in comparison to mathematics, and echoes the Erdgeist's reprimand to Faust, that he fails to grasp the sacred otherness of life:

> You may well despise life. But I pity you. Life will despise *you*, and you'll know it. (*MN*, 12-13)

After her miscarriage Ursula turned from Skrebensky and "from her body, from all the vast encumbrance of the world that was in contact with her", which was "an unreality" (*R*, 456). Lawrence, though, glorified Ursula's repudiation of her past life as a transcendence necessary for her vision of an ideal world; through Gilbert, Lawrence examines the implications of this form of transcendence.

Faust was entranced by Gretchen's physical and spiritual beauty, but to affirm his ideal of individual autonomy which was encapsulated in his wager with Mephistopheles, he was driven to violate and abandon her. Faust reflected on the tragic paradox that "Ich kann sie nie vergessen, nie verlieren" ("I can never forget her, never lose her), and that he was a "Gottverhaßte" ("cursed by God"): "Sie, ihren Frieden mußt ich untergraben!" ("She, I had to undermine her peace!").[6] Gretchen, as the representative of traditional Christian

---

[4] *Ibid.*, 194.
[5] See Boyle, *Goethe: The Poet and the Age*, II, 766-67.
[6] Goethe, *Gedenkausgabe*, VII, 247-48.

values, was the victim of Faust's idealism, and of the revolutionary ideology of the 1790s.

In an analogous situation, Gilbert is a Mephistophelian "snake in the grass" during his attempt to seduce Emmie:

> He was irritable, in a temper, and would not let her go though he did not really want her. Why was he in a temper, and why he hated her he did not know. Doubtful if he ever knew his own state of feeling .... Black devils frisked in his veins, and pricked him with their barbed tails. He was full of little devils.

The "Mephistopheles" in Gilbert is forcing him to pursue his sexual impulse, to violate himself, and Emmie by treating her "rough and hard". Faust is entrapped by his wager with Mephistopheles, while Gilbert is caught "in a ready-made circumstance, going through a ready-made act" and willing himself to be a "womaniser" (*MN*, 27-28, 32). Dissatisfied by Skrebensky, Ursula feared that she wanted "just other men" (*R*, 440) but she refused to acquiesce to a conventional marriage, since she was still aspiring to an ideal.

Gilbert, then, shares Faust and Ursula's idealism of the self over the world at large. Gilbert's idealism threatens to destroy what Lawrence describes in "Democracy" as the "*otherness*" of people, and of the individual's own unconscious desire to relate to them. Although the people on Easter Saturday in *Faust I* and the inhabitants of Woodhouse after the Sunday Service share an easygoing piety, *Mr Noon* is not a tragedy of a lost world, but a comedy of the creation of a new one. Through irony Lawrence makes possible an alternative outcome to the ending of *Faust I*. Gretchen ignored Faust at their first meeting, after confessing her sins to the priest, whereas Emmie rushes out of the Sunday Service to meet Gilbert for a session of erotic "spooning". Emmie does not suffer Gretchen's tragic fate when she becomes pregnant, but chooses another lover as a husband. Gilbert will not find redemption in Emmie, as Faust did in Gretchen's spirit at the end of *Faust II*, or as Ursula anticipated in a man who "would come out of Eternity to which she herself belonged" (*R*, 457) at the end of *The Rainbow*.

Instead, Gilbert will attempt to discover his true "Gretchen" and religion which are beyond the limits of Goethe's political conservatism, and of Lawrence's own idealism. In particular, Gilbert needs to avoid Lawrence's ideal expressed in "Democracy" in the uncompromising choice: "You can have life two ways. Either everything is created from the mind, downwards: or else everything proceeds from the creative quick, outwards into foliage and blossom." Here Lawrence declares that "Ideals, all ideals and every ideal, are a trick of the devil" (*RDP*, 76, 69), yet as we see here, and in Lawrence's novels, the rejection of all ideals is an act of idealism in itself. In *Mr Noon* Lawrence attempts to overturn Goethe's idealism of social duty without placing his own ideal of eroticism in its stead.

Faust in modern Germany

Like Faust and Ursula in *Women in Love*, Gilbert is magically transported to another world at the beginning of Part II of the novel where these themes are pursued in the context of modern Germany. Although Lawrence changes Gilbert's character from Part I to a fictional self-portrait in Part II, the underlying themes and literary references unify the novel in a similar way that the themes of *Faust I* and *II*, and of *The Rainbow* and *Women in Love*, unified these pairs of works. Just as *Faust II* generalized the issues of the hero's personal development into Western civilization as a whole, Lawrence explores the issue of idealism in Germany's cultural traditions and history.

Gilbert becomes an assistant to Professor Alfred Kramer who echoes Faust, "missing life, with his books and his theory and paper" (*MN*, 102). Again, Lawrence deflates Goethe's sublimity by also giving Alfred the qualities of Faust's servant, the pedant Wagner who testifies that through patient reading, "Zwar weiß ich viel, doch möcht ich alles wissen" ("Already I know much, but I would like to know everything").[7] Alfred, like Faust, muses on the opening of St John's Gospel: "In the beginning was the Word, and the Word was with God, and the Word was God." Continuing the theme of Gilbert's alienation from "Life", Alfred "imagines Life to be something and the Word a mere bauble in the hands of buffoons like himself" (*MN*, 103). As we saw in Chapter IV, Faust rewrote St John, from "Im Anfang war das Wort!" ("In the beginning was the Word!") to "Im Anfang war die Tat!" ("In the beginning was the Deed!").[8] Boyle argues that Faust identifies the creation of reality with himself as the individual "doer",

---

[7] *Ibid.*, 62.
[8] Goethe, *Gedenkausgabe*, VII, 180-81.

like Fichte's radical idealism which prioritizes the individual's autonomous subjectivity over Divine Revelation.[9]

In *Mr Noon* German idealism has moved back from the "*Tat*" to the "*Wort*" of Alfred, as one of the "sound and all-too-serious German professors for whom the Word is God, though the Word is not with God, but with them, the professors thereof". lthough Alfred's "Jewish blood" inspires a slight dissatisfaction with this German attitude, his "idealism had stretched his human sensibility at one point" where he is generous to large abstract causes, but not to his "proprietorship" of material things such as his honey dish at breakfast. Alfred's crisis of idealism represents the social crisis of his class; he is "by nature liberal" in politics, while owning various homes and Biedermeier furniture which is associated with the bourgeois conformity of mid-nineteenth century German culture (*MN*, 99-102). Lawrence implies that modern German intellectuals, and the middle class in general, still emulate Faust's individualism in the economic sphere but ethically have returned to the "Word". In this situation the individual becomes a social unit, a bodiless Word. In "Democracy" Lawrence argues, "The one principle that governs all the isms is the same: the principle of the idealized unit, the possessor of property" (*RDP*, 81). Alfred's Word is "*work*" (*MN*, 103), which he constantly repeats to justify his wealth and impress Gilbert, without actually achieving anything.

The individual has become only a Word, and Alfred longs to replace the Word with "Life", yet he can only idealize life back into a meaningless Word like "*work*": "That Life with a big L was also an illusion of his, he had not yet realised" (*MN*, 104). Lawrence's observation is not only directed at German intellectuals, but also at himself, in particular to his youthful attitudes. As we saw in Chapter II, he asserted to Blanche Jennings in 1908 that "No, I don't know much of *life* – but of *Life*" (I, 101), associating "*Life*" with "blood" and Wagnerian opera. In his "Preface to *Sons and Lovers*" of 1913 Lawrence had reversed St John's "the Word was made flesh"[10] with "The Flesh was made Word" (*SL*, 467), to affirm the primacy of physical experience over secondary knowledge. This insight, inspired by Frieda and the ideas of Otto Gross, was the ground upon which

---

[9] Boyle, *Goethe: The Poet and the Age*, II, 208-12, 763.
[10] St John, I.14.

Ursula liberated herself through eroticism in *The Rainbow*, but also on which Lawrence turned the darkness of her eroticism into an ideal, a mere word at the end of the novel. In *Mr Noon* Lawrence repeats the insight of the "Preface": "In the beginning was *not* the Word, but something from which the Word merely proceeded later on …. The first, great, passionately generating God." But the question arises whether this "God" is an ideal like "Life", "blood", "darkness", or has a dynamic, material reality.

Lawrence attempts to answer this question in *Mr Noon* by tracing his development from *The White Peacock* onwards alongside his history of German culture. He recreates his relationship with Frieda in the character Johanna, who introduces herself with "I'm German, and I love Germany". As Gilbert's own Gretchen she embodies Germany before the Enlightenment, threatened by the "nerves and theories and unscrupulous German theorisers just about to devour her" (*MN*, 194, 122, 161), including Goethe himself.

A retrospective across Germany
Lawrence outlines the diverse history of Germany as Gilbert gazes at the Rhine and thinks "of Rome and the naked great Germanic tribes: of the amazing Middle Ages: and then of Luther and the Thirty Years War – and then of Frederick and the great Goethe" (*MN*, 184). In *Movements in European History* Lawrence had characterized Friedrich der Grosse (Frederick the Great, 1712-1786) of Prussia as a child of the Enlightenment, "delicate and sensitive, cultured, almost French in his education, loving books and painting and philosophy". Yet convinced by his father Friedrich Wilhelm I "that force, and force alone, triumphed" (*MEH*, 212-13), Friedrich asserted Prussian power through war.

Friedrich earned his title "the Great" through these military campaigns, and Lawrence implies a dual character in the "great Goethe":

> If only someone had given *you* a good kick in your toga-seat, when you were godlifying yourself and olympising yourself and setting up the stunt of German Godlikeness and superhumanness, what a lot it would have saved the world, and Germany in particular. If only Napoleon had not been taken in. If only that usually sensible person had exclaimed, not *voilà un homme*! but *voilà un dieu gratuite*!, (sic)

and given the gratuitous God-Goethe a good old Napoleonic kick in the rump! ... It would save so many cannons later on. (*MN*, 184)

The expression of Goethe's "superhumanness" connotes Nietzsche's *Übermensch* whose ideal of *Wille zur Macht* had been implicated by Lawrence in German militarism. Lawrence identifies the "God-Goethe" as the origin of the "Word" of German middle-class values. Goethe has "godlified" and "olympised" himself in his work, particularly in the classicism of *Faust II*. In middle-class readers like Professor Kramer, the Word of Goethe only substantiates their political conformity in the face of the aggressive military political elite.

Lawrence presents his alternative to Goethe with his lovers Gilbert and Johanna: "Gentle reader, it was not the silent bliss of two elective affinities who were just about to fuse and make a holy and eternal oneness" (*MN*, 185). Lawrence is referring to Ottilie and Eduard in Goethe's *Die Wahlverwandtschaften*, who are only united in death like Faust and Gretchen, after renouncing their relationship in life. Lawrence interprets the political implications of *Die Wahlverwandtschaften* in a similar way to Walter Benjamin, who described Ottilie's death as a "mythic sacrifice"[11] to redeem the transgression of the French Revolution.

George Eliot had utilized Goethe's scientific rationalization of Ottilie's death as a chemical process to make Maggie Tulliver's tragic fate in *The Mill on the Floss* appear convincing. In *The White Peacock* Lawrence rejected Goethe and George Eliot's use of affinities in favour of Schopenhauer's "The Metaphysics of Love". Schopenhauer helped Lawrence to conceive the tragedy where Lettie and George's sexual desire for each other's opposing qualities was frustrated by their lack of social affinities. In *Die Wahlverwandtschaften* Goethe had resisted including opposition, which Schopenhauer and Lawrence conceive as sexual and asocial, because of its threat to the social hierarchy.

Schopenhauer substituted Goethe's *Entsagung* with the *Verneigung des Willens*, since he lamented the disintegration of the originally unified *Wille* into antagonistic fragments, such as

---

[11] Walter Benjamin, *Selected Writings* (London: Harvard University Press, 1996-), I, 309.

incompatible lovers and rebellious social classes. But like Nietzsche, in *Mr Noon* Lawrence glorifies the implications of Schopenhauer's *Metaphysik* by describing Johanna as Gilbert's "soul's affinity, and his body's mate". Gilbert and Johanna form a "union of indomitable opposites" (*MN*, 186) in the same way as Birkin and Ursula, whose conflicting *Willen zur Macht* generate their desire for one another and their development as individuals together.

Finally, Lawrence emulates Nietzsche's affirmation of the *ewige Wiederkehr* of the Schopenhauerian *Wille*. He rejects the religion of Christ dying on the Cross to become an eternal "abstract spirit", for a "Druid and Germanic" religion in which "the tree of life itself never dies" (*MN*, 189-90). Lawrence began to assimilate the notion of *ewige Wiederkehr* while writing *The Trespasser*, and gave full expression to it in *The Rainbow*. As in the generations of the Brangwen family, eternity exists in the cycles of finite life, universal being in the particular moments of becoming.

In rejecting Goethe's mental affinities for the individual's primal *Wille*, Lawrence dismisses idealism, yet is inconsistent about the relation between the intellect and body. At one point he appears to envisage a dialectic between them: "Yes I love it – the spirit, the mind, the ideal. But not primarily"; it must interact with "sensual individuality". On the other hand, Lawrence echoes Alfred in his comment that the "written-down eternity", or "Word", is only a "bauble". It is ambiguous whether in his repetitive insistence Lawrence is describing life with a capital "L":

> Life does not begin in the mind: or in some ideal spirit. Life begins in the deep, the indescribable sensual throb of desire, pre-mental.

He claims that "Man can live without spirit or ideal" or conscious will for the "dark sap of life, stream of eternal blood": "All the little tricks, all the intensifications of will remain no more than tricks and will-pressure" (*MN*, 189-90). Again, there is the danger that he is celebrating the body to the exclusion of mental consciousness.

Here Lawrence repeats his struggle in *Women in Love* to overcome the idealistic ending of *The Rainbow*. The image of the rainbow in *Mr Noon* takes the form of the "Crown", poised between the irreconcilable lion and unicorn. Lawrence does not describe the gentle gathering of a "faint iridescence colouring in faint colours ... a faint, vast rainbow" (*R*, 458), but "the moment's matching of the two terrible opposites, fire and water" (*MN*, 186). Yet in *Mr Noon* the rainbow is still a universal image on which "we live, all of us balanced delicately", like Ursula's rainbow which unified the people, "arched in their blood" (*R*, 459). The idealism of her rainbow as "the overarching heaven" is retained in *Mr Noon* by describing it as the meeting of "the two eternal, universal enemies", or in Lawrence's preferred expression, "the man and the woman of the material universe" (*MN*, 186). It maintains the integrity of individuals in a sexual relationship, but still compels and reduces them to the terms of an idealized sexuality. In *Mr Noon* Lawrence continues to struggle against his tendency to idealize the body's sensuality over the mind's consciousness.

On the Romanticism of Wagner and Gross

It is uncertain whether these ideas in *Mr Noon* are located in Gilbert's subjectivity, modelled on Lawrence in Germany with Frieda in 1912, or are located in the voice of the omniscient narrator, namely Lawrence writing the novel in 1920. The denunciation of Goethe, and the outline of German history which summarizes Lawrence's treatment of Germany in *Movements in European History*, both appear as the authorial voice but are ascribed to Gilbert, "musing somewhat in this strain" while he travels across Germany before the war. Gilbert thinks of Johanna with "such a lovely sense of fulfilment in the future", then the narrator describes marriage as the necessary condition for the relationship between man and woman, which reflects the early years of Lawrence and Frieda's marriage. But Lawrence ends this section with the narrator voicing the uncertainty of his own position in 1920, that "now alas the English adventure" of marriage "has broken down. There is no going on" (*MN*, 184, 191). There is a crisis of values between Lawrence's authorial subjectivity and his objectified self, by means of which he is attempting to break from the dilemmas of his previous novels.

We see this situation most clearly in Lawrence's treatment of Wagner, and how it affects his characterization of Johanna. Wagner is mentioned alongside the rejection of Goethe's elective affinities: "surely we are entitled to a little Wagnerian language here: it was the bridal peace of Gilbert and Johanna. It was the grail hovering before our hero, shedding its effulgence upon him" (*MN*, 185). Lawrence is alluding to the closing scene of Wagner's *Parsifal* where the hero returned to Montsalvat with the spear on which King Amfortas had wounded himself; Parsifal placed the Grail, which could heal the King, before himself while it glowed with light, and light emerged from above the stage. Through his "spear" Gilbert has discovered his own "Grail" in Johanna. Yet Lawrence's tone is ironic, implicitly dismissing the inadequacy of Wagner's religious alternative to Goethe's classicism.

In *Mr Noon* Lawrence returns to his early fascination for Wagner as a Romantic alternative to the rationalism of modern society. In Part I Lawrence refers to the "grail-like effulgence" of Gilbert and Emmie's "spooning", which he describes with the Wagnerian language of *Tristan und Isolde*. He repeats the word "darkness" with other words in a musical, "*con molto espressione*", rhythm:

> with a second reeling swoon she reeled down again and fell, fell through a deeper, darker sea. Depth doubled on depth, darkness on darkness .... down came his mouth on her unclosed mouth, darkness closed on darkness, so she melted completely, fused, and was gone. (*MN*, 20, 23)

Lawrence parodies his earlier Wagnerian use of darkness, and reveals an awareness of Wagner's idealism. Gilbert and Emmie's "consummation" recapitulates the moments in *The Rainbow* and *Women in Love* where Lawrence believed his characters had transcended material reality: Ursula and Skrebensky in "The Bitterness and Ecstasy" as "one stream, one dark fecundity" (*R*, 414), and Ursula and Birkin's "dark reality" (*WL*, 319) in "Excurse". Through incongruous intrusions Lawrence subverts Gilbert and Emmie's apparent transcendence into darkness, for example in the reference to her ears: "Only let him kiss her ears, and it was consummation .... Ah! – Ah! – and softly came his full, fathomless kiss, softly her ear was quenched in darkness" (*MN*, 22). Paul Eggert interprets this scene as self-parody,[12] but in particular its irony is directed at Lawrence's inheritance of Wagnerian Romanticism.

---

[12] See Paul Eggert, "D. H. Lawrence and His Audience: The Case of *Mr Noon*", *Southern Review*, XVIII (1985), 301-302.

Lawrence also satirizes Wagner in comparing the "god-almighty ferocity" of the German train officials to "a Wotan God". While revealing a sympathy with Wagner's interest in Germanic myth, he dismisses his approach to it when Gilbert observes the landscape of the Tyrol:

> It was hard not to believe in the old, white-skinned muscular gods, whom Wagner travestied. Surely Siegfried tramped through such spring meadows, breaking the god-blond globe-flowers against his fierce, naked knees. (*MN*, 184, 200)

During the composition of *Women in Love* Lawrence had been inspired by the "urzeitig [primal] landscape" of Cornwall; he found "the eternal light washing against the eternal darkness" of the "bare and dark and elemental, Tristan's land" (III, 506, 520, 503) more expressive of primal feeling than Wagner's *Tristan und Isolde*.

Lawrence previously used contradictory statements to relativize their value in terms of each other, especially in the "friction" of male-female relationships. In *Mr Noon* he uses irony, which is more self-conscious than mere contradiction, to break from earlier positions. But Wagner is still an important presence in *Mr Noon*, affecting central figures and issues in the novel by association. Johanna, who personifies primal Germany, is compared to Wagnerian heroines. When Gilbert first sees her, he watches "her rise like a Wagner Goddess through the floor, in the lift", and in their domestic "ballets" she moves like "a Wagner heroine" (*MN*, 120, 255). In associating Johanna with Wagner, Lawrence is casting scepticism on the influence of Frieda, and Otto Gross, on his art. Describing to Frieda "how one must love you – all in flames",[13] Gross had compared himself to Siegfried in his desire to penetrate a wall of fire and reawaken Frieda as Brünnhilde in a kiss. Johanna and Gilbert's arguments about love examine the value of Otto Gross' theories, which were influential on Lawrence's development of eroticism as a utopian ideal from *Sons and Lovers* onwards.

Johanna contrasts her "marvellous lover" Eberhard, based on Otto Gross, with Freud: "Eberhard was spiritual – he may have been

---

[13] *The D. H. Lawrence Review*, XXII, 202: "wie man Dich lieben muss – ganz in Flammen."

demoniacal, but he was spiritual. Which Freud isn't, don't you think." "A genius at love", Eberhard made Johanna "free" of her individuality and marriage. She claims that he located love in sex, which must be expressed "in the proper way", not through the "head". In his bemused question of what "sex" is, Gilbert suggests contradictions in Johanna's summary of Eberhard's theories, of "spirituality" and "freedom" against the physical expression of sex. Johanna attempts to answer without words, which betray the physical immanence of sex, by saying "Just sex". But then she resorts to words, turning sex into theory: "It is the kind of magnetism that holds people together, and which is bigger than individuals" (*MN*, 126-27).

Johanna contradicts herself in the admission that she could not accept Eberhard's inability to be faithful to one woman. Gross attempted to mediate between the jealousies of Frieda and her sister Else, who was also his lover, through idealising his love for them. When Frieda returned to her husband, Gross also suffered this contradiction. He gave a spiritual significance to his relationship with her, arguing that "surely you could take another man who is much dearer than I am, and meanwhile keep your love for me unchanged, preserved as before"; then he expressed the anguish of his frustration and loneliness.[14] Gross and Frieda appealed to spirituality as a consolation for the failure of their relationship. They reflected the historical trend of Romanticism's spiritual escapism after its failure to transform society, from Wagner's political apathy after the 1848 Revolutions to Birkin and Ursula's withdrawal into a "dark ... reality" in "Excurse". This issue becomes the basis of Lawrence's critique of Gross when Gilbert and Johanna resume their discussion about Eberhard in Detsch.

Discussing love, Johanna asserts that "there must be something ideal about it". She approves of Eberhard's dictum to her: "One should love all men: all men are loveable somewhere." She believes that she is "universal", destined to love all men whom she can "understand" (*MN*, 126, 164). In proclaiming sexual relations as a revolutionary alternative to the social relations of power, property and class Johanna is replicating what John Turner describes as Gross'

---

[14] *Ibid.*, 201: "Du könntest wohl einen Andern viel lieber als mich bekommen und dabei unverändert mir Deine Liebe gerade *so* wie bisher bewahren."

"idealism of desire".[15] Lawrence also replicates this idealism in *Mr Noon* with his symbol of man and woman as a rainbow, recalling the utopianism at the close of *The Rainbow*. In glorifying sex as a utopian principle, Gross and Lawrence have transposed sex from the body back to the head. In response to Johanna's use of Gross' ideas, Gilbert argues for "particular love" between two individuals. She interprets his notion as mere conventional marriage, based on jealousy which must be "overcome", as if through a Nietzschean *Wille zur Macht*. Again, Gilbert affirms jealousy as part of physical desire:

> Jealousy is as natural as love or laughter. You might as well overcome everything and have done with it all straight off .... If there is *physical* love, it is exclusive. It *is* exclusive. It's only spiritual love that is all-embracing. (*MN*, 165-66)

Towards the end of *Mr Noon* these issues re-emerge, to undermine Gilbert and Johanna's relationship, and the ideas central to the novel. During her dance with a Tyrolese peasant who is sexually attracted to her, Gilbert recognizes the power at stake in Johanna's "spirituality":

> Given the spiritual recognition, she was a queen, more a queen the more men loved her.... She would go down before no male. The male must go down before her.... And yet how excited she was. And he, Gilbert, must be the instrument to satisfy her roused excitement. It by no means flattered or pleased him. He sympathized with the peasant. Johanna was a fraud. (*MN*, 250)

Lawrence is alluding to Gross' "worship" of Frieda in his letters to her as his *Schicksalsmacht* ("force of destiny") and the *Zukunftsideal* ("ideal of the future")[16] of a matriarchal society. Mind and body are confused: in his spiritual relationship with Johanna, Gilbert is obliged to satisfy Johanna's physical excitement over the peasant. Later, Johanna reverses the situation by asserting her sexual freedom. She confesses that their travelling companion, Stanley, had sex with her. Gilbert responds that only their love matters, not their sexual transgressions: "They don't really mean anything, do they? I love you

---

[15] *Ibid.*, 148.
[16] *Ibid.*, 200, 198.

– and so what does it matter!" She feels humiliated by his forgiveness and "marvellous pearls of spiritual love" (*MN*, 276-77), through which he retains a power over her.

Occasionally Gilbert and Johanna's marriage is undermined by their desire for others, to leave the marriage as only a spiritual bond between them. Like Gerald and Gudrun's relationship in *Women in Love*, their marriage reproduces the power struggles in society and between nations: Johanna demands to be revered and served by Gilbert; in affirming his "spiritual" relationship with Johanna, Gilbert affirms his lack of dependence on her sexually, and leaves her insecure in her material dependence on him. This situation reflects upon Lawrence's conviction of the marriage between man and woman in *Mr Noon*, because in turning it into a utopian principle symbolized in his rainbow of opposites, marriage becomes more than a physical relation between two individuals as an ideal, and independent of its basis in sex. It is diluted into wider social relations, and is subject to their power structures. At the outbreak of war Lawrence had dismissed Freudianism as "only a branch of medical science, interesting", and like Gross as Eberhard, he based his "vision" on getting "our sex right" (II, 218). His vision in *Mr Noon* remains unchanged, despite his recognition of its limitations.

In discrediting Wagner, then, Lawrence has also brought into question the development through Frieda that yielded his greatest novels, of advocating the erotic marriage as an answer to the alienation of capitalism. From affirming the individual through his or her bodily drives, in *Mr Noon* eroticism is revealed as part of the social power structures that it was intended to overturn. From this point the values of *Mr Noon* collapse, where Lawrence looks as far as militarism as a part of the erotic relationship, or even as an alternative to it.

The impasse between eroticism and war
In the military town of Detsch, Gilbert and Johanna's argument about sex is interrupted by a "duty-bound ... dutiful soldier" who threatens to arrest them for spying. Gilbert is not frightened by the soldier, but Lawrence comments that "alas, he has learnt better – or worse" (*MN*, 168). The First World War taught Lawrence that his relationship with a German woman was a political issue. The incident in Metz was

repeated in a far more serious way on 12 October 1917 when police raided the Lawrences' home at Higher Tregerthen and ordered the couple out of Cornwall, on suspicion of spying for the Germans. Although Lawrence conceives Gilbert and Johanna's relationship as a rebellion against militarism, throughout *Mr Noon* their marriage is implicated in German military idealism.

Johanna is associated with the ancient Germans who repulsed Roman civilization; she feels uncomfortable in Trento – "To her fresh, northern, forest-leaved soul it was indescribably hideous" (*MN*, 283). In *Fantasia of the Unconscious*, written in 1921, Lawrence writes that "the true German has something of the sap of trees in his veins even now: a sort of pristine savageness ... under all his mentality" (*PUFU*, 87). In *Movements in European History* Lawrence admired how "the German love of freedom and separateness would not endure either service or control" in its resistance to Roman imperialism, and he glorifies these qualities in Gilbert's combative relationship with Johanna. Like them, the ancient Germans lived by a destructive opposition to each other: "Life was not made for producing. It was made for fierce contest and struggle of destruction, the glory of the struggle of opposition" (*MEH*, 48).

In *Mr Noon* the ancient Germans are depicted in opposition to the "mentality" of Germany at war, but in *Movements in European History* Lawrence's description of the ancient Germans was deeply coloured by Germany's recent militarism. The Germanic tree-religion in *Mr Noon* glorifies life in opposition to Christianity, yet in *Movements in European History* the tree-religion anticipated Christ's sacrifice on the Cross in its nailing of body-parts to trees:

> Life is the fruit of that Tree. But the Tree is dark and terrible, it demands life back again. With its branches spread it becomes a Cross.

For Lawrence the synthesis of pagan violence and Christian suffering is integral to German aggression, which anticipates the modern idealism in war where "honour was everything: and honour in a man meant having killed the greatest number of enemies". In his description of the battles between the German tribes and the Romans Lawrence is haunted by images of the Western Front:

The naked dead piled the fields. But there was little lamentation. It was honour, after all, to die fighting. (*MN*, 49-51)

Despite his reservations, at the end of *Mr Noon* he celebrates these connections between Gilbert's "incalculable fight ... with his German Johanna", and German militarism:

> We don't know what is outside – we can never know till we get out. We have therefore got to fight and fight and fight ourselves sick, to get out. Hence the Germans really made a right move, when they made the war. Death to the old enshrouding body politic, the old womb-idea of our era!

Birth, like war, "is a bloody and horrid and gruesome affair" (*MN*, 290-92). Gilbert and Johanna are implicated in the "cannons" that Lawrence had blamed on Goethe.

In contrast to the "sheer rage" with which Lawrence greeted the "colossal idiocy" (II, 212) of the First World War in early September 1914, his attitude to it became more ambivalent. In "Education of the People" (1919) he distinguishes between the modern Germans who "choose the idea of power, and fix [their] mechanical little will on that", and the positive example for boys today of "the Germans of old" who "look on the black eye and the bloody nose as insignia of honour" (*RDP*, 141, 159). In *Fantasia of the Unconscious* he comments that "the war was really not a bad beginning. But we went out under the banner of idealism", and boys should "be soldiers, but as individuals, not machine units" (*PUFU*, 118-119). Although he still identifies the idealism of industrial progress and nationalism in war, he now defends the primal impulse of violence, and in *Mr Noon* these two sides are conflated.

In the "rampant Germanism of Detsch" Gilbert contrasts its "mechanical heel-clicking" with his "natural ... passionate violence" with Johanna. Yet, even in contrasting the soldiers with Johanna, they are incorporated into his "marriage" with her. He perceives the "handsome ... healthy looking, powerful" soldiers at Trier as if they were ancient warriors in an industrial society who are singing and marching to the mechanical, and pulsating, rhythm of "a terrible, ponderous, splendid heart-stroke, stroke after stroke welding the deep heart into black iron". South of Munich, he watches a cavalcade of soldiers passing, wearing the "hideous neuter, grey neuter of machine-mouths", but he admires a soldier's "strong body", and their "strong, heavy-muscled legs". Again, Gilbert associates their "strange, dark, heavy soldiery, so young and strong with life, reckless and sensual", and their mechanized lives with ancient warriors. He argues with Johanna that the soldiers "want even the vile discipline and the humiliation. They must, or they wouldn't have it!" (*MN*, 159-60, 176, 208-10).

The narrator chides Gilbert as a "fool": "As if there were not sufficient dead eyes of insentience in the world, without his wishing to escape from the magnetism of desire." Yet Gilbert's marriage with Johanna is not an alternative to militarism, but contains his desire to abandon Johanna and become a soldier, to intensify his opposition with her, in which "man remains man, and woman woman, and in their difference they meet and are very happy". Paradoxically, when Gilbert and Johanna are too close to each other, "there was war" (*MN*, 211-12) between them.

As a first draft of a novel, which Lawrence would probably have rewritten from its first page had he later completed it, *Mr Noon* lays bare the ideological contradictions that he confronted in his own thought immediately after the war. In Gilbert, he dramatizes his own development out of a society which has turned its principles of individualism into a conventional ideal that serves the social whole. In terms of German culture, Lawrence represents this situation in Goethe's changing treatment of Faust, and the reception of Goethe in middle-class Germans like Professors Kramer and Sartorius, alias Edgar Jaffe and Alfred Weber. With Johanna, Gilbert learns to express his individuality through his erotic desires. Yet to Lawrence in 1920 this revelation has ossified into another ideal, which he had attempted to impose on society as a whole in *The Rainbow* and *Women in Love*, betraying the physical vitality of the original revelation. Lawrence is caught upon the dilemma of how to mediate between the individual and society, the body and mind: it is imperative to maintain the integrity of each side as an independent entity, while letting each feed into and change the other. Too often he stresses one side, and lets it overwhelm the other.

In *Mr Noon* Lawrence dismantles his value systems, in order to examine this dilemma. He reveals how, from its roots in Wagnerian

Romanticism, Gross' philosophy shared with German militarism an idealized vision of humanity which obliterated the material circumstances of individuals in society, and on the battlefield. Lawrence glorifies war alongside eroticism as a revolutionary event then celebrates military life to the exclusion of sexual love, and finally posits the two as complementary to each other in their opposition.

Although he did not begin to resolve these positions in *Mr Noon*, in *Aaron's Rod*, which he composed between 1917 and 1921, he struggled to find a resolution by affirming individuality to the exclusion of erotic and social relationships. He worked through the potentialities and limitations of this position, to define the scope of the individual in terms of the world beyond itself.

VIII
LEADERSHIP AND THE "DEAD IDEAL":
AARON'S ROD AND *KANGAROO*

In *Kangaroo* Richard Lovatt Somers identifies the Christian "ideal of Love, Self-sacrifice, Humanity united in love, in brotherhood, in peace" as the ideology that contributed to the First World War: "So then, why will men not forgive the war, and their humiliations at the hands of these war-like authorities? – because men were *compelled* into the service of a dead ideal" (*K*, 264). We have seen Lawrence examine contemporary idealism in his post-war novels. In *The Lost Girl* he included his insights in *Psychoanalysis and the Unconscious*, of how the conscious will can dominate the body's centres of the will. Ciccio's physical will liberated Alvina from social convention, yet in this process she was stripped of her individual free will. Her body's impulses became an exclusive ideal. Lawrence attempted to address this problem in Gilbert's relationship with Johanna in *Mr Noon* where he implicated Gross' "erotic ideal" with Wagner, and the idealism of the First World War. Ironically, Gilbert turns from his relationship with Johanna, back to the world of German soldiers. Lawrence returns to his concern with male relationships in *Women in Love*, despite Gerald and Birkin's association with the idealism of war, of Kaiser Wilhelm's "Ich habe es nicht gewollt".

The dilemmas in these novels, between mind and body, the individual and erotic relationships, are incorporated into *Aaron's Rod*. Its composition from 1917 to 1921 spans the completion of *Women in Love* and the writing of *The Lost Girl* and *Mr Noon*. Finishing *Aaron's Rod* in Germany enabled Lawrence to find answers to these dilemmas, and in *Kangaroo*, written the following year, he continued these efforts. Both novels confront the crisis in personal and political relationships which followed the war. Monarchies collapsed across Europe, in Russia, Austro-Hungary and Germany; the values that Somers describes, of "Love", "Self-sacrifice", "brotherhood" and "peace", fell with them. Every programme that was addressed to the crisis, especially liberalism and socialism, was exposed as an ideal because it could not provide an adequate solution to the chaos within individuals and societies as a whole. In *Aaron's Rod* and *Kangaroo* Lawrence suggests new values without turning them into ideals; he explores them in the midst of this crisis, in terms of the characters' disorientated experiences. The ideals that Somers identifies in the war were also to some extent shared by Lawrence, as in Ursula's rainbow and Birkin's love for Gerald.

Aaron's Rod and *Kangaroo* have been criticized for their lack of conventional structure and their anti-liberal ideas. John B. Humma draws attention to the lack of "consecutive thread"[1] in *Kangaroo*, and Eagleton ascribes the "ruptured" form of *Aaron's Rod* to the collapse of Lawrence's beliefs.[2] Diverse ideological positions are thrashed out in the novels, to leave contradiction as one of the tenuous bases of their formal unity. There is a right-wing appeal to leadership and misogyny which symptomizes the male characters' vulnerability against women, and ungovernable social classes. Peter Fjågesund asserts that Lawrence's "leadership ideas are probably more German than anything else, but they are in deliberate opposition to the maternalistic philosophy of Frieda's Schwabing".[3] The German context of these novels provides an important groundwork for understanding Lawrence's most politically controversial novel, *The Plumed Serpent*.

At this later period of Lawrence's career we are no longer exclusively concerned with tracing his influences from Germany, since by and large they are already well in place. Instead, to evaluate the political implications of his novels the priority has shifted to a comparison with the ideas circulating in Germany during the crucial decade of the Twenties. In *Aaron's Rod* Lawrence concentrates on the issue of idealism in the exclusively male relationship between Aaron Sisson and Rawdon Lilly. He tests his characters' capacity to realize themselves independently of sexual and wider social relationships, and to live beyond the traditional conventions encapsulated by the "dead ideal" of war. This project was probably influenced by a contemporary novel, *Demian* by Hermann Hesse, which describes the relationship between Emil Sinclair and Max Demian. More significantly perhaps, the two novels are worth comparing in terms of

---

[1] John B. Humma, *Metaphor and Meaning in D. H. Lawrence's Later Novels* (Columbia: University of Missouri Press, 1990), 32.
[2] See Terry Eagleton, *Criticism and Ideology* (London: Verso, 1978), 157-61.
[3] Peter Fjågesund, *The Apocalyptic World of D. H. Lawrence* (Oslo: Norwegian University Press, 1991), 113.

their relative success and failure to envisage an alternative to the crisis of values at the end of the war.

From the ideal to the individual
On 9 February 1924, in response to a query from Mabel Dodge Luhan, Lawrence described his impression of Hesse's novel: "I read *Demian* in Germany when it first came out, and have almost forgotten it. But the first part interested me" (Letters, IV, 576). *Demian* was published in 1919; its depiction of the relationship between Emil and Demian impressed the younger generation of Germans who had become disillusioned with military hierarchy as the model for male relationships since the outbreak of war.[4] Although Lawrence had begun *Aaron's Rod* in early 1918, it is not known when he began to concentrate on the relationship between Aaron and Lilly. Perhaps *Demian* inspired him to create this relationship, or it only "interested" him in his treatment of it. Certainly, like Lawrence, Hesse developed his self-awareness as a member of society, and as an artist during the war. He denounced the war as a false ideal imposed upon people by social authority; he was attacked by the social authorities, and by pacifists whose rational solutions he disagreed with. Alienated from both political sides, Hesse and Lawrence's isolation inspired their answers to the mass-slaughter of war.

Demian and *Aaron's Rod* reflect the collapse of values in European society through war, especially in terms of Christianity. Both novels depart from the ritual of Christmas, which has been discredited as a celebration of Christian values. Aaron is at home with his family, decorating the tree:

> this was home, this was Christmas: the unspeakably familiar. The war over, nothing was changed. Yet everything changed. (*AR*, 11)

He visits his local public house and buys candles for the tree, only to abandon his family. For Emil, the protagonist of Hesse's novel, Christmas changes from "the evening of festivity and love, of gratitude, and of the renewal of the bond between my parents and

---

[4] See Joseph Mileck, *Hermann Hesse: Life and Art* (Berkeley: University of California Press, 1978), 89.

me", to a "depressing and embarrassing"[5] event since he no longer shares his family's religious values.

This reaction against Christmas, and the values of Christianity, is accompanied by a rejection of the cultural traditions of Goethe and Romanticism. Emil unsuccessfully attempts "to build my 'world of light' [lichte Welt] out of the ruins of my breakdown" through the "Reinheit" ("purity") and "Geistigkeit" ("spirituality")[6] of his desire for an unattainable girl. This *Licht* and *Reinheit* connote Goethe's idealism in *Faust II*, which Lawrence subverted in *The Rainbow* and *Women in Love*. During the war Hesse rejected the conventional image of Goethe, despite appealing to his pacifism: "the essence of love, beauty, and holiness does not lie in Christianity or in antiquity or in Goethe or in Tolstoy – it lies in you and me, in each one of us."[7] Alongside his scepticism of Goethe, Hesse had also lost faith in his early Romanticism. Since his first novel *Peter Camenzind* (1904) which celebrated nature and love, he had struggled to reconcile romantic love with his protagonists' individuality. In *Aaron's Rod* Lawrence too maintains the rejection of Goethe and Romanticism, from Wagner to Otto Gross, that he had shown in *Mr Noon*.

Nietzsche is crucial to Hesse and Lawrence in their break from the conventions of Christianity, Goethe and Romanticism, and in their affirmation of the individual. In *Menschliches, Allzumenschliches* Nietzsche discredited Christian values alongside other Western ideologies. He distinguished from the majority of "gebundenen Geister" ("bound spirits") the individual "Freigeist" ("free spirit"), who is not necessarily right but is liberated from these ideologies.[8] Later, for Nietzsche the death of God coincided with the *Umwertung aller Werte*. Rebelling against the Wagnerian Romanticism of *Tristan und Isolde*, he asserted that in comforting men, women take away

---

[5] Hermann Hesse, *Demian* (Frankfurt am Main: Suhrkamp, 1974), 91: "der Abend der Festlichkeit und Liebe, der Dankbarkeit, der Erneuerung des Bundes zwischen den Eltern und mir"; "bedrückend und verlegenmachend."

[6] *Ibid.*, 94-95: "aus Trümmern einer zusammengebrochenen Lebensperiode mir eine 'lichte' Welt zu bauen."

[7] Hesse, *Politik des Gewissens*, two vols (Frankfurt am Main: Suhrkamp, 1977), II, 228: "das Wesen der Liebe, der Schönheit, der Heiligkeit liegt nicht in Christentum, nicht in Antike, nicht bei Goethe, nicht bei Tolstoy – es liegt in dir, in dir und mir, in jedem von uns."

[8] See Nietzsche, *Werke*, IV 2, 116-17, 193-94.

from them the harshness of experience that inspires them; he concluded that the free spirit needs "allein zu fliegen" ("to fly alone").[9] Demian preaches that "Every man must stand alone": "that is why each one of us must discover for himself what is permitted and what is forbidden – is forbidden to him."[10]

Aaron and Emil develop their individuality by maintaining a degree of hostility with their male partners. In his essay "Zarathustras Wiederkehr" (1919), responding to the immediate popularity of *Demian* in Germany, Hesse quotes Zarathustra's repudiation of his followers: "You should learn to be yourselves, just as I have learned to be Zarathustra."[11] Demian's identity is "singularly and personally stamped"[12] and Lilly has a "half-veiled surety, as if nothing, nothing could overcome him". Aaron admires this quality, while hating it as "basic indifference" and "silent arrogance" towards others. At the beginning of their relationship, Emil feels a mixture "of gratitude and timidity, of admiration and anxiety, of affection and inward hostility"[13] towards Demian. Demian and Emil's bond is comparable to Aaron and Lilly's "brotherhood": "Like brothers, there was a profound hostility between them. But hostility is not antipathy" (*AR*, 289, 106).

Both Lawrence and Hesse use Nietzsche's *Wille zur Macht*, in tandem with psychoanalytic ideas, to define the individualism of their characters. From 1916 to 1922 Hesse underwent psychoanalysis under the Jungian J. B. Lang,[14] and in the same period that he completed *Aaron's Rod* in 1921, Lawrence wrote *Fantasia of the Unconscious*. Both authors identify the *Wille zur Macht* as the source of the individual's energies. Demian explains to Emil the power of the *Wille*: "If an animal or person directs his whole attention and will

---

[9] *Ibid.*, 288.
[10] Hesse, *Demian*, 75-76: "Jeder muß für sich selber stehen"; "Darum muß jeder von uns für sich selber finden, was erlaubt und was verboten – ihm verboten ist."
[11] Hesse, *Politik des Gewissens*, I, 283: "Ihr sollet lernen, ihr selbst zu sein, so wie ich Zarathustra zu sein gelernt habe."
[12] Hesse, *Demian*, 33: "eigen und persönlich gestempelt."
[13] *Ibid.*, 51-52: "aus Dankbarkeit und Scheu, aus Bewunderung und Angst, aus Zuneigung und innerem Widerstreben."
[14] See Mileck, *Hermann Hesse: Life and Art*, 67.

onto a certain matter, then he will achieve it."[15] Lilly uses the same principle towards the end of *Aaron's Rod*:

> We've got to accept the power motive, accept it in deep responsibility, do you understand me? It is a great life motive .... It is a vast dark source of life and strength in us now, waiting either to issue into true action, or to burst into cataclysm. Power – the power-urge. The will-to-power – but not in Nietzsche's sense. Not intellectual power. Not mental power. Not conscious will-power. Not even wisdom. But dark, living, fructifying power. Do you know what I mean? (*AR*, 297)

Like Zarathustra's pupil, Lilly rejects Nietzsche while following his ideas, and in turn, true to the stubbornness of his own *Wille zur Macht*, Aaron answers that he does not know what Lilly means.

According to Demian, the will of the individual disregards impossible ideals for "what he needs, what is indispensable to him" since "truly [his] whole being is filled by it", including his unconscious. If he "wanted to direct his will on a star"[16] he would fail, like the people whom Lilly criticizes, with "their wagon hitched to a star – which goes round and round like an ass in a gin" (*AR*, 292). In *Fantasia of the Unconscious* Lawrence continues his opposition from *Psychoanalysis and the Unconscious* between the "will of the upper centre" and the "will exerted from the lower centre of the solar-plexus" (*PUFU*, 84). Since crossing "the dividing line" between England and Italy, away from "the accursed mechanical ideal" to the "spontaneous life-dynamic", Aaron has faced the "new responsibility" that encompasses his entire being, of getting "a new grip on his own bowels, a new hard recklessness into his heart, and new responsible consciousness into his mind and soul" (*AR*, 151-52).

The ideas of Nietzsche and psychoanalysis offer Lawrence and Hesse an alternative to the war. Yet both novelists are uncomfortable about the cult of Nietzsche in the war and Freud's concentration on sexuality. As in *Women in Love* Lawrence wants to avoid the "bullying" implications of Nietzsche's *Wille zur Macht* that were manifested in the war, and he locates these in the philosopher's

---

[15] Hesse, *Demian*, 66: "Wenn ein Tier oder Mensch seine ganze Aufmerksamkeit und seinen ganzen Willen auf eine bestimmte Sache richtet, dann erreicht er sie auch."
[16] *Ibid.*, 67-68: "was er braucht, was er unbedingt haben muß"; "wirklich [sein] Wesen ganz von ihm erfüllt ist", "seinen Willen auf einen Stern."

emphasis on mental consciousness. Yet for Nietzsche the *Wille zur Macht* was an antidote to idealism; as he argued in one of his uncollected fragments, "the belief in the body is better established than the belief in the spirit".[17] In *Jenseits von Gut und Böse* (*Beyond Good and Evil*) he shares this conviction, that "Leben selbst ist Wille zur Macht" ("Life itself is Wille zur Macht").[18] The problem for Lawrence is the way Nietzsche thinks about the relation between body and mind. Nietzsche outlines the processes of the *Wille zur Macht* as "firstly, a plurality of sensations, ... and then also an accompanying muscular sensation", which function alongside "a commanding thought". The body and mind of the individual enter a relation with the world on the basis of "I am free, 'he' must obey", which also occurs within the individual, since "our body is only a social structure of many souls".[19] This hierarchy resembles that of Gerald over the miners, and of his mind over his body. It also resembles a military hierarchy.

In *Fantasia of the Unconscious* and *Aaron's Rod* Lawrence manoeuvres between different readings of Nietzsche and Freud. He attempts to avoid the potentially oppressive relations of the *Wille zur Macht* by subordinating the mind under what Nietzsche calls the *Unterwillen* within the body, but in so doing Lawrence also transforms Nietzsche's ideas. On the other hand, he is true to Nietzsche's *freie Geist* who must restrain his sexual desire for a woman, in order to maintain his individuality. Lawrence is opposed to Gross' vision of the *freie Geist* and *Übermensch* as a woman whose *freie Liebe* can liberate mankind. In *Fantasia* Lawrence rejects Freud's, and by implication Gross', exclusive concentration on sex, countering it with "the desire of the human male to build a world". Lawrence maintains that this desire is not governed by the "reality principle", or Nietzsche's *Überwillen*, but is an "essentially religious or creative motive" (*PUFU*, 66-67).

---

[17] Nietzsche, *Werke*, VII, 3, 367: "Der Glaube an den Leib ist besser festgestellt als der Glaube an den Geist."
[18] *Ibid.*, VI, 2, 21.
[19] *Ibid.*, 26-27: "erstens eine Mehrheit von Gefühlen, ... dann noch ein begleitendes Muskelgefühl"; "einen kommandierenden Gedanken"; "ich bin frei, ›er‹ muß gehorchen"; "unser Leib ist ja nur ein Gesellschaftsbau vieler Seelen."

Hesse appeals to the idealism of the Expressionists to counter Nietzsche's political dangers and Freud's concentration on sex. In the essay *Eigensinn* (1918), written under the same pseudonym as *Demian*, he dismisses the soldier's honour in heroism for "the law in himself, the 'senses' of the 'individual'".[20] To avoid confusion with the imperialist glorification of the German *Wille zur Macht* in war, Hesse's *Sinn* denotes sense, desire, consciousness, mind, feeling, spirit and meaning – which locates it in the body's sensuality, and in idealist philosophy.

Hesse and Lawrence, then, affirm their characters' individuality in the face of discredited traditions such as Christianity, Goethe and Romanticism. They invoke the ideas of Nietzsche and Freud to outline the core of their characters' individuality in terms of physical impulses, as in the *Wille zur Macht* and libido. Yet both Hesse and Lawrence are uncertain about the relation between body and mind in their readings of Nietzsche and Freud.

Crisis and the *Ewig-Weibliche*
In an attempt to avoid this issue regarding the hierarchy between body and mind Lawrence and Hesse concentrate on the sovereign individuality of each character, which encompasses his whole being. Relationships with a woman or a social group would decentre the individual's will from within himself, and force him to choose how to respond to them, through his intellect or body, or both in varying degrees. Like Lawrence in "Democracy", which discounted "state", "nation", "democracy", "socialism" as "dead ideals" (*RDP*, 66), Hesse underrates the crucial need for political commitment as "das Lied von der Weltverbesserung" ("the song of world betterment"), whether it is the Kaiser, professors, democracy, socialism, the League of Nations, world peace, or new nationalism that claim his allegiance. For Hesse, they have only materialistic value: "why do you not now seek your pain where it is: within yourselves?"[21] For Demian, the *Wille* is manifested in the individual, independent of revolutions and wars in which politicians "cling to ideals that no longer exist"; the

---

[20] Hesse, *Politik des Gewissens*, I, 219: "dem Gesetz in sich selbst, dem 'Sinn' des 'Eigenen'."

[21] *Ibid.*, 297, 286. "warum suchet ihr nicht auch jetzt eure Schmerzen dort auf, wo sie sind. In euch innen?"

individual's *Wille* can "demonstrate the worthlessness of the current ideal". Politics is only manifested through the *Herdenbildung* ("herd instinct").[22] Lilly dismisses the League of Nations, and "all masses and groups": "All I want is to get *myself* out of the horrible heap: to get out of the swarm" (*AR*, 119).

Yet Aaron's individualism is not a quest for fulfilment, but a "hard core of irrational, exhausting withholding of himself" (*AR*, 22-23) to survive. It is "a white fury" resisting his desire for a Romantic darkness:

> Nothing would have pleased him better than to feel his senses melting and swimming into oneness with the dark. But impossible! (*AR*, 251)

Lilly does not offer him fulfilment, but merely a protection from losing himself. Lilly is an alternative to a "woman", or "social ideal" or "social institution" for Aaron, "since yield he must, in some direction or other" (*AR*, 290). For Kinkead-Weekes, *Aaron's Rod* proves the opposite of its opening affirmation of individual freedom, and reveals how the individual is irresistibly drawn into relationships with others. Lawrence attempts to resolve this situation by formulating relationships as expressions of individuals' power towards others, not of the love that they give up to each other. Yet there is the persistent desire to direct power over, not towards, others.[23] The question in *Aaron's Rod* is how to yield, through one's body or mind, and what to yield to, a woman, society, or another man.

Hesse responded to this impasse by reverting to Romantic idealism; towards the end of *Demian* Emil yields to Frau Eva. Lawrence dismissed this section of the novel: "The last part I thought *sau dumm* with its Mother Eva who didn't know whether she was wife or mother or what" (Letters, IV, 576). Eva is Demian's mother, with whom Emil immediately falls in love: "Were she to become a mother to me, a lover, a goddess – if she could just be here!"[24] In Frau Eva Hesse has returned to Goethe, in particular to the ending of *Faust*

---

[22] Hesse, *Demian*, 158-59: "hängen an Idealen, die keine mehr sind"; "die Wertlosigkeit der heutigen Ideale dartun."
[23] See Kinkead-Weekes, *D. H. Lawrence: Triumph to Exile*, 649-53.
[24] Hesse, *Demian*, 165: "Mochte sie mir Mutter, Geliebte, Göttin werden – wenn sie nur da war!"

II. As mother, lover and goddess she is a manifestation of Goethe's *Ewig-Weibliche* ("eternal feminine") whose supreme form is the Mater Gloriosa. Faust addresses her:

> Jungfrau, rein im schönsten Sinn,
> Mutter, Ehren würdig,
> Uns erwählte Königin,
> Göttern ebenbürtig.[25]

> Virgin, pure in the most beautiful way,
> Mother, worthy of honour,
> Our chosen Queen,
> equal to God.

Like Faust as Doctor Marianus, reaching upwards to the Mater Gloriosa, Emil dreams of Frau Eva: "She was a star and I myself was like a star on my way to her."[26] Hesse is contradicting Demian's previous explanation that the *Wille* cannot relate to ideal entities that are detached from its physical needs.

Following this lapse into Goethe's idealism of womanhood, Emil and Demian are seduced by the idealism of war. The crucial issue is their abandonment of a material reality of their individual experiences to serve a bodiless ideal of womanhood and love, which Lawrence has associated with the ideal of self-sacrifice in war since Birkin's rage against "love" in *Women in Love*. Demian echoes Franz Marc's initial attitude in September 1914, that "I feel so strongly the spirit [Geist] which hovers behind the battles, behind every bullet, so that the realistic, the material, disappear completely".[27] Like most officers, Demian predicts that: "it won't in itself give me any pleasure to command artillery fire at living people, but that will be merely incidental. Now it will catch up each one of us in the great wheel."[28]

---

[25] Goethe, *Gedenkausgabe*, V, 526, 523.
[26] Hesse, *Demian*, 177: "Sie war ein Stern, und ich selbst war als ein Stern zu ihr unterwegs."
[27] Marc, *Briefe aus dem Feld*, 11: "ich fühle den Geist, der hinter den Schlachten, hinter jeder Kugel schwebt so stark, daß das realistische, materielle ganz verschwindet."
[28] Hesse, *Demian*, 187: "Es wird ja im Grund kein Vergnügen machen, Gewehrfeuer auf lebende Menschen zu kommandieren, aber das wird nebensächlich sein. Es wird jetzt jeder von uns in das große Rad hineinkommen."

In the narrative Hesse provides no counter against Demian's identification of the individual with the nation. Heinz Stolte observes in *Demian* the dangerous consequences of imposing the incongruous needs and characteristics of each character upon the other, whereupon the reality of both is denied.[29]

At the close of the novel Hesse is ambiguous about the meaning of the war. Emil observes that: "all people were capable of dying for an ideal. Only it could be no personal, no free, no chosen ideal; it had to be a common and accepted one." The majority of soldiers are dying in the name of "war, heroism, ... honour and other old ideals", which Emil rejects, but they are also dying for Demian's alternative ideal. In imagining that "in the depths something was developing. Something like a new humanity",[30] Emil shares Ursula's vision at the close of *The Rainbow*, of humanity "in the husk of an old fruition, but visible through the husk, the welling and the heaving contour of the new germination ... the new liberation" (*R*, 458). Both glorify the war's idealism of renewal which looks beyond the mortality of individual soldiers.

Lawrence is opposed both to the lingering idealism of *Demian*, and the threat of Gross' vision of womanhood as an alternative to patriarchy. Yet, as Kinkead-Weekes observes, Aaron's individual resistance is not a creative, fulfilling condition in itself. The novel as a whole threatens to disintegrate into the uncompromising positions of the characters. We can see Lawrence's ideological confusion, and an accompanying misogyny, when Aaron reflects on his separation from his wife Lottie in the chapter "Wie es Ihnen Gefällt". At first Aaron denounces Lottie's will as if it were mental consciousness: "Her will, her will, her terrible, implacable, cunning will!" He identifies his wife's will with her notion of herself as a woman, "the first great source of life and being, and also of culture", which "was formulated for her in the whole world". Through this ideal Lottie, like Johanna in

---

[29] See Heinz Stolte, *Hermann Hesse: Weltscheu und Lebensliebe* (Hamburg: Hansa, 1971), 119.

[30] Hesse, *Demian*, 189-90: "alle Menschen fähig sind, für ein Ideal zu sterben. Nur durfte es kein persönliches, kein freies, kein gewähltes Ideal sein, es mußte ein gemeinsames und übernommenes sein"; "Krieg und Heldentum, ... Ehre und andre alte Ideale"; "In der Tiefe war etwas im Werden. Etwas wie eine neue Menschlichkeit."

Mr Noon, demands that a man "yield" (*AR*, 158-59) himself to her. Like Goethe and Gross, Hesse believes in this "religious" "worship" of the female as Frau Eva, despite its link with idealized war, to which millions of men have yielded themselves in its denial of their individual lives.

Yet Lawrence has celebrated this religion in his previous novels, and betrays a sympathy for it by identifying it with Lottie's whole being: "She held it not as an idea, but as a profound impulse and instinct: an instinct developed in her by the age in which she lived." It is not located in her conscious mind, but her "deep unconscious instinct". Her will in these terms is the equivalent to Lilly's formulation of it as "a vast dark source of life and strength in us" (*AR*, 159, 297). Despite being instinctual, Lottie's will is historically linked to war.

Lawrence struggles to give a negative portrayal of this eroticism. He writes that Aaron, who represents every man in this context, never gave himself to this Romanticism, and that it was only his wife's delusion:

> He withheld the very centre of himself. For a long time, she never realised ... for her every veil seemed rent and a terrible and sacred creative darkness covered the earth – then – after all this wonder and miracle – in crept a poisonous grey snake of disillusionment.

The language is as powerful as in the erotic experiences of each generation of the Brangwen family in *The Rainbow*, but here Lawrence is arguing against it – or even claiming that it was always a sham. From being a mutual loss of self and then recovery and flourishing of the self in the earlier novel, in *Aaron's Rod* Lottie's erotic experience is treated as a mere dead-end: "all her instinct, all her impulse, all her desire, and above all, all her *will*, was to possess her man in very fulness once: just once: and once and for all. Once, just once: and it would be once and for all" (*AR*, 161). Lawrence repeats together "once" and "all", as if this single act of possession contained everything within it, and only death could follow it. He foregrounds the "*will*" as if it were mere consciousness, yet in conjunction with her desire and instinct the will signifies the whole of her being, as Lilly formulates it.

From this ambiguous position Lawrence then describes Lottie's conscious will as the dominant force upon the body, "fixed" and solidified into "stone", in opposition to her "unbearable desire" for Aaron. On the other side, Aaron's will liberates him from his wife's attempt to possess him, and is still identified with his whole being as an individual:

> His will was still entire and unabated .... His intrinsic and central aloneness was the very centre of his being. (*AR*, 161-62)

Lawrence's language of the will collapses because its formulation is rooted in the body's impulses. While attempting to break from his previous idealism inspired by Gross, Lawrence remains entangled in it. Anxious that the reader is unconvinced, Lawrence concedes that Aaron "wasn't half clever enough to think all these smart things", but then challenges the reader: "yet it all resolved itself in him as I say, and it is for you to prove that it didn't" (*AR*, 164).

The novel's unresolved tension in language, and accompanying misogyny and "ruptured" form, are due to Lawrence's unbending insistence on his male characters' individuality. Even this insistence is contested by the characters among themselves, in order to confirm their individual resistance to any encompassing idea. Lilly argues that "no man who was awake and in possession of himself would use poison gases: no man", and Aaron replies that "it's the wide-awake ones that invent the poison gas, and use it". Lilly's declaration that "every man is a sacred and holy individual, *never* to be violated", is bracketed by his proposal for "a proper and healthy and energetic slavery" (*AR*, 119, 281-82), and a bomb explosion. In *Aaron's Rod* every statement has its contradicting rebuttal.

A similar ambivalence, which has set Emil and Demian apart as developing individuals, becomes vaguer over the course of Hesse's novel, until their synthesis at the end with Demian's *Liebestod*. He kisses Emil and advises him to "listen inside yourself, then you will realize that I am within you".[31] At Covent Garden Lilly makes "a certain call on his, Aaron's soul: a call which he, Aaron, did not at all intend to obey". Yet in rejecting Lilly, Aaron is like Zarathustra's follower, and is faithful to Lilly's sense of individuality. Aaron's last

---

[31] *Ibid.*, 193: "dich hinein hören, dann merkst du, daß ich in dir drinnen bin."

words to Lilly, "And whom shall I submit to?" (*AR*, 121, 299) are perhaps beseeching, or mocking. Lawrence even resists turning individuality into an ideal by discussing it in fiercely contested, individual statements.

German politics in *Aaron's Rod*

Kinkead-Weekes describes Lawrence's burst of creativity in Baden-Baden from 26 April 1921, until his move to Zell-am-See in Austria on 10 July. Lawrence completed more than the final third of *Aaron's Rod* in May alone, including Aaron's relationship with the Marchesa and his subsequent return to Lilly.[32] A year later Lawrence reminisced that "only Germany helped me to the finish of *Aaron*". He was inspired, perhaps by the stillness of the trees as he claimed, or by "all that the German professors flung in my face when I was in Germany" (Letters, IV, 259, 133) of the upheaval in society and politics. Throughout this period he was aware of developments in Germany, partly in his correspondence with Else Jaffe, his mother-in-law Baroness von Richtofen, and his publisher in Germany Dr Anton von Kippenberg.

The riot and bomb explosion in *Aaron's Rod* have been traced back to Lawrence's experience of Florence in autumn 1920 by Kinkead-Weekes.[33] However, Germany offered Lawrence intellectual ideas to analyse these political events, just as they did for his analysis of the Nottinghamshire mining industry in *The Rainbow* and *Women in Love*. This factor has made *Aaron's Rod* appear ominous in relation to the crisis that Germany, and the world, were drawn into over the next two decades. It has inspired Lawrence's most violent critics, including Bertrand Russell and Kate Millett. For Eagleton and Kinkead-Weekes the power relationship advocated in *Aaron's Rod* finds its political realization in fascist oppression which tragically dispossesses individuals of their freedom.

In turning their novels towards political issues, both Lawrence and Hesse shift from the notion of male friendship to leadership. In his solitary despair Emil refers to Demian as his *Freund und Führer* ("friend and leader"):

---

[32] See Kinkead-Weekes, *D. H. Lawrence: Triumph to Exile*, 647.
[33] *Ibid.*, 599.

Leadership and the "Dead Ideal" 255

A leader [Führer] has abandoned me. I am standing in utter darkness. I cannot take another step alone. Help me![34]

Demian is gathering around himself a circle of followers who have grouped together as a pseudo-political movement, and he anticipates the renewal of mankind in the communal experience of war. Demian, like any other army officer, leads Emil to risk his life on the battlefront for an ideal. For Lawrence, an authoritarian leadership is the only viable alternative to the political structures that fostered war in the first place.

Lilly's alternative to current political ideologies is "for no one but myself", in other words, each individual should formulate his own ideology. Yet Lilly's personal philosophy demands that everyone be "brought to agree – after sufficient extermination – and then they will elect for themselves a proper and healthy and energetic slavery ... of inferior beings to the responsibility of a superior being", enforced by "military power". Then Lilly asserts the opposite, that "I think every man is a sacred and holy individual, *never* to be violated" (*AR*, 281-82). Later, in his concluding dialogue with Aaron, he identifies the "will-to-power" as "a great life motive", yet which demands the obedience of women to men, and men "to the greater soul in a man", "a leader" (*AR*, 297-99).

Lilly is reflecting current anti-democratic ideas, including those that Adolf Hitler would articulate in *Mein Kampf* (1925-27) on leadership: "This principle of the unconditional bond of absolute responsibility with absolute authority will gradually breed an elite of leaders, such as today, in this age of irresponsible parliamentarianism, is unimaginable."[35] Once elected, Hitler's leader would have unconditional power, secured by the army. Yet for Lilly, individual freedom and slavery are not exclusive alternatives, but necessarily function together, despite their incongruity. In expressing individual power, Lilly implies, one must either dominate or submit to the power of others. These ideas form the core of debates over *Aaron's Rod*, and

---

[34] Hesse, *Demian*, 194, 152-53: "Ein Führer hat mich verlassen. Ich stehe ganz im Finstern. Ich kann keinen Schritt allein tun. Hilf mir!"
[35] Adolf Hitler, *Mein Kampf*, 2 vols (Munich: Zentralverlag der NSDAP, 1940), II, 90-91: "Dieser Grundsatz unbedingter Verbindung von absoluter Verantwortlichkeit mit absoluter Autorität wird allmählich eine Führerauslese heranzüchten, wie dies heute in Zeitalter des verantwortungslosen Parlamentarismus gar nicht denkbar ist."

are at the root of its alleged fascism and misogyny; they are also elaborated in *Kangaroo*. The question that begs to be answered is why Lilly's two antipodal positions, of individual freedom and its submission to an outside authority, should be placed alongside one other as his answer to the problems of Lawrence's age.

In 1921 Germany was in a period of short-term stability. Lawrence had sent food parcels to his German relatives before the embargoes were lifted with the ratification of the Versailles Treaty, but through state intervention employment had been provided for demobilized German soldiers immediately after the war, and industry was already recovering.[36] There could be no foresight of the hyper-inflation and right-wing putsches of 1923. Yet Lawrence was exceptional in his foreboding of future warfare beyond the impasse in politics and peoples' attitudes: "one feels, the old order has gone – Hohenzollern and Nietzsche and all. And the era of love and peace and democracy with it. There will be an era of war ahead: some sort of warfare, one knows not what" (Letters, III, 732). Lawrence's premonition was informed by the failure of his acquaintances to bring "peace and democracy" to German politics. Most important was Edgar Jaffe's role as the Finance Minister of the Bavarian Republic in 1919; he died on 29 April 1921, a few days after Lawrence's arrival in Germany. Lawrence also met Alfred Weber in May 1921, who was struggling to establish a liberal party in Germany.

Although Lawrence dismisses Nietzsche in his letter in 1923, it is clear, and confirmed by his direct appeal to the philosopher in *Aaron's Rod*, that he is referring to those Nietzschean ideas that Germany had glorified in the war, for instance that of the national *Wille zur Macht*. In the section "Wir Heimatlosen" ("We homeless ones") of *Die Fröhliche Wissenschaft* Nietzsche anticipates Lilly's ideas most closely. He notes that "in this fragile and crumbling period of transition", "we are resentful of ideals", and do not even believe in "Realitäten" ("realities"), since they do not last. We are no longer liberal since we do not work for "Fortschritt" ("progress"), and neither do we conserve the past. Yet in our enjoyment of danger and war, "we think about the necessity of new orders, also new slavery – every strengthening and ennobling of the 'human' type belongs also

---

[36] See Richard Bessel , *Germany after the First World War* (Oxford: Oxford University Press, 1993), 128-29, 163.

to a new type of slavery – does it not?" Nietzsche is ambiguous here, perhaps sincere, perhaps ironic about the German sense of vitality after the wars of national unification. He describes how one reads in the word "deutsch dem Nationalismus und dem Rassenhaß" ("nationalism and racial hatred"), since politics only "makes the German spirit empty".[37] Party politics fail to satisfy the needs of people, leaving a political vacuum filled by aggressive nationalism which is the equivalent to slavery.

During the political crisis in post-war Europe Nietzsche's thoughts were taken up by socialists and liberals. Edgar Jaffe's collaborators in the Bavarian Revolution, Kurt Eisner and Gustav Landauer, believed that the proletariat would exert its *Wille zur Macht* through a revolution,[38] but they rejected Nietzsche's anti-socialist attitudes.[39] In 1925 Alfred Weber published *Die Krise des modernen Staatsgedankens in Europa* (*The Crisis of modern Political Systems in Europe*), in which he attempts to envisage how democracy, despite being determined by large-scale economic interests, could provide the conditions for the freedom of its citizens. In relation to this question Weber is fiercely ambivalent towards Nietzsche, who advocated "individual self-integration, personal leadership and professed communal awareness" that was based on the principle of *Menschenrechte* ("human rights"). At the same time Weber rejects Nietzsche's *riesenhaften Pessimismus* ("gigantic pessimism") of *Machtgedanken* ("power-thought"), *Nationalgedanken* ("nationalist thought") and racial and biological ideas. Nietzsche has destroyed man's "background of ideals" to leave a "slavery of pure egocentric, state-power political will".[40]

---

[37] Nietzsche, *Werke*, VI 2, 310-13: "in dieser zerbrechlichen, zerbrochenen Übergangszeit"; "Wir sind allen Idealen abgünstig"; "wir denken über die Notwendigkeit neuer Ordnungen nach, auch einer neuen Sklaverei – denn zu jeder Verstärkung und Erhöhung des Typus 'Mensch' gehört auch eine neue Art Versklaverung hinzu – nicht wahr?"; "den deutschen Geist öde macht."
[38] See Aschheim, *The Nietzsche Legacy in Germany*, 170-78.
[39] See Allan Mitchell, *Revolution in Bavaria 1918-1919: The Eisner Regime and the Soviet Republic* (Princeton: Princeton University Press, 1965), 37-40.
[40] Alfred Weber, *Die Krise des modernen Staatsgedankens in Europa* (Stuttgart: Deutsche Verlags-Anstalt, 1925), 164, 107: "individuelle Selbsteingliederung, persönliches Führertum und vorgegebenes Gemeinschaftsbewußtsein"; "ideellen Hintergrundes"; "Sklaven eines rein egozentrisch eingestellten staatlich=machtpolitischen Wollens."

Jaffe's socialism and Weber's liberalism take only one side of Nietzsche's analysis of Germany. After Jaffe's socialist revolution was suppressed by conservative forces, the SDP joined an uneasy alliance with the victors, and the German political stage echoed the extremes of Nietzsche's earlier analysis. As Lawrence predicted, the Weimar Republic proved to be "an era of war" between these opposing ideologies, later polarized between Communists and National Socialists. This "war" is present throughout *Aaron's Rod*, in the conflict between characters, and their values. Lilly does not offer a solution to the ideological crisis of this period; instead he embraces the conflicting ideologies of this crisis. He avoids the political idealism of Jaffe and Weber who were political failures, and Hesse's idealism. In advocating slavery and freedom, he is a true inheritor of Nietzsche's thought. Lawrence avoids any idealistic solutions to the political condition of Europe; by this first step, he hopes to place a political responsibility onto the individual, not onto mass movements.

German politics in *Kangaroo*

In *Kangaroo* Lawrence imagines the future consequences of Lilly's political attitudes by placing them onto the political stage of Australia. In particular, the ambiguous character of Benjamin Cooley, or Kangaroo, embodies the political alternatives open to Germany, and Europe, in the Twenties. He is both a "leader" who demands absolute compliance, and a prophet of freedom for his unwilling "subjects".

After his stay in Germany and Austria Lawrence left for Italy, then Ceylon, and Australia where he wrote the novel in June and July 1922. A year on, *Kangaroo* looks back to Lawrence's impressions of Germany; trying to harness inspiration to write the novel, he recalled to Frieda's mother that "letztes Jahr habe ich es in Ebersteinburg gefunden" ("last year I found it in Ebersteinburg"). The Australian basis of *Kangaroo* has been repeatedly examined,[41] but the memory of Europe forms a backdrop which also gives political significance to the characters and their actions. While writing the novel Lawrence wrote to Kippenberg in Germany: "The world is all alike – weary with its old forms. But here the earth and air are new, and the spirit of place

---

[41] See Bruce Steele's introduction to *Kangaroo*, xix-xxxiv.

untouched" (Letters, IV, 254, 360). Australia shares Europe's democratic politics, industrialization and scars of the war, but its geographical isolation from Europe gives it scope to choose its future direction.

Richard Lovatt Somers and his German wife Harriett, who have followed the Lawrences' journey from Europe to Australia, bear the residues of Europe. Their neighbour Jack Callcott at first suspects that Somers is German, and Harriett lives by her "pure Teutonic consciousness", singing Schubert and wearing a Bavarian dress. In Australia itself, Germany is present in the memories of war. Somers discounts its threat to the rest of the world: "As a war-machine, she's done, and done for ever. So much scrap-iron, her iron fist." At the local war monument there is a German machine gun, looking "scrapped and forgotten" but also "exotic, a thing of some higher culture, demonic and fallen". Yet the war lies beneath the surface of events in the novel; it erupts after Somers' confrontation with Kangaroo in the "Nightmare", which includes memories of "German military creatures" whom Somers "would never forgive … in his inward soul" (*K*, 238, 41, 191, 213). The war encompasses the "dead ideal" that Lawrence's protagonists are trying to escape from.

War veterans, such as Jack, constitute most of Kangaroo's political movement. Jack reiterates Lilly's most extreme assertions. He shares Hitler's idea of a leadership based on a military hierarchy where "you've got to command, you don't have to ask your men if it's right, before you give the command". With the "trained fighting men" behind it, he believes the Diggers movement could "*make* the will of the people". Hitler argued that one could "win the broad masses" through "will and strength".[42] Like Hitler, Jack is also concerned racial purity: "if we let in coloured labour, they'll swallow us." At the beginning of the novel Somers is moved by Jack's rhetoric, just as Gilbert Noon was attracted to the German soldiers. Somers believes that he can be Jack's leader, but Harriett points out that Jack only "wants a chance of keeping on being a hero" (*K*, 88, 94, 90, 98).

Michael Wilding comments that that the Diggers movement cannot be categorized politically, and that despite being Jack's chosen

---

[42] Hitler, *Mein Kampf*, I, 331: "die breite Masse gewinnen"; "Wille und Kraft."

leader, Kangaroo is not exclusively fascist in his philosophy.[43] On the contrary, as a Jew Kangaroo has been linked to Lawrence's Jewish acquaintances. Lawrence, though, asserted that "Kangaroo was never Kot[eliansky]" (Letters, V, 143), his long-term Jewish friend. As a Jew trying to lead a people to regeneration, Edgar Jaffe is a more plausible model; it is mentioned that Kangaroo "had been a student in Munich" (*K*, 117). Also like Kangaroo, Jaffe's Jewish comrades in Munich, Eisner and Landauer, were murdered by their political opposition.

One detail in the novel that directly links Kangaroo to Jaffe is the episode when Somers stares at Albrecht Dürer's engraving "St Jerome in his Study" in Kangaroo's house. This detail recalls the "genuine Dürer engravings" (Letters, II, 63) noted by Lawrence during his stay at Jaffe's house in Irschenhausen in 1913. Dürer's engraving of St Jerome, alongside "Knight, Death and Devil" and "Melencolia I", expresses the humanist values of the Renaissance. St Jerome was admired during the Renaissance as a founder of the Church who rejected its rituals through his individualism by living alone in a desert, and later as a scholar translating Biblical texts; he considered the Bible as the core of Christian belief, anticipating the values of the Reformation. In Lawrence's novel the engraving relates Kangaroo to Jaffe as a Jew who has followed the traditions of Renaissance and Enlightenment humanism. But it is an idealism which Somers rejects.

Both Kangaroo and Jaffe break from their ethnic roots and assimilate themselves into their host cultures. Yet their sense of communal unity, or "love", over and above individual differences, has become an oppressive ideal. For Kangaroo "permanency, everlastingness is ... the root of evil", in contrast to "life". Yet, instead of being married to a woman, he is "wedded to my ideals", or rather, to the one ideal of love in his "Abraham's bosom". For Kangaroo, "the one fire of love" is God, the only creative force. Somers feels entrapped by Kangaroo's love, believing it to be only an idea in his head, not an impulse from his body. Kangaroo resembles Jaffe as "an order-loving Jew" with "one central principle in the world", of love (*K*, 113, 119, 133, 137, 207).

---

[43] See Michael Wilding, *Political Fictions* (London: Routledge and Kegan Paul, 1980), 165.

This scene set before Dürer's engraving is the dramatic climax of the novel: Kangaroo demands that Somers accepts his love, and threatens to kill him if he resists. The engraving includes a lion, whom Jerome has tamed, sitting in the foreground beside a lamb, the symbol of Christ. The tamed lion represents the omnipotence of spiritual love over violent nature. Kangaroo is like St Jerome, with his back to the fire as he works, trying to "tame" Somers. And yet Kangaroo roars "like a lion at Somers", as a violent, predatory being. In Lawrence's scene the idealism of love is exploded from within by the violence that it conceals.

Wilding comments that Kangaroo's love denies class struggles.[44] In *Kangaroo* Lawrence ascribes the political failure of Edgar Jaffe and Alfred Weber to their idealism of social unity, which denies a reality of class divisions. Jaffe and Eisner's programme for the Bavarian Republic had been to reconcile the parliamentary system with revolutionary councils, but was flawed by lack of democratic support. Even after this programme became impractical Jaffe adhered to it, making his contribution, as Allan Mitchell puts it, "more a matter of confusion than of clarification". In the elections of early 1919 he was humiliated by winning only 2,331 votes.[45] Alfred Weber had supported Jaffe's programme and made his own appeal for a middle-class alliance with the working class in a united liberal party. The initial public support for his Deutsche Demokratische Partei (DDP) dwindled away after just eighteen months.[46] Like Jaffe and Weber, Kangaroo fails to attract wide public support, yet still believes he can unify the different classes in Australia. Lawrence had little sympathy for Jaffe's fate, commenting to Else:

> I was glad Edgar died: better death than ignominious living on. Life had no place for him after the War. (Letters, III, 717)

Somers feels a similarly resigned cynicism at Kangaroo's deathbed.

We can understand Somers' attitude to Kangaroo in the "Nightmare" that is triggered by the confrontation between them.

---

[44] See Wilding, *Political Fictions*, 168.
[45] Mitchell, *Revolution in Bavaria*, 172, 217.
[46] See E. J. Feuchtwanger, *From Weimar to Hitler: Germany, 1918-33* (London: Macmillan, 1995), 35-36.

Somers' nightmare is of the war, especially in terms of its idealism that has lingered on in politicians like "Kaiser Kangaroo", as Harriett calls him. Under the banner of "Love" the "filthy little stay-at-home officers" used their "beastly *little* wills ... to fight for a dead ideal, and to bully every other man into compliance" (*K*, 124, 264). Even in Australia this "dead ideal" retains its wartime character of the sacrifice of individual free will, and life.

In the symbolism of *Kangaroo* Lawrence's political analysis switches between such apparently diverse political movements as Jaffe's socialists and the fascists, by revealing the violence within their ideals of social unity. At the end of the novel Jack kills people in a political riot, as "a killer in the name of love" (*AR*, 328). Jack's sexual gratification in killing men during the riot at the political meeting – "there's *nothing* bucks you up like killing a man" (*K*, 319) – anticipates Hitler's fond memory of hearing gun-shots at a Communist meeting: "The heart almost rejoiced again in the face of such a renewal of old war experiences."[47]

Martin Buber and Zionism

Another possible source for Kangaroo is Lawrence's friend David Eder, who was active in the Zionist movement during this period. Zionism shares Lawrence's aspirations in *Kangaroo* for a political state in which "a new religious inspiration, and a new religious idea must gradually spring up and ripen before there could be any change" (*K*, 99), as Somers puts it. Immediately after the war, Palestine was one of the countries that Lawrence considered settling in. He wanted to write "a Sketch Book of Zion" there, and hoped that through Zionism the emerging Jewish nation would be a realization of his "Rananim". Consistently critical of assimilated Jews, Lawrence hoped that they could recover their native culture. He criticized Louis Golding's novel *Forward from Babylon* (1920), which described a son's rebellion from Jewish tradition as embodied by his father Reb Monash, for lacking "the passional truth of Reb Monash's Yiddishkeit". Lawrence was interested in "the sacred and ineradicable *differences* between men and races" (III, 687, 690).

---

[47] Hitler, *Mein Kampf*, II, 145: "Fast jubelte einem doch wieder das Herz angesichts solcher Auffrischung alter Kriegserlebnisse."

As a socialist and Jew, Edgar Jaffe's fate sums up that of Jews in Central Europe during the post-war period, when their assimilation into society came to a tragic halt. The Enlightenment had emancipated German Jews in the early nineteenth century. To transcend the gulf between themselves and native Germans, Jews concentrated on their *Bildung*, especially as it was expressed in *Wilhelm Meisters Lehrjahre*, as the development of one's inherent abilities through self-education.[48] It was said that Jews were "Deutsche von Goethes Gnaden" ("German by Goethe's grace"),[49] and consequently education was identified with work.[50] Yet since the representatives of the Enlightenment hated Judaism, acceptance for Jews demanded abandonment of their religious tradition. Over the course of the nineteenth century *Bildung* became identified with patriotism, duty, and discipline for the nationalist cause in the universities and *Gymnasien*, till it was appropriated by the Nazis as exclusively German.[51] During the First World War, when anti-semitism was rife in Germany, the Enlightenment principles of liberalism and Jewish assimilation were discredited. In response to these developments, German Jews rallied round the Zionist cause to recover their identity as a religion, community and race. In this process they drew on both German and Jewish culture to find a national identity, yet with different results to the nationalism of Germans.

Lawrence, though, became critical of the "Zionist stunt" (Letters, IV, 690) for being indistinct from European politics. Zionists debated whether the movement should be a nationalist movement, like those in Germany and Italy in the previous century, or whether its nationalism should only be a means to a religious end. One of the central figures of the Zionist movement was the German philosopher Martin Buber. In his writings on Judaism, politics and Zionism he bears many similarities with Lawrence's Kangaroo, and through comparing them we can open up a new perspective on the politics of *Kangaroo*.

---

[48] See George L. Mosse, *German Jews beyond Judaism* (Bloomington: Indiana University Press, 1985), 3.
[49] Paul Mendes-Flohr, *German Jews: A Dual Identity* (New Haven: Yale University Press, 1999), 5.
[50] See George L. Mosse, *Germans and Jews* (New York: Howard Fertig, 1970), 43.
[51] *Ibid.*, 13, 74.

Buber attempted to establish an alternative to Enlightenment, liberal values for Jews by reviving the eighteenth century Hasidic movement, which he believed could bridge medieval and modern Jewish culture. Hasidism could provide the model of a Zionist state as "the living double kernel of humanity: genuine community and genuine leadership".[52] Lawrence's Kangaroo shares the responsibilities of Buber's zaddik, the leader of each Hasidic community. The zaddik helps the members of his community to relate to God by guiding their sensual experiences of the world towards Him: "Through the zaddik, all the senses of the hasid are brought to perfection, and indeed not through conscious directing, but through their bodily nearness."[53] Kangaroo wants to be a "tyrant", or rather, "a patriarch, or a pope", "to establish my state of Australia as a kind of Church, with the profound reverence for life, for life's deepest urges, as the motive power". He wants to relieve man "from this terrible responsibility of governing himself when he doesn't know what he wants" (*K*, 112, 113), to guide his will towards God. Buber argues that "man cannot take himself in hand, in order to hallow himself";[54] as "the helper in the spirit, the teacher of the meaning of the world, the leader to the divine sparks",[55] the zaddik links man to God. Like Lawrence's characterization of Kangaroo, Buber sees the relationship between the zaddik and his community as the "germ of future orders",[56] after the imminent collapse of political structures in Europe.

Yet Buber was confronted with the historical problem of the decline of Hasidism. He describes the tragic fate of one of the later zaddikim, Rabbi Nachman, who became "'the soul of the people', but the people had not become his", because they were "not pure

---

[52] Martin Buber, *Werke*, 3 vols (Munich: Kösel, 1963), III, 961, 964: "der lebendige Doppelkern des Menschentums: wahrhafte Gemeinde und wahrhafte Führerschaft."
[53] *Ibid.*, 83: "Alle Sinne des Chassids werden durch den Zaddik zur Vollendung gebracht, und zwar nicht durch dessen bewußtes Einwirken, sondern durch seine leibliche Nähe."
[54] *Ibid.*, 940: "Der Mensch kann sich zwar nicht in die Hand nehmen, um sich zu heiligen."
[55] *Ibid.*, 963-64: "der Helfer im Geist, der Lehrer des Weltsinns, der Führer zu den göttlichen Funken."
[56] *Ibid.*, 964: "Keim künftiger Ordnungen."

enough".[57] Here we see Buber's early idealism, which he shares with Kangaroo in his ideal of love.

Buber reflected that his early representations of Hasidism had stressed its "Reinheit und Höhe" ("purity and loftiness") at the expense of its "crude and ungainly but living folk-tone".[58] In "Das Leben der Chassidim" (*The Life of the Hasidim*, 1908) he valued man's unity with God at the expense of his individuality. In this work Buber described man's existence as lying between "Awoda" ("Dienst", "duty") and "Hithlahawuth" ("Entbrennen", "burning of ecstasy"). Man's *Awoda* to God made possible his unity with Him in *Hithlahawuth*. In both sides man is only part of a unity. The everyday world of *Awoda* is like that of the Bavarian peasant in Lawrence's *Twilight in Italy*. Buber describes it as when the individual "collects and unifies himself, he approaches the unity of God"; *Awoda* is every act of life.[59] This "Einheit" is the basis of "Gemeinschaft" ("community"):

> The souls bind themselves to each other into a larger unity and power. There is a service that only the community can fulfil.[60]

From this *Gemeinschaft* man joins "God's I, the simple unity", "above nature and above time and above thoughts".[61] The unity in *Awoda* and *Hithlahawuth* are only possible through "Liebe", which "lives in a kingdom greater than the kingdom of the individual ... *between* the creatures, that is, it is in God".[62]

Buber believed that Zionism could realize the "holy insignia of mankind, rootedness, solidarity, wholeness",[63] which was modelled on the Hasidic community. In German Zionism this unity became a

---

[57] *Ibid.*, 905: "'die Seele des Volkes', aber das Volk war nicht sein geworden"; "nicht rein genug."
[58] *Ibid.*, 935-36: "volkstümlich lebendigen Ton."
[59] *Ibid.*, 27: "sich sammelt und vereint, nähert er sich der Einheit Gottes."
[60] *Ibid.*, 30: "Die Wollenden binden sich aneinander zu größerer Einheit und Macht. Es gibt einen Dienst, den nur die Gemeinde vollbringen kann."
[61] *Ibid.*, 22: "Gotts Ich, der einfachen Einheit"; "Über der Natur und über der Zeit und über dem Denken."
[62] *Ibid.*, 44: "in einem Reich lebt, größer als das Reich des Einzelnen ... *zwischen* den Kreaturen, das heißt: sie ist in Gott."
[63] *Ibid.*, 967: "heiligen Insignien des Menschentums, Wurzelhaftigkeit, Verbundenheit, Ganzheit."

dominant ideal in which the individual Jew would be redeemed in the *Volksorganismus*.[64] Nationalism was incorporated into this ideal, since the Jewish drive towards unity demanded a unified community in a single, national homeland. Through this idealism the Zionists ignored the material and power struggles necessary to establish their nation in Palestine, as we will see more fully in the following chapter.[65] Lawrence claimed that Zionism only reproduced the political idealism of Europe. On crossing the Arabian Sea in March 1922 on his journey to Australia, he described Mount Sinai to Baroness von Richthofen:

> Alles ist Semitisch und grausam – nakt, scharf, kein Baum, kein Blatt, kein Leben: der mörderliche Wille und Eisen von Idee und Ideal .... Das Ideal ist schlimm gegen den Mensch gewesen: und Jahveh ist Vater von dem Ideal. (Letters, IV, 210)

> (Everything is Semitic and cruel – naked, sharp, no tree, no leaf, no life: the murderous will and iron of idea and ideal .... The ideal has been wicked against man: and Jahveh is father of the ideal.)

His language of *Eisen* evokes Bismarck and Gerald Crich, and *Wille* and *Ideal* reflects his perception of Judaism in terms of German culture. Kangaroo's Diggers partly reproduce the idealism of the Zionists.

Somers decides to "leave mankind to its own connivance, and turn to the gods" (*K*, 162). He reflects:

> There *is* God. But forever dark, forever unrealisable forever and forever. The Unutterable Name, because it never can have a name. (*AR*, 265-66)

He cannot formulate this "God", or turn it into an ideal. It is not "the Universal Mind", or *Geist*, in Hegel's terms. Nor is it "Hardy's Blind Fate", which had fascinated Lawrence in his youth, alongside the Schopenhauerian "will-to-live". Rather, it is a Nietzschean "will-to-change, a will-to-evolve, a will towards further creation of the self".

---

[64] See Stephen M. Poppel, *Zionism in Germany 1897-1933: The Shaping of a Jewish Identity* (Philadelphia: Jewish Publication Society of America, 1976), 128.
[65] *Ibid.*, 147.

Like Lilly and Aaron, Somers is one of Zarathustra's pupils, asserting his individual will, regardless of larger political events: "like Nietzsche, I no longer believe in great events. The war was a great event – and it made everything more petty." He affirms "the true majesty of the single soul ... not the tuppenny trick-majesty of Kaisers" (*K*, 263, 295, 161, 303). And yet, he is inspired by the inscription on Harriett's wooden heart, "a Black Forest trifle which she had bought in Baden-Baden for a penny":

"Dem Mutigen gehört die Welt."

"To the manly brave belongs the world."

Despite this being "a rather two-edged motto just now for Germany", and loaded with "destructive surprises", he envisages it as an alternative to Kangaroo's destructive love. Given these contradictions and uncertainties, Somers discounts his "dark god" as "Blarney – blarney – blarney!" (*K*, 150, 272), but this crisis of faith is necessary to avoid idealism, and to renew his humility before the unknown.

Somers pursues, then, the "dark, living, fructifying power" that Lilly struggled to convey to Aaron. And yet, as in *Aaron's Rod*, this assertion of individuality is only a preliminary to his return to wider social relationships; it is a notion that he believes can revitalize society, and release it from the trauma of the war. The experience of the First World War made Buber realize, like Somers, "that the human spirit is either bound to existence or ... is nothing before the decisive judgement". He became aware "of human life as the possibility of a dialogue with being",[66] not as an ideal form of being in itself, but in a tendentious relation with God, who is unknowable and unreachable. Somers concedes that "man must have some idea of himself", an "absolute", and like Buber and his friend, the Jewish philosopher Franz Rosenzweig, he maintains that it is "the great dark God who alone will sustain us in our loving one another" (*K*, 263, 199). In *The Plumed Serpent* Lawrence will attempt to realize this

---

[66] Buber, *Werke*, III, 936: "daß der menschliche Geist entweder existenz-verbindlich oder ... vor der entscheidenden Instanz nichtig ist"; "des Menschenlebens als der Möglichkeit eines Dialogs mit dem Seienden."

"great dark God" in Mexico as an answer to the dilemmas of his novels, and of his age.

IX
THE *VÖLKISCH* IDEOLOGIES OF
THE PLUMED SERPENT

The Plumed Serpent can be regarded as a summation of Lawrence's concerns since the First World War. Like *The Lost Girl* it envisages a *Mignons Land* as an alternative to modern, capitalist society. Like Gilbert Noon, the heroine Kate Leslie struggles to overcome her cynicism in this society, quoting Goethe's Mephistopheles, "ich bin der Geist der stets verneint!" (*PS*, 214). The ending of *The Plumed Serpent* recapitulates that of *Aaron's Rod*, where Lilly advises Aaron that "your soul will tell you" (*AR*, 299) whom to submit to. Ramón Carrasco, the leader of the Quetzalcoatl cult, reassures Kate to "listen to your own best desire" (*PS*, 444) in her choice of whether to stay in Mexico; meanwhile he uses his power to compel her to him. Finally, *The Plumed Serpent* attempts to create an alternative to the political struggles in Europe between right and left, with the principle of Somers' "dark god" in *Kangaroo* which demands submission, and offers liberation.

The Plumed Serpent is probably Lawrence's most politically controversial novel. Its symbolic language of the blood gives substance to Bertrand Russell's accusation that Lawrence's "mystical philosophy of 'blood' ... led straight to Auschwitz".[1] The great majority of Lawrence's defenders, from Leavis onwards, have stopped short at *The Plumed Serpent*. In a recent summing up of where the controversy stands, David Ellis has acknowledged the novel's similarities to the *völkisch* literature that contributed to the fascist movement in Germany; he describes Diego Rivera's impression of a similar cult in Berlin with the German President Paul von Hindenburg as Wotan and Marshall Ludendorff as Thor. Yet Ellis resists identifying *The Plumed Serpent* with Nazism, despite the authoritarianism of its principal male characters.[2]

Having followed Lawrence's direct relationship with Germany in his writing career, we are in a position to judge *The Plumed Serpent* directly in terms of contemporary German politics, including Hitler

---

[1] Russell, *The Autobiography of Bertrand Russell*, II, 22.
[2] See Ellis, *D. H. Lawrence: Dying Game*, 218, 656.

and the philosopher of Nazism Alfred Rosenberg. However, we can also turn away from the example of Nazism and continue our comparison with contemporary German Jews, including Buber and Franz Rosenzweig, who share the *völkisch* discourse of *The Plumed Serpent*, particularly in its language of blood.

The debate on the politics of *The Plumed Serpent* can be approached at the level of style. The question it poses is whether Lawrence's religious, mythological vision of Mexico forms a totality that compels the action of his characters, or whether the characters disrupt his mythology while they enact it. In his defence of the novel L. D. Clark admits that "*The Plumed Serpent* is a flagrant piece of propaganda".[3] John B. Humma observes that in the relationship between Kate and the Aztec cult "the outcomes seem, indeed, predisposed". For Humma, Kate's marriage to Cipriano Viedma is unconvincing because the imagery compels her behaviour, instead of there being a mutual relation between the two characters.[4] Ellis voices a similar criticism about the ceremonies and hymns weakening the drama of the novel.[5] Michael Bell argues that the "ontological vision" of Lawrence's symbolic language in the novel fails to transform the physical reality of characters like Kate, because Lawrence is "trying to graft it on to a resistant sensibility". Lawrence's myth is "too much an authorial idea", or an ideal, like those of liberalism and rationalisation to which it is opposed. The failure of Lawrence's language, Bell observes, gives rise to "a doctrinal extremism"[6] which, in its political form, approaches the totalitarian ideas of contemporary right-wing movements.

In Lawrence's first version of the novel, now referred to as *Quetzalcoatl*, the balance between Realist and mythological discourses is more even, leaving its characters with an apparently greater freedom to realize their individuality. Between composing *Quetzalcoatl* during the summer of 1923 and *The Plumed Serpent* from late 1924 to early 1925 in Mexico, Lawrence returned to

---

[3] L. D. Clark, *Dark Night of the Body* (Austin: University of Texas Press, 1964), 4.
[4] Humma, *Metaphor and Meaning in Lawrence's Later Novels*, 66, 74.
[5] See Ellis, *D. H. Lawrence: Dying Game*, 219.
[6] Bell, *D. H. Lawrence: Language and Being*, 172, 174.

England and Germany; first we shall look at how this visit inspired the nature of his revisions.

Mexico and Germany
Travelling through Strasbourg from Paris, Lawrence stayed in Baden-Baden between 7 and 20 February 1924, writing the article "A Letter from Germany" on his last day there. He remarks upon developments in Germany since his last stay in 1921:

> Then it still looked to western Europe for a reunion, for a sort of reconciliation. Now that is over .... The positivity of our civilization has been broken .... The ancient spirit of pre-historic Germany [is] coming back, at the end of history.

Lawrence recognizes the historical causes of this change, of the liberal and industrial "old peace-and-production hope of the world" destroyed first by the war, and then by the economic chaos of 1923: "Money becomes insane, and people with it" (*P*, 108-109).

Nineteen-twenty-three had been a critical year in German history. In January the French had occupied the Ruhr, Germany's industrial heartland, and brought the economy to the verge of collapse, especially since the German government had run out of money to subsidize it. By 20 November hyperinflation reached the level of 4,200 billion marks to the dollar. The Ruhr occupation, reminding the Germans of the defeat and the Treaty of Versailles that France was attempting to enforce, inflamed their sense of nationalism and fostered the rise of extreme right-wing groups, including Hitler's Nationalsozialistische Deutsche Arbeiterpartei (NSDAP). On 1 October 1923 Major Buchrucker and the Black Reichswehr attempted the first putsch at fortresses near Berlin, but were defeated. On 8 November at a meeting of Munich military associations Hitler declared himself leader of the Reich government, intending to capture the government buildings in Munich and then march on Berlin. The Munich Putsch on the following day, though, was repressed by the Reichswehr and police.[7]

In the "Letter" Lawrence comments that the change in Germany "is a happening of far more profound import than any actual *event*. It

---

[7] See Feuchtwanger, *From Weimar to Hitler*, 119, 112, 130-34.

is the father of the next phase of events" (*P*, 109). This transitional phase stretched over the rest of the Twenties while economic prosperity ensured political stability, facilitated by the Dawes Plan. However,

In Germany the liberals were gradually ousted from power, until the "children" of the chaos of 1923 fully emerged with Hitler's seizure of power in 1933. In December 1924 a centre-right coalition was formed, which excluded the socialist and liberal SPD and DDP. In the following year Hindenburg became president as an *Ersatzkaiser* ("substitute-kaiser"), despite his opposition to the parliamentary democratic system. The Republic moved further and further right, since the liberals and socialists were weakened by their lack of nationalist appeal and their inability to organize themselves into an effective opposition. Democracy was only tolerated as a safeguard for economic prosperity, until the 1929 Wall Street Crash and ensuing depression; the parliamentary system was discarded as a front for Germany's political hierarchy when Hitler was appointed as Chancellor by Hindenburg.[8] Michael Burleigh describes this period in Europe as

> a time when liberalism was regarded as a waning force, rapidly being superseded by authoritarianism, Communism, fascism and Nazism – the alleged forces of the future. Liberal democracy was in danger of becoming an extinct species in inter-war Europe, where by 1939 undemocratic regimes already outnumbered constitutional democracies by sixteen to twelve.[9]

Lawrence's diagnosis and prophecy of Germany proved extremely accurate; Thomas Mann remarked in his diary for 19 October 1934 on the "admirably insightful letter by Lawrence ... about Germany and its return to barbarism – when Hitler was hardly even heard of as a factor".[10] But, of course, after the Munich Putsch

---

[8] *Ibid.*, 151, 166, 169, 184, 186, 190, 194, 200.
[9] Michael Burleigh, *The Third Reich: A New History* (London: Macmillan, 2000), 61. For a more in depth analysis of the political developments during this period, see 61-84.
[10] Thomas Mann, *Tagebücher 1933-34*, (Frankfurt am Main: Fischer, 1977-), 551: "Bewundernswert instinktsicherer Brief von Lawrence ... über Deutschland und seine

Hitler was a prominent figure in Germany's political situation; and Mann does not register the deeper complexity of "A Letter from Germany", in Lawrence's partial sympathy, privately at least, for the changes taking place in the country.

The similarities between Germany in the "Letter" and Mexico in *The Plumed Serpent* are not explicit, but are nonetheless distinct. Lawrence describes the Black Forest, where "at night you feel strange things stirring in the darkness .... Out of the very air comes a sense of danger" (*P*, 109). It anticipates the "primitive darkness" of the Mexican landscape in *The Plumed Serpent*, with "strange noises in the trees" and "a panic fear, a sense of devilment and horror thick in the night air" (*PS*, 133-34). Lawrence wrote to Koteliansky from Germany:

> Germany is queer – seems to be turning – as if she would make a great change, and become manly again, and a bit dangerous in a manly way. I hope so ... there is a certain healthiness, more than in France, far more than in England, the old fierceness coming back. (Letters, IV, 574)

In Germany Lawrence saw a European equivalent of Mexico, devastated by revolutions and economic collapse, within which a new consciousness was emerging from the "old fierceness" of tribal ancestors. In October 1923 Lawrence had praised the Mexicans in similar terms to the Germans:

> there is a sort of *basic* childishness about these people, that for me is the only manliness. When I say childishness, I only mean they don't superimpose ideas and ideals, but follow the stream of the blood. A certain innocence, even if sometimes evil.

Lawrence is appealing to the qualities that he has approved of in his previous novels, such as the masculinity of Jack Callcott, Aaron Syson and the German soldiers in *Mr Noon*, and a corresponding resistance to ideals through affirming the body's impulses in the "blood". Lawrence continued, that for England to recover its power it "must be juxtaposed with something that is in the dark volcanic blood" of the Mexicans, in "a polarity of the two" (Letters, IV, 522).

Rückwendung zur Barbarei – als von Hitler noch kaum die Rede war."

On arriving in England he was disappointed, but in Germany he found potential for this racial regeneration from within the blood. Lawrence, then, anticipated the German swing to right-wing politics as the equivalent to his vision of Mexican regeneration in *Quetzalcoatl*. He would have understood that Germany was turning from liberalism, but could not foresee the precise form that the new power would take.

In his short story "The Border-Line", written immediately after "A Letter from Germany" in early 1924, he attempts to transpose aspects of *Quetzalcoatl* into a German context, and anticipates the style of *The Plumed Serpent*. Katherine Farquhar re-enacts his journey to Baden-Baden via Strasbourg, during which she meets the spirit of her husband Alan who was killed in the war. He murders her second husband Philip, to possess her again. Like Kate in both of the Mexican novels, Katherine is modelled on Frieda, but more directly with her German aristocratic background; and both Katherine and Kate Leslie in *The Plumed Serpent* are forty years old.

Alan's reclamation of Katherine from his substitute while she crosses the "everlasting border-line" from French to German territory, symbolizes Lawrence's vision of Germany reclaiming Alsace-Lorraine. Strasbourg is "a conquered city ... empty, as if its spirit had left it" (*WWRA*, 84), where shop-signs are in French and goods are from formerly German factories while the inhabitants continue to speak German. In the earliest manuscript version of the story this political meaning is more pronounced. At Strasbourg Cathedral Katherine feels "the mystery and the terror of the war, that seemed to her forever unfinished", and the murder of her second husband evokes images of "the ghosts of the old skin-clad Germans" (*WWRA*, 298, 303) attacking French civilization.

The themes of "The Border-Line" are shared by *Quetzalcoatl* and *The Plumed Serpent*, suggesting that Germany is the European equivalent of Mexico. Like Kate in both of the Mexican novels, Katherine identifies with "her queen-bee love, and queen-bee will" (*WWRA*, 80), which Alan opposes with his "destiny" by going to war. Alan is partly based on Cipriano; he is a captain in a Highland regiment but has the natural authority of a general. Alan's "destiny", like Cipriano's "natural destiny" in *Quetzalcoatl*, is to possess Kate through "the will of the gods in me", regardless of "her own empty will" (*Q*, 171). Katherine experiences Strasbourg Cathedral as if it were a monument to Quetzalcoatl, or more appropriately, to the German pagan gods: "the great, blood-dusky Thing, blotting out the Cross it was supposed to exalt." The language of blood and darkness from *Quetzalcoatl* is used to describe the Cathedral: "looking down like darkness out of darkness ... a flush in the darkness, like dark flesh ... a faint rust of blood out of the upper black heavens ... an ancient, indomitable blood seemed to stir in it." The symbolic language is more concentrated than in *Quetzalcoatl*, and anticipates the symbolism in *The Plumed Serpent*. Later she reaches the Black Forest, whose "silence, and waiting, and the old, barbaric undertone" (*WWRA*, 84-85, 89) again mirror Mexico.

In the presence of Philip, "dead in a pool of blood", Alan's spirit has sex with a submissive Katherine, who feels he "could possess her through all the pores of her body ... as a cloud holds a shower" (*WWRA.*, 96). This scene conflates Cipriano's execution of the enemies of Quetzalcoatl and his sexual relationship with Kate in *The Plumed Serpent*. From Cipriano's "body of blood could rise up that pillar of cloud ... till it swept the zenith, and all the earth below was dark and prone, and consummated", including Kate. Katherine submits to Alan's "power", while "the heavy power that lay unmerged in [Cipriano's] blood" overwhelms Kate's "will" (*PS*, 310). Yet the macabre imagery of blood in "The Border-Line" is ironic, and turns Lawrence's story more into a parody than a pastiche of Edgar Allen Poe's tales. This irony undermines the power of the symbolism expressing Alan's possession of Katherine, and the political subtext of the story. It distances us from the rhetoric of the symbolism, enabling us to objectify its ideological significance. *The Plumed Serpent* shares this tension between the power of the symbolic imagery over physical reality; there is a need to undercut this power through irony, and yet an anxiety about dismantling the political vision of the novel. Lawrence struggles between exploiting the power of his symbolism for an ideological purpose, where his characters' actions appear to be determined by it, and countering its power with their personally motivated actions.

"The Border-Line", then, can be seen as a transitional piece between *Quetzalcoatl* and *The Plumed Serpent*. Germany's *völkisch* turn from capitalism proved to Lawrence that his vision of a new religion in Mexico need not be limited to its local circumstances, but could be widened out across the world. Consequently, *The Plumed Serpent* is more metaphysical than its earlier version, and its mythology is more dominant over its realistic incidents. In *The Plumed Serpent* Lawrence adds Ramón's appeal for other countries to revive their native religions, for instance where "the Teutonic world would once more think in terms of Thor and Wotan" (*PS*, 248).

But do the changes from *Quetzalcoatl* to *The Plumed Serpent*, partly effected by Lawrence's experiences of Germany in 1924, follow the ideological direction of German politics in the Twenties towards fascism, or do they follow the very different direction towards Zionism? Lawrence's symbolic language is crucial in answering this question: its terms of blood, darkness, will and power were fundamental to both the German right and German Zionists in their rejection of the political language of liberalism.

The ideology of blood in *Quetzalcoatl*

In many respects *Quetzalcoatl* offers an alternative to the stylized excesses of *The Plumed Serpent*. In his Introduction to *Quetzalcoatl*, Louis L. Martz discusses how the novel's greater realistic tendency counters the static effect of the hymns, songs and long sermons in *The Plumed Serpent*. In *Quetzalcoatl* hymns are presented as they are performed by singers with native instruments to preserve their specific, local character, unlike the written form in *The Plumed Serpent* which gives the hymns a more generalized significance. In accordance with this greater emphasis on characters' individual volition, at the end of *Quetzalcoatl* Kate rejects the cult, to "preserve her individual soul". Martz ascribes Lawrence's attempt to "create a complete mythology for his new religion" (*Q*, xii-xiii) in *The Plumed Serpent* to his disappointment with post-war Europe and his greater urgency for change. Given Lawrence's impression of Germany as turning away from civilization, it could be argued that Germany inspired him about the possibility of a European rejection of Enlightenment values.

In *Quetzalcoatl* he re-introduces his symbolic language of blood, darkness, will and power. Ramón asserts that life lies in "the power of the blood ... from the darkness"; he dismisses the individual's "free will", since "there is no liberty, only the will of some God" (*Q*, 39). In the philosophy of Nazism formulated by Hitler, and elaborated by Rosenberg, the *Wille zur Macht* and *Blut* were crucial terms, alongside *Rasse* ("race"), *Volk*, *Reich* and *Ideal*. The Romantic language of Wagner, of darkness and night, was not essential to their political discourse, but incorporated into their world-view. The crucial issue is how these words function in the narrative of *Quetzalcoatl*.

In *Quetzalcoatl* blood signifies a racial identity, instead of the vitality of the individual's body. Ramón, a Mexican in this version, muses that "a race must produce its own heroes, its own God-men", and he wants to release "the religious energy native to our own blood" (*Q*, 117, 174). Cipriano reiterates these thoughts in a cruder form:

> We're the best blood in America, the blood of the Montezuma. We've gone against our own blood, serving the gringos' gods, and kneeling down on our own knees.

He wants his soldiers to concentrate on changing "all the people of his blood" (*Q*, 250, 252).

In his opening declaration in *Mein Kampf* Hitler defined the German Reich by its race, or *Blut*: "*The same blood belongs to the same Reich*."[11] Fundamental to the Reich were the "universally valid drives to racial purity in nature".[12] In his demand for "the ability and will of the individual to sacrifice himself for the totality" as the Reich, Hitler asserted that "the right of personal freedom recedes before the duty of preservation of the race".[13] The *Reich*, as a *Gesamtheit*, was the *Ideal* and larger *Wille* to which the individual *Wille* must be sacrificed: "true idealism is nothing more than the subordination of the interests and lives of individuals to the totality"; "it corresponds in its innermost depths to the ultimate will of nature."[14] In Hitler's

---

[11] Hitler, *Mein Kampf*, I, 13: "*Gleiches Blut gehört in ein gemeinsames Reich.*"
[12] *Ibid.*, 281: "in der Natur allgemein gültige[n] Triebe[s] zur Rassenreinheit."
[13] *Ibid.*, 157: "Aufopferungsfähigkeit und Aufopferungswille des einzelnen für die Gesamtheit"; "das Recht der persönlichen Freiheit tritt zurück gegenüber der Pflicht der Erhaltung der Rasse."
[14] *Ibid.*, 294: "wahrer Idealismus nichts weiter ist als die Unterordnung der Interessen und des Lebens des einzelnen unter die Gesamtheit"; "entspricht er im innersten Grunde dem letzten Wollen der Natur."

philosophy, then, the individual *Wille* is sacrificed to the national and racial *Ideal* or *Wille*, of the *Blut*.

For Hitler, "military instruments of power" were required "to serve high ideals".[15] Individuals must be bred to concentrate, and trained to strengthen, their "Willenskraft" ("will-power") to serve the larger "Bluteinheit" ("blood unity") and "Einheit des Willens= und Entschlußkraft" ("unity of will-power and resolve").[16] He seems to acknowledge to his own committed readership the lies in his own rhetoric, that *Reich, Rasse, Blut, Ideal* are only devices to win over the German population to his personal power. He asserts that political power lies in controlling the "crowd of the simple or credulous" through propaganda and physical brutality.[17]

As a general of the army, Cipriano approaches Hitler's attitude to the significance of the individual in the larger "will". Kate recognizes "the powerful, inhuman quality of his will", and that he is "a soldier who sees beyond human lives, counts human lives as nothing, having some further, dangerous purpose" (*Q*, 207). He declares to Ramón that "I'd rather smash Mexico to bits, and spill every drop of blood in the country, than let him [*sic*] become like New Mexico" (*Q*, 119).

One question that arises is whether Cipriano serves the larger interests of the Mexican people, or whether in his disregard for their value as individuals he sees their united will as only an instrument for his will to power. Cipriano declares to Ramón his desire to be dictator of Mexico, since "I can see no clean thing in the country but my own will", and he wants "to be the power that could exterminate the universe in its folds" (*Q*, 122). Ramón warns him of the danger of military dictatorship being only "blind personal power" (*Q*, 118), and it is implied that Cipriano's "will" to kidnap Kate is another example of his dominating will to power. Ramón suggests the counter-influence of religion against the individual will, but it is ambiguous throughout *Quetzalcoatl* whether his religion only legitimates Cipriano's individual power.

---

[15] Hitler, *Mein Kampf*, II, 15-16: "militärischer Machtmittel"; "höheren Idealen zu dienen."
[16] *Ibid.*, 47, 55, 37.
[17] Hitler, *Mein Kampf*, I, 240, 242: "Haufe der Einfältigen oder Leichtgläubigen."

In these situations, where blood is identified with race, and will and power are defined by dictators and armies over the population, the symbolism of Romantic darkness also has a political significance. Lawrence was fascinated with Wagner's *Nacht* in *Tristan und Isolde* as an expression of the loss of individual self and consciousness through the sexual act, sometimes resulting in death. Wagner's structural principle of the *Leitmotiv* enacts this process through the use of repetition. Rosenberg comments on the political implications of this technique: "*However, the essential part of Western art has become manifest in Richard Wagner: that the Nordic soul is not contemplative, that it does not lose itself in individual psychology, but that it wilfully experiences cosmic-spiritual laws and is architectonically constructed.*"[18] Rosenberg describes how individual characters are subsumed in the larger, *kosmisch=seelische Gesetze* of Wagner's structural framework. For Rosenberg an ideal fascist state is like a Wagnerian opera, in which each individual is like a *Leitmotiv*, functioning within the laws of the totality.

In Lawrence's novels there is the danger of the individual characters being subsumed in the *motivisch* imagery of darkness where Ramón locates "life". In *Quetzalcoatl* individuals do not lose themselves in the darkness of the sexual act, but in a religious act. Cipriano confesses to Ramón that "I still feel a bit shy of stepping into history as a divine, or semi-divine character" of Huitzilopochtli, since his individual consciousness resists it. Immediately, his body is "darkened" by Ramón's touch:

> He was passing into death, into all complete darkness: but it was warm, and infinitely grateful. Slowly, slowly he passed away into the inner darkness. He had no consciousness any more, was just a darkness within the dark, that was warm, and infinitely satisfying. (*Q*, 253-54)

Through this religious experience of darkness Cipriano is convinced that "the depths of me is God", and he resolves this new status with

---

[18] Alfred Rosenberg, *Der Mythus des 20. Jahrhunderts* (Munich: Hoheneichen, 1935), 433: "*Das Wesentliche aller Kunst des Abendlandes ist aber in Richard Wagner offenbar geworden: daß die nordische Seele nicht kontemplativ ist, daß sie sich auch nicht in individuelle Psychologie verliert, sondern kosmisch=seelische Gesetze willenhaft erlebt und geistig=architektonisch gestaltet*" (italics in original).

his role as general by using it to justify his military power to serve his race:

> He was keeper of the Lord's vengeance, the living Huitzilopochtli. He had many men with him, and power over them. He wanted his race to live, his breed to continue. (*Q*, 256)

Here we see a process that was central to Nazi ideology: the individual authorizes his military power through semi-religious mystification, and uses that power to serve the blood of his race. In *Quetzalcoatl* Lawrence offers no opposing perspective to subvert this construction. Louis L. Martz is mistaken in reading Kate's rejection of the Quetzalcoatl cult as his rejection of the symbolic mystification of his novel. She does not assert her individual, conscious self against Cipriano and Ramón's religion of the racial blood, but reinforces its construction by rejecting it on the grounds that her blood cannot be mixed with that of Mexicans. Blood is a fixed, material entity, not a dynamic symbol of life. When Cipriano suggests she become the goddess Malinchi, she refuses on the basis that there was absolutely no communication between his blood and hers (*Q*, 221). In her final refusal to stay in Mexico and become Cipriano's wife, she argues:

> If I were free to choose, in the same way that I am free to choose my hat or my dress, I would stay. Yes, I would. But I am not free. My race is part of me, it doesn't leave me free. My blood *is* me, and that doesn't let me become Mexican. (*Q*, 318)

Kate's conscious, individual choice, then, would be to marry Cipriano. It is the imperative of her blood and race that prevents her from doing so.

Quetzalcoatl and Jewish thought

Yet we should not conclude too rashly that *Quetzalcoatl* is a fascist novel, even though it bears many aspects of Nazi ideology. Its ideological problems are shared by *völkisch* movements in general, including the contemporary German Jewish ones of Buber and his associate Franz Rosenzweig.

Buber introduced to the Zionist movement the notion of a Jewish "Gemeinschaft des Blutes" ("community of blood") in his speech of 1911, "Das Judentum und die Juden" ("Judaism and the Jews"). *Blut* unified each geographically dispersed Jew with his race through a common ancestry: "He feels in this immortality of generations the community of blood, and he feels it as the past life of his self, as the duration of his self in the infinite past."[19] In his major work *Der Stern der Erlösung* (*The Star of Redemption*, 1921) Rosenzweig adopts Buber's notion as a "Blutsgemeinschaft" of "blood kinship, brotherhood, national traditions, marriage".[20] *Blut*, then, for these German Jews is racially determined, as it is for Hitler, Rosenberg, and Lawrence in *Quetzalcoatl*.

At the Nuremberg Trials Rosenberg attempted to exploit Buber's racial use of *Blut*, to neutralize the political ramifications of Nazi ideology. As we have seen, Hitler and Rosenberg combined *Blut*, *Wille zur Macht* and nationalism into an ideal which would be realised through an aggressive foreign policy. Having experienced this idealism in the First World War, Buber warned against a similar interpretation of Jewish blood in his speech of 1921, "Nationalismus" ("Nationalism"):

> Will-power, which is not the effect "from itself" of a power developed from within, but the striving for attainment and production of power, is problematic. A will-power, that has less to do with being powerful than with being "more powerful than", becomes destructive.[21]

Buber valued a *Wille zur Macht* was is internal to each individual.

Yet Cipriano has an inner will to power which he combines with his military power to devastating effect. At this early point of the

---

[19] Martin Buber, *Der Jude und sein Judentum: Gesammelte Aufsätze und Reden* (Cologne: Joseph Melzer, 1963), 13: "Er fühlt in dieser Unsterblichkeit der Generationen die Gemeinschaft des Blutes, und er fühlt sie als das Vorleben seines Ich, als die Dauer seines Ich in der unendlichen Vergangenheit."
[20] Franz Rosenzweig, *Der Mensch und sein Werk: Gesammelte Schriften*, 3 vols (The Hague: Martinus Nijhoff, 1976-84), II, 268-69: "Blutsverwandtschaft, Brüderschaft, Volkstum, Ehe."
[21] Buber, *Der Jude und sein Judentum*, 311: "Machtwille, der nicht die Auswirkung einer »von selber« entstannen innern Macht, sondern die Erlangung, die Herstellung von Macht erstrebt, ist problematisch. Ein Machtwille, dem es nicht darum zu tun ist, mächtig, sondern darum, »mächtiger als« zu sein, wird zerstörerisch."

migration of Zionist settlements into Palestine, Buber was not aware that in the relations of power between modern states, a sense of one race's will to power over another usually follows a fixed, exclusive ideology of racial blood. In these political circumstances blood has become a fixed signifier of race, community and culture, providing a totality of experience that subsumes the individual; subsequently, it can provide the ideal that nationalism exclusively serves to fulfil. This notion pervades Buber's sense of a Jewish *Gemeinschaft des Bluts* established over hundreds of generations, and it left him powerless to counter the conflict between Jew and Arab in Palestine. In "Das Judentum und die Juden" he envisaged Zionism as an ideal that could establish unity of land, language and culture, as well as of blood.[22] This ideal of unity would have demanded excluding non-Jews. As we have seen, Buber did not support Zionism for the sake of Jewish nationalism, but for Judaism. Nevertheless, the problems inherent in his political idealism still threatened to fuel an aggressive nationalism between Jews and Arab Palestinians. Stephen M. Poppel criticizes Buber's idealistic avoidance of the power struggles in Palestine between Jew and Arab.[23] In his treatment of Cipriano Lawrence struggles with the association between a racial notion of blood and the military power of a race as a nation.

Rosenzweig shared Buber's notion of a community of blood, but he rejected Zionism and insisted that Jews continue their unredeemed lives on foreign lands. For Rosenzweig a shared racial blood was not crucial as the basis of Jewish identity in shared land, language and culture. On the contrary, it was crucial because the Jews had sacrificed these things to the exclusion of *Blut*: "We alone trusted in blood and left the land; and so we saved the priceless sap of life which offered us the guarantee of our own eternity."[24] The vitality of blood in each living individual could only be obstructed by state organization, which Rosenzweig associated with political idealism. In contrast to the dangers of Buber's nationalistic appeal to blood,

---

[22] *Ibid.*, 14.
[23] See Poppel, *Zionism in Germany*, 146-47.
[24] Rosenzweig, *Gesammelte Schriften*, II, 332: "Wir allein vertrauten dem Blut und ließen das Land; also sparten wir den kostbaren Lebenssaft, der uns Gewähr der eigenen Ewigkeit bot."

Rosenzweig has been criticized for overestimating the value of blood in creating a community independently of political institutions, and leaving the Jewish population vulnerable to the threat of right-wing extremism. In *Quetzalcoatl*, with its concluding resignation in Kate's departure from Mexico, Lawrence shares the political impotence of Rosenzweig in their racial notion of blood. They refuse to let cultural and political institutions interrelate with it, and change it.

Like Rosenzweig's philosophy, *Quetzalcoatl* fails to articulate a viable alternative to post-war Europe because its racial notion of blood denies the possibility of cultural ideas crossing racial boundaries. There is a determinist logic in the novel, where the Aztec religion lies dormant in the blood of the Mexicans and is inaccessible to foreigners such as Kate. However, there are glimpses of an alternative; for instance, towards the end of the novel the Mexican people perceive Kate as equal to them in their blood, but out of pride for her social status and "fine blood" she rejects them. In *The Plumed Serpent* Kate submits to the Mexican belief that "The blood is one blood" (*PS*, 291, 417), but how does this compare to Hitler, that "*Gleiches Blut gehört in ein gemeinsames Reich*"?

The politics of Lawrence's racial thinking

After writing *Quetzalcoatl* and returning to Europe Lawrence believed that Germany could emulate his vision of a Mexican *völkisch* revival. To explore and encourage this idea he extended and broadened his mythological language so that it could give the novel significance beyond its immediate setting. This use of mythology is the focus of most critical reservations about *The Plumed Serpent*, as we saw earlier. In making this change Lawrence weakens the racial thinking of the novel, but also its realistic description of the characters, whose consciousness is dominated by the mythological language. The transition from *Quetzalcoatl* to *The Plumed Serpent*, then, is both progressive and regressive.

Lawrence's racial thinking in the early Twenties does not conform to contemporary stereotypes, let alone Nazi ones. Writing to Koteliansky, he denounced Robert Mountsier's "generalised detestations: his particular ones being Jews, Germans and Bolshevists. So unoriginal" (Letters, IV, 113). When John Middleton Murry recommended to him the notion of the "Ursprung of the Aryan races",

Lawrence responded that "hell can have the Aryan races" (Letters, IV, 544). On the other hand, he was outraged by the French introduction of Africans to work in the occupied Ruhr in 1922 (Letters, IV, 182-83). This event became a rallying point for the Nazis, and in "A Letter from Germany" Lawrence alludes to the occupation as a cause of Germany's turn from Western civilization. Lawrence's notion of race is idiosyncratic because it is subject to his greater concern of the individual's relation to a community and religion.

Towards the end of *The Plumed Serpent* Kate imagines in Mexico "the old prehistoric humanity" of Atlantis when the seas were frozen into glaciers, and people could wander around the globe. After the glaciers melted, the "flood" cut people off from each other on high plateaux, where they developed into various races (*PS*, 414-15). Lawrence's interest in primitive cultures was indebted to the research of the German explorer Leo Frobenius, especially *The Voice of Africa* (1913), which he read in the spring of 1918 (Letters, III, 233), and to which he refers in *Aaron's Rod* and *Fantasia of the Unconscious*. Frobenius believed that he had discovered the remains of Atlantis in south-western Africa, a civilization that preceded the Negro race. Ramón is attempting to revive Atlantis in Mexico, which we can compare to the Atlantis of another reader of Frobenius, Alfred Rosenberg.

In *Der Mythus des 20 Jahrhunderts* (*The Myth of the Twentieth Century*, 1924) Rosenberg speculates that Frobenius' Atlantis was a "Nordic, prehistoric culture-centre", not the original diaspora as it is for Lawrence. In his following historical survey of ancient races, Rosenberg reaches opposite conclusions to Lawrence. He celebrates how the Romans destroyed the Etruscans who, as their "rassisch=völkisch"[25] enemies contributed nothing to European culture. Lawrence was fascinated by Etruria as an Atlantis, destroyed by the aggressive and rationalistic Romans. Compared to Roman military power, the Etruscans had "religious power" through "the power of the symbol"; as in "all the great old civilisations", including Frobenius' Yorubans and the Aztecs, Etruscan art expressed a religion of the universe, manifested in each moment of life (*SEP*, 56-59).

---

[25] Rosenberg, *Der Mythus des 20. Jahrhunderts*, 24, 61: "nordisches vorgesichtliches Kulturzentrum."

Lawrence identifies the Italian peasant with the Etruscans, in defiance of the fascists who were glorifying ancient Rome. He comments that "the will-to-power is a secondary thing in an Italian, reflected on to him from the Germanic races that have almost engulfed him", including historians such as Theodor Mommsen who discounted the Etruscans in favour of "the Prussian in the all-conquering Romans" (*SEP*, 166, 9).

On the issue of tribal Germany, though, Lawrence and Rosenberg share more common ground. Lawrence celebrates the violence of German tribes in opposition to the civilization of Rome but as we see in their various manifestations in his work, they also have negative associations. In *Movements in European History* and *Mr Noon* Lawrence recognized the principles of duty to military honour, self-sacrifice and indiscriminate aggression that the ancient Germans shared with German soldiers in the First World War. Without reservations Rosenberg celebrates the ideals of 1914 as those of the German *Volk*:

> Millions upon millions were ready for sacrificial death for the sake of only *one* password. This password was: for the honour and freedom of the *Volk*.[26]

He identifies the Nordic race with "the notion of honour and the idea, bound up inseparably with it, of the sense of duty arising out of the consciousness of inner freedom".[27] But where Rosenberg celebrates these qualities unconditionally, Lawrence is profoundly ambivalent about the ancient Germans, and by implication, about the Germans in the Twenties who hark back to their ancestors.

Lawrence admired the primitive impulse in Germans as an antidote to the bourgeois values that he associated with idealism. In "A Letter from Germany" he compares the students travelling from Heidelberg, where the Webers and Jaffes were based, to "loose, roving gangs of broken, scattered tribes" (*P*, 109). In the later essays "Flowery Tuscany" and "Germans and English" of early 1927,

---

[26] *Ibid.*, 698: "Millionen und aber Millionen konnten nur hinter *einer* Losung zum Opfertod bereit gemacht werden. Dieses Losungswort hieß: des Volkes Ehre und seine Freiheit."
[27] *Ibid.*, 147: "der Begriff der Ehre und die Idee der mit ihr untrennbar verbundenen, aus dem Bewußtsein der inneren Freiheit stammenden Pflichtgewesen."

Lawrence would identify these "Wandervögel" as rebels against the self-conscious, "*so* bourgeois" German tourist; more generally, they opposed the tendency in Germany where "the mass-consciousness has been *taken over*, by great minds like Goethe or Frederick [II of Prussia], from other people, and does not spring from the Teutonic race itself ... always in terms of somebody else's experience, and almost never in terms of its own experience" (*SEP*, 241-42). Lawrence sees this primal urge of the younger generation as a rebellion against the "world of pure idea" that spawned militarism and industrialization (*SEP*, 249). Similarly, he envisages Ramón and Cipriano's Quetzalcoatl cult as a break from these European values. Rosenberg instead quotes Goethe on the necessity to limit one's aspirations to master a vocation, and to "attempt to do your duty and you will know what you are. Duty, though, is the requirement of the day";[28] according to Rosenberg, even primitive Germans shared this ethic of duty.

Kate's own "Atlantis" is the "Tuatha Dé Danann", a mythological race who inhabited Ireland before the ancestors of the modern Irish. She feels that her "innermost blood" from this race must be re-united with the blood of Cipriano and Ramón, in defiance of the "scientific, fair-and-square Europe" (*PS*, 415) to which Goethe, Frederick II, and Rosenberg belong to. This reunion of diverse races is a central theme in *The Plumed Serpent*.

A dualistic mythology

For Lawrence, Atlantis, primitive Germany and Aztec culture are significant as alternatives to the political status quo in Europe, despite their potential dangers. Lawrence was inspired by Frobenius' description of the Yoruban religion, which is local to the people, in that each God is a founder of a family, and each person is a part of that God, to whom the family prays and dances for fertility. At the same time, the religion is a universal "expression of the need of searching for a final cause, of the endeavour to find a concrete idea of a Universe which transcends native intellectual capacity".[29] Lawrence

---

[28] *Ibid.*, 260-61: "Versuche deine Pflicht zu tun, und du weißt gleich, was an dir ist. Die Pflicht aber ist die Forderung des Tages."

[29] Leo Frobenius, *The Voice of Africa*, 2 vols (New York: Benjamin Blom, 1968), I,

stresses this dualistic quality of the Quetzalcoatl religion, in its apprehension of the particular and universal significance of human experience. The danger that threatens in *The Plumed Serpent*, however, is of the universal language of myth swallowing up the characters' experience, and becoming another ideal.

The fundamental duality of the Quetzalcoatl religion, in its universal and particular aspects, is shared by Buber and Rosenzweig's versions of Jewish religion. For Lawrence, Buber and Rosenzweig this duality provides a model against the idealist thought that was dominating Europe, especially Germany. We saw in the previous chapter how Buber was part of the German Jewish reaction against Enlightenment values, including idealism. The notion of blood was used against political and philosophical liberalism. Through the experience of the First World War Buber developed his philosophy of "dialogue" to prioritize the duality within man, and between himself and the world and God, over the ideal of *Einheit*. Buber emphasizes the physical vitality of the Hasidic *völkisch* culture, and the diversity of Jewish identity: "No other people has produced such lowly adventurers and betrayers, such exalted prophets and redeemers."[30] He resists trying to reconcile these oppositions in Jewish culture.

According to Buber, Hasidism consecrates the individual's physical desires. He quotes Rabbi Nachman:

> One can serve God with the evil drive if one directs his passion and his longing ardour to God. And without the evil drive there is no perfect service.[31]

Buber even quotes the founder of Hasidism, Baal-Shem Tov, that "Prayer is a coupling with the Glory of God", in which one imitates the sexual motion of moving up and down. Baal-Shem Tov taught that "Out of my flesh shall I see God",[32] and Buber explains that Hasidism

---

188-89, 229.

[30] Buber, *Der Jude und sein Judentum*, 20: "Kein anderes Volk hat so niedriglträchtige Spieler und Verräter, kein anderes Volk so erhabene Propheten und Erlöser hervorgebracht."

[31] Buber, *Werke*, III, 908: "Man kann mit dem bösen Triebe dienen, wenn man sein Entbrennen und seine begehrende Glut zu Gott lenkt. Und ohne bösen Trieb ist kein vollkommener Dienst."

[32] *Ibid.*, 58-59: "Das Gebet ist eine Paarung mit der Einwohnenden Herrlichkeit";

involves the individual transforming and realizing himself through God, not giving himself up to God.

Rosenzweig envisages traditional Judaism as an alternative to German idealism, by concentrating on the individual's relation to God. Having served in the First World War, Rosenzweig confronted the inadequacy of German idealist philosophy in reassuring the individual of his significance within the whole of humanity while facing death:

> As long as he lives on earth, he shall also remain in the anxiety of the earthly. And philosophy deceives him about this imperative as it weaves the blue mist of its all-encompassing idea of the earthly.[33]

Throughout *Der Stern der Erlösung* (1921, *The Star of Redemption*) Rosenzweig criticizes *Idealismus* in a similar way that Lawrence had done since the war: "[Idealism] had been unable to comprehend [phenomena] as 'spontaneous', because it would have involved denying the omnipotence of the logos ... the basic relationships must ... run from categories to individuals."[34] Like Lawrence, Rosenzweig associates idealism with materialism, progress, rationalism and modern state organization.

In his rejection of idealism, Rosenzweig shares Lawrence's development through Schopenhauer to Nietzsche. The individual who faces the terror of his mortality fractures the idealism of the whole. According to Rosenzweig, Nietzsche gives voice to the individual in the larger will and the idealist whole: "The person in the utter singularity of his individual nature ... stepped out of the world which knew itself as the conceivable world, out of the All of philosophy."[35]

"Aus meinem Fleisch heraus werde ich Gott schauen."
[33] Rosenzweig, *Gesammelte Schriften*, II, 4: "solang er auf der Erde lebt, soll er auch in der Angst des Irdischen bleiben. Und die Philosophie betrügt ihn um dieses Soll, indem sie den blauen Dunst ihres Allgedankens um das Irdische webt."
[34] *Ibid.*, 50, 54-55: "[Idealismus] hatte [die Erscheinung] nicht als ‚spontan' begreifen dürfen, weil er damit die Allherrschaft des Logos geleugnet hätte ... Die grundlegenden Beziehungen müssen von den Gattungen zu den Individuen ... laufen."
[35] *Ibid.*, 10: "Der Mensch in der schlechthinnigen Einzelheit seines Eigenwesens ... trat aus der Welt, die sich als denkbare wußte, dem All der Philosophie heraus."

Individual vitality disrupts the idealist whole, and for Rosenzweig constitutes the basis of man's relation to God as *Trotz* ("defiance"):

> Defiance, this dark, boiling over, original evil in man, is the subterranean root out of which the sap of faithfulness rises into the soul beloved of God. Without the sombre reticence of the self no bright opening of the soul, without defiance no faithfulness.[36]

As in Buber's Hasidism, the *Böse* ("evil") in man, the vitality of his individual will empowers him to cleave to God, whom he gives himself up to. This loss and retention of self characterizes the religious experience of Lawrence's characters. Rosenzweig's Romantic imagery of the body's vitality "bubbling up darkly" resembles Lawrence's description in 1913 of sex as "where life bubbles up into the person from the unknown" (Letters, II, 102). In *The Plumed Serpent* Lawrence gives a more religious significance to this insight, as in his description of Ramón praying: "In his eyes was only darkness, and slowly the darkness revolved in his brain too, till he was mindless." Ramón alternates the exertion and relaxation of his will to realize himself through God, not to give himself up to Him:

> Only a powerful will stretched itself and quivered from his spine in an immense tension of prayer .... Then suddenly, the clenched and quivering arms dropped, the body relaxed into softness. (*PS*, 169)

This concentration on the individual before God, and within a community of blood, distinguishes Lawrence, Rosenzweig and Buber from Hitler and Rosenberg's emphasis on the sacrifice of the individual for the *Volk*. Nazi ideology recapitulates the values of the First World War, of the individual serving the national ideal; Lawrence, Rosenzweig and Buber are dedicated to overturning the idealism of the war. They use blood as an antidote to idealism, to express the physicality of each individual in his relation to his community, and to God. Rosenzweig identifies the individual's *Trotz*

---

[36] *Ibid.*, 190: "Der Trotz, dieses dunkel aufkochende Urböse im Menschen, ist die unterirdische Wurzel, aus der die Säfte der Treue in die gottgeliebte Seele steigen. Ohne die finstre Verschlossenheit des Selbst keine lichte Offenbarung der Seele, ohne Trotz keine Treue."

with life: "life achieves resistance; it resists, specifically, death."[37] In turn, life constitutes the *Blutsgemeinschaft*. This difference is crucial in *The Plumed Serpent* because it enables blood to express the physical vitality of the individual, not race. Furthermore, Kate is free to join the Quetzalcoatl cult and marry Cipriano, and by implication, Europeans share her freedom to change their blood and develop a more immanent relation with their community and God, without rationalizing these into ideals.

The ideology of blood in *The Plumed Serpent*

In *The Plumed Serpent* Lawrence revises his previous notions about blood. From identifying it with race in *Quetzalcoatl*, he locates the vitality and passion of the blood in the individual. From the beginning of *The Plumed Serpent* Kate has fixed notions of race and blood that pressurize her to leave Mexico. At one point she is so exasperated by her Mexican neighbours that she muses on the failure of "rich people, white people, superior people" to maintain their "leadership" over the "dark races". Her argument undermines itself as it graduates to comparing the Indians to the Irish, whom she and her husband fought for, as "the backward races!" (*PS*, 148-49). She refuses marriage to Cipriano on the grounds that there should be no physical contact between different races, and yet the real reason for her refusal lies in her greater sexual attraction to the physically more beautiful Ramón. In *Quetzalcoatl* the conflict between Ramón and his wife Carlota seemed to lie in their different races, he being Mexican and she Spanish; in *The Plumed Serpent* both are Spanish, and he later marries the Mexican Theresa. Cipriano's glorification of "Montezuma blood" as the "best blood in America" is toned down in *The Plumed Serpent* as: "We are the blood of America. We are the blood of the Montezuma" (*PS*, 361).

Lawrence sets out prevailing racial ideas through an elderly man, Julio Toussaint. He argues that "you may mix Spanish and French blood" because "Europeans are all of Aryan stock, the race is the same", but in Mexico the mixture of European and Indian races has created "the half-breed":

---

[37] *Ibid.*, 248: "Leben leistet Widerstand; es widersteht, nämlich dem Tode."

> He is neither one thing nor another, he is divided against himself. His blood of one race tells him one thing, his blood of another race tells him another.

Lawrence makes "the didactic Toussaint" verge on the ridiculous in his concentration on the act of interbreeding: "What was the moment of coition like? – Answer me that, and you have told me the reason for this Mexico which makes us despair." Perhaps Lawrence is even parodying his own preoccupation with the procedures of the sexual act. To Toussaint's assertion that "the blood is homogeneous, so the consciousness automatically unrolls in continuity", Kate retorts that she hates "automatic continuity" (*PS*, 64-65).

In *The Plumed Serpent* Lawrence transforms the image of blood from a *Motiv* of fixed ideological meaning, like Hitler and Rosenberg's use of it, into a variation that is semantically open. He draws attention to its physicality in the description of the horse's blood and bowels (*PS*, 16) during the bull-fight, and in the repetition of blood when Ramón is struggling for his life against a bandit: "blood running down his arm and his back ... blood shot out like a red projectile ... the bloody knife ... black hair wet with blood, and blood running into his glazed, awful eyes ... blood-soddened hair, blood running in several streams down the narrow, corrugated brow" (*PS*, 295). In this section Lawrence disrupts the ideological meanings of blood by forcing to our attention its physicality in maintaining the body's life. This quality is not as extreme as in the comically grotesque description of Alan lying in a pool of blood in "The Border-Line", but Lawrence approaches this self-deflating style.

Still, the relation between blood, race and the individual is uncertain in *The Plumed Serpent*. Halfway through the novel Ramón outlines a middle position, that "the races of the earth are like trees, in the end they neither mix nor mingle"; only the "flowers" of each race, "Natural Aristocrats" like Cipriano and Kate, can mix with each other. In this sense, Quetzalcoatl gives voice to the Mexican blood, and if "the Teutonic world would once more think in terms of Thor and Wotan, and the tree Igdrasil", they could express the German blood (*PS*, 248).

At the end of the novel Kate discovers a more radical solution. From her desire for Cipriano's "blood-stream to envelop hers", she learns that "the clue to all living and to all moving-on into new living lay in the vivid blood-relation between man and woman" (*PS*, 317, 399). The racial associations of blood are discarded for its evocation of the body's drives. Through Cipriano, she discards her "English, Germanic idea of the *intrinsic* superiority of the hereditary aristocrat", and accepts the Mexican peoples' "primeval assertion", that she had rejected in *Quetzalcoatl*:

> *The blood is one blood. We are one blood.* It was the assertion that swept away all individualism, and left her immersed, drowned in the grand sea of the living blood, in immediate contact with all these men and all these women. (*PS*, 417)

This belief differs profoundly from Hitler's imperative of racial purity. In "Das Judentum und die Juden" Buber anticipated Lawrence's position by combining his racial notion of blood with one determined by individual experience. He argued that for German Jews, native German culture had "been assimilated by the innermost forces of our blood, and has become right for us". As a "Mischung" ("mixture"), German Jews needed to master, not be enslaved to, their diverse heritage by choosing aspects of it that were most rewarding for their lives.[38] The most important product of this German-Jewish cultural dialogue by Buber and Rosenzweig was their translation of the Hebrew Bible into German in the Twenties. In this project they attempted to "Hebraise" German, to encourage the German-Jewish reader to seek out the original, and his own native culture. They were indebted to the German Romanticism of Herder and Grimm in attempting to capture the *völkisch* character of the Hebrew in its sound, poetic quality and immanence of the action. Their success was compared to the achievements of Wagner's poetry in the *Ring*.[39]

In the Mexican novels Lawrence is attempting to achieve a fusion between two distant cultures, to inspire in his English-speaking readers a concern with their own primal religious impulses by reviving the Mexican cult of Quetzalcoatl. As for Buber and

---

[38] Buber, *Der Jude und sein Judentum*, 16: "von unseres Blutes innersten Kräften verarbeitet und uns eingeeignet worden ist."
[39] See Michael Brenner, *The Renaissance of Jewish Culture in Weimar Germany* (New Haven Yale: University Press, 1996), 103-109.

Rosenzweig, the problem lies in the scope of his freedom within these distinct cultures, in his capacity to choose from among them a vision that can liberate his readership from its native conventions without enslaving it to the political conventions of Mexican culture. In particular, his use of German culture is exposed to the danger of importing its political extremes into his vision, of not liberating his characters to act spontaneously, but entrapping them within a totalitarian ideology.

Both Buber and Rosenzweig believed that Judaism had global significance, that by its example it could show a way forward for other nations and religions out of the modern European crisis that had climaxed in the First World War. George Mosse sums up Buber's approach: "Only by first becoming a member of the 'Volk' could the individual Jew truly become part of humanity."[40] Lawrence's vision in *The Plumed Serpent* shares this regenerative ambition across national and cultural boundaries, to re-establish the historical roots of each culture, partly by their fusion with each other.

Between "horror" and liberation

The problem that still threatens Lawrence's cross-cultural project in *The Plumed Serpent* is the overwhelming power of its symbolic discourse. The language of blood, darkness, will and power sweeps away European ideas of both racism, and liberalism in its denial of the consciousness of individuals such as Kate. She is freed from her racial identity, but dispossessed of her free will. The mythology is the only source of values left in the novel, becoming an ideal in place of the European ideals that Lawrence is attempting to break from. As in *Quetzalcoatl* mythology is hijacked by Cipriano who uses it to idealize, and authorize, his own will to power. And yet in its dualistic quality Lawrence's mythology can undermine idealism through a tactile expression of ideal entities, such as God. We see these two tendencies compete with each other to determine the ideology of *The Plumed Serpent*.

While supporting Ramón's attempt to revive a Mexican Atlantis, Kate acknowledges that "the old way had its horror" (*PS*, 415). In *The Plumed Serpent* Lawrence is true to the horror of Frobenius' Atlantis,

---

[40] George L. Mosse, *Germans and Jews* (New York: Howard Fertig, 1970), 89.

where the Yorubans' "wealth and piety" was judged by how many human sacrifices they could afford; the ensuing feasts united the Yorubans in a "tie of a certain mystic and religious strength".[41] In *The Plumed Serpent* there is the horror of ritual executions, and of an aggressive nationalism based on the Quetzalcoatl cult. Lawrence does not flinch from the political consequences of his creation, but the question is whether he considers them an acceptable price to pay for the abolition of a capitalist state.

In her marriage with Cipriano, Kate feels "the constitution of her very blood" "changing" (*PS*, 421). In "A Letter from Germany" Lawrence described how "within the last three years, the very constituency of the blood has changed in European veins. But particularly in Germanic veins." He recognized that the change in Germany had been caused "by a Ruhr occupation, by an English nullity, and by a German false will. We have done it ourselves" (*P*, 110). When blood is not racially bound but subject to individual experience, it develops a political significance that is subject to the historical events impinging upon it. It can be manipulated for political ends, as the Nazis would do in Germany, and as Cipriano does in Mexico.

The change in Kate's blood with Cipriano has occurred through material circumstances that have political significance. Cipriano emits "dark rays of dangerous power" over others, such as the "Jefe politico" ("police chief") who "put their wills entirely in his power", and Kate whose "will had left her. He was carrying her on his will" (*PS*, 319). The change in her blood is both an erotic and political process: it liberates her body, but dispossesses her of an independent will. Cipriano's will over her and the Mexican population legitimates itself through its power: "when she remembered his stabbing the three helpless peons, she thought: Why should I judge him? He is of the gods"; sex with Cipriano leaves Kate "insouciante like a young girl. What do I care if he kills people?" (*PS*, 394).

Cipriano's inner will is the source of his power in religion, sex and war – there are no distinctions, and one must accept the horror and creativity of his will to power. He wants a "Holy War" with "the

---

[41] Frobenius, *The Voice of Africa*, I, 148, 13.

rest of the world", and often acts as "the inevitable Mexican general, fascinated by the opportunity for furthering his own personal ambition and imposing his own personal will" (*PS*, 248, 253) by harnessing the will of his soldiers. Like Ciccio in *The Lost Girl*, whose power over Alvina derived from both his physical vitality and social convention, Kate has to accept both aspects of Cipriano's will-to-power.

Ramón is only able "to keep free from the taint of politics" (*PS*, 247) while spreading his religion, because Cipriano's army hunts down opposition and supervises the removal of Christian objects from the church. Of course, these scenes relate to contemporary political events in Mexico,[42] but Lawrence is also reflecting on the political idealism that he had perceived in Edgar Jaffe and the Bavarian Revolution, and Ramón shares this idealism. In *The Plumed Serpent* Lawrence does not shy away from the political implications of the Quetzalcoatl cult. Ramón proves to be a political idealist like Jaffe and Buber. He resists changing the material situation of people, believing that religious belief is enough to change them. Towards the end of the novel Lawrence describes how "the Quetzalcoatl movement had spread in the country, but sinisterly", turning into "a religious war" against the Catholic church. Through Cipriano's military success, Quetzalcoatl becomes "the national religion of the Republic"; all churches are closed and priests are forced to declare allegiance to the Republic or are exiled. There is a great sense of excitement and released energy, but also "a sense of violence and crudity in it all, a touch of horror" (*PS*, 419-20) like the spirit of 1914 on the outbreak of the First World War. Kate participates in the atmosphere of the events through her submission to Cipriano. By the end of the novel Ramón is exhausted, ghostly, as if dispossessed of his own revolution, convinced that somebody will murder him, like Gerald at the end of *Women in Love*.

Through his mythology Ramón legitimates the power of Cipriano's will, on a larger scale than in *Quetzalcoatl*. Cipriano's dictatorial power can only be restrained if the power of the Quetzalcoatl religion, including the symbolic language that expresses it, is checked by the material reality that it imposes itself upon. The symbolic language must express the individual's relation to God, just

---

[42] See Ellis, *D. H. Lawrence: Dying Game*, 214.

as blood expresses the religious vitality within each individual. Mythology should remain physically immediate while reaching out to the cosmos, without being able to grasp it as a whole, or an ideal. It must be the unknowable, ungraspable God that Somers pursued as an alternative to the oppressive political ideals of Kangaroo.

In their emphasis on the physicality of man, Lawrence, Buber and Rosenzweig value mythology and ritual as concrete means of relating the individual to a remote God. In *The Plumed Serpent* Kate reflects on the Quetzalcoatl cult: "Gods die with men who have conceived them. But the god-stuff roars eternally, like the sea, with too vast a sound to be heard" (*PS*, 59). For Buber, the *völkisch* character of Hasidic legends provides a medium for the dialogue between man and God, who is unknowable. Buber values a mythology of God that splits Him into various "Gewalten" ("powers") or personifies Him as a divine hero who crushed the "Untier des Chaos" ("monster of chaos"). Buber believes that myth can enable modern man to grasp God, not "by thoughts", but "by the wide-awake power of the senses, the ardent vibrations of the whole person ... as a vivid, multifaceted reality".[43]

In Lawrence's Mexican novels ritual is used for communal expression of religious mythology. In *Der Stern der Erlösung* Rosenzweig examines how the physical acts in Jewish festivals symbolize man's position in history between creation and redemption. During prayer in the synagogue, individual worshippers unite with each other to glimpse their future redemptive unity with God on the Day of Judgement. In communal eating the "life" and "blood" of the individual is given sustenance, in the company of others, to anticipate mankind's future providence from God.[44] Similarly, after Ramón has prayed alone, he joins others in a ritual of drum-playing and singing, where they evoke the primeval world of creation as individuals, and anticipate redemption in their unity: "they were singing from the oldest, darkest recess of the soul, not outwards, but inwards, the soul singing back to herself.... in the peculiar unison like a flock of birds

---

[43] Buber, *Der Jude und sein Judentum*, 83-84: "mit dem Gedanken"; "mit der wachen Kraft der Sinne und dem glühenden Schwingen der ganzen Person ... als eine anschauliche, in aller Vielheit gegebene Wirklichkeit."
[44] See Rosenzweig, *Gesammelte Schriften*, II, 321-30, 339-64.

that fly in one consciousness" (*PS*, 175). Individual and communal experience are held in balance.

For Buber and Rosenzweig, the fundamental quality of myth and ritual, and blood, is in how their physicality denies any ideal unity for man, since the ideal is the unknowable God. To avoid the *Wille zur Macht* being an ideal, Rosenzweig isolates man's *Wille* as "free will, not free power" from God's power: "God, visible in the Creation, can do anything he wills."[45] The individual's will acquires power through loving God, during which he maintains the individual vitality of his "defiance".

The problem threatening *The Plumed Serpent* is of directly evoking God in the narrative, and relating it to the will and power of the characters, to give the lie of their redemption and turn the Quetzalcoatl cult into an ideal. In Lawrence's two versions of the opening of the church, we see him move towards this danger, while remaining aware of it. In *Quetzalcoatl* he undermined the religious significance of the scene with a few satirical details, such as Cipriano being dressed in lurid stripes, while "the curious stiff Indian poise and the balance of the great hat saved him from any suggestion of ridicule", and how "the men in the congregation were too dense or stupefied to understand" (*PS*, 229, 233) the priest's order to stand up. In *The Plumed Serpent* Lawrence removes these details, but most crucial is his change to the chant. In *Quetzalcoatl* it was:

> God is One God.
> No man can see Him.
> No man can speak to Him.
> No man knows His Name.
> He remains beyond. (*Q*, 230)

But in *The Plumed Serpent* it is reduced to "What is God, we shall never know!" (*PS*, 336). Where God was inaccessible to all men in the first version, in the second version He is accessible to individuals such as Ramón and Cipriano, but cannot be conceived rationally by the multitudes. Ramón embodies God, in "the heart of all darkness in front of him, where his unknowable God-mystery lived and moved";

---

[45] *Ibid.*, 72, 125: "nicht freie Macht, sondern freier Wille"; "Gott der Schöpfer ist wesentlich mächtig. ... Gott, der in Schöpfung Sichtbare, kann alles, was er will."

he has "the power of his heavy, strong will over the people", while "the crowd began to fuse under his influence". God is the source of his will and power over others. Meanwhile, Cipriano remains at the gate of the church with his soldiers, his voice "clear and military" (*PS*, 337).

Lawrence tries to counter the effect of this difference between the two versions in his treatment of Carlota's death. In *Quetzalcoatl*, after her initial outburst she loses consciousness and later dies; she is the sacrifice, symbolizing the death of Catholicism. In *The Plumed Serpent* her death is described in harrowing detail, in which she regains consciousness and quarrels with Cipriano on her death-bed. She gives Kate "her old footing" (*PS*, 345) from which to criticise Ramón and Cipriano's venture:

> The business of living? Were they really gone about the great business of living, abandoning her here to this business of dying? (*PS*, 349)

Kate's criticism echoes the insight that Lawrence made into the idealism of the First World War, where its apparent affirmation of vitality hid a denial of the deaths of individual soldiers. Nonetheless, her resistance has been disparaged as extremely weak by critics, especially since she is silenced by the overwhelming power of Cipriano while making love to her afterwards.

In placing Lawrence's Mexican novels against the contemporary political situation in Germany, then, we are still struck by their political ambiguity. Lawrence does not merely follow Germany's lurch towards right-wing politics in his increasingly totalizing use of myth in *The Plumed Serpent*. He also mirrors other political developments, such as the German- Jewish attempt to create a community for its race and religion, a community that was open to other cultures, and whose mythology confirmed man's autonomy, not his unity in relation to God. Crucially, over the period of composing *Quetzalcoatl* then *The Plumed Serpent* Lawrence detaches his mythology of the blood from a racial meaning so that it is a symbol of man's freedom from the state, not of his enslavement to it. The vitality of each person's blood connects him to others across racial divides. Lawrence's vision of Mexico, too, cuts across cultural boundaries. And yet, there are the lingering dangers of his mythology:

it empowers Cipriano and Ramón with absolute political authority as "gods", and it deprives Kate and the Mexican population of their free will against these gods.

In his post-war novels Lawrence belongs to those diverse tendencies in Europe that were anti-liberal, but not exclusively fascist. Liberal politics proved weak against the onslaught of fascism. Rosenzweig's refusal to combine a notion of Jewish *Blut* with national politics was also impotent in this struggle. Buber's Zionist assertion of Jewish *Blut* as the basis of a nation state finally protected Jews against persecution, but could not extricate them from it, as we see today. It is an unanswerable question as to whether Lawrence's alternative vision of society could have provided any greater resistance to these problems. His achievement, at least in *The Plumed Serpent*, lies in his acknowledgement of the limitations of his vision against them.

CONCLUSION:
THE LADY CHATTERLEY NOVELS

As in the case of *The Plumed Serpent* Lawrence wrote the final version of *Lady Chatterley's Lover* (1928) immediately after visiting Germany, between late August and mid-October 1927. Unlike *The Plumed Serpent*, however, the political and social climate of Germany did not significantly affect the direction of his revisions. Instead, the contrast between Germany's situation and his writing confirmed to him the values of his earlier drafts.

For Lawrence Germany was economically "much revived and prosperous", despite remaining "dead" in spirit (Letters, VI, 169). A couple of months after leaving the country, though, he suggested to his younger friend Rolf Gardiner that perhaps beneath its prevailing materialism there was "a stir of life". Having corresponded with Lawrence since 1924, Gardiner considered him to hold the answers to the post-war decline of Europe. He had been inspired by what he interpreted as Lawrence's rejection of democracy in *Aaron's Rod* for a "leadership, of inspired authority evoking ready obedience and loyalty in the cause of creative change". Following developments in Central Europe, particularly Germany, Gardiner rejected the Communist movement for the *Buende* of youth movements and ex-servicemen's organizations that represented "the beginnings of a conservative revolution which harked back to earlier forms of non-tyrannic government in which the leaders were acclaimed rather than voted into office, and to whom unbreakable allegiance was given". Writing in 1956, he denied any link between this notion of a leader and the fascist "strutting little heroes", despite the two most important "leaders" in Britain, Oswald Mosley and Owen Hargrave, being committed fascists in the Thirties.

In a letter to Gardiner in early 1928 while completing *Lady Chatterley*, Lawrence recognized a primal impulse resistant to the materialism in German society, yet he intuited with remarkable accuracy the direction that history would take in the decade following his death. In one sense Germans satisfied the terms of his erotic manifesto in *Lady Chatterley*, as he observed how they "take their shirts off and work in the hay: they are still physical: the English are so wofully disembodied". Yet he could not envisage this physicality as a source of liberation from Germany's social ills. Instead, the bodies of individuals would merge into a collective "*fighting* body":

> Even the German Bünde, I am afraid, will drift into nationalistic, and ultimately, *fighting* bodies: a new, and necessary form of militarism. It may be the right way for them. But not for the English. The English are over-tender. They must have kindled again their religious sense of atoneness.

While the German youth is fusing into a "fighting unity" of "us against the world", Lawrence observes that the English are "weary even of victory": "What we need is reconciliation and atoning" (Letters, VI, 258-59). In this letter he conflates his notion of England with his vision of what it should be in *Lady Chatterley*, and sets them in opposition to his prognosis of Germany.

In all three of its versions the novel is interspersed with cultural references that extend its significance beyond its local setting in Nottinghamshire. Lawrence is addressing his current concerns about the condition of England, and of Europe, while reflecting allusively upon the concerns of his career as a whole. He recapitulates themes that have run through all of his novels, of the contest between the sensual and materialistic *Willen zur Macht*, individual and society, the conscious mind and unconscious body.

In the first and second versions of the novel Lawrence refers to Oswald Spengler's *Der Untergang des Abendlandes* (*The Decline of the West*, 1918, 1922), to imply that he is providing an alternative to Spengler's vision of the inevitable decline of Western civilization. Clifford Chatterley's relation to Germany evokes its materialistic culture. He has studied in Bonn, where Gerald Crich was a student; he reads "the latest things on mining and the chemistry of coal and of shale which were written in German" (*LCL*, 107). In the second version the mines revive him beyond a mere Schopenhauerian "will to live", towards an "insentient will to assert himself", that is, "to make money" (*FLC*, 347). Then in the final version he echoes Gerald's Nietzschean *Wille zur Macht* over the mines: "Power! He felt a new sense of power flowing through him: power over all these men, over the hundreds and hundreds of colliers" (*LCL*, 108).

In the first version Clifford reads to Connie the works of Hauptmann and Rilke, but in the second version they are generalized to "modern German books" which could include such writers as Thomas Mann whose classical detachment reflects Clifford's own style of writing. In a letter of November 1928 Lawrence reiterated his opinions in the review of 1913, that Mann "leaves out the shady side. He is so good – and yet I feel, ultimately, he is nothing" (Letters, VII, 563). Furthermore, Clifford is associated with the classical, rationalistic tradition in German culture, such as Immanuel Kant, of whom Lawrence wrote in one of his last essays, "we cannot feel ... ever had a soul" (*LEA*, 300). Goethe remains the most important representative of this tradition for Lawrence in his last years, with the poem of 1929, "Goethe and Pose":

> When Goethe becomes an Apollo, he becomes a plaster cast.
> When people pose as gods, they are Crystal Palace statues,
> made of cement poured into a mould, around iron sticks.
>
> (*CP*, 673)

Lawrence identified a "peculiarly bourgeois and Goethian" culture in Germany where sexuality was at best marginalized, as he inferred from *Wilhelm Meister* in a letter from March 1928:

> Goethe *began* millions of intimacies, and never got beyond the how-do-you-do-stage, then fell off into his own boundless ego. He perfected himself into perfection and Godliness. (Letters, VI, 342)

Clifford's physical paralysis, which is described by Lawrence as both symbolic and literal, resembles that of Goethe's classical statue. Also, mirroring Goethe's desire to "perfect himself into perfection", in the first version Clifford imagines his disembodied relationship with Connie as "two souls going hand in hand along the upper road that skirts the heaven of perfection". He believes in Plato's notion of the soul as a chariot drawn by two horses representing the body and spirit, yet feels "so anxious for immortality" (*FLC*, 23-24), given the possibility that his lost physical impulses will prevent him from reaching it. In the final version of the novel he solves this problem with his motorized chair, needing "no steeds at all, only an engine!" (*LCL*, 179). In the development between these passages Lawrence articulates his long held belief that contemporary industrial civilization has emerged from a rationalistic, classical culture that includes Goethe.

Despite this industrial, mechanized power Clifford feels "a secret dread" (*LCL*, 109) of Connie's sensual power. In version 1 he responds to the prospect of her having a child by another man with "I'm getting off cheap, in deferred payments, really" (*FLC*, 68). He is referring to the reparations demanded by the Allies at the Treaty of Versailles, and the subsequent negotiations which culminated in the Treaty of Locarno in December 1925; Germany struggled to re-establish its economic power in the Twenties while being dragged back by the punitive terms of the peace. And yet if we follow the logic of the novel, the greatest threat to this resurrection of material, bourgeois interests is not the fallout from the war, but the erotic vitality of the individual. It comes from within Germany, that is, from Otto Gross who had revolutionized Lawrence's artistic career before the war.

Lawrence suggests the influence of Gross' philosophy upon *Lady Chatterley's Lover*, while withholding acknowledgement of the debt he owes. Connie's upbringing in Dresden just before the war is drawn from Frieda's experiences in her native country, but with significant differences. Lawrence combines Gross with Frieda's German lovers before her marriage to Weekley, to foreground Gross' traditional romantic sentiments at the expense of his revolution in sexuality. The "impassioned interchange of talk" that dominates Connie and her sister's relationship with their *Wandervogel* lovers alludes to Frieda and Else's affairs with Gross. In particular, it continues Lawrence's scepticism regarding Gross' idealism of desire that was implicit in *The Rainbow* and overtly expressed in Johanna's complaint about Eberhard in *Mr Noon*. He suggests the lasting importance of Gross in the "subtle but unmistakeable transmutation [sex] makes, both in the body of man and woman", as experienced by Connie and her lover. At the same time, though, Lawrence stresses the relationship of power that sex initiates between them, with Connie becoming "either anxious or triumphant", and her man "less assertive, more hesitant". This is not the liberation that Lawrence imagines for Connie and Mellors. Both German lovers are killed in 1914, which identifies Connie's with one of Frieda's earlier lovers, Udo von Henning who died in October at Châlons. Gross is merged with him. Lawrence forcefully denies any lasting significance for the lovers, or for Gross, in stating that "they didn't exist any more" (*LCL*, 7-9).

In denying the impact of the left-wing revolutionary Gross, Lawrence has denied himself one of the most important defences for the politics of his own ideas which advocate a "democracy of touch" (*FLC*, 277). My aim in this book has been to address the lingering doubts of even Lawrence's most sympathetic readers since Bertrand Russell and Kate Millett's denunciations of him. I have demonstrated the inaccuracy of their criticisms, especially in the links between Lawrence, Freud and fascism. The direct influence of Freud's ideas on Lawrence, at least through British psychoanalysts such as Ernest Jones, David Eder and Barbara Low, would have been comparable to the influence of other middle-class intellectuals, such as Max Weber and Thomas Mann. They revealed the tragic quality of modern man in his highly developed consciousness of his individuality, and his service to social and economic systems that fail to serve his own sensual needs. These intellectuals were, in turn, taking their cue from Goethe, the archetypal figure of German middle-class culture. In *Faust*, the *Wilhelm Meister* novels and *Die Wahlverwandtschaften* Goethe explored the freedom of each individual to choose his path in life, while revealing how this choice was circumscribed by oppressive social demands. Together, Freud, Weber, Mann and Goethe constitute my notion of Realism, in their location of the individual within social structure, and their consequent resistance to envisaging a freedom for him outside this structure.

Although profoundly influenced by them, Lawrence rejected the ideological conclusions of sublimation, *Dienst* and *Entsagung* reached by Freud, Weber, Mann and Goethe. His notion of idealism after the War includes these elements, in their denial of the individual's desires. His use of Freud through Otto Gross challenged these ideological assumptions, asserting the primacy of the individual's sensual impulses against the restrictions of society. In *The Rainbow* and *Women in Love* Tom and Lydia, Will and Anna, Ursula and Birkin, realize their desires in the midst of a modernizing world. Its *Fluch*, to use Wagner's term, of religious disintegration is countered by an increasing social conformity in characters such as Anton Skrebensky and Gerald Crich, reaching its zenith in Lawrence's era with the self-sacrifice of conscripted men to the First World War. Contrary to Millett and Russell, Gross' use of Freud was part of his left-wing programme for a revolution of Germany's capitalist and militarist society.

In characters such as Ursula and Birkin, Lawrence attempted to incorporate both the revolutionary and conservative, the Romantic and Realist, aspects of German culture. Tom and Lydia aspire to a light of greater consciousness of themselves that is associated with Goethe, while they reach into the darkness of their erotic will which can be traced back to Schopenhauer and Wagner. Between Will and Anna this duality becomes polarized, as he turns exclusively towards the darkness. This situation is more extreme in the darkness of Ursula's sexual encounters with Skrebensky. Darkness expresses the idealism of Lawrence's own thinking, in his tendency to reject the conscious mind for the body's needs. In *Women in Love* this problem recurs, and Lawrence dramatizes it in the characters to demonstrate his own "idealism" to the reader. Gerald monopolizes the language of Goethe in the purity and light of his mechanical ideal, while Ursula and Birkin turn from his industrial world, into an exclusively dark reality.

Here we see the dangers within Lawrence's work: in attempting to transform social values through his rejection of Realist culture, he often lapses into a Romantic escapism. This danger predominated in his early novels, before he had discovered Otto Gross' eroticism. During the composition of *The White Peacock* Lawrence turned from the Realist style of Goethe and George Eliot to the ideas and artistic qualities of Schopenhauer and Wagner. Through them he envisaged his characters, not in terms of their social relationships, but their sexual and emotional experiences. Yet central to this vision was the tragic inability of his characters to realize themselves as individuals through these experiences. He further elaborated this style in his

Conclusion 307

second novel *The Trespasser* in which Siegmund and Helena escape from the dreariness of their social reality into an operatic, Wagnerian world of feelings. Lawrence expressed these feelings in a poetic style similar to *Tonsprache* which prioritizes the musical quality of language over its objective signification. Yet this Romanticism is only an escape from society, and leaves the characters powerless as individuals on their return to it.

We see here a weakness of Lawrence's early novels, but it is present even in his greatest achievements, and resurfaces in *The Plumed Serpent* in a political guise. In this novel Lawrence aspired to a society that could foster the individual's primal impulses, unlike the materialism of post-war European societies. Since the individual's consciousness and physical drives are irreconcilable, Lawrence struggled to balance them in a mutual relationship. Kate faces the choice of either maintaining her conscious volition as a modern European, or of fulfilling herself physically in her sexual relationship with Cipriano and her identity as a goddess in his Quetzalcoatl religion. In the last chapter I compared the politics of the Quetzalcoatl movement to those of National Socialism. Although there are strong parallels between them, the Quetzalcoatl movement is more similar to the contemporary *völkisch* movement of Zionism in their shared focus on the individual's vitality in his blood. Nazism's focus on the blood of the race demands the individual's self-sacrifice to society that characterized the war.

In the final analysis, it is impossible to answer the question of how Lawrence would have responded to the political events leading up to the Second World War. And yet, my contextualization of his writing in German culture has revealed his tragic dilemmas, between body and mind, individual and society, consciousness and unconscious, that are characteristic of both his and our eras. His lifelong struggle with these dilemmas in his novels has at least opened up to us the possibility of objectifying them for ourselves, and of imagining strategies for living through them.

SELECT BIBLIOGRAPHY

Primary Texts: D. H. Lawrence
Lawrence's texts are cited with abbreviated titles listed below and page numbers in brackets. I follow the conventions for abbreviations set out in the Cambridge edition of Lawrence's works.

Letters
Letters, I *The Letters of D. H. Lawrence*, Volume I, ed. James T. Boulton (Cambridge: Cambridge University Press, 1979).
Letters, II *The Letters of D. H. Lawrence*, Volume II, eds George J. Zytaruk and James T. Boulton, (Cambridge: Cambridge University Press, 1982).
Letters, III *The Letters of D. H. Lawrence*, Volume III, eds James T. Boulton and Andrew Robertson (Cambridge: Cambridge University Press, 1984).
Letters, IV *The Letters of D. H. Lawrence*, Volume IV, eds Warren Roberts, James T. Boulton and Elizabeth Mansfield (Cambridge: Cambridge University Press, 1987).
Letters, V *The Letters of D. H. Lawrence*, Volume V, eds James T. Boulton and Lindeth Vasey (Cambridge: Cambridge University Press, 1989).
Letters, VI *The Letters of D. H. Lawrence*, Volume VI, eds James T. Boulton, Margaret H. Boulton and Gerald M. Lacey (Cambridge: Cambridge University Press, 1991).

Works
AR *Aaron's Rod*, ed. Mara Kalnins (Cambridge: Cambridge University Press, 1988).
EmyE *England, My England and Other Stories*, ed. Bruce Steele (Cambridge: Cambridge University Press, 1990).
FLC *The First and Second "Lady Chatterley's Lover"*, eds Dieter Mehl and Christa Jansohn (Cambridge: Cambridge University Press, 1999).
FWL *The First "Women in Love"*, eds John Worthen and Lindeth Vasey (Cambridge: Cambridge University Press, 1998).

Hardy	*Study of Thomas Hardy and Other Essays*, ed. Bruce Steele (Cambridge: Cambridge University Press, 1985).
IR	*Introductions and Reviews*, eds N. H. Reeve and John Worthen (Cambridge: Cambridge University Press, 2005).
K	*Kangaroo*, ed. Bruce Steele (Cambridge: Cambridge University Press, 1994).
LEA	*Late Essays and Articles*, ed. James T. Boulton (Cambridge: Cambridge University Press, 2004).
LAH	*Love Among the Haystacks and Other Stories*, ed. John Worthen (Cambridge: Cambridge University Press, 1987).
LCL	*Lady Chatterley's Lover*, ed. Michael Squires (Cambridge: Cambridge University Press, 1993).
LG	*The Lost Girl*, ed. John Worthen (Cambridge: Cambridge University Press, 1981).
MEH	*Movements in European History*, ed. Philip Crumpton (Cambridge: Cambridge University Press, 1989).
MN	*Mr Noon*, ed. Lindeth Vasey (Cambridge: Cambridge University Press, 1984).
P	*Phoenix: The Posthumous Papers of D. H. Lawrence*, ed. Edward D. McDonald (New York: Viking Press, 1936).
PM	*Paul Morel*, ed. Helen Baron (Cambridge: Cambridge University Press, 2003).
PO	*The Prussian Officer and Other Stories*, ed. John Worthen (Cambridge: Cambridge University Press, 1983).
PUFU	*Psychoanalysis and the Unconscious and Fantasia of the Unconscious*, ed. Bruce Steele (Cambridge: Cambridge University Press, 2004).
Q	*Quetzalcoatl: The Early Version of "The Plumed Serpent"*, ed. Louis L. Martz (Redding Ridge: Black Swan Books, 1995).
R	*The Rainbow*, ed. Mark Kinkead–Weekes (Cambridge: Cambridge University Press, 1989).
RDP	*Reflections on the Death of a Porcupine*, ed. Michael Herbert (Cambridge: Cambridge University Press, 1988).
SEP	*Sketches of Etruscan Places and Other Italian Essays*, ed. Simonetta de Filippis (Cambridge: Cambridge University Press, 1992).

Studies	*Studies in Classic American Literature*, ed. Ezra Greenspan, Lindeth Vasey and John Worthen (Cambridge: Cambridge University Press, 2003).
SL	*Sons and Lovers* Baron, eds Helen and Carl Baron (Cambridge: Cambridge University Press, 1992).
SS	*Sea and Sardinia*, ed. Mara Kalnins (Cambridge: Cambridge University Press, 1997).
T	*The Trespasser*, ed. Elizabeth Mansfield (Cambridge: Cambridge University Press, 1981).
TI	*Twilight in Italy and Other Essays*, ed. Paul Eggert (Cambridge: Cambridge University Press, 1994).
WL	*Women in Love*, eds David Farmer, Lindeth Vasey and John Worthen (Cambridge: Cambridge University Press, 1987).
WP	*The White Peacock*, ed. Andrew Robertson (Cambridge: Cambridge University Press, 1983).

Primary Texts: English
De Quincey, Thomas, *Works*, 15 vols (Edinburgh: Adam and Charles Black, 1862-71).
Eliot, George, *Middlemarch* (Oxford: Oxford University Press, 1988).
———*Selected Essays, Poems and Other Writings* (London: Penguin, 1990).
———*The Mill on the Floss* (London: Penguin, 1979).
Garnett, Edward, *Friday Nights* (London: Jonathan Cape, 1922).
Hardy, Thomas, *Far From the Madding Crowd* (London: Penguin, 1985).
———*Jude the Obscure* (London: Penguin, 1998).
———*Tess of the d'Urbervilles* (London: Penguin, 1994).
———*The Notebooks of Thomas Hardy*, ed. Lennart A. Björk (London: Macmillan, 1985).
Keynes, John Maynard, *The Collected Writings of John Maynard Keynes* 30 vols (London: Macmillan, 1971-94).
Low, Barbara, *Psychoanalysis: A Brief Account of Freudian Theory* (London: Allen and Unwin, 1920).
Orage, A. R., ed., *The New Age*.

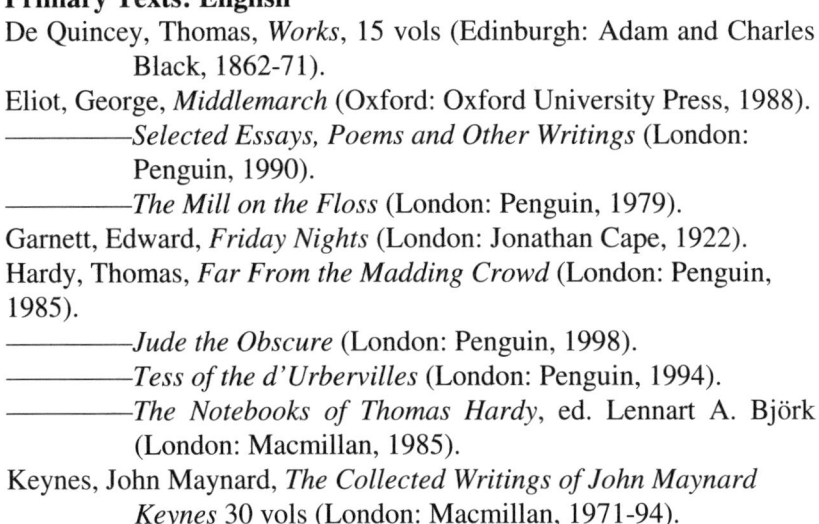

Primary Texts: German
Berliner Tageblatt, 3 August, 1915, 1.
Bismarck, Otto von, *Werke in Auswahl*, 8 vols (Stuttgart: W. Kohlhammer, 1962-84).
Buber, Martin, *Der Jude und sein Judentum: Gesammelte Aufsätze und Reden* (Cologne: Joseph Melzer Verlag, 1963).
───── *Werke*, 3 vols (Munich: Kösel, 1962-4).
Freud, Siegmund, *Gesammelte Werke*, 18 vols (Hamburg: Fischer, 1940-52).
Frobenius, Leo, *The Voice of Africa*, 2 vols (New York: Benjamin Blom, 1968).
Goethe, Johann Wolfgang von, *Werke*, 14 vols (Hamburg: Christian Wegner, 1948-60).
───── *Gedenkausgabe der Werke, Briefe und Gespräche*, 26 vols (Zurich: Artemis, 1948-64).
Gross, Otto, *Von geschlechtlicher Not zur sozialen Katastrophe* (Berlin: Nautilus, 2000).
Gross, Otto and Frieda Weekley, "The Otto Gross – Frieda Weekley Correspondence", ed. John Turner, *D. H. Lawrence Review*, 2 (1990), vol. 22,137-227.
Haeckel, Ernst, *The Riddle of the Universe* (London: Watts, 1900).
Hauptmann, Gerhart, *Die Versunkene Glocke* (Frankfurt am Main: Ullstein, 1959).
───── *Sämtliche Werke*, 11 vols (Frankfurt am Main: Propyläen, 1962-73).
Hesse, Hermann, *Demian* (Frankfurt am Main: Suhrkamp, 1974).
───── *Politik des Gewissens*, 2 vols (Frankfurt am Main: Suhrkamp, 1977).
Hitler, Adolf, *Mein Kampf*, 2 vols (Munich: Zentralverlag der NSDAP, 1940).
Kandinsky, Wassily and Franz Marc, eds, *Der Blaue Reiter* (Munich: R. Piper, 1965).
Kandinsky, Wassily and Franz Marc, *Briefwechsel* (Munich: R. Piper, 1983).
Kandinsky, Wassily, *Über das Geistige in der Kunst* (Bern: Benteli Verlag, 1973).
Lawrence, Frieda, *The Memoirs and Correspondence*, ed. E. W. Tedlock (London: Heinemann, 1961).

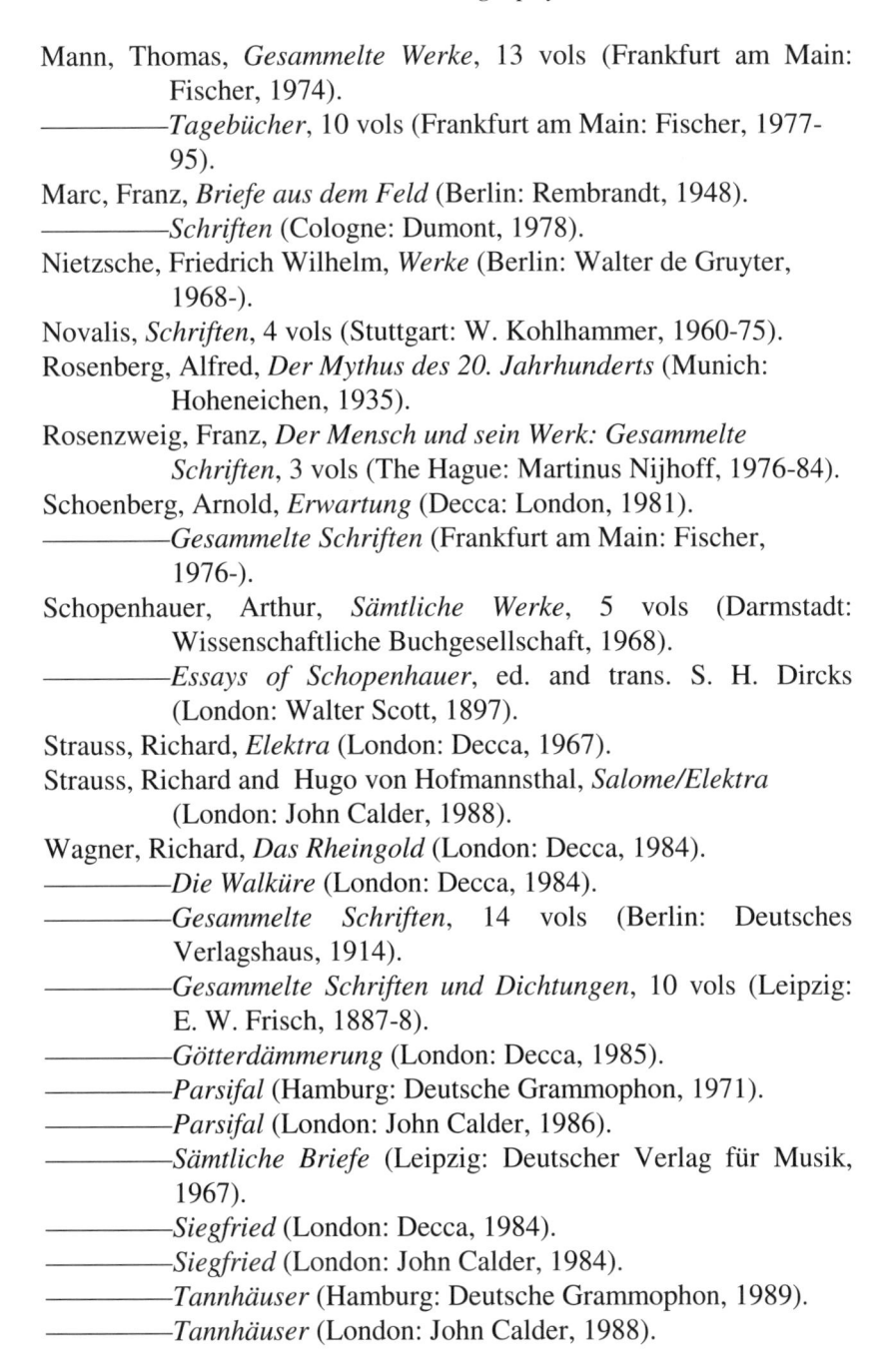

Mann, Thomas, *Gesammelte Werke*, 13 vols (Frankfurt am Main: Fischer, 1974).
———*Tagebücher*, 10 vols (Frankfurt am Main: Fischer, 1977-95).
Marc, Franz, *Briefe aus dem Feld* (Berlin: Rembrandt, 1948).
———*Schriften* (Cologne: Dumont, 1978).
Nietzsche, Friedrich Wilhelm, *Werke* (Berlin: Walter de Gruyter, 1968-).
Novalis, *Schriften*, 4 vols (Stuttgart: W. Kohlhammer, 1960-75).
Rosenberg, Alfred, *Der Mythus des 20. Jahrhunderts* (Munich: Hoheneichen, 1935).
Rosenzweig, Franz, *Der Mensch und sein Werk: Gesammelte Schriften*, 3 vols (The Hague: Martinus Nijhoff, 1976-84).
Schoenberg, Arnold, *Erwartung* (Decca: London, 1981).
———*Gesammelte Schriften* (Frankfurt am Main: Fischer, 1976-).
Schopenhauer, Arthur, *Sämtliche Werke*, 5 vols (Darmstadt: Wissenschaftliche Buchgesellschaft, 1968).
———*Essays of Schopenhauer*, ed. and trans. S. H. Dircks (London: Walter Scott, 1897).
Strauss, Richard, *Elektra* (London: Decca, 1967).
Strauss, Richard and Hugo von Hofmannsthal, *Salome/Elektra* (London: John Calder, 1988).
Wagner, Richard, *Das Rheingold* (London: Decca, 1984).
———*Die Walküre* (London: Decca, 1984).
———*Gesammelte Schriften*, 14 vols (Berlin: Deutsches Verlagshaus, 1914).
———*Gesammelte Schriften und Dichtungen*, 10 vols (Leipzig: E. W. Frisch, 1887-8).
———*Götterdämmerung* (London: Decca, 1985).
———*Parsifal* (Hamburg: Deutsche Grammophon, 1971).
———*Parsifal* (London: John Calder, 1986).
———*Sämtliche Briefe* (Leipzig: Deutscher Verlag für Musik, 1967).
———*Siegfried* (London: Decca, 1984).
———*Siegfried* (London: John Calder, 1984).
———*Tannhäuser* (Hamburg: Deutsche Grammophon, 1989).
———*Tannhäuser* (London: John Calder, 1988).

────────*Tannhäuser* (Zurich: Eulenburg, 1961).
────────*Tristan und Isolde* (Hamburg: Deutsche Grammophon, 1982).
────────*Tristan und Isolde* (London: John Calder, 1981).
Weber, Alfred, *Die Krise des modernen Staatsgedankens in Europa* (Stuttgart: Deutsche Verlags-Anstalt, 1925).
Weber, Max, *Gesammelte Politische Schriften* (Tübingen: J. C. B. Mohr, 1958).
────────*Gesammelte Aufsätze zur Religionssoziologie*, 2 vols (Tübingen: J. C. B. Mohr, 1947).

Secondary sources on D. H. Lawrence

Atkins, A. R., "Textual Influences on D. H. Lawrence's 'The Saga of Siegmund'", *D. H. Lawrence Review*, XXIV/1 (1992), 6-26.
Balbert, Peter, *D. H. Lawrence and the Psychology of Rhythm* (The Hague: Mouton, 1974).
Bedient, Calvin, *Architects of the Self* (Berkeley: University of California, 1972).
Bell, Michael, *D. H. Lawrence: Language and Being* (Cambridge: Cambridge University Press, 1991).
────────"D. H. Lawrence and Thomas Mann: Unbewusste Brüderschaft", *Études Lawrenciennes*, X (1994), 187-97.
Beauvoir, Simone de, *The Second Sex* (London: Everyman, 1993).
Björkén, Cecilia, *Into the Isle of Self: Nietzschean Patterns and Contrasts in D. H. Lawrence's* The Trespasser (Lund: Lund University Press, 1996).
Black, Michael, "A Bit of Both: George Eliot and D. H. Lawrence", *Critical Review*, XXIX (Canberra, 1989), 89-109.
────────*D. H. Lawrence: Sons and Lovers* (Cambridge: Cambridge University Press, 1992).
────────*D. H. Lawrence: The Early Fiction* (London: Macmillan, 1986).
Blissett, William, "D. H. Lawrence, D'Annunzio, Wagner", *Wisconsin Studies in Contemporary Literature*, VII (Winter/Spring, 1966), 21-46.
Bonds, Diane S., *Language and the Self in D. H. Lawrence* (Ann Arbor: UMI Research Press, 1987).

Brown, Keith, ed., *Rethinking Lawrence* (Milton Keynes: Open University Press, 1990).
Brunsdale, Mitzi M., *The German Effect on D. H. Lawrence and His Works* (Berne: Peter Lang, 1978).
Burwell, Rose Marie, "Schopenhauer, Hardy and Lawrence: Toward a New Understanding of Sons and Lovers", *Western Humanities Review*, XXVIII (1974), 105-17.
Caudwell, Christopher, *Studies in a Dying Culture* (London: Bodley Head, 1938).
Chambers, Jessie, [E. T.], *D. H. Lawrence: A Personal Record* (London: Frank Cass, 1965).
Clark, L. D., *Dark Night of the Body* (Austin: University of Texas Press, 1964).
Clarke, Colin, *River of Dissolution: D. H. Lawrence and English Romanticism* (London: Routledge and Kegan Paul, 1969).
Corke, Helen, *D. H. Lawrence: The Croydon Years* (Austin: University of Texas Press, 1965).
────── *In our Infancy* (Cambridge: Cambridge University Press, 1975).
Dix, Carol, *D. H. Lawrence and Women* (London: Macmillan, 1980).
Drain, R. L., *Formative Influences on the Work of D. H. Lawrence* (Cambridge University, 1962).
Draper, R. P., *D. H. Lawrence: The Critical Heritage* (London: Routledge and Kegan Paul, 1970).
Eggert, Paul, "D. H. Lawrence and His Audience: The Case of *Mr Noon*", *Southern Review*, XVIII/3 (1985), 298-307.
Ellis, David and Ornell de Zordo, eds, *D. H. Lawrence: Critical Assessments*, 4 vols (Mountfield: Helm Information, 1992).
Ellis, David, *D. H. Lawrence: Dying Game* (Cambridge: Cambridge University Press, 1998).
Fernihough, Anne, *D. H. Lawrence: Aesthetics and Ideology* (Oxford: Clarendon Press, 1993).
Fjågesund, Peter, *The Apocalyptic World of D. H. Lawrence* (Oslo: Norwegian University Press, 1991).
Green, Eleanor Hewson, *The Works of D. H. Lawrence with Relation to Schopenhauer and Nietzsche* (University of Nottingham: 1973).

Green, Martin, *The von Richtofen Sisters* (New York: Basic Books, 1974).
Hoffmann, Regina and Michael Weithmann, *D. H. Lawrence and Germany: A Bibliography* (Passau: University Library of Passau, 1995).
Holderness, Graham, *D. H. Lawrence: History, Ideology and Fiction* (Dublin: Gill and Macmillan Humanities Press, 1982).
Humma, John B., *Metaphor and Meaning in D. H. Lawrence's Later Novels* (Columbia: University of Missouri Press, 1990).
Hyde, G. M., *D. H. Lawrence* (London: Macmillan, 1990).
Kermode, Frank, *Lawrence* (London: Fontana, 1985).
Kestner, Joseph, "The Literary Wagnerism of D. H. Lawrence's *The Trespasser*", *Modern British Literature*, Fall (1977), II, 123-38.
Kinkead-Weekes, Mark, "D. H. Lawrence and the Dance", *The Journal of the D. H. Lawrence Society* (1992-94) 45-62.
——— *D. H. Lawrence: Triumph to Exile* (Cambridge: Cambridge University Press, 1996).
Lawrence, Frieda, *"Not I, But the Wind ..."* (London: Granada Publishing, 1983).
Leavis, F. R., *D. H. Lawrence: Novelist* (London: Penguin, 1955).
MacLeod, Sheila, *Lawrence's Men and Women* (London: Heinemann, 1985).
Michaels-Tonks, Jennifer, *D. H. Lawrence: The Polarity of North and South, Germany and Italy in His Prose Works* (Bonn: Bouvier, 1976).
Millett, Kate, *Sexual Politics* (London: Fontana, 1977).
Milton, Colin, *Lawrence and Nietzsche: A Study in Influence* (Aberdeen: Aberdeen University Press, 1987).
Murfin, Ross C., *Swinburne, Hardy, Lawrence and the Burden of Belief* (Chicago: University of Chicago Press, 1978).
Oates, Joyce Carol, "Lawrence's *Götterdämmerung*: The Tragic Vision of *Women in Love*", *Critical Enquiry*, Spring (1978), vol. 4, 559-78.
Pace, Billy James, *D. H. Lawrence's Use in His Novels of Germanic and Celtic Myth from the Music Dramas of Richard Wagner* (University of Arkansas: 1973).
Pinkney, Tony, *D. H. Lawrence* (London: Harvester Wheatsheaf,

1990).

Ragussis, Michael, *The Subterfuge of Art: Language and the Romantic Tradition* (London: John Hopkins University Press, 1978).

Russell, Bertrand, *The Autobiography of Bertrand Russell* (London: George Allen and Unwin, 1968).

Rylance, Rick, ed., *New Casebooks: Sons and Lovers* (London: Macmillan, 1996).

Sagar, Keith, ed., *A D. H. Lawrence Handbook* (Manchester: Manchester University Press, 1982).

Schorer, Mark, ed., *Sons and Lovers* (Berkeley and London: University of California Press, 1977).

Scott, James F., "D. H. Lawrence's Germania: Ethnic Psychology and Cultural Crisis in the Shorter Fiction", *D. H. Lawrence Review*, 2 (1977), X, 142-64.

Simpson, Hilary, *D. H. Lawrence and Feminism* (London: Croom Helm, 1982).

Squires, Michael and Keith Cushman, eds, *The Challenge of D. H. Lawrence* (Wisconsin: University of Wisconsin Press, 1990).

Squires, Michael, *The Pastoral Novel* (Charlottesville: University Press of Virginia, 1974).

Stewart, Jack F., "Expressionism and the Prussian Officer", *D. H. Lawrence Review* (1986), 275-89.

——— *The Vital Art of D. H. Lawrence: Vision and Expression* (Carbondale: Southern Illinois University Press, 1999).

Whelan, P. T., *D. H. Lawrence: Myth and Metaphysics in* The Rainbow *and* Women in Love (Ann Arbor: UMI Research Press, 1988).

Williams, Raymond, *The English Novel: From Dickens to Lawrence* (London: Chatto and Windus, 1970).

Worthen, John, *D. H. Lawrence* (London: Macmillan, 1989).

——— *D. H. Lawrence and the Idea of the Novel* (London: Macmillan, 1979).

——— *D. H. Lawrence: The Early Years* (Cambridge: Cambridge University Press, 1991).

Zoll, Alan R., "Vitalism and the Metaphysics of Love", *D. H. Lawrence Review* (1978), XI, 1-20.

Other Secondary Sources

Adorno, Theodor Adorno, and Max Horkheimer, *Dialectic of Enlightenment* (New York: Herder and Herder, 1972).

Adorno, Theodor, *Beethoven: The Philosophy of History* (Cambridge: Polity Press, 1998).

———*In Search of Wagner* (London: NLB, 1981).

———*Introduction to the Sociology of Music* (New York: Seabury Press, 1976).

———*Philosophy of Modern Music* (New York: Seabury Press, 1973).

Ashheim, Steven E., *The Nietzsche Legacy in Germany 1890-1990* (Berkeley: University of California Press, 1992).

Ashton, Rosemary, *George Eliot* (Oxford: Oxford University Press, 1983).

———*George Eliot: A Life* (London: Hamish Hamilton, 1996).

———*The German Idea* (Cambridge: Cambridge University Press, 1980).

Benjamin, Walter, *Illuminations* (London: Fontana, 1968).

———*Selected Writings* (London: Harvard University Press, 1996-).

Bessel, Richard, *Germany after the First World War* (Oxford: Oxford University Press, 1993).

Bindschedler, Maria and Paul Zinsli, eds, *Geschichte, Deutung, Kritik* (Berlin: Francke, 1969).

Boyle, Nicholas, *Goethe: The Poet and the Age* (Oxford: Oxford University Press, 1991-).

Bradbury, Malcolm, *The Social Context of Modern English Literature* (Oxford: Basil Blackwell, 1971).

Brenner, Michael, *The Renaissance of Jewish Culture in Weimar Germany* (New Haven: Yale University Press, 1996).

Bronner, Stephen Eric and Douglas Kellner, eds, *Passion and Rebellion: The Expressionist Heritage* (South Hadley: J. F. Bergin, 1983).

Carr, William, *A History of Germany 1815-1990* (London: Edward Arnold, 1991).

Dabrowski, Magdalena, *Kandinsky Compositions* (New York: Museum of Modern Art, 1995).

DiGaetani, John Louis, *Richard Wagner and the Modern British*

Novel (New Jersey: Associated University Press, 1978).
Eagleton, Terry, *Criticism and Ideology* (London: Verso, 1978).
————*The Ideology of the Aesthetic* (Oxford: Basil Blackwell, 1990).
Feuchtwanger, E. J., *From Weimar to Hitler: Germany, 1918-33* (London: Macmillan, 1995).
Firchow, Peter Edgerly, *The Death of the German Cousin* (London: Associated University Press, 1986).
Fischer-Dieskau, Dietrich, *Wagner und Nietzsche* (Stuttgart: Deutsche Verlags-Anstalt, 1974).
Furness, Raymond, *Wagner and Literature* (Manchester: Manchester University Press, 1982).
Garwood, Helen, *Thomas Hardy: An Illustration of the Philosophy of Schopenhauer* (John L. Winston, 1911).
Goldman, Harvey, *Max Weber and Thomas Mann: Calling and the Shaping of the Self* (Berkeley: University of California Press, 1988).
Grimm, Reinhold, ed., *Deutsche Romantheorien* (Frankfurt am Main: Athenäum, 1968).
Harrold, C. F., *Carlyle and German Thought* (New York: AMS Press, 1978).
Heilbut, Anthony, *Thomas Mann: Eros and Literature* (London: Macmillan, 1995).
Heller, Erich, *The Disinherited Mind* (London: Bowes and Bowes, 1971).
————*Thomas Mann: The Ironic German* (New York: Paul P. Appel, 1973).
Hobman, J. B., *David Eder: Memoirs of a Modern Pioneer* (London: Victor Gollancz, 1945).
Hollinrake, Roger, *Nietzsche, Wagner, and the Philosophy of Pessimism* (London: Allen and Unwin, 1982).
Jacquette, Dale, ed., *Schopenhauer, Philosophy, and the Arts* (Cambridge: Cambridge University Press, 1996).
Jameson, Fredric, *Late Marxism* (London: NLB, 1990).
Janaway, Christopher, *Schopenhauer* (Oxford: Oxford University Press, 1994).
Jarvis, Simon, *Adorno: A Critical Introduction* (Cambridge: Polity Press, 1998).

Lamport, F. J., *A Student's Guide to Goethe* (London: Heinemann, 1971).
Leavis, F. R., *The Great Tradition* (London: Chatto and Windus, 1960).
Lewes, George Henry, *The Life of Goethe* (London: J. M. Dent, 1908).
Lukács, Georg, *Essays on Thomas Mann* (London: Merlin Press, 1964).
——*Goethe and His Age* (London: Merlin Press, 1968).
Magee, Bryan, *Aspects of Wagner* (London: Alan Ross, 1968).
——*The Philosophy of Schopenhauer* (Oxford: Clarendon Press, 1983).
Maurer, Warren R., *Understanding Gerhart Hauptmann* (Columbia: University of South Carolina Press, 1992).
Mendes-Flohr, Paul, *German Jews: A Dual Identity* (New Haven: Yale University Press, 1999).
Michaels, Jennifer E., *Anarchy and Eros* (New York: Peter Lang, 1983).
Miller, J. Hillis, *Thomas Hardy: Distance and Desire* (Cambridge, Mass.: Harvard University Press, 1970).
Mitchell, Allan, *Revolution in Bavaria 1918-1919: The Eisner Regime and the Soviet Republic* (Princeton: Princeton University Press, 1965).
Mitzman, Arthur, *The Iron Cage: An Historical Interpretation of Max Weber* (New York: Alfred A. Knopf, 1970).
Mommsen, Wolfgang J., *Max Weber and German Politics 1890-1920* (Chicago: University of Chicago Press, 1984).
Mommsen, Wolfgang J. and Jürgen Osterhammel, eds, *Max Weber and His Contemporaries* (Hemel Hempstead: Allen and Unwin, 1987).
Moore, Kevin Z., *The Descent of the Imagination: Postromantic Culture in the Later Novels of Thomas Hardy* (New York: New York University Press, 1990).
Mosse, George L., *Germans and Jews* (New York: Howard Fertig, 1970).
——*German Jews beyond Judaism* (Bloomington: Indiana University Press, 1985).
——*The Crisis of German Ideology* (New York: Grosset and

Dunlop, 1964).
Murry, John Middleton, *Between Two Worlds: An Autobiography* (London: Jonathan Cape, 1935).
Neubauer, John, *Novalis* (Boston: Twayne Publishers, 1980).
Newman, Ernest, *A Study of Wagner* (London: Bertram Dobell, 1899).
———*Wagner* (London: Bodley Head, 1904).
———*Wagner Nights* (London: Putnam, 1949).
Nipperdey, Thomas, *Deutsche Geschichte 1866-1918*, 2 vols (Munich: C. H. Beck, 1990).
Orlow, Dietrich, *A History of Modern Germany: 1870 to the Present* (New Jersey: Prentice-Hall, 1987).
Pese, Claus, *Franz Marc: Life and Work* (Stuttgart: Belser, 1990).
Poppel, Stephen M., *Zionism in Germany 1897-1933: The Shaping of a Jewish Identity* (Philadelphia: Jewish Publication Society of America, 1976).
Reed, T. J., *Thomas Mann: The Uses of Tradition* (Oxford: Clarendon Press, 1996).
———*Goethe* (Oxford: Oxford University Press, 1984).
Reiss, Hans *Goethe's Novels* (London: Macmillan, 1969).
Ridley, Hugh, *Thomas Mann: Buddenbrooks* (Cambridge: Cambridge University Press, 1987).
Röder-Bolton, Gerlinde, *George Eliot and Goethe: An Elective Affinity* (Amsterdam: Rodopi, 1988).
Sagarra, Eda, *A Social History of Germany 1648-1914* (London: Methuen, 1979).
See Mileck, Joseph, *Hermann Hesse: Life and Art* (Berkeley: University of California Press, 1978).
Schwartz, Frederic J., *The Werkbund: Design Theory and Mass Culture before the First World War* (London: Yale University Press, 1996).
Sessa, Anne Dzamba, *Richard Wagner and the English* (London: Associated University Press, 1979).
Simpson, James, *Matthew Arnold and Goethe* (London: The Modern Humanities Research Association, 1979).
Stahl, E. L. and W. E. Yuill, *German Literature of the Eighteenth and Nineteenth Centuries* (London: Cresset Press, 1970).
Stolte, Heinz, *Hermann Hesse: Weltscheu und Lebensliebe* (Hamburg: Hansa, 1971).

Thatcher, David S., *Nietzsche in England* (Toronto: University of Toronto Press, 1970).
Thórlemann, Felix, *Kandinsky über Kandinsky* (Bern: Benteli, 1986).
Watanabe-O' Kelly, Helen, ed., *The Cambridge History of German Literature* (Cambridge: Cambridge University Press, 1997).
Wellek, René, *Confrontations* (Princeton: Princeton University Press, 1965).
Wilding, Michael, *Political Fictions* (London: Routledge and Kegan Paul, 1980).
Zweite, Armin, *Der Blaue Reiter im Lenbachhaus, Munich* (Munich: Prestel, 1989).

INDEX

Adorno, Theodor Wiesengrund, 5-8, 34, 41-42, 44, 47, 57, 99-100
Africa, 284, 286, 293
Ajanta Frescoes, 132
Alsace-Lorraine, 274
America, United States of, 1-2, 16, 159, 199, 201
Archer, William, *Fighting a Philosophy*, 170
Arnold, Matthew, 26
Ascona, 93
Asquith, Lady Cynthia, 1
Atlantis, 284, 286, 293
Auschwitz, 3, 269
Australia, 2, 258-59, 262, 264, 266
Austria, 90, 112, 219, 254, 258

Baal-Shem Tov, 287
Baden-Baden, 220, 254, 267, 271, 274
Bamberg Cathedral, 125
Barber-Walker family, 164
Bauhaus, 190
Bavaria, 2, 110-13, 115, 219, 259, 265, 271
  Republic, 256
  Revolution, 15, 257, 295
Bayreuth, 7-8
Beethoven, Ludwig van, 6-7, 34-35, 44, 59
Bell, Michael, 10, 113, 270

Benjamin, Judah P., "Nietzsche the Olympian", 62
Benjamin, Walter, 228
Bennett, Arnold, *Anna of Five Towns*, 197, 205
Berlin, 118, 162, 268, 271
Berliner Tageblatt, 194
Bern, 137
Bible, The, 21, 260, 292
Biedermeier, 226
Bismarck, Otto von, 14, 98, 162-64, 169-71, 176, 266
Bizet, George, *Carmen*, 92
Björkén, Cecilia, 63
Black Forest, 267, 273, 275
Black, Michael, 10, 31, 73, 75-76, 81
Black Reichswehr, 271
Blake, William, 9
Blaue Reiter, der, 13, 107, 110-11, 146, 154
  Almanac, 111, 120
Böckmann, Paul, 205
Bolshevism, 283
Bonaparte, Napoleon, 162, 227
Bonds, Diane S., 149, 160
Bonn, 162, 302
Botticelli, 133
Boyle, Nicholas, 198, 203-204, 211, 213, 221, 225-26
Bradbury, Malcolm, 162
Brenner Pass, 110
British Medical Association, 172

British Psychoanalytic Movement, 171
Brontë, Charlotte, 19
Brücke, die, 111
Buber, Martin, 263-65, 267, 270, 280-87, 289, 292-93, 296, 299
  "Das Judentum und die Juden", 281-82, 287, 292, 296
Buchrucker, Major, 271
Buende youth movement, 301-302
Burleigh, Michael, 272
Burrows, Louie, 84, 91

Calvinism, 141
Carlyle, Thomas, 19, 200
Carswell, Catherine, 1
Catholicism, 166, 168, 206, 295, 298
Ceylon, 2, 258
Chamberlain, Houston Stewart, 4
Chambers, Jessie, 20, 26-28, 31, 33, 101
Christianity, 23, 26, 38, 120, 169, 206, 223-24, 236, 242, 295
Clark, L. D., 270
Coleridge, Samuel Taylor, 19
Communism, 258, 262, 301, 272
Cooper, James Fenimore, 199
Corke, Helen, 39, 44, 51, 55, 58, 61-62, 70, 85

Dawes Plan, 272
Dax, Alice, 101
De Quincey, Thomas, 199
Deutsche Demokratische Partei, 261, 272
Deutsches Werkbund, 190-91
Dickens, Charles, *Hard Times*, 197
Dircks, S. H., transl., *Essays of Schopenhauer*, 27-28, 33, 219
Dix, Carol, 6
Dodge Luhan, Mabel, 243
Dresden, 304
Dunlop, Thomas, 168
Dürer, Albrecht, *Melencolia I*, 260

Eagleton, Terry, 242, 254
Eder, David, 172, 262, 305
Eggert, Paul, 231
Eisner, Kurt, 257, 260-61
Eliot, George, 9, 306
  Middlemarch, 11, 19-20, 22, 43, 47
  The Mill on the Floss, 11, 19, 21, 23, 25-26, 29, 75, 228
Ellis, David, 4, 10, 269-70
Expressionism, 2, 103, 107, 110-14, 129-31, 136, 248

Fernihough, Anne, 5, 9-10

Index

Fichte, Johann Gottlieb, 226
First World War, 1-2, 5, 14, 19, 114, 129, 131, 139, 141, 152, 160, 162-64, 170-71, 175-178, 182, 184-85, 189-90, 192-195, 199-200, 202, 204, 218, 219-20, 222, 227, 230, 235-39, 241-44, 246, 248, 250, 252, 255-59, 262-63, 267, 271-72, 275, 276, 283, 288-89, 294-95, 299, 302, 305
Fjågesund, Peter, 242
Ford, Ford Madox, 1
Forster, E. M., 162
Fowler, Roger, 206-207
France, 4, 20, 163, 198, 271, 273
   Revolution, 25, 198, 221, 228
Frankfurt, 99, 162
   Parliament, 163
Frederick the Great of Prussia, 227, 286
Friedrich Wilhelm I, 227
Freud, Sigmund, 3, 6, 12, 16, 72, 75-76, 79-80, 85, 89-94, 96-97, 99-101, 103, 129-30, 133, 161, 175, 181-82, 200, 208, 212-14, 232-33, 235, 246-48, 305-306
   Die Traumdeutung, 92, 183
   Studien über Hysterie, 172, 177
   Zur Psychopathologie des Alltagslebens, 183
   "Bemerkungen über einen Fall von Zwangneurose", 172
   "Bruckstück einer Hysterie-Analyse", 174
   "Das Unbewusste", 174, 180
   "Die Verdrängung", 174
   "Drei Abhandlungen zur Sexualtheorie", 173
   "Formulierungen über die zwei Principien des psychischen Geschehens", 173
Franklin, Benjamin, 199
Frobenius, Leo, *The Voice of Africa*, 284, 286, 293-94

Gardiner, Rolf, 301
Garnett, Edward, 60-62, 76, 93, 95
Germany
   Analogies to Mexico, 16, 268, 273-76, 283, 291, 294-95
   Ancient, 228-29, 233, 236-38, 274-75, 284-85
   Biblical criticism, 25
   Democracy, 163, 248, 255-57, 261, 272
   Enlightenment, 3, 5-8, 16, 25, 67, 119, 121, 129, 227, 260, 263-64
   Folk songs, 2
   Gothic, 119, 125

Idealism, 9, 12, 14-16, 30-31, 42, 104-105, 113-14, 129, 131, 136, 152-53, 160, 171, 185, 191, 193-95, 202, 208, 213-14, 220-22, 224-26, 231, 233-34, 236, 244, 247-51, 253, 258, 265-67, 277, 281-82, 285, 298, 302-303
Industry, 4-6, 75, 119, 37, 162-65, 170, 190-91, 194, 199, 237, 256, 259, 271, 274, 286, 302
Junkers, 4
Language, 1, 70, 210
Liberalism, 3, 14-16, 118-19, 136-37, 140, 163, 198, 256, 261, 268, 271-72, 299
Liberal Imperialism, 13, 114, 129, 138, 171, 198
Militarism, 2, 163-64, 166, 171, 175, 182, 193, 220, 227-28, 235-39, 243, 255, 259, 271, 278, 280, 285-86, 300, 306
Nationalism, 138, 175, 220, 223, 249, 257-58, 272, 281,
Realism, 6-7, 11-12, 14, 16, 30, 40, 48, 70, 92, 100, 198, 200-201, 204-205, 208, 212, 218, 305-306
Revolutions (1848), 32, 163

Romanticism, 2, 5, 12-15, 19, 80, 126, 132, 292, 306
Socialism, 175, 241, 248, 257-58, 262-63
Unification, 98, 163-64, 170, 257
Gertler, Mark, 190
Girondins, 198
Goethe, Johann Wolfgang von, 7, 13, 15, 33, 43, 47, 49, 51, 107, 114, 116, 121, 124-26, 129, 136-38, 140, 143, 153, 166, 168, 170, 184, 186, 192, 213, 216, 218, 231, 238, 248, 252, 264, 286, 303, 306
Die Wahlverwandtschaften, 7, 11, 16, 19-29, 23, 27-28, 43, 228, 305
Farbenlehre, 119
Faust, 15, 37, 114, 119-21, 138, 147-149, 151-52, 169, 171, 186, 199, 204, 220-226, 228, 238, 244, 249-50, 269, 305
Italienische Reise, 216
Urfaust, 119, 200
Wilhelm Meister novels, 14, 16, 22, 199, 201, 217, 269, 303, 305
Wilhelm Meisters Lehrjahre, 14, 16, 137, 197-218, 219, 221-22
Wilhelm Meisters Theatralische Sendung,

198, 200, 202-204, 209, 211, 216, 218, 221-22
Wilhelm Meisters Wanderjahre, 137, 198-199, 203
"Die Absicht ist eingeleitet", 117
Golding, Louis, *Forward from Babylon*, 262
Goldman, Harvey, 141
Graz, 134
Green, Martin, 145
Grimm, Jacob and Wilhelm, 292
Gropius, Walter, 191
Gross, Otto, 6, 12-13, 15-16, 72, 75, 90-95, 97, 100, 102-106, 114, 118, 129-30, 132-35, 136, 139-40, 145-46, 153, 178, 181, 220, 226-27, 230, 232-35, 239, 241, 244, 247, 251-53, 304-306
Das Freud'sche Ideogentitätsmoment, 102
"Ludwig Rubiners 'Psychoanalyse'", 135
"Zur Überwindung der kulturellen Krise", 130

Hardy, Thomas, 19-20, 39, 117, 171, 266
Far From the Madding Crowd, 31-32, 48
Jude the Obscure, 29, 31, 36, 48
Literary Notebooks, 32-35
Tess of the D'Urbervilles, 31, 36
Hargrave, Owen, 301
Hasidism, 264-65, 287, 289, 296
Hauptmann, Gerhart, 303
Die versunkene Glocke, 62, 66-67
Einsame Menschen, 62
Elga, 62-63, 69-70
Hegel, Georg Wilhelm Friedrich, 7, 266
Heidelberg, 118-19, 137, 184, 285
Heller, Erich, 21, 74, 77
Henning, Udo von, 305
Herder, Gottfried, 292
Hesse, Hermann, 258
Demian, 15, 242-46, 248-51, 253-55
Eigensinn, 248
Peter Camenzind, 244
"Zarathustras Wiederkehr", 245
Heym, Georg, 103
Hitler, Adolf, 3, 8, 269, 271-73, 281, 283, 289, 291-292
Mein Kampf, 255, 259, 262, 277-78, 283
Hofmannsthal, Hugo von, *Elektra*, 100
Hohenhausen, 168
Hohenzollerns, 256
Holbrook, May, 33

Holderness, Graham, 73, 159-62, 165-66, 171, 176
Hopkin, Sally, 92
Horkheimer, Max, 5-6
Humma, John B., 242, 270
Hyde, George, 10, 65, 116, 176-77, 197, 202-203, 205

Irschenhausen, 118, 146, 260
Italy, 2, 14-15, 52, 89, 91, 110, 115, 133-34, 187, 208-12, 215-18, 246, 258, 263, 265, 284

Jaffe, Edgar, 16, 111, 118, 137-39, 144, 146, 162, 191, 238, 257-58, 260-63, 285, 295
Jaffe, Else, 117, 137, 144, 162, 191, 200, 254, 261, 285
Jennings, Blanche, 24, 52-53, 55, 58, 91, 226
Jerome, St, 260
John, St, 225-26
Jones, Ernest, 172, 305
Judaism, 16, 191, 226, 260-61, 263-64, 267, 281-283, 287, 292-293, 298-99
Jung, Carl Gustav, 245

Kandinsky, Wassily, 13-14, 111-12, 115, 121, 152
Bild mit schwarzen Bogen, 153, 158
Klänge, 111
Komposition IV, 154, 157
Komposition VI, 112
Über das Geistige in der Kunst, 111, 121
Kant, Immanuel, 303
Keats, John, 48
Kestner, Joseph, 55
Keynes, John Maynard, *The Economic Consequences of the Peace*, 162, 164-66
Kinkead-Weekes, Mark, 10, 30, 45, 109-111, 152, 159, 219-20, 249, 251, 254
Kippenberg, Anton von, 254, 258
Koteliansky, S. S., 179-80, 184, 273, 283

Landauer, Gustav, 145, 257, 260
Lang, J. B., 245
Lawrence, D. H.
Aaron's Rod, 3, 8, 15-16, 204, 239, 241-59, 267-68, 269, 273, 284, 302
Fantasia of the Unconscious, 236-37, 245-47, 284
First Lady Chatterley's Lover, The, 302-304
First "Women in Love", The, 181, 187, 194
Kangaroo, 15-16, 241-42, 256, 258-68, 269, 296
Lady Chatterley's Lover, 3, 301-304

Movements in European History, 163, 175, 227, 230, 236, 285
Mr Noon, 15, 119, 135, 199-200, 204, 219-40, 241, 244, 252, 259, 269, 273, 283, 304
Plumed Serpent, The, 4, 242, 267, 269-299, 301, 307
Psychoanalysis and the Unconscious, 13, 213-15, 241, 246
Quetzalcoatl, 16, 270, 274-83, 285-86, 290-292, 295-297, 307
Rainbow, The, 8-9, 13-14, 73, 90, 107-54, 159-60, 169, 170, 180, 185-88, 204, 212, 220-22, 224-25, 227, 229-31, 234-35, 238, 242, 244, 251-52, 254, 304-305
Sea and Sardinia, 84, 200, 200, 216
Second Lady Chatterley's Lover, The, 302, 305
Sons and Lovers, 7, 8, 12, 15, 46, 49, 72, 73-104, 107, 108, 112, 113, 117, 123-25, 129, 142, 148, 162, 171, 180, 213, 226, 232
Studies in Classic American Literature, 199
Studies in Etruscan Places, 286

Touch and Go, 161-62
Trespasser, The, 12, 39, 51-72, 73, 85, 91-92, 96, 100-101, 105, 109, 132, 229, 306-307
Twilight in Italy, 109, 114, 133, 135, 209, 215, 265
White Peacock, The, 7-8, 11-12, 19-49, 51-52, 57-58, 71, 75, 77, 96, 104, 116, 227-28, 306
Women in Love, 8-9, 14, 49, 73, 90, 151, 159-96, 207, 212, 214-15, 217, 220, 223, 225, 229, 231-32, 235, 239, 241, 244, 246, 250, 254, 295, 305-306
"Border-Line, The", 274-75, 291
"Crown, The", 168, 173, 178, 190, 229
"Democracy", 222, 224-26, 248
"Education of the People", 199, 237
Foreword to *Women in Love*, 159
"German Books: Thomas Mann", 140
"Germans and English", 285
"Goethe and Pose", 303
"Letter from Germany, A", 271-74, 284-85, 294
"Mortal Coil, The", 138

"Modern Lover, A", 16, 24
"Paul Morel", 58, 73, 76-77, 93-94, 103
"On Human Destiny", 174
"Prussian Officer, The", 8, 107-110, 123-24, 148
"Saga of Siegmund, The", 50, 58
"Sisters, The", 107
"Study of Thomas Hardy", 13, 117, 120, 132, 139, 178

Lawrence, Frieda, 1-3, 6, 12, 15, 71, 73, 75, 84, 90-95, 103-105, 118, 135, 164, 219-20, 226-27, 230, 232-35, 242, 258, 274, 304
League of Nations, 248-49
Leavis, F. R., 1-4, 8-10, 26, 73, 152, 159-60, 197, 269
Lerici, 119
Lewes, George Henry, 19
The Life of Goethe, 21
Lodge, David, 203
Low, Barbara, 171-72, 174, 183, 305
Ludendorff, Marshall, 269
Lukács, Georg, 4, 22, 74, 81-82, 198, 209
Luther, Martin, 227

Macartney, Herbert, 50, 57, 61
Macleod, Sheila, 6

Mann, Thomas, 114, 129-30, 136, 153, 303, 305
Betrachtungen eines Unpolitischen, 76, 141
Buddenbrooks, 12, 73-77, 79, 81-83, 89, 97-100, 105, 107, 142, 146
Tagebücher, 272-73
Tod in Venedig, Der, 13-14, 140-48
"Leiden und Größe Richard Wagners", 81

Marc, Franz, 13-15, 111-112, 114, 121, 129-31, 132, 136, 140, 143, 147, 153, 251
Kampfende Formen, 131
großen blauen Pferde, Die, 150, 155
Turm der blauen Pferde, 152, 156
Marsh, Edward, 164
Martz, Louis L., 276, 280
Mexico, 16, 269-78, 280, 283-84, 290-96, 298-99
Michaels-Tonks, Jennifer, 10
Millett, Kate, 3-4, 6, 9-10, 73, 254, 305-306
Milton, Colin, 10
Mommsen, Theodor, 284
Moore, George, *A Mummer's Wife*, 197
Mosley, Oswald, 301
Mosse, George L., 3-4, 293

Index

Mountsier, Robert, 283
Munich, 84-85, 109, 111, 118, 137, 150, 237-38, 260
Secession, 110
Putsch, 16, 256, 271-72
Murry, John Middleton, 172, 283

Nachman, Rabbi, 265, 283
National Socialism, 3-4, 6, 258, 263, 269-72, 277, 279-81, 283, 289, 294, 307
Neubauer, John, 205
New Age, The, 60, 62
Newman, Ernest, 84
Study of Wagner, A, 55, 58-59, 103
Wagner, 55, 57, 59
Newton, Isaac, 120
Nietzsche, Friedrich, 13, 19, 32, 34, 39, 51, 61-62, 67, 72, 74, 91, 93, 97, 107, 113-15, 129-35, 136, 138-40, 141-43, 145-48, 151, 166, 168-70, 174, 178, 180-81, 193, 200, 208, 212, 214, 219-20, 228-29, 234, 244-48, 256-58, 266-67, 288, 302
Also Sprach Zarathustra, 12, 63, 65-66, 171, 179, 181-82, 245-46, 253, 266-67
Fall Wagner, Der, 92, 96
Fröhliche Wissenschaft, Die, 68, 178, 256

Geburt der Tragödie, Die, 63-65, 68, 88, 94, 96, 100
Jenseits von Gut und Böse, 247
Menschliches, Allzu Menschliches, 62, 64, 244, 251
Morgenröte, 178
Novalis, 107, 113, 135, 139, 146-48, 153, 219
Heinrich von Ofterdingen, 15, 200, 204-206, 209
Hymnen an die Nacht, 13, 125-29, 134, 204
Nuremberg Trials, 281

Pace, Billy James, 10
Palladio, Andrea, 211
Pantheism, 23, 37-39
Pawling, Sidney, 73, 76
Plato, 49, 199, 303
Poe, Edgar Allan, 275
Poland, Revolution (1863), 116
Poppel, Stephen M., 282
Positivism, 3, 120
Pound, Ezra, 63
Pritchett, V.S., 2
Prussia, 6, 163, 175, 227, 284-85

Renaissance, 260
Reformation, 260
Reich, Wilhelm, 6
Richtofen, Baroness, 254, 266
Rilke, Rainer Maria, 303

Rosenberg, Alfred, 2, 270, 277, 281, 285-86, 289, 291
Mythus des 20. Jahrhunderts, Der, 279, 284
Rubiner, Ludwig, 130-32, 135
Ruskin, John, 126
Russell, Bertrand, 2-4, 6, 8-10, 159, 162, 179-81, 185, 254, 269, 305-306
Russia, 19, 175, 219, 241

Savage, Henry, 126-27
Schiller, Friedrich von, 192, 205
Schlieffen Plan, 193
Schoenberg, Arnold, 8, 47, 97, 122, 148, 161
  Erwartung 107-109
  Pelleas und Melissande, 108
Schopenhauer, Arthur, 12-13, 16, 41-45, 47, 52-54, 59-60, 62, 66-71, 74, 77-78, 80, 82-85, 87-92, 95-96, 98, 113, 116, 122, 124, 129, 132, 136, 142, 153, 174, 214, 219-20, 228-29, 266, 288, 302, 306
  "Metaphysik der Geschlechtsliebe" ("The Metaphysics of Love"), 11, 19, 24-29, 33, 36, 39, 44, 47-48, 62, 76, 79, 125, 229
  "Nachträge zur Lehre von der Nichtigkeit des Daseyns" ("The Emptiness of Existence"), 33-38
  Welt als Wille und Vorstellung, Die, 30, 61, 63, 81
Schubert, Franz, 37, 259
Schulz, Gerhard, 207
Second World War, 2, 307
Shaw, George Bernard, "The Perfect Wagnerite", 85
Simpson, Hilary, 215, 217
Social Democrat Party, 165, 258
Sophocles, *Oedipus Tyrannus*, 90
Spengler, Oswald, *Untergang des Abendlandes, Der*, 302
Stewart, Jack, 110
Stolte, Heinz, 251
Strasbourg, 271, 274-5
Strauss, D. F., 25
Strauss, Richard, *Elektra*, 46, 99
Swift, John N., 161, 172

Taylor, Rachel Annand, 76
Thirty Years War, 227
Tolstoy, Leo, 244
  War and Peace, 74
Trakl, Georg, 102
Treaty of Locarno, 304
Treaty of Versailles, 256, 266, 304
Turner, John, 104, 233-34
Turner, J.M.W., 121

Vienna,

Revolution (1917), 140
Congress, 163

Wagner, Richard, 7-8, 13-16, 19-20, 31, 34-35, 47, 51, 60-62, 64, 67-68, 71, 74, 81, 83, 90-91, 96-97, 99-100, 104-105, 112-14, 140, 145, 149-50, 161, 173-74, 189, 219-20, 226, 233-34, 241, 244, 277, 279, 306
Lohengrin, 52, 59, 97
Ring des Nibelungen, Der, 30, 32, 58, 82, 84-90, 115-17, 124-26, 129, 136, 145, 153, 233, 235, 238-239, 292, 305
Oper und Drama, 55-56
Parsifal, 44, 46, 104, 230-31
Tannhäuser, 30, 39-46, 52
Tristan und Isolde, 12, 44, 53-54, 57-59, 64-66, 81, 85, 88, 96, 108-10, 116, 121, 125, 185, 191-93, 231-32, 244-45, 279
Wall Street Crash, 272
Waugh, Evelyn, 162

Weber, Alfred, 16, 119-20, 137, 143, 162, 190, 198-200, 238, 256, 261
Die Krise des modernen Staatsgedankens in Europa, 257
Weber, Max, 13, 16, 115, 119, 129-31, 136-38, 140, 145-48, 153, 162, 184, 190, 200, 217, 285, 305
Die protestantische Ethik und der Geist des Kapitalismus, 14, 138-40, 142, 163-70, 198-99
"Freiburger Antrittsrede", 138, 171
Wilding, Michael, 259-61
Wilhelm II, Kaiser, 118, 138, 194-95, 241, 263, 268
Williams, Raymond, 73
Worthen, John, 10, 23, 27-28, 30, 76, 79, 90, 124, 148, 159-62, 165-66, 170, 176, 178, 197, 219

Zionism, 15-16, 262-66, 276, 281-83, 299, 307-308